ERRORS IN POSTAGE STAMP DESIGN

D E G Irvine & M. Seshold

DISCOURS
SUR LA
MÉTHODE
1637
DESCARTES
90c
H. CHEFFER
RÉPUBLIQUE FRANÇAISE
POSTES
DISCOURS
DE LA
MÉTHODE
1637
DESCARTES
90c
H. CHEFFER
RÉPUBLIQUE FRANÇAISE
POSTES
DISCOURS
SUR LA
MÉTHODE
1637
DESCARTES
90c
H. CHEFFER
RÉPUBLIQUE FRANÇAISE
POSTES
DISCOURS
DE LA
MÉTHODE
1637

ERRORS IN POSTAGE STAMP DESIGN

D E G Irvine & M Seshold

Published by
National Philatelic Society
1 Whitehall Place
LONDON

1979

ISBN 0 906291 01 1

Printed in Great Britain by

Crampton & Sons Ltd, Sawston, Cambridge

CONTENTS

Chapter		Page
	Preface	vi
	Foreword	vii
1.	SPELLING AND GRAMMATICAL ERRORS	1
2.	ERRORS IN IDENTIFICATION	26
3.	DENOMINATION ERRORS	45
4.	MIS-STATEMENTS	52
5.	ERRORS IN PORTRAYAL OF SUBJECT	84
6.	ANACHRONISMS	128
7.	IMPOSSIBLE COMPOSITIONS	137
8.	COMMEMORATION OF NON-EVENTS	142
9.	DIPLOMATIC ERRORS	147
10.	INTENTIONAL ERRORS	159
11.	OTHER THAN STAMPS	165
	ADDENDUM	175
	INDEX	183
	12 PLATES OF ILLUSTRATIONS	

PREFACE

by the President of the National Philatelic Society

From 1972 to 1975 there appeared in ' The Stamp Lover ' an intriguing series of articles by Dr David Irvine and Mr Maxwell Seshold entitled ' Errare est Humanum '.

It is human to err—but it is even more human to enjoy detecting others in erring.

Since their series ended the authors have been patiently at work discovering more stamp design errors. This has been partly aided by response to their queries from the membership of the National Philatelic Society (the largest in the U.K.), some of this response being highly technical in nature. In early 1977, when the present work was decided upon, they had already amassed twice as much material as had fed their series.

The range of subjects which are susceptible to error is unexpectedly extensive; anything which can form the subject of a stamp design, or part of it, is liable to error. The scope is virtually infinite. The authors have sorted their specimens into types and the chapter-headings alone give a fascinating glimpse of what the book holds in store. A small number of the errors reported here will already be known because of being published in general or specialist catalogues, but the majority have not been published until now in a form available to the stamp-collector, much less to the public at large, to whom also this book will be attractive. The philatelist who can point to a design error in stamps which he is discussing or displaying will always score a point especially where, in many cases, the stamp itself is well-known but the error of design had not been noticed.

The amount of effort, and the depth of study, which is supplied enthusiastically by a philatelist in pursuing his research, is prodigious. The authors of the present work possibly surpass all in this regard because they have had to look at the designs of all issued stamps and ask themselves the question ' what is wrong with...' when applied to perhaps twenty or more features contained in the design.

This book opens up a new field in the study and collecting of stamps, wide though the scope of philately is already. This is relevant to the developing mode of collecting on a thematic basis and philatelists who travel this road will have an enjoyable and deeply satisfying journey.

Because of the impetus which a reading of this book will give to a collector minded to search for stamp design errors, possibly in a field in which his everyday work gives him some advantage, as much as because of the wealth of carefully-researched examples presented here, the authors are to be congratulated on their collaboration which has produced possibly the most important philatelic literary work of the decade.

John A. Grimmer

FOREWORD

Having searched separately for errors in design for several years, and in the process contacting various dealers, we were introduced to each other by Mr. and Mrs. R. Hickman of Libritz Stamps about the end of 1970. We compared notes and found that each of us had many errors that the other did not have, which led us to believe that there were very likely a couple of hundred or so more awaiting discovery. Admittedly the ever-increasing flood of new issues meant that errors were being perpetrated more frequently than hitherto, but we imagined that we could cope with these. *Amabilis insania.* We wished to contact like-minded collectors so that we could compare notes, but how? One way was to write and have published a few articles listing our discoveries and appealing for further information. The choice of magazine was obvious to members of the N.P.S., namely *The Stamp Lover,* and we were fortunate to have the enthusiastic support of its Editor, Mr. Philip Halward, to whom we owe much. Response from fellow-members was gratifying and swift, and several new lines of research opened up. We had the great good fortune to meet Col. C. F. Black, at that time attached to the Canadian High Commissioner's Office in London, who had been developing a collection along similar lines, but with the emphasis on areas little explored by us. Through Col. Black we made contact with Herr Hans-H. Beu of Hamburg who very kindly made available to us his published articles in the *Deutsche Zeitung für Briefmarkenkunde.*

With these assistances we went from strength to strength, and the originally projected series of about seven or eight articles extended to nineteen; we found that we then had remaining enough material to duplicate that number if we so wished. Indeed the number of errors we have uncovered is positively frightening, and certainly provides food for thought.

Our definition of a design error is one inherent in the basic design or conception of a stamp or series of stamps, item of postal stationery or associated officially issued material such as stamp booklets; it is not, as a rule, caused through faults in printing processes, so typically affects all the stamps of an issue. In this book we have followed the classification chosen for our original articles, but with a few exceptions have segregated errors not involving stamps to a chapter of their own.

In a work of this type it is not possible to list all the works of reference, philatelic articles, books and catalogues from which we have gleaned our information, nor to name all the individuals who have helped in various ways. We have already stressed our debt to Herr Hans-H. Beu of Hamburg, probably the *doyen* of this field of philately, and to Col. C. F. Black of Charlottetown, Prince Edward Island; both have published many articles of their own, and have freely shared with us their extensive knowledge of design errors. We are grateful to the late Mr. Michael Gordon of Hampstead and Mrs. Margaret Stern of Swiss Cottage for assistance in translation of Herr Beu's publications and letters, and to Mr. T. M. Doust, formerly Acquisitions Librarian of the Polytechnic of North London, for invaluable assistance in ferreting out information necessary to prove or disprove suspected errors. We are grateful to our many friends in the trade who have helped us with material and information, and to the members of our own local and specialised philatelic societies who have assisted us likewise. We should like to give particular thanks to some who have given valuable help in specialised fields:

Mr. W. Stuart Clark (places, buildings and monuments)
Mr. B. Davis (map stamps)
Sr. E. M. Guerra (stamps of Spanish-speaking countries)
Dr. L. B. Holthuis (Crustacea)
Mr. H. W. A. Linecar (railway stock)
Mr. R. McDougall (South Africa)
Mr. C. Sharp (zeppelins)
Prof. W. R. Taylor (flowers, U.S.A.)
Mr. H. S. Taylor-Young (medicine, first aid).

For general help and encouragement we would like to thank: Mr. Derek Bebb, Mrs. Ethel Bloesch, Mr. Norman Gladstone and Dr. Ferenc Pásthy.

The following publications have been particularly useful to us:

C. O. Enhagen (1961) *Sports stamps.* Stanley Paul, London.

A. M. Goodbody (1973) Letter on Railway anachronisms, *Stamp Magazine,* August: p. 58.

I. T. Hamilton (1950) Musical extracts on stamps. A survey and criticism. *Stamp Magazine* October and November issues and correspondence.

R. J. Sutton (1957) *Stamp curiosities.* Stanley Paul, London.

Les Winick (1969) Space variety checklist. *Topical Times*, November-December 1969: 22-24.

The *Bapip Bulletin.* Official journal of the British Association of Palestine-Israel Philatelists.

The *Baton.* Official journal of The Philatelic Music Circle.

Special thanks are also due to Mr. Charles Grimsey for designing the dust jacket.

The critical study of stamp design is a very neglected field—alarmingly so, for surprisingly many collectors accept unquestioningly the information purveyed to them by the catalogue or philatelic agency handout, or on the stamp itself. Indeed, we have seen many award-winning exhibits of international standard which have incorporated uncritically such misinformation in the writing up. If our book spurs designers and their patrons to check their issues more carefully, and fellow collectors to be less trusting and more critical, we shall feel that it has served a useful function. For our own errors, both of omission and commission, we beg your forgiveness and hope that you will let us know (with full documentation) wherein we have erred.

DAVID E. G. IRVINE

MAXWELL SESHOLD

CHAPTER 1

Spelling and Grammatical Errors

The first category of design error which we propose to discuss in detail is that of mistakes in spelling, grammar, punctuation, typography and associated fields. Those errors which concern the face value of the stamp are, however, placed in a separate category of their own.

As might be expected, names of places and of people form a trap for the unwary stamp designer. One of the earliest and best known of such errors is that of the New Zealand 2½d. stamp of 1898 featuring Lake Wakatipu and Mount Earnslaw, which as originally produced was inscribed "Lake Wakitipu". (Figs. 1 & 2). This error had been noted by the Government printer in Wellington at the proof stage, and a corrected die had been prepared by the British printers (Waterlow & Sons), but when the entire issue of 218,000 'error' stamps sold out in less than a fortnight, the Government ordered and received a further 50,000 'kits', although by then the corrected 'kats' were already available! Other errors involving a single wrong letter appear often to be due to confusion between similar letters at some stage. Examples are "Virgin Corda" for Virgin Gorda on the $4.80 Virgin Islands stamp of 1952 (though spelt correctly on the 8c. stamp of the same issue) and "Beouia" for Bequia on the 1c. St. Vincent definitive of 1965, corrected in 1967. The Polish mountain resort of Niedzica appears as "Niedziga" on a 1z. stamp of 1952, although corrected subsequently, and the small island of Toku as "Taku" on the ½d. Tongan definitive of 1951 (given correctly on the 1s. definitive of 1953). The Place d'Armes parade ground on St. Lucia was renamed Columbus Square in 1893, but the 1d., 2½d. and 6d. definitives of 1936 misspell it "Colombus", corrected on the 6d. stamp of 1938. The 1934 Italian issue commemorating a direct flight from Rome to Buenos Aires spells the destination as "BUENOS-AYRES", an old-fashioned and generally discarded spelling which may be fairly considered erroneous here. Halbturn Castle is misspelt "Halbthurn" on a 2s. Austrian stamp of 1968, and a 2s.50 East African stamp of 1973 featuring the Interpol H.Q. at St. Cloud, France, somehow manages to convert this to "St. Clans" (corrected on a 1974 stamp). The 1897-1900 issue for the Marshall Islands carried the overprint "Marschall-Inseln". They had been named after Marshall, who discovered them in 1788, and introduction of a ' c' into the name was quite incorrect. The German Foreign Office demanded a new issue with correct spelling of the name, duly produced (1899-1900).

A more complex case is that of the Sudanese £1 stamp of 1962 featuring the camel postman—a long-suffering design involved in many different kinds of error. The original design of 1898 showed the postman carrying mailbags inscribed KHARTOUM and BERBER, but with the pannier straps covering the 'R' of KHARTOUM and the second 'R' of BERBER. Displacement of these straps in the 1962 version left BERBER misspelt "BERBE".

Transposition of letters also occurs, as in the 50c. 1950 definitive of North Borneo in which Jesselton is misspelt "Jessleton", corrected in 1952. The 40p. 1961 Nepalese stamp featuring Mt. Manaslu, the tenth highest mountain in the world, is wrongly inscribed "Mansalu". A 10l. Greek stamp of 1937 portrays a court lady of Tiryns, wrongly spelt "ΤΥΡΙΝΘΟΣ" (of Tyrins), corrected on a 1938 issue to "ΤΙΡΥΝΘΟΣ", while the Ivory Coast definitives of 1936-40 include several values featuring a Baoulé woman, on the stamp wrongly designated "Femme Baloué". The correct spelling is shown on a 5c. Liberian stamp of 1971 featuring native masks. Another West African tribe is misspelt on a 1933 5d. stamp of Sierra Leone showing a Bullom canoe, wrongly given as "Bullam", but spelt correctly on a 1s. stamp of 1956.

In the Hungarian Castles series of 1960, the first photogravure printing cylinder for the 1fo.70 value was wrongly inscribed "SOMLYÓ", an error only noticed in the final proof. A new cylinder with the correct "SOMLÓ" was prepared, and the stamps from this were issued. However the old cylinder was inadvertently used when a further printing was required, and these erroneous stamps were issued in 1962, an unusual case of the correction appearing well in advance of the original error! The town of Greenville is spelt "Grenville" on a 10c. registration stamp of Liberia of the issues of 1893, 1903, 1919 and 1920, though correctly spelt on subsequent issues. Saulte Sainte Marie is spelt "SAULT DE STE MARIE" on an 8c. 1901 stamp of the U.S.A., but this may have been the accepted form at that date. The 1972 issue of the Tokelau Islands marking the 25th anniversary of the South Pacific Commission omits the first 'i' of Pacific on the 15c. value. Two further cases of missing letters are not, however, errors. The U.S.A. 1948 3c. stamp commemorating the 150th anniversary of Mississippi portrays the State seal, which bears the spelling "Missisippi"; this was the spelling on the original seal. Similarly the 1964 Italian 30l. and 130l. stamps commemorating the opening of the Verrazano Narrows Bridge, New York, feature the man after whom it was named, G. de Verrazzano, but the second 'z' is indeed missing from the name of the bridge.

Countries sometimes even get their own names wrong, at least where given in a language other than their own. Afghanistan in particular has come up with several variants. Thus the 15p. of 1938 for the International Anti-Cancer Fund reads "AFGHANESTAN", 1956 issues commemorating the International Exhibition, Kabul, and the 10th anniversary of admission to the U.N. have "POSTES AFGHANNES" instead of AFGHANES, and the 1949 125p. Child Welfare stamp has "AFGANES", as well as an erroneous "JOURNEE D'ENFANCES" (Childhoods' Day) instead of D'ENFANCE. Travancore has managed at various times between 1899 and 1939 on one particular design to have "TRAVANOORE", but this may be due to bad printing. Similarly in 1892 Sirmoor released for postage stamps that had been reprinted for collectors in 1891 all inscribed "SIRMDOR". Several issues of Norway (1951 Garborg centenary, 1963 Aasen 150th birth anniversary, 1964 centenary of Norwegian Folk High Schools, 1968 Vinje 150th birth anniversary, 1977 herring fishing *et seq.*) bear the spelling "NOREG" rather than the more usual NORGE; this is not an error, but the form advocated by Garborg and others as being more correct. Post-independence Libyan

1

2

3

4

5

6

7

8

9

10

11

12

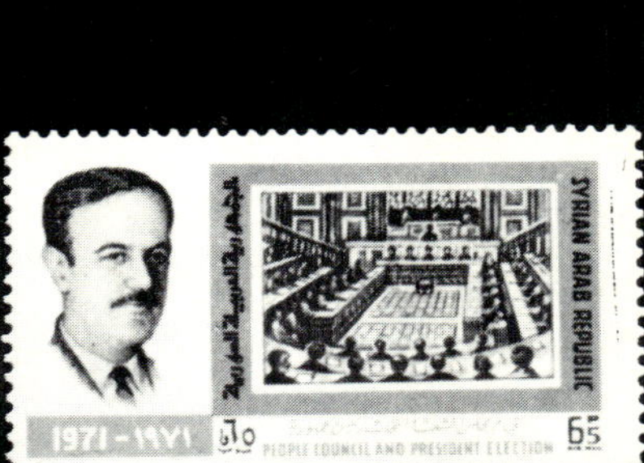

13

14

15

16

17

18

19

20

21

26

25

24

22

23

issues have all been inscribed "LIBYA" when that country has adhered to UPU regulations concerning the use of the Latin alphabet, except for the 1966 Tourism issue, which was printed in Italy and carries the Italian spelling "LIBIA". Two miniature sheets produced by Ajman in 1972, with paintings by Tiepolo and Titian, and a 12r. miniature sheet of 1969 commemorating Mozart, use the spelling "AYMAN". This may be an acceptable transliteration, but it can be argued that countries should be consistent in such matters. Similarly the Iranian 1965 issues marking Women's Rights and the World Eradication of Illiteracy Congress carry the spellings "Tehran" and "Teheran" respectively, and the omnibus issues to mark the "Deir Yasin massacre" is so spelt by Syria and Iraq in 1965 and Saudi Arabia (1966) but as "Deir Yassin" by the Yemen Arab Republic, Egypt, Lebanon, Jordan and Kuwait in 1965 and again by Kuwait in 1968 and as "Dir-Yacine" by Algeria in 1966. The 1977 West German 140pf. stamp showing the Palais de l'Europe places it in "Strassburg", but if French this should be ' Strasbourg ', if German ' Straßburg'. Perhaps it was considered more diplomatic to use neither! Germany has had trouble with the middle ' s ' of ' DEUTSCHES ' on several issues: the 1902 2m. definitive with Gothic script lettering has a round ' s ' in this position instead of the required long ' s '. The 15pf. value of the 1919 issue marking the National Assembly at Weimar wrongly has a round ' s ' in the middle of "NATIONALVERSAMMLUNG", while a 70pf. East German stamp of 1965 featuring a bilateral demonstration of Communist and Socialist parties correctly has the long ' s ' in "Sozialistische Einheitspartei" on the banner figured, but not in "Deutschlands". This last word was not on the original banner, shown correctly on a 5pf. stamp of 1966. Likewise the numeral issues of 1921-22, in which the 75pf. value, the last issued, alone has the long ' s '. Hong Kong has never been able to make up its mind as to whether its name is one word or two, and has often compromised by placing both words only fractionally further apart than individual letters. In general all Victorian postage stamps have one word, issues of Edward VII and George V have two words, issues of George VI and Queen Elizabeth II also have two words except for the 1938 and 1954 definitives, postage due stamps have one word and postal fiscals have two words. Two words are generally accepted as correct. In 1922 the Turkish Nationalist Government at Angora issued a series of definitives, the 50p. of which was inscribed in Turkish "Ottoman Government Posts". This was corrected to match the rest of the series as "Turkish Posts".

To get other countries wrong is perhaps more understandable. Iraq in 1970 overprinted a Freedom from Hunger 50f. M.S. with the adjuration "REMEMBER PALISTINE". The 1959 ½d. stamp of Ghana, part of a set intended to mark the West African football championships (which did not take place), spells Portuguese Guinea as "Portugese". Since all the other names are given an English spelling this can fairly be counted an error. One might also mention here the 1936 2c. stamp of Ecuador which shows a map of the Galapagos Islands, giving the Spanish names for ten of the islands but naming the eleventh by its English name (Tower Island), instead of the Spanish 'Genovesa'. The 2½b. and 10b. miniature sheets of the Yemen Arab Republic which commemorate the Inauguration of the U.P.U. Building, Berne, include a background with names of U.P.U.

countries mostly (though not all) in English, but with Norway as "NORVAY". A South Korean 10w. miniature sheet of 1970 commemorating the visit of the President of El Salvador was hurriedly withdrawn and replaced by a corrected version when it was seen to have the misspelling "El Salvadol". A 5f. 1949 stamp of Monaco showing the research ship *Princess Alice II* spells Spitzberg with the 'z' reversed.

Names of people are often spelt wrongly. The 1969 set of three stamps issued by Dominica commemorating the centenary of Gandhi's birth spells his name throughout as "Ghandi". In 1956 Russia commemorated the 148th birthday of Mahmud Aivazov and incorrectly gave his first name as "МЧХАМЕД" (Muhamed). This was corrected to "МАХМЧД", but the corrected version was only put into circulation in Baku—the old man's birthplace—and in limited quantities at that. The 1966 air stamps of Syria featuring the deities Astarte and Tyche have the former spelled "Astrate". On the tab of the 1967 40a. stamp of Israel, issued after the Six Day War, the quotation from Isaiah carries the spelling "Isiah". The 10c. Costa Rican definitive of 1901 featuring the former President Braulio Carrillo has his given name spelled "Branlio". This was corrected in 1907. In the Olympic Games issues of 1957 by the Dominican Republic the Irish 1500 metre Olympic winner Ron Delany has his name misspelt "Delaney" on the 2c. value, while in the 1960 issue Terence Spinks has his given name spelled "Terrence" on the 5c. value. In a 1968 issue of Honduras marking the Summer Olympics, the 10c. value has Marielle Goitschel misspelt "GOITSHELL" and on the 12c. Dr. R. Klimpke is misspelt "KLEINKE". The 1962 Egyptian issue commemorating Dag Hammarskjöld has his name spelt "Hammarskjölds" while Panama on an issue of 1961 omitted the umlaut, and on a U.N. Day set of 1964 spelled it "Hammerskjöld", and Ecuador (1966; 10c.) spelt it "HAMMERSKJOLD". On a 60fi. Hungarian stamp of 1966 the astronaut W. Schirra Jr. is misspelt "Schira" and on a 5c. Panamanian stamp of 1963 marking the visit of four American astronauts to Panama, A. Shepard Jr. has his name misspelt "SHEPPARD". Admiral Martin Guise is featured on a 10c. Peruvian stamp of 1921, but his name is misspelt "Guisse". A Norwegian issue of 1942 marks the centenary of the birth of the poet Johan Herman Wessel, but spells his name "Hermann". Conversely Johann Sebastian Bach has his forename misspelt "Johan" on 5f. and 45f. 1967 stamps of Togo in an issue marking the 20th anniversary of the inauguration of UNESCO. The founder of Windhoek, Curt von Francois, has his forename misspelt "Kurt" on a 15c. 1965 stamp of South West Africa. West Germany commemorated Florence Nightingale on a charity stamp of 1955, but named her "Florentine". The England footballer Bobbie Charlton is commemorated on a 10d. 1970 stamp of Fujeira as "B. Charlton"—it should of course by ' R ' (for Robert) as on the 5cor. Nicaraguan stamp of 1970. A 1d. 1965 stamp of Tristan da Cunha features the flagship of Tristão D'Acunha, discoverer of the islands, but misspells his name "Tristão da Cunha". The U.S.A. destroyed a first printing of 40 million stamps of the 1973 21c. issue featuring Amadeo P. Giannini when it was seen that his name was misspelt "Amedeo", and only the corrected version was released to the public. The Indian scholar and statesman (and onetime British M.P.) Dadabhai Naoroji has his name rendered "Dadabhoy", an obsolete and pedantic version, on an Indian 15n.p. stamp of 1963. Nawab Shah Jahan Begam becomes "EEGAM" on an 1876-77 ¼a. issue of Bhopal. The great painter Rafaello has his name spelt "Rafaelo" on a 70pf. East German stamp of 1955—it is given correctly on, for instance, the Italian 1970 issue featuring paintings of his. East Germany also got Rembrandt's name wrong on a 20pf. stamp of 1955 calling him "HARMENSZ REMBRANDT van RYN" instead of 'REMBRANDT HARMENSZ van RIJN'. A miniature sheet issued by Sharjah in 1972 misspells Galileo "Galilee" and features the well-known painters "LEONARD DE VINCI" and "MICAEL ANGELO" and someone called "DENTE" who is certainly not Dante but probably Dante Gabriel Rosetti the poet—his portrait is accompanied by a sheet of music lying on a painter's palette. The composer of the National Anthem of Ecuador, J. L. Mera, has his name wrongly spelt "Meran" on a 1965 issue, although correct on a 1s.30 stamp of 1961. The Cuban composer Jorge Anckermann has his name so spelt on a 7c. stamp of 1966, but it is spelt "Ankerman" on a 13c. stamp of 1977—one of these must be wrong. The founder of the Bucharest Botanical Gardens, Dr. Dimitrie Brandza, is misspelt "Brindza" on a Rumanian miniature sheet of 1961. The owner of a painting of Shakespeare and Johnson featured on a Nicaraguan 5cor. stamp of 1975, the Rev. William M. de Heyman, has his name spelt as one word "DEHEYMAN" on the stamp. The stamp designer Clive Abbott has his name misspelt "Abbot" on the 1975 'fish' issue of the Virgin Islands and this was unaltered on the 1977 re-printing. The Grenadines of St. Vincent issued definitives in 1977 which correctly have the designer's name as "Granger Barrett" instead of "Granger Barratt" as previously. The designer of the Swedish 1965 issue commemorating Prince Eugen, David Tägtström, has his name misspelt "D. Tägström" on the stamps. The painter Cornelius Krieghoff has his name correctly spelt on the 1972 Canadian 8c. stamp which features his painting "The Blacksmith's Shop", but the marginal inscription has it as "Kreighoff".

When names are transcribed from a non-Latin alphabet it is not always easy to determine if a spelling error is involved. For example, the 1947 Ethiopian issue marking the 150th anniversary of the founding of the Selassie dynasty spells it "Sellassie", but elsewhere, *e.g.* on the 1952 issue marking the 60th birthday of the Emperor, it is spelt "Selassie", although the inscription would not satisfy a purist as it reads "COMMEMORATING H.I.M. HAILE SELASSIE FIRST 60th BIRTHDAY, 23rd July, 1952". The ancient Indian astronomer Aryabhatta gave his name to the Indian satellite featured on a 25p. stamp of 1975. On the stamp it is given as "ARYABHAT" in Hindi and as "ARYABHATA" (which would mean 'menial of the Aryans') in English, which has given some offence in India. The murdered Hungarian Prime Minister Imre Nagy becomes "Naghi" on a Greek issue of 1959. On the Albanian 2l. stamp of 1964 featuring Karl Marx his name is spelt "KARL MARKS". This is not an error but is due to a peculiarity of Albanian pronunciation of the letter 'x' as 'dz', which means that the appropriate way of writing Marx in Albanian to get the proper pronunciation is Marks. The film director Sergei Eisenstein becomes "Serghei" on a 250f. 1971 stamp of the Congo (Brazzaville), while the composer Haydn becomes "Hayden" on a 1971 Ras Al Khaima issue.

The South African 1964 and South West African 1965 issues commemorating the death of the Protestant reformer John Calvin both have the name spelled "Calvyn"; although this is the generally accepted Afrikaans spelling, it was never so spelt by Calvin himself. The more usual spelling is given on a West German 20pf. stamp of 1964. Leifr Eiricksson, Icelandic explorer of the New World, has his name so spelt on various Icelandic stamps of 1938, but a 6c. 1968 stamp of the U.S.A. gives it as "Leif Erikson". The Albanians spell their great 15th century patriot Castriota Skanderberg as "SKANDERSBERGU" on the 1913 issue but as "SKENDERBEU" on a 1951 issue. East Germany honours the two Russian space-faring dogs on a 5pf. stamp of 1962, but transliterates their names according to different systems, as "Bjelka" and "Strelka" (for consistency the former should be ' Belka ').

The lake steamer *Chauncy Maples* on the 1/6d. stamp of Malawi of 1967 has its name spelled "*Chauncey Maples*"; it is given correctly on a 15t. stamp of 1975. The liner *Quezaltenango* is misspelt "*Quetzaltenango*" on a 6c. Guatemalan stamp of 1959 which commemorates the Central American Merchant Marine. A 1949 4c. Canadian stamp and a 10c. stamp of Newfoundland issued in 1897 show Cabot's ship, here spelt "*Matthew*" but earlier records spell it as *Mathew* (1496) or more commonly *Mathewe* (1503-04). The 3-D 1971 series of Bhutan which features veteran cars includes on the 10ch. value an Alfa Romeo, but spelled "Alfa Rameo" (correctly spelled on a 2c. 1967 stamp of Monaco).

Proliferating initials and acronyms make it easy to sympathise with Syria for getting "UNECEF" instead of UNICEF on the Children's Day set of 1969, but a more charming error is found in the 1970 issue commemorating the first Youth Week of the Revolution's Youth Union, inscribed "Youth's First Weak". Afghanistan is particularly prone to make spelling mistakes. On the 125p. stamp of 1952 marking the 21st anniversary of the Faculty of Medicine, médecine is spelt "MADECINE". On the 125p. stamp of 1953 marking the 22nd anniversary this mistake is repeated, and this time *Anniversaire* is also misspelt "ANNIVERAIRE" (fig. 3); a corrected version was produced this time (fig. 4). Anniversary appears to be curiously susceptible to misspelling. It is wrongly abbreviated to "ANVERS" on the 1956 issue marking the 38th anniversary of Independence and to "ANV." on the 1955 issue marking the 10th anniversary of the U.N.O. and on the 1957 issue marking the 39th anniversary of Independence. Mongolia marked the 40th anniversary of its independence with several issues: the three miniature sheets of 1961 carry both French and Russian inscriptions, the French with the misspelling "ANNIVERSSAIRE". The Iranian 5r. stamp of 1956 marking the 10th anniversary of the National Olympic Committee has in the French text "ARNNIVERSAIRE". Lastly Haiti, in a 1959 issue marking the 10th anniversary of the Declaration of Human Rights with overprints in English, French, Portuguese and Spanish, got understandably confused and in the Spanish version put "ANIVERSARIE" instead of ANIVERSARIO.

Returning to Afghanistan, as we shall frequently throughout this book, this country appears also to have had trouble in numbering in French, for the 1948 and 1949 U.N.O. anniversary issues are given as "3EM" and "4EM" instead of 3ME (TROISIÈME) and 4ME (QUATRIÈME) respectively, and the 1957 Independence Day commemorative has "39^{em}" where it should have been 39ème. The Canadian 1908 Quebec Tercentenary issue has "IIIE' on all but the 10c. and 15c. values, which correctly have "IIIe" ("CENTENAIRE"). On the 1967 Red Crescent Day issue of Afghanistan the French CROISSANT is misspelt "CROISSAN". The Yemen intended in 1963 to overprint a Freedom from Hunger miniature sheet with the inscription "Red Crescent", to commemorate the centenary of the Red Cross, but it came out "Red Grescent", so the sheet was not issued. Later, however, it was over-printed "Periodicals" and issued as a newspaper stamp. Another overprint which went wrong occurred on the 45c.+50c. value of the 1943 semipostals of Curacao, surcharged for Dutch Prisoners of War Relief, in which the overprint reads "Voor Krljgsgevangenen" instead of the slightly less unpronouncable Krijgsgevangenen, although correct on other values. The 1891 issue for Johore featuring Sultan Aboubaktar was to be overprinted KEMAHKOTAAN to commemorate the coronation of his successor, Sultan Ibrahim. However due to an error on a telegram from Johore to the printers De La Rue, the word was rendered "KETAH-KOTAAN". De La Rue duly so overprinted and shipped 56,000 stamps. Although the error was speedily rectified and correctly overprinted stamps produced and despatched, the erroneous overprints also got into circulation. An almost certainly bogus overprint of Netherlands Indies stamps of about 1949 states "REPOEBLIC INDONESIA TWO DAYS OF INFAMY! 7 Dec. 1941—Pearl Harbour 18 Dec. 1948 Jogjakarta"—the correct spelling should be REPOEBLIK. The German Jubilee pattern propaganda ' stamp ' of World War II with the denomination of ½d (the ' d ' being composed of a hammer and sickle) carries the slogan "THIS WAR IS A JEWSH WAR" omitting the ' I ' of JEWISH. The overprints on the K.G.VI ' definitives ' in the "Liquidation of the Empire" series include "Bahama Is" for the Bahamas.

The 1971 Christmas issue of Fujeira labels the 60d. scene "NAISCANCE DE JÉSUS" instead of NAISSANCE. On the 10m. Egyptian stamp of 1959 issued as part of the UNESCO campaign for the preservation of the Nubian Monuments threatened by the completion of the Assouan High Dam, Safeguard is misspelt "Saveguard". The 20c. 1973 stamp of Lesotho's issue to mark an International Kimberlite Conference carries the misspelling "KIMERLITE VOLCANO". A 5f. Jordanian stamp of 1971 marking Racial Equality Year is inscribed "KINIGDOM" for KINGDOM. Republics can err also, for the 20c. Colombian 1886 issue featuring General Marino is inscribed "REPULICA", corrected to "REPUBLICA" in 1889, and the Syrian Peasants' Union issue of 1965 has "RERUBLIC". The 5c. 1913 stamp for Sonora, issued during the Mexican civil war, has the error "MARO" (for MARZO) on stamps in positions 1, 2, 6 and 7, the remaining six being correct, so this should be counted as a production rather than a design error. Similarly the 25c. stamp of Plate III of 1903 for the Venezuelan state of Guayana has the spelling "Coreos de Venezuela" instead of Correos as on plates I and II. A 1976 issue of the Dominican Republic commemorating the fire service spells it with three ' R 's as "CORRREOS". Another well-known production error affects two stamps per sheet of the 2/3t. 1912 Tibetan stamps, which are inscribed "POTSAGE" instead of POSTAGE. South

Korea's miniature sheets of 1962 marking in English the first anniversary of the May 16th revolution had the ' E ' of POSTAGE omitted. Corrected sheets (on unwatermarked paper) were speedily produced. Antigua in a U.P.U. centennial issue of 1974 spelt English as "Enlish" on the ½c. and Postal as "Fostal" on the 2c. value. The 1900 Cuban 10c. express stamp is inscribed "immediata", corrected to "inmediata" on the 1902 issue.

Amongst more debatable cases, it has been claimed that the 10c. 1966 stamp of British Honduras portraying "Half Moon Caye" should have the more usual spelling Cay. A Swiss 1968 50c. semipostal shows the zodiacal sign Fish (Latin PISCES) inscribed "PICES". This is not, however, an error, for the design is taken from a 14th century stained glass window at the Cathedral of Lausanne, and PICES is perfectly acceptable mediaeval Latin. On the 2c. 1910 Newfoundland stamp of the issue marking the tercentenary of the founding of the Colonisation Company there occurs the word "Colonising", while the 6c. bears the word "Colonization". This inconsistency, although a permissible spelling, was noted, and the latter altered to "Colonisation" with a somewhat angular ' s ' which the catalogues usually describe as a reversed ' z '.

In the motto for the arms of Bolivar province in the 1951-54 Venezuelan Arms series, Deciembre is wrongly spelt "DECIEMBER", On the 1p. 1886 stamp for the Colombian state of Antioqua the words "LIBERTAD Y ORDEN" (Liberty and Order), correct on the lower values, read "LIBERTAD Y ORDNE". A 1971 sheet of stamps showing Kings and Queens of England produced by Umm Al Qiwain includes the Royal coat of arms (very poorly produced) with "HONNI" instead of HONI in the motto, reputedly first coined by Edward III concerning a lady's dropped garter, while a 1974 Hungarian 2fo.50 stamp featuring a lady who has lost considerably more of her clothing spells it "HONNY". A much more reputable error of considerably longer standing (indeed very probably the first indisputable design error on a stamp) occurs on the 1852 1c. and 4c. stamps of British Guiana, which show the badge and motto of the colony. The motto should read "Damus petimusque vicissem" (we give and seek in return) but was misspelled "Patimus". Fortunately reprints of those very rare stamps were made in 1885, and are relatively readily available (fig. 5).

The 1942 Panamanian issue had a 2c. value showing oxen drawing a sugar cart which initially was entitled "ACARRERO DE CAÑA", then corrected to "ACARREO DE CAÑA". Grenada has Careenage spelled "Carenage" on the 6c. definitive of 1966 (the correct English spelling occurs on the 60c. definitives of Barbados for 1950 and 1956), but this place-name is of French origin and hence correct. Australia switched to the American spelling "Harbors" on a 5c. stamp of February 1969 issued on the occasion of the Sixth Biennial Conference of the International Association of Ports and Harbours, yet in June 1969 retained the English spelling of Labour for the 50th anniversary of the I.L.O., and previously, as for example in the Sydney Harbour Bridge series, had used the spelling ' Harbour '. It has been argued that ' Harbors ' is the correct spelling in the title of the Association, but whether it should have been used here is nevertheless debatable.

The East German miniature sheet of 1970 which commemorates the 25th anniversary of Freedom from Fascism has a border formed of a series of vows, each beginning "WIR SCHWOREN" (we swear), but the second has the misspelling "WIR SCWOREN". On the 10pf. stamp of 1970 issued by East Germany to commemorate 25 years of D.D.R. radio, "INTERNATIAONAL" occurs in place of INTERNATIONAL. A 2b. 1968 stamp of Yemen marking the 20th anniversary of UNESCO features Sheban Funerary Carvings, misspelt "Funeiary". An Egyptian 20m. stamp of 1974 indicting alleged Israeli misbehaviour towards refugees features a sheaf of leaflets, the front one reading "CONTINIOUS AGRESSION ON REFUGEE CAMPS" instead of CONTINUOUS AGGRESSION.

Spelling mistakes do, naturally enough, tend to slip past where designers and printers are unfamiliar with the language. Latin, being a dead language, is particularly prone to errors. On the 15c. 1970 definitive of St. Christopher, Nevis and Anguilla a Spanish ' piece of eight ' is featured, inscribed "HISPANIANUM" instead of HISPANIARUM, to which it was speedily corrected. A Mongolian miniature sheet of 1973 commemorates the astronomer Copernicus but misspells the title of his book ' DE REVOLUTIONIBUS URBIUM COELESTIUM ' with "IRBIUM" in place of URBIUM. The title is given correctly on a 1973 Venezuelan issue. Surprisingly enough the Vatican City itself has erred in a Latin inscription for the 1955 issue commemorating Pope Nicholas V. The inscription, taken from his tomb, should have read ' Excoluit doctos doctior ipse viros '—A scholar himself, he taught others to learn—but has in error "Escoluit". Another spelling error associated with a Pope is shown on the 20cr. stamp issued by Brazil in 1964 to honour the late Pope John 23rd, which instead of ' In Memoriam ' is inscribed "In Memorian". The 1970 Christmas stamps of Great Britain (4d. value) and Cook Islands (4c.) both show an illustration from the De Lisle Psalter with the phrase ' Gloria in Excelsis Deo ' wrongly rendered "Excelris". Here, however, the error lies not with the stamp designer (Sally Stiff) but with some long-forgotten restorer of the manuscript who converted a long ' s ' into an ' r ' in the manuscript itself. Thailand on a 50s. 1970 stamp marking an I.C.W. conference in Bangkok has the Latin tag 'OMNIA QUACUMQUE VULTIS UT FACIANT VOBIS HOMINES ET VOS FACITE ILLIS ' but runs HOMINES and ET into one word.

The specific names of plants and animals, often derived from classical sources, are likewise subject to error. In the first place designers often do not appreciate that each name consists of two parts, a generic name (comparable to a surname) which must be capitalised, and a specific name or epithet which in general should not be capitalised. Uncapitalised generic names occur on issues of Albania (1965), Bulgaria (1968, 1972), Czechoslovakia (1962), Gambia (1966), Hungary (1973), Malagasy Republic (1973), Nicaragua (1974), Norway (1970), Philippines (1962), Poland (1968) and Yugoslavia (1964, 1965 and 1967). Capitalised specific names and epithets occur on issues of British Honduras (1967, 1969 and 1970), Burundi (1972), Cuba (1969), Czechoslovakia (1960), Ecuador (1961), Fiji (1968), Gambia (1973), Greece (1970), Guinea (1963, 1964), Guyana (1972), Mali Republic (1971), Mauritius (1969), Monaco (1960), Paraguay (1974), Ras Al Khaima (1975), St. Pierre et Miquelon

(1962), Samoa (1967), San Marino (1972), Uruguay (1969), Venezuela (1969) and North Vietnam (1966). Doubtless there are many more in both categories. However spelling errors occur also (though one must beware of the frequent typographic errors in the catalogues themselves). Butterflies, which because of their beauty feature frequently on stamps, seem curiously liable to be misnamed. The handsome 1958 Cuban issue commemorating the naturalist Felipe Poey shows on the 12c. and 14c. values butterflies of the genus *Terias*, in each case wrongly spelled "*Teria*". The Peacock butterfly, *Nymphalis io*, is wrongly spelt "*Nymphalis Jo*" on a 60h. Czechoslovakian stamp of 1961, and the Purple Emperor butterfly, *Apatura iris*, as "*Apatura ilia*" on a 60fi. Hungarian stamp of 1959. The 1f. and 2f. values of the 1960 butterflies issue of the Central African Republic feature *Charaxes mobilis* but misspelt "*Charaxe*"—the generic name is correctly spelt on 10f. and 20f. values of the same issue—while on the 20c. value of the 1967 Ethiopian set of butterflies, *Charaxes varanes* is misspelt "*varans*" (it is correct on a 30c. Senegalese stamp of 1963). On the 5c. value of the same Ethiopian set confusion between the name of the family (*Papilionidae*) and of the genus (*Papilio*) has led to the latter being entirely omitted for *Papilio aethiops*. A 4r.+1r. semipostal Indonesian stamp of 1963 misspells *Charaxes dehani* as "*dehaani*". A 20c. 1970 stamp of Ecuador and a 50c. 1966 Venezuelan stamp both spell *Papilio zabreus* as "*zagreus*". A 1967 60c. Nicaraguan stamp has the butterfly *Anaea cleomestra* misspelt "*Ananea*". The Milkweed Monarch's genus *Danais* appears to have caused orthographic problems, as it is sometimes given as "*Danais*" (Mozambique 1953, 2$.30, Ifni 1966 40c., 4p.), sometimes as "*Danaus*" (Tanzania 1973 30c.). Other types of insect appear less frequently on stamps, and errors are accordingly less numerous. A 5c. Panamanian stamp of 1950 illustrates the mosquito *Aedes aegypti* which transmits yellow fever, but names it "*Aeedes egity*", while the Solifuge *Galeodes arabs* on a 130f. 1972 stamp of Chad, which sounds in error and is given as *araba* in some catalogues, is actually correct.

Crustaceans also get misspelt at times. An 8c. Panamanian stamp of 1965 showing the shrimp *Penaeus occidentalis* misspells its name "*Penacus*" (the correct spelling can be seen on a 1965 12x. North Vietnamese stamp). A 1f. 1965 Moroccan stamp shows a prawn labelled (on the tabs) "*Aristeomorpha foliacea*". It is the wrong prawn, but the name should in any case be spelt *Aristaeomorpha*. Both mistakes also occur on a 25c. Algerian stamp of 1970. Could this be an example of plagiarism? A 20b. Rumanian stamp of 1966 misspells the crab *Pachygrapsus marmoratus* as "*Pachigrapsus*". The 1c. 1960 Monégasque stamp showing the crab *Macrocheira kaempferi* misspells it "*kampferi*".

Although many mistakes involve molluscs, simple spelling errors are relatively rare. Kenya illustrated the Pearly Nautilus (*Nautilus pompilius*) on a 70c. definitive of 1971, but with the misspelling "*pompileus*", finally corrected in 1974, and that is the only unequivocal spelling error of a mollusc's name on our lists so far. Echinoderms are uncommonly figured on stamps, but the 70q. 1966 Albanian stamp featuring the sea urchin *Sphaerechinus granularis* has it misspelt "*Sphaereclinus*".

Fish do appear often on stamps, and spelling mistakes are frequent. The sea horse on the 3c. definitive of Barbados, issued in 1965, is wrongly labelled "*Hippocanpus* species", corrected to "*Hippocampus*" in 1967.

The swordfish on the 80q. Albanian stamp of 1967 is labelled "*Xiphias gladiolus*"—the correct "*Xiphias gladius*" can be seen on a 3s. Peruvian stamp of 1970. The Cuckoo wrasse on a 50p. 1968 Lebanese stamp is named "*Labrus ossifagus*" in error for *ossiphagus*, and *Lutjanus fulniflamma* is misspelt "*Lutyanus*" on a 2r. Iranian stamp of 1973. The Orange-striped trigger fish *Balistapus undulatus*, correctly spelled on a 90g. Polish stamp of 1967 is misspelt "*Balistipus*" on a ½c. Panamanian stamp of 1968. *Acanthurus triostegus* is misspelt "*Acauthurus*" on a 3e. stamp of Mozambique issued in 1951—the correct spelling of the generic name can be seen on a 50c. 1963 stamp of the New Hebrides. The Spanish hogfish, *Bodianus rufus*, is misspelt "*Bodiana*" on a 2c. Cuban stamp of 1969, and the Stone bass on the 1l. 1966 stamp of San Marino is wrongly called "*Cernia bruna*" but should in any case be spelt *Cerna*. The 1964 Guinean set of fishes carries a curious mixture of German and scientific names with at least one spelling error—the Senegal herring on the 2f. and 300f. stamps should in German be named 'Senegalhechtling', not as on the stamps "Senegalchechtling".

Turning to reptiles, the 12x. 1966 stamp of North Vietnam depicts a gecko inscribed "GEKKO GECKO" instead of GECKO GECKO. A 25m. Mongolian stamp of 1972 shows the lizard *Phrynocephalus versicolor* misspelt "*Phrynoephalus*". The python on a 5b. Rumanian stamp of 1964 is named "*Pyton molurus*", but the generic name is *Python*, as shown on a 60f. Mauritanian stamp of 1969. The dinosaur *Talarurus* is misspelt "*Talararus*" on a 10m. Mongolian stamp of 1967, and the dinosaur on a 15f. 1970 stamp of the Congo (Brazzaville) is inscribed "Kentrosaure" in fact more correct than the later published synonym Kentrurosaure.

A bird genus which causes particular spelling difficulties is that of the sea eagles—*Haliaeetus*, which was correctly *Haliaeëtus* until a change of rule (in 1961) abolished the diaeresis. It is misspelt "*Haliaëtus*" on a 1fo. Hungarian stamp of 1962, "*Haliaetus*" on a 4n. Zambian stamp of 1975 and a I£3 Israeli stamp of 1963, "*Haliaëtus*" on a 50m. Mongolian stamp of 1970, and "*Haliaeëtus*" on a 60g. Polish stamp of 1960. It is correct on a Swedish 75ore stamp of 1973. The Golden eagle *Aquila chrysaetus* appears as "*chrysaetos*" on a 60b. 1968 Rumanian stamp and a 10q. Albanian stamp of 1966, "*chrysaëtos*" on a 11.30 Rumanian stamp of 1960, and "*chrysaëtus*" on an 80m. Mongolian stamp of 1976. The osprey *Pandion haliaetus* is correct on a 75b. Rumanian stamp of 1967, but "*haliaëtus*" on a Polish 60g. stamp of 1964. The Bateleur eagle *Terathopius ecaudatus* is misspelt "*Terathopis*" on the 1r. South African definitive of 1974, and on the 15c. value of the same issue the Sunbird *Nectarinia afra* is mislabelled "*afer*" (strictly speaking not a spelling error but a mistake in gender). The King vulture *Sarcoramphus* is misspelt "*Sarcaramphus*" on 5c. 1963 stamps of El Salvador, and the Cinereous vulture *Aegypius monachus*, correctly spelt on a 70q. Albanian stamp of 1966, is misspelt "AEGYPTUS" on a 1a. 1968 stamp of Afghanistan. The Plantain eater *Musophaga* is misspelt "*Musophuga*" on a 10s. Gambian stamp of 1966, the Waxwing *Bombycilla garrulus* is "BOMBY-CILA" on a 15q. Albanian stamp of 1968, and the Mount Apo lorikeet *Tricoglossus johnstoniae* is "*jopnstoniae*" on a 10c.+5c. 1969 semipostal of the Philippines. The Niger Republic gives the Buff-backed cattle egret *Bubulcus ibis* as "*Bulbucus*" on a 50f. stamp of 1972, and the Flamingo

Phoenicopterus ruber ruber is "*ruber rubur*" on a 25c. 1973 stamp of Grenada. A 200f. 1963 stamp of Gabon shows the beautiful bird *Melittophagus muelleri,* but spells its name "*müllleri*", which is not permissible. A curious non-error is the 20f. 1963 stamp of the Congo (Kinshasa) showing the African jabiru, where several editions of Gibbons' catalogues carry a note pointing out that the inscription on the stamp is wrongly spelt "JARIBU", for in fact the stamp is perfectly correctly inscribed.

Turning to the mammals we find that a 50c. Venezuelan stamp of 1963 has the Three-toed sloth *Bradypus tridactylus* misspelt "*trydactilus*", and a 100p. Uruguayan stamp of 1970 has the Armadillo *Dasypus hybridus* as "*hibrydus*". The Raccoon *Procyon lotor* is misspelt "*lothor*" on a 3c. 1963 stamp of El Salvador, and on a Czechoslovakian issue of 1959 the Marmot *Marmota marmota* is misspelt "*Marmotta marmotta*" on the 30h. value and the European bison *Bison bonasus* is misspelt "*bonassus*" on the 40h. value. The Malayan bear *Ursus malayanus* is misspelt "*malynus*" on both a 20x. 1961 stamp of North Vietnam and a 70k. 1969 stamp of Laos, and the Leopard *Panthera pardus* is misspelt "*Phanthera*" on a 12a. 1973 stamp of Afghanistan. In 1966 Czechoslovakia produced a set showing indigenous wild animals. The Hare *Lepus europaeus* on the 80h. stamp was misspelt "*europaens*" on 40 out of 50 stamps on each sheet, while correct on the remaining 10. This might more rightly be considered a production error, but at least the error predominates. A 4k. 1971 stamp of Malawi shows the Grey Duiker, but uses the American spelling "Gray" which is now rarely used in Britain or the Commonwealth in Africa. The correctness or otherwise here is therefore debatable. The oft-cited 1950 2c. stamp of Sarawak showing a Tarsier labelled "THE TARSIUS" is not, strictly speaking, a spelling error, but a slightly pedantic use of the scientific generic name, the full scientific name of the animal being *Tarsius spectrum*.

When we come to plants we find that the vast majority of those shown on stamps are flowers, and spelling mistakes are numerous. The 20e. Portuguese stamp of the 1968 Lubrapex set spells *Musschia aurea* as "*Muschia*" on both front and back of the stamp. British Honduras issued a 5c. stamp in 1971 showing the flower *Hymenocallis littoralis* misspelt "*littorallis*", and on a 6c. stamp of 1972 *Petrea volubis* is misspelt "*Petrae*", while on a 25c. stamp of 1969 the Mahogany tree *Swietenia macrophylla* is misspelt "*macrophylia*". The 1963 Cameroun postage due set has *Hibiscus rosa-sinensis* wrongly spelt "*Hybiscus rosa sinensis*" on a 0.50f. value. The hyphen is also missing on stamps of the Congo (Brazzaville) (20f. 1971), Surinam (8c.+4c. 1962), Wallis & Futuna (21f. 1973) and Upper Volta (50c. 1963). It is given correctly on a Rumanian 1l. stamp of 1965. The Cameroun issue also has *Amorphophallus* as "*Amorphophalus*" on a 40f. stamp, the family Zingiberacée without the acute accent on the other 40f. value, and *Crinum* misspelt "*Grinum*" on a 1f.50 stamp of the same issue. A 10c. 1955 stamp of Somalia has *Crinum scabrum* also misspelt "*Grinum*", while a 1s. express letter Somalian stamp also of 1955 has *Erythrina melanacantha* misspelt "*Erihrina*". A 4f. 1963 stamp of Upper Volta has *Ipomoea stolonifera* misspelt "*Ipomaea*" (it is correct on a 40f. 1952 stamp of the Belgian Congo), and a Mauritanian 20f. stamp of 1966 also has "*Ipomaea*". A 40f. stamp of Upper

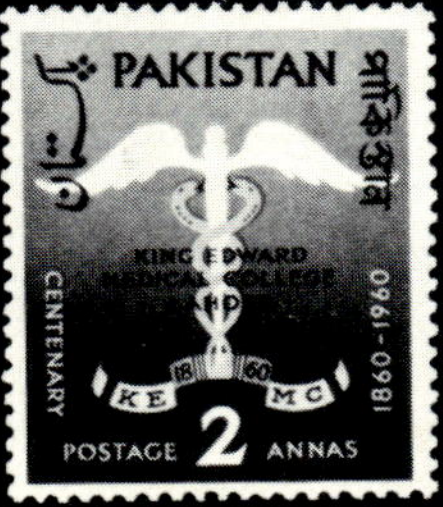

27

28

29

30

31

32

33

34

35

36

37

38

39

40

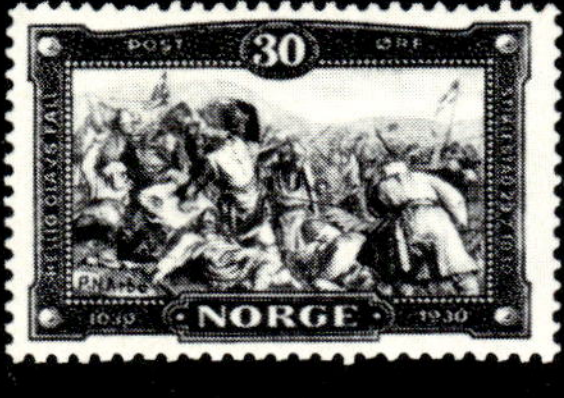

41

43

42

Volta in the same 1963 series features the water lily *Nymphaea lotus* but misspelt "*Nymphea*". The correct spelling appears on a 5f. Mauritanian stamp of 1965, while a 5st. 1963 Bulgarian stamp showing the White water lily *Nymphaea alba* misspells its name as "NIMPHAEA". The 6st. value of the same set has *Tulipa urumoffii* as "*Urumovii*" and the 13st. value has *Anemone narcissiflora* incorrectly spelt "*Anemona*". *Campanula persicifolia* is misspelt "*persicaefolia*" on a 10l. 1967 stamp of San Marino. On a 1t. Mongolian stamp of 1973 the flower labelled "*Pulsatilla tlavescens*" should be *Anemone* (*Pulsatilla*) *flavescens*, and "*Rhododendron dahuricum*" on the 30m. value should be *Rhododendron dauricum*. "*Antirrhinum romosissimum*" on 5c.+5c. and 20c. 1956 stamps of Spanish Sahara should be *Antirrhinum ramosissimum*, and "*Eminium lehemannii*' on a 16k. Russian stamp of 1975 should have been *Eminium lehmanni*, or more properly *Helicophyllum lehmanni*. *Cyclamen graecum* on a 5d. 1958 Greek stamp is misspelt "*greacum*", and a Russian 40k. stamp of 1960 has *Tulipa greigii* misspelt "*gregii*", Albania spells *Camellia williamsi* as "*Camelia*" on a 5q. 1967 stamp although *Camellia* is spelt correctly on the 1972 set devoted to the genus. On a 5q. 1970 stamp *Lilium cernuum* has lost a '*u*' to become "*cernum*", and on a 5l. stamp of 1965 *Rosa*...var. *shquiperia* has lost its specific epithet altogether. On a 1965 set illustrating fruits Albania spells *Mespilus* as "*Mesphilus*" on the 2l. value (it is correct on a Bulgarian 1st. stamp of 1969), and on the 3l. value spells the Persimmon *Diospyros kaki* as "*Dyospyros*". Tunisia gets the Pear *Pyrus communis* wrong on a 5c. 1971 stamp, misspelling it "*Pirus*".

Orchids are popular subjects for stamps, but their names are often misspelt. For instance the orchid *Trichoglottis fasciata* is misspelt "*fasiata*" on a 70k. Laotian stamp of 1971. Israel, on a 12a. value of 1970 shows the Jersey orchid *Orchis laxiflora* (spelt correctly on a 7½p. 1972 stamp of Jersey), as "*laxiflorus*". Colombia spells *Masdevallia nycterina* correctly on a 4c. stamp of 1950, but as "*nicterina*" on a 1c. stamp of 1947. Venezuela has "*Cycnoches chlorochilon*" instead of *chlorochilum* on a 20c. stamp of 1962. *Cypripedium hookerae* var. *volonteanum* is misspelt "*volunteanum*" on a 3c. Cuban stamp of 1966, and *Brassocattleya sindrossiana* appears as "*Brasso catleya*" on a 1c. stamp of 1972. Laos has misspelt *Ascocentrum miniatum* as "*miniatur*" on a 50k. stamp of 1971, *Rhynchostylis giganteum* as "*Rynchostylis giganterum*" on a 40k. stamp of 1972, and *Cattleya* as "*Catteleya*" on an 80k. stamp of the same series.

Botanists do not always agree amongst themselves as to correct spelling of scientific names. The rival merits of *Plumieria* and *Plumeria* are still arguable. The Ivory Coast (1962, 5f.), Congo (Brazzaville) (1971, 5f.), Samoa (1969, 2s.) and Laos (1967, 80k.) have "*Plumeria*", Cuba (1967, 13c.) and Niger Republic (1965, 45f.) have "*Plumieria*", but whichever of these is right "*Plumera*" as on a 10l. 1973 Maldivian stamp is certainly wrong. The cactus *Mammillaria boolii* is shown on an East German 30pf. stamp of 1970, there spelt "*Mamillaria*", but this spelling is accepted by some authorities. *Polyanthus* and *Polyanthes* provide another disputed pair—"*Polyanthes tuberosa*" appears on both a 10f. 1971 stamp of Congo (Brazzaville) and a 1d.15 1972 Algerian stamp. A 1s.50 1969 Ugandan stamp illustrates *Clerodendrum myricoides*. On etymological grounds this should be "*Clerodendron*" as on an 18f. 1968 stamp of Rwanda Republic, but both forms are used.

The genus *Strophanthus,* correctly spelled on a 10c. 1963 stamp of the Congo (Kinshasa), is misspelt "*Strophantus*" on an 85f. 1961 stamp of the Ivory Coast and on 15c. and 50c. stamps of Spanish Guinea. The Rwanda 20c. stamp of 1970 commemorating the discovery of quinine misspells *Cinchona* "CHINCHONA". The Mangosteen *Garcinia mangostana* is misspelt "*Guarcinia*" on a 12x. 1964 stamp of North Vietnam, and the Breadfruit *Artocarpus integrifolia* is misspelt "*intregrifolia*" on a Laotian 180k. 1968 stamp. The Cannonball tree *Couroupita guianensis* is misspelt "*Coroupita*" on a 3c. Cuban stamp of 1967 (it is spelt correctly on a 6c. 1971 stamp of Guyana), while the "*Limoniastrum ifniensis*" on 15c. and 20c. 1956 stamps of Ifni should be *ifniense.* A 1966 Mongolian issue has *Physochlaina physalioides* misspelt "*Physochlaena*" on the 5m. value and *Allium polyrhizum* misspelt "*polyrrchizum*" on the 10m. value, and a 15m. stamp of 1960 has *Polemonium caeruleum* misspelt "*coeruleum*". The Congo Republic has *Helichrysum mechowiam* misspelt "*Helicrysum*" on a 100f. stamp of 1961, South Africa has *Zantedeschia aethiopica* misspelt "*ethiopica*" on a 4c. definitive of 1974. This was in any case an out-of-date name for the plant now known as *Richardia africana.* Liberia has *Barteria nigritana* incorrectly spelt "*nigritiana*" on a 25c. stamp of 1955, Senegal has *Opuntia engelmannii* misspelt "*engelmanni*" on a 150f. 1967 stamp, and Somalia has *Sesamothamnus busseanus* misspelt "*bussernus*" on a 1s.20 stamp of 1955. A 5c. 1966 stamp of Papua and New Guinea spells *Mucuna nova-guineensis* as "*novoguinensis*", and a 1f. 1964 stamp of New Caledonia has "*Freycinettia*" in mistake for *Freycinetia.* Nicaragua misspells *Schomburgkia tibicinis* as "*tibicinus*" on a 5c. stamp of 1962. A 1967 North Vietnamese issue featuring bamboos has *Arundinaria rolloana* as "*rollana*", *Bambusa binghami* as "*bingami*" and *Bambusa arundinacea* as "*arundinaceu*" on the 12x. values, while Israel has "*Oenothera drummondii*" instead of *drummondi* on a 32a. stamp of 1960.

Turning to Europe we find that the Mediterranean cypress *Cupressus sempervirens* has become two words "*semper virens*" on a 55l. 1968 Italian stamp, that Belgium has "*Hypochoeris*" instead of *Hypochaeris maculata* on a 5f. stamp of 1974, and that in 1973 Bulgaria issued a 2st. stamp with "*Leucantheum*" for *Leucanthemum* and the 28st. value has "*Ranunculus acer*" for the correct *acris.* Andorra has a curious flower labelled "*Heleborus coni*" on a 10p. 1966 stamp of the Spanish post offices. The identity of the flower is dubious, but the name certainly should be spelled *Helleborus,* possibly *Helleborus bocconi,* as no *Helleborus coni* is known. Spain spells *Helianthemum* as "*Helianthemun*" and *Teucrium* as "*Teucriun*" on 8p. and 1p. stamps respectively of 1974.

Mistakes in spelling of vernacular names are surprisingly rare. Pakistan on a 15r. stamp of 1958 refers to the Coconut tree as "COCOANUT TREE", an incorrectly derived spelling through confusion with cocoa—a quite different plant. This spelling was also used on the local stamps of the Central Pacific Cocoanut (sic) Plantations Ltd. of Christmas Island from about 1916 to 1934. The more acceptable spelling "Coconut" is found on a 10c. 1951 stamp of Ceylon. An indisputable and amusing error is the Water Lily on a 4c. 1967 Cook Islands stamp which was named "WALTER LILY' . This error is strictly speaking a production one, for it occurred on all stamps of only one of the four post office sheets which together make up a printing sheet; it was later corrected.

Inscriptions in languages with non-Latin alphabets frequently have spelling errors through misplaced dots and squiggles. Thus the 1961 lower definitive values for Pakistan when first produced had the Bengali inscription wrongly engraved, the lack of a small projection on the first letter converting it from a ' p ' to a ' sh ', so that it read "Shakistan"; this was corrected for later issues, on the die of the 1p., 2p. and 5p. values and on the plate for the 3p. and 7p. values. In the 1951 set commemorating the 4th Anniversary of Independence an extra dot engraved in the lower loop of the middle character of the central inscription for the 8a. and 10s. design (an archway and lamp) makes it read "Pakisnatan". Moving to Persia (Iran), the 5sh. value of 1882 had at first three dots at the right end of the Farsi inscription on the scroll: in a later version these became only two, the equivalent of changing the ' p ' of ' postes ' into a ' y '. The 1952 35c. definitive of Ceylon (now Sri Lanka) omitted a dot from above the third character of the Tamil inscription, changing it from ' Ilanggai ' (Ceylon) to "Ilangagai"; this was duly corrected in 1954. On the 1918 1a. definitive of Cochin a small mark extra to the Malayalam equivalent of ' revenue ' changed it into a word non-existent in the vernacular and with no meaning in this context; this also was corrected. The Saudi Arabian 1966 issue commemorating the burning of Algiers Library was withdrawn shortly after issue because of small errors in the Arabic inscription—a small dotted line in one case, a missing dot in another, each converting one letter into another. In 1922 Egypt issued a 15m. stamp with the Arabic in the nominative instead of the accusative. This was duly corrected (figs. 6 & 7), as eventually were the several Sudanese camel postman stamps issued in 1898 which, amongst other errors, used the singular instead of the plural for the inscription which transliterates the Italian "Posta Soudaniya" (Sudan Postage) into Arabic script. This was duly corrected to the proper Arabic term "Bariyd il Sudan". The 1907 Nepalese issue misspells the name of Sri Pashupati (Patron God of Nepal) as "Pasupati" in the 3rd ideogram at the top of the stamp. This was corrected for the 1929 issue. The Japanese 10s. 1940 stamp in the Kirishima National Park issue has a horizontal stroke missing from the second character from the right (=shima), although this is correct on the remaining values of the issue. The tab of the Israeli 15m. 1948 definitive spells the word ' L'gulat ' (redemption) with a letter ' vov ' which is incorrect (and indeed is missing from the coin itself, which is reproduced on the stamp). It is correctly omitted from the tab of the 3m. value, and also from the inscription incorporated in the designs of the 3, 15 and 50pr. values of the 1949 definitives, and in subsequent issues. The name "Yisroel" (Israel) is always shortened to "Yisro" on coins of the type illustrated on the 15pr. stamp (second coin set) of 1949. As the designs had been modified to include the descriptions which previously were on the tabs, the error is in the stamp itself and is that the Hebrew translation of the ancient coin inscription is given as "l'gulat Yisroel" instead of ' l'gulat Yisro '. This appears on the 15pr. definitives of 1949 and 1950, the 15pr. official of 1951, the 45pr. definitive of 1952 and the 15pr. postcards of 1950 and 1952. The 1949 10pr. stamp shows a coin depicting an amphora, with the inscription transliterating to "Schnat sholosh" (year 3). The word ' sholosh ' is always found with a ' vov ' as on the tab of the 1948 10m., but the ' vov ' is omitted on this stamp. This error also occurs on the 10pr. and 40pr. of the 1950-54 coin issues and the 10pr. postcards of 1950-51. The left-hand characters of the inscription in the top right-hand corner of the 3½a. value of the Burmese 1949 U.P.U. anniversary issue lacks a small circle inside the large one, compared with other values of this issue. Whether or not this is particularly significant we do not know.

Overprints, being generally relatively hurried productions, are particularly subject to error, though we would only consider these within the scope of design error where constant throughout the issue. However the error made in the Siamese date inscription overprinted on the 1a. value of 1908 to commemorate 40 years rule by King Chulalongkorn was constant. It involved a single character, and was discovered and corrected by hand after 60 sheets had been printed. A more dubious error is in the circular overprint on South Korean stamps during the North Korean occupation in 1950, where a slight change in one character converts ' democratic ' into "inferior" the status or even existence of such an error is questionable, and indeed it sounds too good to be true.

Plurals often create difficulties of various kinds. The centenary of the International Telecommunication Union was commemorated by many countries, but Syria, Egypt and Ghana gave it wrongly in 1965 as "TELECOMMUNICATIONS", although to be inconsistent Ghana got it right on the miniature sheet of this issue. In 1967 Ghana commemorated the Ghanaian boy scout movement with three values and a miniature sheet but labelled them "BOYS SCOUT MOVEMENT", which is not quite correct. Conversely, Afghanistan in 1968 commemorated the Mexican Olympics with a set of three values inscribed "MEXICO OLYMPIC". A Syrian 60p. stamp of 1965 reading "MEDICAL DAYS OF THE NEAR AND MIDDLE EAST DAMASCUS 19.25 AP. 1965" does seem a bit involved. Australia on an 8½d. definitive of 1950 portrayed a native, Djungarai (better-known as "One Pound Jimmie") labelled "Aborigine". ' Aborigines ' is a plural noun for the native inhabitants of a country, the correct word for a single inhabitant being ' aboriginal '. The incorrectly derived singular ' aborigine ' is by now widely accepted, but at the time of this issue its use was deplored by many purists. However it was unchanged on the 1952 2/6d. issue with the same portrait. A faulty plural occurs on a 1976 miniature sheet of Ajman labelled "FAMOUS MENS" (incidentally including Queen Elizabeth II as one of the subjects). A Nicaraguan issue of 1974 shows flowers which on the 2c., 4c. and 1cor. values are given only their generic names, *viz.* "*Malachra* spp", obviously intended to indicate ' a species of *Malachra* '. However ' spp.' is an abbreviation for species in the plural, and the correct abbreviation for a single species is ' sp.'.

Another type of error which often resembles a spelling error is the use of a word or phrase in the wrong language. On a 10m. Egyptian definitive of 1953 the word "DEFENCE" appears, but as French was the occidental language used for other inscriptions on the stamp this ought to have been ' DEFENSE ', and a corrected version was produced within the same year. A 9c. 1973 stamp of Christmas Island shows a ship labelled "H.M.S. *Imperious*", but the ship of Capt. H. W. May who annexed Christmas Island in 1888 was given as H.M.S. *Imperieuse* in the Navy List of that year. A 1959 40p. Syrian stamp overprinted for the Second Damascus Conference gives it the French spelling "CONFERANCE" but with the English "2nd" (fig. 8). Conversely the 1961 Moroccan series marking an African Postal and Telecommunications Union Conference has "CONFERENCE DE TANGER" instead of 'CONFERANCE'. Saudi Arabian stamps formerly carried inscriptions in French, but changed over to English in the nineteen sixties, and during the transition period mixtures occur: thus on the 1966 issue commemorating the burning of the Algiers Library in 1962 the commemorative inscription is in English but the stamps also bear the French "postes", and the Deir Yasin Massacre commemorative issue of 1966 has a similar mixture. A Jordanian issue of January 4th 1964 marking the visit of Pope Paul to the Holy Land gives him the Italian title of "Papa Paulus" in the English inscription, and the issue commemorating the meeting of the Pope with the Oecumenical Patriarch on January 5th 1964 repeats this error but also refers to "Their Holiness" rather than 'Their Holinesses'. Lebanon on a 1974 air issue has "MISS UNIVERS", which should have been 'MISS UNIVERSE' (whatever that may mean) or 'MADEMOISELLE UNIVERS', but not a mixture of both languages. The Morales 1874 issue for Republican Revolutionary Cuba carried the Latin tag "CUBA LIBRA" instead of the Spanish 'CUBA LIBRE', so the issue was rejected. An East German 20pf.+10pf. semipostal of 1965 shows a 'Freedom for Ernst Thälmann' demonstration, but the Spanish slogan given as "Libertad pro Thälmann" should of course have read 'Libertad para Thälmann'. Hungary in 1965 on a 1fo. stamp shows the Russian astronaut Leonov dangling in space from a capsule labelled "VOSZHOD 2" in Roman alphabet letters—it should of course have been in Cyrillic, as shown on a 10k. Russian stamp of 1965. Finally, East Germany in 1968 produced an issue honouring the Sachsenhausen National Memorial Museum. The word 'peace' is included in the design in 12 different languages, but in the Russian word МЧР (mir) the Latin letter 'R' is given in place of the corresponding Cyrillic letter 'P' —an error of the stamp design for the original panel is correct.

Expression of the genitive case often seems to create trouble for stamp designers. Frequently this is merely the omission of a necessary apostrophe, presumably to simplify fitting lettering into a given space. For example, the 1d. St. Vincent stamps of 1938 and 1949 both omit the apostrophe of 'Young's Island'. The early Tasmanian stamps did not treat the apostrophe of 'Van Diemen's Land' very seriously, for it is omitted from the 1d. design of 1853 and from all values of the 1855 design, while retained on the 1853 4d. and also the Australian 1953 3d. Centennial commemorative. Similarly the 1860 2½d. stamp of British Columbia & Vancouver Island is inscribed "Vancouvers Island" with no apostrophe. Newfoundland has been a prime offender in omitting apostrophes, *e.g.* from 'Heart's Delight' (1933 10c.), 'Colony's' (1897 5c., 6c., 8c., 15c.), 'Cabot's' (1897 10c.), and 'Heart's Content' (1928 8c.), although in this last case there was some doubt as to the correct spelling, and the Canadian Board of Geographical Names did not settle this (in favour of including the apostrophe) until November 1953. Other cases include South Georgia, 1963 2s. (Shackleton's Cross), Swaziland, 1969 50c. (Burchell's Zebra), British Solomon Islands, 1973 9c. (Ship's hour-glass), Iraq, 1967 200f. (Aladdin's Cave), Manama, 1971 60d. (Grocer's Daughter), Malta, 1956 4½d. (Roosevelt's Scroll, third paragraph, ' Malta's '), Sudan, 1961 15m., 3p. and 55m. (Girls' Education), Sharjah, 1965 50p. (Man's early flight), British Virgin Islands, 1970 issue (Centenary of Charles Dickens' Death), Dubai, 1968 and Libya, 1968 (Children's Day issues). In some cases it might be argued that the word with the apparently missing genitive is a noun in apposition, so that Dubai's 1968 "Arab Mothers Day" issue, Syria's 1959 80p. "Emigrants Congress", Israel's 1962 12a. "Heroes and Martyrs Day" (on the tab) and Pakistan's 1964, 1965, 1967 (15p.) and 1971 (20p.) "Universal Children Day" could be as intended. On the other hand Manama's 1968 issue for Mothers' Day is clearly wrong in being labelled "Mother's Day". Arab countries do appear to have trouble in expressing the genitive case in English: for instance Syria in 1966 commemorates "LABOURS' UNION" which is certainly wrong as it stands and ought to read either ' LABOUR'S UNION ' or more probably ' LABOUR UNIONS '. Iraq in 1969 issued a 15f. stamp commemorating "Prophet's Mohammed Birthday", corrected on the 1970 issue, and Saudi Arabia in 1974 produced an issue labelled "BLINDS' DAY" instead of ' BLIND'S DAY ', while Siam in 1920 produced two issues of semipostals supporting the ' Wild Tiger ' Scouts organisation overprinted "Scout's Fund".

Similar errors occur for countries which should know better, for instance Norfolk Island, 1953 8½d. has "Barrack's Entrance" instead of ' Barracks' Entrance ', and New Zealand, 1900 1½d. has "THE EMPIRES CALL", which does not mean quite the same thing as the intended ' THE EMPIRE'S CALL'. Sierra Leone in 1969 produced an issue commemorating the World's first self-adhesive postage stamps, but omitted the apostrophe. The Yemen Arab Republic (1964) and Jordan (1965) commemorated the New York World's Fair, but labelled their stamps simply "WORLD FAIR". Bermuda, on the other hand, created a non-existent genitive on 3d. and 1/3d. stamps of 1953 which show a map of the main island divided into its eight parishes, each named after one of the important members of the first colony, to whom it was assigned. One of these was named Sir Edwin Sands or Sandys, but Sandys Parish had been wrongly changed to "Sandy's Parish" on the Colonial Office map supplement followed by the stamp designer (possibly the marking for a house had been mistaken for an apostrophe). This was not corrected until 1957. Another missing apostrophe case is that of Saudi Arabia in various issues from 1937 to 1956 which omit the apostrophe from L'ARABIE SOUDITE. A regrettable tendency is the sloppy use of an apostrophe where only the plural is intended, and we see examples of this daily in newspapers and in advertisements. Perhaps the ultimate can be seen on a Kenyan 2s. stamp of 1976 marking advances in the telephone, which illustrates a "Contemporary telephone", an "Early phone 1880's" and a "Classic of 1930's" (fig. 9).

Hyphens can also cause trouble. Lord Baden-Powell's name ought to be hyphenated, as shown on his tombstone (East Africa, 1973 70c.), but the hyphen has been omitted on issues of Ajman (1967, 30d.), Anguilla (1970, 50c.), Barbados (1972, 15c.), Belgium (1957, 4f.), Brazil (1957,

3cr.30), Dahomey (1973, 20f.), Dubai (1967, 1r.), Grenada (1968, 3c., $1), Iran (1957, 10r.), Luxemburg (1957, 2f., 2f.50), Mali (1973, 130f.), Netherlands Antilles (1957 set), Nicaragua (1957 set), Panama (1970, 15c., 50c.), Paraguay (1962 set, 1965, 15g.), Togo (1961, 1f.) and Uruguay (1968, 9p., which gave him an apparent award of "U.K." after his name). On the other hand "Smithie"—Kingsford Smith—did not spell his name with a hyphen, although it is hyphenated on stamps of Fiji (1968 set) and Samoa (1968, 20s.). Kingsford was his mother's maiden name; it was the final given name of all her seven children and was later prefixed to the surname by all the family to distinguish them from neighbouring Smiths. 'Transatlantic' is hyphenated on stamps of Newfoundland (1919, 3c., $1 on 15c.; 1928, 8c., 9c., 14c.; 1930, 50c. on 36c.; 1932, $1.50 on $1), but is usually spelt as a single unhyphenated word, as for instance on the 20c. stamp of 1937. The hyphen of 'Vickers-Vimy' is omitted from a 1931 50c. stamp and also from "South-West Arm" on a 2c. stamp of 1923, all Newfoundland issues.

Pan-Arab is spelt "PAN ARAB" on stamps of Egypt (1965 set), Pan-African as "PAN AFRICAN" on a 1976 issue of the Seychelles marking an ornithological congress, Petro-chemical as "PETRO CHEMI-CAL" by Iran (1964 set) and Inter-colonial as "INTER COLONIAL" by Barbados (1950 8c.). A five-masted schooner on a 12c. Canadian stamp of 1977 appears without its hyphen, although correct in the text on the official advertising leaflet of the Canadian Philatelic Service. Gandhi is called "Apostle of Truth and Non Violence" on a 2r.50 1969 Mauritian stamp.

A hyphen is missing between "JUBILAUMS" and "KONGRESS" on a 3s.50 Austrian stamp of 1971. Numerous German issues carry compound words split on two lines or carried round the corner on a stamp without the necessary hyphen to indicate this, and designers often fail to form such compound words correctly even when they have no such excuse. Several values of an overprinted 1940 issue for German occupied Poland omit the hyphen between "General" and "Gouvernement". For German New Guinea the issues of 1898-99, of 1901 and the 3pf. value of 1919 have the spelling "DEUTSCH-NEU-GUINEA". This is against the rules of German spelling, for the geographical concept is 'NEUGUINEA' with the political elucidation 'DEUTSCH'. The correct "DEUTSCH-NEUGUINEA" appears on the 1914 issue. In the same way the 1897 issue for German South-west Africa wrongly has the overprint "Deutsch-Südwest-Afrika", corrected to "Deutsch-Südwestafrika" on the 1898 issue. Further examples of superfluous or missing hyphens in German words include West Germany, 1949 10pf. and 20pf. (Opening of West German Parliament issue), "BUNDES TAG" instead of 'BUNDES-TAG'; 1951 (700th anniversary of St. Mary's Church, Lübeck), "MARIEN KIRCHE" instead of 'MARIEN-KIRCHE'; 1951 (National Philatelic Exhibition), "BRIEFMARKEN AUSSTELLUNG" instead of 'BRIEFMARKEN-AUSTELLUNG'; 1954 (500th anniversary of the Gutenberg Bible), "GUTENBERG BIBEL" instead of 'GUTENBERG-BIBEL'; 1956 (125th birth anniversary of von Stephan), "WELTPOST VEREINS" instead of 'WELTPOST-VEREINS'; 1957 10pf. (350th anniversary of Justus Liebig University), "Justus Liebig-Hochschule" instead of 'Justus-Liebig-Hochschule'; 1958 (500th anniversary of Hospice of St. Nicholas), "CUSANUS

STIFT" instead of ' CUSANUS-STIFT '; 1959 (International Stamp Exhibition), "POSTWERTZEICHEN AUSSTELLUNG" instead of ' POSTWERTZEICHEN-AUSSTELLUNG '; 1959 (Inauguration of Beethoven Hall), "Mendelssohn Bartholdy" instead of ' Mendelssohn-Bartholdy '; (the same error occurs for East Germany, 1959, on an issue marking the 150th anniversary of his birth); 1961-64 (also for West Berlin 1961-62) (Famous Germans), "DEUTSCHE BUNDES POST" instead of ' DEUTSCHE BUNDES-POST '; 1961 (centenary of the telephone of Philipp Reiss), "Philipp Reiss-Telephon" instead of ' Philipp-Reiss-Telephon '; 1970 (SABRIA 70), "Briefmarken ausstellung" instead of ' Briefmarken-ausstellung '. West Berlin 1956 (Air Lift Monument), "Luftbrucken Denkmal" instead of ' Luftbrucken-Denkmal '; 1956 (Lilienthal Monument), "Lilienthaldenkmal" instead of ' Lilienthal-Denkmal '; 1957 (Mothers' Convalescence Fund), "MUTTER GENESUNGSWERK" instead of ' MUTTER-GENESUNGSWERK '. East Germany 1961 (High-voltage switchgear) "380 Kilo-Volt-Schalter" instead of ' 380-Kilovolt-Schalter '. Austria 1953 issue 1s.+25g. surcharged to commemorate the 60th anniversary of the Austrian Trade Union Movement "GEWERKSCHAFTS BEWEGANG" instead of ' GEWERKSCHAFTS-BEWEGANG '; 1961 3s.+70g. (Day of the Stamp semipostal) "POST AMT" instead of ' POST-AMT '.

The French Overseas Propaganda semipostals of 1940 incorrectly have "LA FRANCE D'OUTREMER", correctly given on the corresponding 2f. stamp of 1945 as "D'OUTRE-MER". Russia has two types of the 1951 issue marking the anniversary of the opening of the Lenin Volkhovsky Hydro-electric station, one with hyphen and the other as two unhyphenated words.

We have earlier indicated some of the errors perpetrated in biological nomenclature. Since the scientific name of a species consists of two words, an epithet which would normally itself be two words must be run into one, with or (for zoological names) without a hyphen. The 1f. 1971 Ivory Coast stamp showing the mollusc *Aporrhais pesgallinae* wrongly gives it as "*pes gallinae*". Colombia omits the hyphen in two values of a 1960 issue of the orchid *Odontoglossum luteo-purpureum* and Yugoslavia (1957, 50d.) for the fern *Dryopteris filix-mas*. On the other hand East Germany (1966, 10pf.) hyphenates the name *Gentiana pneumonanthe* to fit into the stamp format, splitting it as "*pneumo-nanthe*" instead of the etymologically more natural ' *pneumon-anthe* ' (=lung-flower), and in the same issue on the 20pf. value the name of the orchid *Cephalanthera rubra* is wrongly divided "*Cepha-lanthera*"—it should be ' *Cephal-anthera* '. The Cook Islands have *Bauhinia bipinnata* as "*bi-pinnata*" on a 5c. stamp of 1967. Jordan on a set of paintings of 1975 spells ' The club-footed boy ' without a hyphen on the 5f. value, ' Mona Lisa ' as one word on the 20f. value, and wrongly entitles ' Hope ' as "The Hope" on the 30f. value. Syria on a 15p. 1970 stamp marking a Scout Jubilee gives "BOYSCOUTS" as one word instead of two. The Christmas overprints of Anguilla in 1969 have the word ' CHRISTMAS ' split on two lines with no hyphen and on all values except the 25c. wrongly split as "CHRIS" and "TMAS" instead of ' CHRIST ' and ' MAS '. The Kuwaiti 1977 80f. value marking the 4th Asian Basketball Championship gives "BASKET BALL" as two words.

Abbreviations can also create problems—and errors. A full scientific name for a plant or animal species includes the name of the authority who conferred it, often in abbreviated form, but designers (and cataloguers) often simply add this to the name as an extra epithet. Thus in the 1970 Cambodian set illustrating aquatic plants Willd. (for Willdenow) and Solms. (for Solmsbach) have lost the full stops that mark abbreviations on the 3r. and 4r. values respectively. Venezuela (1970, 25c.) has 'Griseb.' (Grisebach) without the stop and (1971, 75c.) has 'Hook.' (Hooker) also without the stop. Cuba (1967, 20c.) correctly includes the abbreviation stop of 'Walp.' but does not capitalise the first letter of his name. Venezuela (1968, 20c.) shows a species of *Systena* (an insect) but omits the stop after 'sp.' (for species), while the Central African Republic (1962, 2f.) shows a species of *Ceroplesis* labelled "CEROPLESIS S.P"! Venezuela also puts an unwanted stop after the specific epithet but before the authority in the names of flowers of a 1970 issue.

Elsewhere stops marking abbreviations may be considered optional, but there should at least be consistency within an issue. The 1973 issue of Ghana marking the anniversary of the Organisation of African Unity has "O.A.U" with no stop after the 'U'. West Germany commemorated the poet Hans Jacob Christoffel von Grimmelshausen on a 40pf. stamp of 1976, but gave his initials as "H.J.C" with no stop after the 'C'. The 8c. 1973 Canadian stamp of the issue commemorating the Royal Canadian Mounted Police portrays Commissioner G. A. French, but while his initials are so given in the inscription in French, the English has simply "GA" with no stops and without even a space between the initials. Many modern issues, particularly for African countries, have stops after adjectival numerals, *e.g.* "25th.". Although these are not strictly necessary they should not be considered erroneous except where an issue is inconsistent, *e.g.* Fiji in the 1969 issue marking the 25th anniversary of the Solomons Campaign, where the 25c. value has "25th." and "23rd." while other values are without stops. A somewhat unusual but nevertheless logical error appears on a Syrian 60p. stamp of 1966 marking Labour Day, which is inscribed "May 1rst". A space after the figures of an abbreviated ordinal number might also be considered erroneous, *e.g.* "100 TH" on a Jordanian issue of 1976 marking the 100th anniversary of the first telephone call, and "30 TH" on a 1977 issue of Iraq marking the 30th anniversary of the Al Baath Party. Another example can be found on a 40f. stamp issued by the Cameroun Republic commemorating their admission to the World Scout Conference on "MARCH 26 TH 1971". A non-constant positioning of quotation marks can be seen on the tabs of the Israeli Jewish New Year issue of 1974, the 25a. tab having in English "The "Istanbuli" Synagogue Jerusalem", the 70a. has "The "Emtzai,, Synagogue Jerusalem" and the I£1 has "Raban Yohanan Ben Zakkay Synagogue Jerusalem" with no quotes at all.

Accents and other diacritical marks are also often treated rather casually on stamps. The accent is missing from 'Réunion' (1852, 15c., 30c.), 'St. Dévote' (Monaco 1960-61 set)—though present on stamps of the 1944 issue with the name in lower case, 'à percevoir' (France, 1882 30c. postage due; French Colonies, General Issue, 1884, 30c. postage due)—though present on other values of these issues, 'AÉREO' (Costa Rica 1930, 20c. on 50c., 40c. on 50c.)—though present on a slightly earlier 1930 air mail issue and on the 5c. on 10c. air mail stamp of 1932. The Compagnie des Transports Aèriens Guyanais of French Guiana has ' AÉRIENS ' on some of the 1921 stamps and "AERIENNE" on others. French Equatorial Africa has grave instead of acute accents on ' aérienne ' and ' Équatoriale ' on the 50c. value of the 1946-57 air mails, while the 2f. stamp of 1943 has what appears to be a circumflex instead of an acute accent on ' Équatoriale '. Afghanistan has "MÉRES" for ' MÈRES' on a 1968 Mothers' Day issue, and Ecuador has "réve" for ' rêve ' on a 1966 10c. stamp commemorating Dante. France commemorated the laying down of the French cruiser *Clemenceau* in 1939 with a 90c. stamp which included a portrait of the former Premier Georges Clemenceau, but spelt his name "Clémenceau", although he had always insisted that the name should not be accented. The Ivory Coast in 1904 issued a number of colonial general issue stamps overprinted "Cote d'Ivoire" instead of ' Côte ', while the 17c. Canadian express stamp of 1946 had "EXPRÊS", corrected to "EXPRÈS" in 1947. Burundi in 1967 commemorated the World Fair, Montreal, spelling the city's name without an accent on the stamp but as "Montréal" on the tab. The French Canadian spelling does use an accent, so one can at worst only accuse Burundi of inconsistency here. The spelling of ' Liege ' on Belgian stamps varies, with an acute accent in issues of 1919, 1930, 1938 and 1940, but a grave accent on a 20c. stamp of 1955. This is not, however an error, for the spelling was controversial until settled by decree of 17th Sept., 1946, which ratified the spelling ' Liège ' with a grave accent. Portugal seems to have been somewhat uncertain about the spelling "PORTUGUESA" or "PORTUGUÉSA", for most of the 10c. and 15c. stamps of the 1935-41 issue commemorating Prince Henry the Navigator have the latter spelling, but some are unaccented, as are other values of the issue, and indeed all other Portuguese issues. The Irish Republic has likewise been inconsistent in accenting its name. The 1952 issue commemorating the death of Moore first omitted the accent, and questions were immediately raised in the Dail (for ' eire ' without the accent could mean ' an encumbrance '!), but other issues since, *e.g.* the Europa issue of 1968, have also omitted the accent, even from Celtic script. It is, admittedly, general practice to omit accents from upper case Roman lettering for display purposes, so omission from, for instance, the 1963 Europa issue might be justified on these grounds. When Czechoslovakia commemorated the International Olympic Congress in Prague in 1925 by overprinting three values to mark the event "CONGRES" appeared instead of ' CONGRÈS '. One could argue that the letters, being upper case, did not have to have an accent, but the special postcards issued on the same occasion do have an accent.

Newfoundland in 1923 omitted the tilde from ' Cañon ' on a 10c. stamp. Carlist Spain omitted the tilde from ' ESPAÑA ' in the first issue of 1873, but cunningly created a straight line one by removal of part of a thin white line except just above the ' N '. In the final setting of 1874 a properly curved tilde was finally produced. The Spanish Protectorate in Morocco omits the tilde of ' ESPAÑOL ' from overprints on Spanish stamps issued from 1915 to 1921.

The Polish city of Czestochowa is given an accent under the ' z ' on a 150l. 1966 stamp of the Vatican City, although it should really have been under the neighbouring ' e '. Mongolia omits the accent from ' TORUŃ', the birthplace of Copernicus, on a miniature sheet of 1973 in his honour—the correct spelling can be found on a 90g. Polish stamp of 1960. Canada omits the diaeresis from ' Noël ' on the 1970 Christmas issue, although it is present on other Christmas issues, *e.g.* that of 1976, Turkey omitted the diaeresis from "CÜMHURIYETI" on the 1929 definitive issue, but rectified this in 1930. Israel omits two small dots from under the penultimate letter of the Arabic territory name on the 1975 Protected Wildbirds issue.

Individual letters and words can be wrong in various ways other than simple misspellings. A 10h. South Korean stamp of 1955 marking Rebirth of Industry has a faulty character on the upper right, redrawn in 1956. Great Britain in the 1973 British Explorers set does not dot any of the ' i 's except for one of the two in ' Livingstone '. Conversely a 1952 U.N. Day issue of Afghanistan inexplicably has a lower case ' i ' in the otherwise upper case name of the country. The Colombian state of Bolivar has no crossbar to the ' A ' of COLOMBIA on a 20c. stamp of 1903, and likewise French Polynesia—Tahiti in the A of TAHITI in the surcharge of the 1884 5c. on 20c. value, and the Confederate States of America in the word ' STATES ' on a 10c. 1861 stamp featuring James Madison (U.S.A. President, 1809-17, though often wrongly stated to be a portrait of Thomas Jefferson). Kishangarh, on the other hand, has a crossbar on the ' V ' of ' REVENUE ' on an 8a. 1904 stamp. Reversed letters are surprisingly common. Luxembourg has a reversed ' z ' in the name of the designer (Gonzague) of the 1956 Europa set, although it is correct for all the corresponding Europa issues of other countries. A reversed ' S ' appears to the left of the circle enclosing the numeral of value in the abbreviated name (F Sch) of the engraver Ferdinand Schirnbock of a Vatican City issue of 1933 featuring the Vatican Palace. However ' N ' is the most frequently reversed letter. The ' N ' of ' NAWAB ' is reversed on the 1886 issue of Bhopal, although correct on most stamps of other issues. A number of issues of the Colombian state of Bolivar have reversed ' N 's, such as the 1903 20c. registration stamp (correct in "CENTAVO" but reversed in ' VIENTE ' for at least part of the issue), the 1904 5c. registration stamp (reversed in ' CENTAVO ' and in ' CINCO '), the 1903 Too Late stamps (reversed in ' DEPARTAMENTO'), the 1904 2c. Acknowledgement of Receipt stamp (which also omits the ' DE ' of ' REPUBLICA DE COLOMBIA '), and in the 1904 postage issue (reversed in ' CENTAVO '). However the most striking case is that of the 12½p. Syrian stamp of 1960 commemorating Evacuation Day with the boldly printed slogan ' WE DEMAND ABSOLUTE INDEPENDENCE '—with all four ' N 's reversed! (fig. 10).

Whole words and phrases may also be reversed. On the 75c. 1932 Syrian issue the printer's imprint (Vaugirard) is reversed, and on a 30f. French stamp of 1957 commemorating the French Public Works the name of the engraver, J. Piel, is reversed along the framework on the right-hand side. On the obelisk on an Italian issue of 1933 marking the International University Games, Turin, the inscription "MUSSOLINI" appears, but reading from base to apex. A 2½d. 1890 stamp of New South Wales shows an allegorical figure with a banner inscribed "ADVANCE AUSTRALIA" reading from the hoist but inverted—a strange device indeed! The Mexican constitutionalist issues of the Civil War, 1913-15, bore a vertical overprint with an inverted $ sign, and the 10c. and 30c. values of the Saarland 1927-34 official stamps carry the overprint "DIENSTMARKE" inverted.

Lastly in this section we may turn to grammatical errors. The 1897 Chinese issue bore the inscription "Imperial Chinese Post", corrected to "Chinese Imperial Post" in the 1898 issue. The Japanese issues of 1876-96 all bore the inscription "Imperial Japanese Post" except one design which got round the problem of grammatical correctness by putting "Japanese Empire" at the top and "post" down each side, but subsequent issues were in Japanese only, breaching U.P.U. regulations. Korea likewise had "Imperial Korean Post" on its 1900 issue, but later issues of the short-lived Korean Empire evaded the problem by using French instead of English. Returning once more to Afghanistan, on the 1948 issue marking the 3rd anniversary of the U.N.O. we have "Afghanes postes" instead of 'Postes Afghanes', on the 1967 U.N.E.S.C.O. anniversary this is compounded by having "Afghan Postes", thus mixing English and French, and on various newspaper and parcel stamps from 1928 to 1930 this is only slightly bettered as "Postes Afghan". The Afghan airmails of 1939 and 1948 are inscribed "POSTES AERIENNE", a singular epithet qualifying a plural noun. The 1928 Persian airmails are correctly overprinted 'poste aérienne' on the lower values (to 2kr.), although with an accent which veers from acute to grave, but the higher values (from 3kr. upwards) have 'Poste aérien', wrongly making 'poste' masculine. The 1958 U.N. Day Iranian commemoratives likewise have "NATIONS-UNIS", restored to the correctly feminine "NATIONS-UNIES" on the comparable issue of 1959 (figs. 11 & 12). Sex also rears its head in the Mexican issue of 1964 marking 400 years of Mexican-Philippine Friendship, for the inscription "AMISTAD MEXICANO-FILIPINA" should read 'MEXICANA-FILIPINA', because AMISTAD (Friendship) is feminine.

The 1902 2m. German stamp portraying allegorically the union of North and South Germany has the inscription "Seid Einig, Einig, Einig" (Be one, one, one), but should not have capitals for the adjective 'einig'. Conversely the 42pf. German miniature sheet of 1936 commemorating the 'Brown Ribbon' of Germany horse-race in Munich, is inscribed "Das braune Band", but for a set phrase like this the epithet should also be capitalised, as on the special commemorative postmark used on this issue, and on the equivalent semipostal issue of 1939. The East German 25pf. value of a 1969 Forest Fire Prevention issue has the ungrammatical slogan "Erholungsstätte Wald SCHUTZT IHN", but should have SIE, not IHN. A 1959 40pf.+10pf. semipostal of West Germany portrays the brothers Grimm, but labels them "Gebrüder Grimm" instead of the more grammatical 'Die brüder Grimm'. Venezuela on a 1975 issue marking the 14th Scout Jamboree has "14 Jamboree", a Jordanian 1973 issue marking the 5th anniversary of the Battle of Karama has the slightly stilted caption "5th ANNIVERSARY FOR THE KARAMA BATTLE", and an Australian 2½d. stamp of 1950 is labelled rather clumsily "N S WALES' FIRST STAMP" instead of the preferable 'FIRST N.S. WALES STAMP'. Syria labels its 1971 issue marking the People's Council and Presidential Election as "PEOPLE COUNCIL AND

PRESIDENT ELECTION" (fig. 13), and the Yemen Arab Republic in 1972 marked the 25th anniversary of the Establishment of SOFAR with an issue labelled "ESTABLISH OF SOFAR". Linguistically incorrect inscriptions appear on Labour Day anniversary commemoratives of East Germany (1950) and West Germany (1965) stating enigmatically "60 JAHRE 1. MAI" and "75 Jahre 1 Mai" respectively.

CHAPTER 2

Errors of Identification

The errors to be dealt with in this section are cases in which the wrong subject is portrayed, an incorrect name is applied, or the wrong event is celebrated. While considerably less numerous than spelling errors, these have nevertheless occurred surprisingly frequently, and often there is an interesting story connected with the error.

If we look first at the portrayal of historical personages, the designer is obviously in difficulty if no authentic portrait is available for reference. On the other hand the likeness equally cannot be faulted, provided that it is not contradicted by contemporary descriptions or is not attributable to some quite different person. For example, no known portrait of the etcher V. Hollar exists, so the 'portrait' on the Czechoslovakian issue of 1953 is quite imaginary, and this also applies to the portrait of the Antarctic explorer John Biscoe on a 2p. 1973 stamp of the British Antarctic Territory. Bolivia, however, commemorated Dr. Bernardo Monteaguda, a minister under San Martin, on 10c. stamps of 1897 and 1909 with two completely different portraits, and it has been claimed that the 1897 portrait is in fact that of the Argentinian Dr. Bernardo de Vera y Pintado (author of the original words of the Chilean National Anthem, though he gets no credit for it on the Chilean 40c. stamp of 1947 which commemorates the centenary of the anthem as modified by Eusebio Lillo). The 1909 portrait remains unidentified. Similarly on the 1c. stamp of the 1908 Canadian issue for the Tercentenary of Quebec, the absence of an authentic portrait of Champlain is made good by substitution of a portrait (by Montcornet) of Michel Particelli, an Italian who became Comptroller of Finance in France under Louis XIV. The statue to the Hawaiian King Kamehameha I shown on a 25c. Hawaiian stamp of 1883 and a 3c. 1937 stamp of the U.S.A. was in fact modelled from a young Kanakan athlete named Kaopuiki, as no likeness of the king was known.

It has been claimed that the portrait of St. Clare (Clara Favarone) on the 25l. Italian stamp of 1953 marking the 7th centenary of her death actually portrays Jacope dei Sette Soli, a friend of St. Francis of Assisi. The portrait on the 90l. Vatican City stamp of the 1971 issue marking the 8th centenary of the birth of St. Dominic is that shown in *The Italian Catholic Encyclopedia* as that of St. Vincent Ferrer, a Spanish Dominican monk born some two centuries later. An 80c. Mexican stamp of 1969 commemorated Father Serra, coloniser of California, but by mistake the designer copied the picture of Father Francisco Palou, a co-worker, from a painting which included both. An Italian 100l. stamp of 1975 marking the 450th anniversary of the birth of Palestrina features part of the title page of his first book of Masses (1554 edition). This is dedicated to Pope Julius III and carries his purported likeness, but in fact the portrait is cribbed from the Masses of Morales, dedicated to Pope Paul III, published in 1544 and presumably representing the latter Pope. Equally the portrait allegedly of Palestrina is that of the Spanish composer

Cristóbal de Morales and the music reproduced is also that of Morales. However, some part of this confusion can be traced back to the 16th century. A 1935 issue of the Vatican City claims to portray, on three values, Pope Gregory IX handing over Decretals to a jurist, but the pope illustrated is in fact Julius II.

Confusion between relatives appears not infrequent. Australia in 1947 produced an issue marking the sesquicentenary of the city of Newcastle, New South Wales, portraying Lt. John Shortland on the 2½d. value. However the Lt. John Shortland who in 1797 discovered the Hunter River on which Newcastle stands was the son of the gentleman on the stamp—a clue that all is not right is given by the absence of epaulettes, which became part of naval uniform in 1795 and hence would have been worn by the son. A 2c. 1897 stamp of Newfoundland bears a portrait entitled CABOT "hym that found the new isle". The full quotation (from a Royal account book now in the British Museum) is "12 Hen. VII, Aug. 10 To hym that founde the new Isle...£10", so that if the archaic spelling 'hym' was retained 'founde' should also have been kept. It is not clear whether this sum went to John Cabot who commanded the *Matthewe* or to the unknown look-out who first descried Newfoundland, but in any case can not have referred to Cabot's son Sebastian, who sailed with his father as an 11-year old youngster—but it is Sebastian's portrait by Holbein, now in the National Maritime Museum, which is on the stamp. A French 20c.+10c. semipostal of 1964 was meant to portray Prof. Jean-Nicolas Corvisart, physician to Napoleon, but in error has the portrait of his nephew L. R. P. Corvisart. A West German 30pf. stamp of 1967 marks the centenary of the Bethel Institution, founded in 1867 and taken over by Friedrich von Bodelschwingh in 1872. The portrait on the stamp is of his son, who bore the same name and was also connected with the Institution, but it seems probable that the intention had been to commemorate the father and not the son. The Hungarian 1fo.70 value of the 1954 issue depicting Hungarian scientists purports to show the physician Tivadar Puskás but the likeness is of his brother Ferenc. An Austrian 2s. stamp of 1970 commemorated the composer and poet Thomas Koschat, and a report was published that the portrait on the stamp was not of him but of his son; however this is not so—the design is based on a genuine portrait now in the National Library of Vienna, and in any case Koschat had no son!

A particularly interesting problem is that of the two issues of Monaco of 1948 and 1968 commemorating the Monégasque sculptor François Joseph Bosio, 'the French Canova'. The first set gives his initials correctly except on the 4f. value, a portrait stamp on which they are transposed, the date of his birth in this set being given as 1769 (he was born on 1768). For the second set his birth date has been given correctly, a similar portrait is shown, but the initials have been transposed throughout and also on the commemorative First Day Covers. It appears possible that this is through confusion with his brother Jean François Bosio (1767-1832), Professor of Drawing at the Ecole Polytechnique, Paris. The question which we have not so far been able to resolve is whether the portrait is *of* his brother or *by* his brother, either of which might have led to the error.

A confusion between father and son is illustrated on a 2c. Nicaraguan stamp of 1975 and a 22s. 1976 stamp of Western Samoa. Both form part of series commemorating the bicentenary of American Independence, and both show reproductions of a painting by Karl Anton Hickel entitled "Interior of Old House of Commons in St. Stephen's Chapel at Westminster in 1793", showing William Pitt the Younger addressing the House of Commons. However the Nicaraguan stamp gives the date (14th Jan. 1766) of a speech by William Pitt *the Elder*, Earl of Chatham, which was largely responsible for the repeal of the notorious Stamp Act that helped to trigger off the revolution of the American colonists, and the stamp also bears a quotation from this speech. The Samoan stamp dates the illustrated speech as 1782, implying that the scene is part of the debates of that year which ended the American War of Independence; this is of course not so, and in any case the Younger Pitt took little part in these debates. At least Samoa gets the right Pitt (his father had died in 1778), but gets the painter's initials wrong, listing him as "R. A. Hickel".

An interesting but rather academic case is the 50l. Greek stamp of 1956 showing a coin bearing a portrait: below the coin is the Greek inscription "ΦΙΛΙΠΠΟΣ" (Philip), implying that this is a portrait of Philip II of Macedon (359-336 B.C.) in whose reign it was issued, but in fact it should have been the inscription from the reverse of the coin—' ΦΙΛΙΠΠΟΥ '—(a coin) of Philip. The portrait actually represents Zeus.

Misidentifications are sometimes due to similarity of names of quite unrelated people. Thus a 45g. Polish stamp of 1951 marking the Siege of Paris was intended to portray Jaroslav Dabrowski (1836-1871), Commander-in-chief of the Paris Communard, but in fact shows the pianist and composer Henrik Dabrowski, after a photograph published in the magazine "L'Illustration" in 1861. This photograph had been mistakenly used by the French painter Achilles-Isodore Gilbert as the model for his portrait of Jaroslav Dabrowski and hence by the stamp designer R. Brordt. This also appears to have been the basis of the portrait of J. Dabrowski on the 60g. Polish stamp of 1971. Similarly the 10g. value in a Polish series of 1957 commemorating Polish physicians was intended to show Dr. Johann Innozenz Petrycy, but instead shows the philosopher and politician Sebastian Petrycy. In this same issue Dr. Jedrzej Sniadecki on the 40g. value is out of place, for although he was a distinguished naturalist, physicist, chemist, philosopher and Professor of Pharmacy, he was never a practising physician.

An Austrian issue of 1937 features ' Austrian doctors ', but although all these gentlemen taught and lived in Vienna, only three of the nine were born within the confines of modern Austria—Karl von Rokitansky (12g.) was born in Moravia (in modern Czechoslovakia), Joseph von Skoda (20g.) in Pilsen, Bohemia, Ferdinand Ritter von Arlt (30g.) in Graupen, Bohemian Sudetenland, Gerard van Swieten (5g.) was Dutch, while Theodor Billroth (60g.) and Theodor Meynert (64g.) were both German. Another gentleman who has little right to his place in an issue is Sir Wilfred Laurier, the first French-Canadian to become Prime Minister of Canada, who appears on the 5c. value of the Canadian issue of 1927 marking the 60th anniversary of Confederation. At the time of Confederation Laurier was only 26, and as editor of the French extremist publication *Le Défricheur* was in fact strongly opposed to the whole principle of Confederation.

44

45

46

47

48

49

50

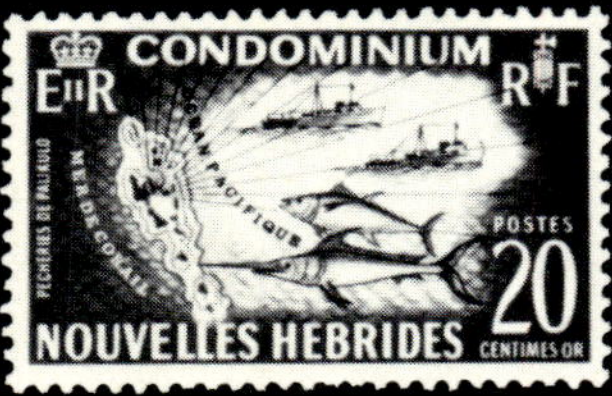

51

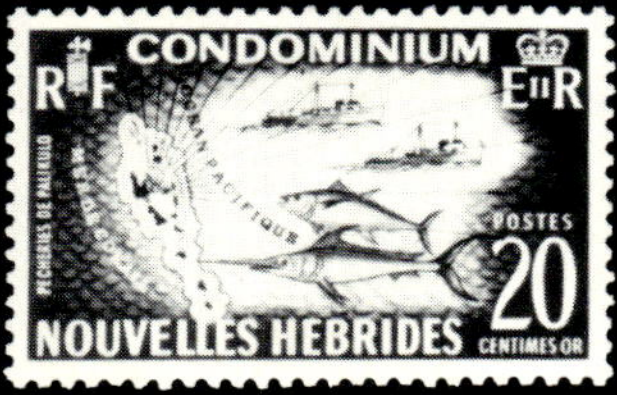

52

53

54

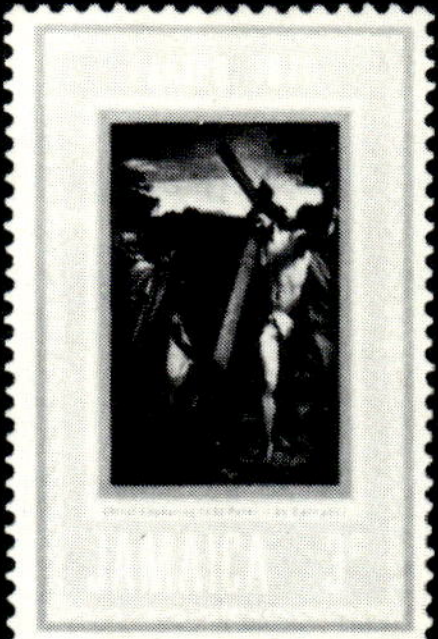

55

56

57

58

59

60

61

62

63

64

65

66

67

70

68

69

71

The Gulf states show their admiration of Western classical music by the frequency with which they commemorate the great composers, but they are sometimes a little hasty in their choice of illustrations. Thus both Sharjah (3d. and 60d.) and Manama (1r.) in 1971 show what purports to be young Mozart at the piano but is in fact his friend Carl Graf Firmien, while a Yemen Arab Republic issue and a 10r. miniature sheet of Fujeira show what purports to be Beethoven at the piano but is in fact Franz Schubert, after the painting "A Schubert evening in a Vienna townsman's house" by Julius Schmid, in the Historisches Museum, Vienna.

Two cases of apparently doubtful identity may be mentioned here. The portrait on a 10c. 1866 stamp of Newfoundland was described in early catalogues as being of Edward, then Prince of Wales, from a photograph taken at the time he paid his only visit to the colony, in July 1860, yet modern catalogues assign this to Albert, Prince Consort. The subject is not identified on the stamp, so this is at worst a catalogue error only. A 50p. 1967 stamp of Pakistan shows the Shah and Empress of Persia, but malicious rumours hinted that although the stamp commemorated the coronation of Shah Mohammed Riza Pahlavi and Empress Farah, the Empress portrayed was her predecessor Soraya. This was indignantly denied by the Pakistani postal authorities who claimed that the portrait was taken from a photograph of Farah provided by the Iranian Embassy.

Another category of perhaps debatable error is where an actual person is portrayed, implicitly at any rate, as a representative of the stamp-issuing country, yet has no connection with it. Thus the Nyasaland 1d. definitive of 1945 shows a sergeant of the King's African Rifles. The stamp portrait is a singularly ugly one, with the sergeant's neck drawn out like a Modigliani portrait, and furthermore he himself came from Tanganyika, so in 1947 this stamp was replaced by one bearing the symbol of the Protectorate. The 1949 8y. Japanese stamp commemorating the 1st National Scout Jamboree, Tokyo, portrays an American scout, George P. Russell, and the Australian 2½d. (1948) and 3½d. (1952) scout stamps feature an English scout, Kenneth Courtenay. Athletic events provide several such cases. The 1935 Colombian 7c. stamp of the set marking the "Third National Olympiad" features Kolchmainen (Finland) and Bouin (France) in the 5,000m. race of the 1912 Olympics. The 1940 6k. Turkish stamp of the issue commemorating the Eleventh Balkan Games portrays the American Meadows, the Olympic pole vault champion, and the 1947 1y.20 Japanese stamp from the set marking the Second National Athletic Meeting, Karagawa, is adapted from a photograph of the American discus thrower Carpenter. The 5y. stamp of the 1952 Japanese issue marking the Seventh National Athletic Meeting features wrestlers, but although Japan had taken a wrestling gold medal in the 1952 Olympics the wrestlers actually depicted were the Estonian Kristyan Palusala holding the German Kurt Hornfischer. A 1948 3d.+1d. Yugoslavian semipostal of an issue marking projected Balkan Games has a design adapted from a photograph of Nancy Cowperthwaite, the American hurdling champion, though with Yugoslavian colours substituted for American! (fig. 14). Even more remarkably, the designer of the 70pf. West German stamp of 1976 marking the Olympic Games illustrates a rowing event not, as one might expect, with the rowing four which had won a gold medal for the

Federal Republic at Munich but with the rowing four of the D.D.R.! (fig. 15).

Another sporting event error occurs on the 1956 100f. stamp issued by Monaco to commemorate the 26th Monte Carlo Rally, illustrated by a route map from Glasgow which is actually that of the 1954 rally. The Peruvian issue of 1930 to commemorate the Sixth Pan-American Child Congress held in Lima, wrongly entitles it the Seventh (which was, in the event, held in Mexico City in 1935). The 1930 Japanese issue commemorating the national census of that year calls it the second, while catalogues insist it was the third; this may, however, be a matter of definition of a national census, and we are still not quite convinced on this one. A more subtle error in commemorating the wrong event is that of the Australian 3d. stamp of 1951 inscribed "100 YEARS RESPONSIBLE GOVERNMENT IN VICTORIA", which in reality was marking the centenary of *representative* government. Truly responsible government only came with the new constitution of 1855, unobtrusively commemorated by the issue of a 3½d. stamp of 1956 to mark centenaries of responsible government for New South Wales, Tasmania *and* Victoria. A Spanish issue of 1976 intended to mark the bicentennial of Independence of the U.S.A. is wrongly inscribed as marking the 200th anniversary of the American Constitution, which was not signed until 17th September, 1787.

Another case in which we might consider that the wrong event is being commemorated is the 3c. 1948 stamp of the U.S.A. which is labelled "A CENTURY OF FRIENDSHIP UNITED STATES-CANADA", for the centenary of American-Canadian friendship might more properly be dated from 1814, the end of the War of 1812, and the stamp really marks the centenary of the opening of the Niagara Railway Suspension Bridge on August 1st, 1848, although the bridge on the stamp is the third on that site, after an 1861 print by A. H. Peters. It was opened in 1855 and replaced by an arch bridge in 1897, so its relevance to any kind of centenary in 1948 is questionable. Incidentally, the 25c. U.S.A. stamp of 1922 shows the Niagara Falls from the Canadian side, while the 20c. Canadian stamp of 1935 shows the Falls from the American side! A near error involved a 1969 issue of Afghanistan intended to mark the 50th anniversary of the League of Red Cross Societies, which was produced with an inscription indicating that it marked the 50th anniversary of the International Red Cross (which was founded in 1863!). Before issue the error was spotted and the offending inscription obliterated with gold bars.

There are interesting problems connected with the issues of Afghanistan commemorating Independence (usually reckoned from the Declaration of Independence proclaimed on 28th February, 1919), for the issues of 1923-25 mark the 5th-7th Independence Days, *i.e.* 4th-6th anniversaries of Independence by Western reckoning, although the issues of 1926-28 confusingly mark the *anniversary*, Western style. From 1931 onwards Independence was reckoned to start with the armistice of 24th August, 1919, and once again counted by numbers of Independence Days, although some, *e.g.* the issues of 1956 and 1957, are wrongly inscribed as *anniversaries* on the stamps, in the former as "38em ANVERS DE L'INDEPENDANCE" when the 38th Independence Day is meant. All very confusing! This may also explain how the 1953 issue marking the 22nd anniversary of the Faculty of Medicine in Kabul came to be inscribed as the

23rd anniversary in Arabic on the 35p. and in Roman numerals on the 125p., errors which were speedily corrected (figs. 3 and 4).

Sometimes commemorative issues bear illustrations which do not seem relevant to the event commemorated. Thus a Turkish 2½l. stamp of 1959 which for some obscure reason commemorates the 888th anniversary of the Battle of Malazgirt shows only a mounted warrior and a tent, which have no obvious connections with the Battle. A 5d.50 Yugoslavian stamp of 1940 marks the 500th anniversary of Gutenberg's printing press, mysteriously with an illustration of the Bridge at Obod in Montenegro. Here, however, there is a connection, for it was in Obod that the first Slav printing press was established, in 1493, but there is no mention of this on the stamp.

We have earlier dealt with the confusion over Cabot's portrait, but this also extends to his ship the *Matthew* (or more properly *Matthewe*). The design of the 1897 10c. stamp of Newfoundland which purports to feature it is obviously copied from the 1893 American 3c. stamp featuring the *Santa Maria* of Columbus with little changed but for the flags. The same illustration of the *Santa Maria* was also used for a Costa Rican issue of 1936—economical fellows these stamp designers (figs. 16, 17 and 18). There is no contemporary illustration of either ship, the American design having been copied from an old Spanish engraving, but the *Matthewe*, being only of 50 tons and with a crew of 18 must have been considerably the smaller of the two, and it does not seem likely that the same design could equally serve for both. An engraving based on a woodcut by Erhart Reuwich of Utrecht in 1483 was used in 1494 to illustrate the *Santa Maria* on a printed copy of Columbus's letter, also the flagship *Santamaria-gallante* of his second voyage on a 1c. 1970 stamp of the Virgin Islands, and what is presumably the flagship of his third voyage on the Colony Badge of Grenada, which appears on numerous issues, *e.g.* on the 2½d. of 1898 marking the 400th anniversary of the island's discovery. The $2 miniature sheet of Grenada of 1976 shows a ship named as the *Santa Maria* of 1492 which is at variance with the American version. The American ship S.S. *Adriatic* appears on a 12c. 1869 stamp of the U.S.A. and then reappears (economically but quite inappropriately) on a Peruvian postage due set of 1874.

A 1d. 1906 stamp of Barbados marks the tercentenary of annexation of the island with an illustration of the *Olive Blossom*. This ship (possibly spelt *Oliph Blossom* as on a 50c. 1973 stamp of St. Lucia, though modern research now suggests the name was *Olive Branch*) sailed from England in 1605 en route for Guiana, and was long believed to have called at Barbados and claimed it for England—hence this issue, which incidentally was 8½ months late. However in fact it called at St. Lucia, leaving 67 colonists there, and Barbados was not annexed until 1625 by men from the *Olive* (hence the confusion) en route home to England; colonisation was not undertaken until 1627. It has been claimed that the 2d. 1955 Jamaican stamp labelled "Man-o'-war at Port Royal" in fact shows H.M.S. *Britannia* off Portsmouth. It is from a hand-coloured lithograph by J. B. Kidd, but we have not yet been able to verify the subject. The 2c. 1925 stamp of the U.S.A. which claims to show the sloop *Restaurationen* which brought Norwegian immigrants to the U.S.A. in 1825 in fact shows a ship of similar size from the same shipyard, since no illustration of the

Restaurationen was available. The designer who wished to illustrate the Nova Scotian schooner *Bluenose* winning the fishery race championship from the American contender *Columbia* on a 50c. Canadian stamp of 1929 had the same problem, for no illustration of the *Columbia* was available, so *Bluenose* stood model for both vessels. Ironically the number "1" shown on the sail of the winner should have been a '2', for the *Columbia* was No. 1. A 25c. 1976 stamp of Turks and Caicos in the American bicentennial commemorative issue features a frigate labelled as the American frigate *Grand Turk*, but no such ship appears in the American Naval List of that period: there may have been some confusion with the American privateer of that name, but the latter was only a sloop, not a frigate.

Lack of a suitable illustration of the correct ship has probably been the main reason why so many designers have featured the wrong one. Thus a 1973 issue of Christmas Island purports to show H.M.S. *Egeria* which visited the island in 1887, shortly before conversion from a man-of-war to a survey ship. However the ship actually featured is a coastal defence monitor, probably the *Hecate*, which never left British home waters and could have had no connection with Christmas Island. The 25c. of the same issue shows a brig labelled "H.M.S. *Gordon*", but no such brig ever served in the Royal Navy. Possibly this is a confused reference to the paddle-steamer frigate H.M.S. *Gorgon* which visited the island in 1864. Similarly an 8d. 1969 stamp of St. Helena shows a ship labelled "R.M.S. *Dane*", which in fact is her sister ship *Phoebe*, also belonging to the Union Castle Line, and a 30f. 1955 French stamp marking the centenary of the voyage of *La Capricieuse* is claimed to illustrate the corvette *Galathée* instead. A 6d. 1959 stamp of St. Helena shows the *London* which brought the first colonists in 1659. As no details of this ship were known, the artist drew it after a painting of a Portsmouth-based frigate of 1670 by Van de Velde in the National Maritime Museum, Greenwich, but he truncated the bows to such an extent that the ship appears blunt at both ends. Crossing to the Indian Ocean we have a 15c. 1969 stamp of the Seychelles which purports to show the *Koenigsberg* at Aldabra in 1915. The sharp eyes of a German naval historian spotted that the ship actually portrayed is the *Koenigsberg II* (later the French cruiser *Metz*); the date in any case should have been 1914, not 1915. A Portuguese issue of 1970 marks the centenary of the laying of the submarine telegraph cable from Falmouth to Lisbon, and two values show the cable being laid, but portray the *Great Eastern* (at that time laying the Bombay-Aden cable) instead of the *Hibernia* which laid this cable. A German 40pf.+35pf. semipostal of 1937 was intended to illustrate the S.S. *Bremen*, but in error the designer was sent a picture of the S.S. *Europa*, which differed in the positions of derricks, the windows below the bridge and other minor details. The ship is not named on the stamp, but is misnamed in many of the contemporary catalogues. The Bermudian 2d. stamps of 1936, 1938 and 1940 all feature an unnamed yacht. It has been claimed that this was intended to be the Bermudian yacht *Viking*, a winner of the Prince of Wales Cup, but in fact the American built and owned *Lucie* is shown, which at that date had never won a race. The design was replaced by a Bermudian racing dinghy in the 1953 definitive issue. The S.S. *Arab* shown on a 1d. 1967 stamp of Gibraltar is not the intended ship of M. H.

Bland & Co., a small ship of only 24 tons which used to cruise between Gibraltar and Tangiers, but a much larger vessel, probably the S.S. *Arab* of the Bedouin Steamship Navigation Co. Ltd. of Liverpool, built in 1890.

Ship canals can also be in error. The U.S.A. commemorated completion of canalisation of the Ohio River in 1929 with a 2c. stamp, which however is from a photograph of 4th October 1920 showing the Carnegie Steel Co. stern-wheeler *H. D. Williams* in Lock 5 of the Monongahela River—nothing to do with the Ohio River project (fig. 19). A near error was the 1913 2c. American stamp showing the Pedro Miguel Locks of the Panama Canal (from a model, for the Canal itself was not completed until 1914), for these were originally labelled "Gatun Locks". The mistake was discovered in time and the entire first printing was destroyed, the issued stamp simply bearing the inscription "Panama Canal". About three die proofs of the erroneous first printing are still in existence. A 200f. 1955 air stamp of French Equatorial Africa features a dockland scene, but this does not appear to correspond to any part of French Equatorial Africa, and it has been suggested that the scene featured is in fact Douala, in the Cameroons. Similarly the portion of the Victoria-Buea Road shown on Nigerian 2/6d. stamps of 1936 and 1938 is not in Nigeria but in the then British Mandate of Cameroons, which did at that time use Nigerian stamps. Numerous Armenian issues (also the 1923 issues of the Transcaucasian Federation) feature Mt. Ararat, which is in eastern Turkey. When Turkey protested that Armenia had no right to portray territory which they did not possess, the Armenians are reported to have blandly replied that they would stop featuring Mt. Ararat when Turkey stopped featuring the Moon on her stamps! Jamaican 2d. stamps of 1932, 1938 and 1951 show a place labelled "Columbus Cove", but no such place exists in Jamaica, and it would appear to be Don Christopher's Cove, an inlet in St. Ann's Bay, in this case therefore just a confusion over the name. The 5c. 1962 stamp of Trinidad and Tobago with an undersea panorama labelled "Buccoo Reef" created much local criticism, for it is based on a photograph of a portion of the mural by Carlisle Chang behind the bar of the Hotel Normandie, Port of Spain. This in turn was based in part on illustrations in the National Geographic Magazine of reefs in quite different parts of the world, and has no connection with Buccoo Reef, which the artist had never visited; indeed, some of the fish may not even be found in the Caribbean! (fig. 20). ½d. stamps of the Cook Islands (both general issue and for separate islands) from 1920 to 1950 purport to show Capt. Cook landing. This indeed they do, but the scene is copied from a photograph of Point Venus, Tahiti, (where Cook did land) reproduced in an 1882 book on Tahiti. He did not land on any of the Cook Islands except Niue (June 20th, 1774) where he landed briefly with two men, meeting such a fierce reception from the natives that he beat a hasty retreat. The two-masted ship shown on the 1920 stamp could not be the (three-masted) *Resolution*, and it has been claimed that date palms (here shown flourishing) were only subsequently introduced to the Cook Islands from Samoa.

An even more blatant case of the wrong scene being portrayed occurs on the 1932 18c. Philippine Islands stamp which is labelled "Pagsanjan Falls" but shows the Vernal Falls of Yosemite National Park, California, some 5,000 miles away! The real Pagsanjan Falls, which are not nearly so impressive, are shown on a 30s. Philippine stamp of 1971. The 1952 3d. stamp of Western Samoa which is labelled "Aleisa Falls" in fact shows falls near Malifa, in this case because the stamp designer had been provided with a wrongly captioned photograph by the Samoan Government. A wrong map appears on the 5c. Canadian stamp of 1957 honouring the explorer and cartographer David Thompson, for the map in the background of this stamp is not his ' Map of the North West Territory of the Province of Canada ', which he made for the North West Company in 1813-1814, but a fictional one of that general area.

Wrong buildings quite often appear on stamps. The 1957 4d. Pitcairn Islands definitive stamp purports to feature Pitcairn School, which appeared on the 1951 8d. stamp. It is clearly a different building and the stamp was re-issued in 1958 with the inscription amended to "SCHOOL-TEACHER'S HOUSE". The 1915 1c. postage due stamp of Panama is inscribed "Castillo de San Lorenzo Chagres" but really shows San Geronimo Castle Gate, Portobelo. A Chinese 8f. stamp of 1964 commemorating the centenary of the First International was intended to show St. Martin's Hall, Long Acre, in which British Trades Union representatives, organised and directed by Marx and Engels, had founded the International Working Men's Union in 1864. However this Hall, shown on a 5l. Albanian stamp of 1964, no longer existed, and by mistake the issued stamp bears an illustration of St. Martin-in-the-Fields Church, Trafalgar Square, which happens to be the Parish Church for Buckingham Palace. This error can hardly have amused the Chinese Communists! (fig. 21). Two Russian stamps of 1969 show Lenin's house in Ulyanovsk, but wrongly label it the Lenin Museum. This Museum, erected in 1929, is correctly shown on a different stamp of the same issue. A 21c. Panamanian stamp of 1964 features the Church of the Holy Cross, Warsaw, but labels it wrongly as St. John's Cathedral, Warsaw, a quite different building. Another 21c. stamp of this issue shows the Czechoslovakian Cathedral of Košice but labels it of Kassa, Hungary. Kassa is the Slovak town of Košice which belonged to Hungary until 1918. It was handed back to Hungary in 1938 but was reincorporated into Czechoslovakia in 1945. A Czechoslovakian 60h. stamp of 1967 purports to show St. Sophia, Istanbul, but in fact illustrates the Selimiye Mosque of Edirne, some 150 miles from Istanbul. The building shown on a 7½d. 1953 stamp of Norfolk Island is labelled "First Governor's Residence" but is in fact an old crank mill built in 1827 on the site of the First Governor's Residence. A 12c. Liberian stamp of 1956 in an issue marking the Olympic Games, Melbourne, shows the Main Stadium (normally the Melbourne Cricket Ground) with the caption "Olympic Park, Melbourne", but this latter, the site of swimming pool, velodrome and two smaller arenas, was a quite different site some distance from the Main Stadium. A 1940 Nicaraguan issue depicts a scene which the caption claims is President Somoza addressing the United States Senate, but in fact shows him in the House of Representatives. An amusing slip on the Italian 1964 issue marking the Seventh European Municipalities Assembly, which attempts to illustrate symbolically the city halls of various participating municipalities, represents London by the Clock Tower of the Palace of Westminster, hardly a mere municipal symbol. The Clock Tower also appears on a 10c. 1968 stamp of the Bahamas, on which it is labelled

"BIG BEN", but strictly speaking Big Ben is the name of the hour bell of the clock within the tower, not the tower itself.

The 3c. 1950 stamp of the U.S.A. honouring ' Casey ' Jones, a railway engineer who met his death trying to minimise the seriousness of an imminent collision, numbers his locomotive "382" on the stamp. It has been claimed (*cf.* R. J. Sutton, 1957, pp. 270, 271) that his locomotive was No. 638, but although the locomotive he drove earlier in his career was a 2-8-0 Consolidation No. 638, the engine he drove to his death was indeed a Rogers 4-6-0 No. 382, so this is no error. The 5c. Uruguayan definitives of 1895, 1897 and 1899 show a locomotive used by the Great Northern Railway, its only connection with Uruguay being that Waterlow and Sons who produced the stamps had a die on hand of a G.N.R. locomotive for use on railway stationery, which they also produced. A 10c. Cuban stamp of 1937 marks the centenary of Cuban railways with an overprint on a 25c. stamp showing an outline of the ' De Witt Clinton ', the first locomotive to run in New York State but with no known Cuban connection. A 4c. Canadian stamp of 1951 marking the centenary of Canadian stamps portrays on the lower part of the stamp a locomotive which is NOT Canadian; it is the Albany Springfield Express of the Western Railroad of Massachusetts! The 50f. value of a 1963 Central African Republic issue promoting the Bangui-Douala Railway project (later abandoned) shows an engine bearing the monogram "C.F.M." (Chemins de fer Malgaches), although supposed to be representing the Cameroons Railway! The locomotive shown on a 45ore Norwegian stamp of 1947 is NOT the first Norwegian locomotive as intended. Similarly the first Swedish locomotive was NOT the *Fryckstad* shown on a Swedish 25ore stamp of 1956 (which was delivered in 1855) but the *Förstlingen* (delivered to the Norrbergsbanen in 1853). The locomotive shown on an 80f. 1970 stamp of the Mali Republic is a 4-6-0 from the series numbered 1101-1120 (actually No. 1107), not a Pacific (231) as described on the stamp.

Aeroplane stamps have also had their troubles. The 1934 2s. and 5s. stamps of Peru appear to show a Fairey Firefly fighter, a type never used by Peru, though there has been some controversy on this point. The 1962 1/3d. stamp of Rhodesia and Nyasaland in the set marking the 30th anniversary of the first London to Rhodesia airmail service, shows an Empire "C" flying boat on the Zambesi, but in fact only "Solent" flying boats operated from the Zambesi on this scheduled service. A 50c. 1963 stamp of Ceylon marks the 25th anniversary of the airmail service and features a DH85 Leopard Moth, but no aircraft of this type was registered in Ceylon at that time, and the inaugural flight of the airmail service was in fact made by an American WACO biplane. The 1971 issue of Seychelles which marks completion of the airport very inappropriately includes flying boats, which could not possibly use its facilities. The aircraft on a 1l. 1962 San Marinese stamp labelled "Wright 1904" and that on a Latvian 20-100s. semipostal of 1932 labelled "Wright 1903" is in both cases the improved Wright A type of 1908, in which the aviator sat up instead of having to lie flat as in earlier models. The 5c. value of a Spanish issue of 1930 features Santos-Dumont and a scene labelled "First mechanical flight 1906". This must have been intended to mark the first mechanical flight of a heavier than air machine *in Europe*, which was indeed carried out by Santos-Dumont in 1906, not in the Wright Flyer

No. 1 of 1903 featured on the stamp but in the '14 Bis', which is shown on a 500r. Brazilian stamp of 1929. The 10c. value of the same Spanish issue features Teodoro Fels, who made the first flight across the Rio de la Plata in 1912 (not 1913 as on the stamp) but for some unexplained reason the aircraft pictured with him is a Douglas 0-2M military biplane of the late 1920s. Airship stamps seem less frequently at fault, but a 200f. 1976 stamp of the Malagasy Republic marking the zeppelin flight over Berlin for the Olympic Games of 1936 portrays the Graf Zeppelin (with five engines) whereas the flight was actually performed by the Hindenburg (with four engines, and with special Olympic markings for this flight). A 2l. 1968 stamp of the Maldive Islands portrays the Graf Zeppelin II, but from the flight date given this should be the Graf Zeppelin I. The French airship Ville de Paris on a 60f. 1977 stamp of the Ivory Coast has no rightful place in an issue commemorating zeppelins.

Stamp designers have had considerable trouble in coming to terms with the Space Age, and errors here are many and various. An East German 10pf. stamp of 1957 bears the date of launching of Sputnik I, the first artificial earth satellite, but an official Russian press release was at pains to point out that the satellite depicted bore no resemblance to the real Sputnik I. Similarly a Bulgarian 2l. stamp of 1959 marking the launching of the first Russian Moon probe portrays an entirely imaginary spacecraft. An Albanian 1l. stamp of 1962 commemorated the dog Laika, the first living being carried in an earth satellite, but the stamp features Sputnik III, not Laika's Sputnik II, as can be seen by comparison of the three Sputniks as figured on a 4k. Russian stamp of 1964. (Figs. 22 and 23.) A Hungarian 2fo.50 stamp of 1965 purports to show "Sjondag" but in fact shows Lunik III, as can be seen by comparing with the illustration of Lunik III on a 40k. Russian stamp of 1960. A 5ch. North Korean stamp of 1960 is meant to be illustrating Lunik III (which first photographed the far side of the Moon), but instead shows Lunik I (which missed the Moon altogether). A Rumanian 10b. stamp of 1966 shows Venus I instead of the intended Venus III (which is correctly shown on a 6k. Russian stamp of 1966). A Bulgarian 13st. stamp of 1963 and a Russian 10k. stamp of 1962 both show a spacecraft labelled as "Mars 1", which it certainly is not, as can be seen by comparison with the authentic Mars I on a Russian 6k. stamp of 1964. A Hungarian 30fi. stamp of 1965 depicts the Transit 2A satellite, though labelled as the "San Marco" satellite, while a 2s.50 1966 stamp of Ecuador labelled "Gemini VI" is clearly a Mercury capsule, as shown by comparison with a 1f. Jordanian stamp of 1966 (Gemini VI) and a 2n.p. 1964 stamp of Dubai (Mercury capsule). A Mongolian 10m. issue of 1961 commemorating Yuri Gagarin's historic space flight of 1961 shows him alongside a Mercury capsule instead of the Vostok I capsule in which the orbital flights were made (it is correctly depicted on a 10k. Russian stamp of 1963). A Mongolian 10m. stamp of 1971 shows Vostoks II and III with the date "12-15 August 1962", but this refers to the flights of Vostoks III and IV, as given correctly on a Polish 2z.50 stamp of 1963.

Qatar and Ras Al Khaima produced in 1966 very similar issues marking achievements in space flight, each making the same numerous errors. The 1r. value of Ras Al Khaima and the 60n.p. stamp of Qatar show Cooper with a capsule which is certainly not his proper Faith VII, while the 50n.p. stamp of Ras Al Khaima and the 20n.p. stamp of Qatar show the American astronaut J. Glenn Jnr. with Sputnik III instead of his own Friendship VII.

Returning to earth we may next look at misidentified or mislocated plants and animals. The seaweed with the shrimp on a 1d. Moroccan stamp of 1965 is the Serrated wrack (*Fucus serratus*) which does not occur further south than Spain, and hence does not occur in Morocco. The fungus on a 1l. Rumanian stamp of 1958 is not "*Morchella conica*" as labelled but an elongated form of *M. esculenta.* The 1966 10p. stamp of Andorra (Spanish Post Offices) is inscribed "*Heleborus coni*", but there is no such species; possibly *Helleborus bocconi* (a synonym for *Helleborus viridis*) was intended. The flower shown appears from its hairy sepals to be *Pulsatilla vulgaris,* but the single undivided stem leaf shown does not fit any species of *Pulsatilla.* Could this be a figment of the artist's imagination? For comparison look at the Polish 1z.50 stamp of 1962 (*Pulsatilla vulgaris*), and the 1fo. Hungarian stamp of 1958 (*Helleborus purpurascens*). There is some doubt as to whether the lily and hazelnuts on 15pr. and 220pr. values respectively of an Israeli 1952 issue are indeed the plants referred to in the Scriptural verses quoted on their tabs; the Rose of Sharon is thought by many to have been the Narcissus, which grew abundantly in the Plain of Sharon, and the nuts referred to in the Song of Solomon may have been walnuts, once luxuriant around the Lake of Gennesareth, according to the Jewish historian Josephus. An Ethiopian 15c. stamp of 1965 is labelled "SUGAR CANES". As a crop it should more properly be labelled ' SUGAR CANE ', but the plants shown appear much more likely to be sisal rather than sugar cane. The plants labelled "ALOES" on 2c. stamps of Lesotho for 1967 and 1971 are also more likely to be sisal than aloes. Iraq in 1970 produced 10f. and 15f. stamps showing grapes and oranges respectively, but transposed their scientific names. On the stamps overprinted for official use in 1972 these erroneous names were blacked out. Similarly a Jordanian floral set of 1970 has the names transposed of several of the plants depicted. Thus the 5f. value is labelled "Desert Scabious" but features the pomegranate flower, the 25f. value labelled "Pomegranate" actually depicts the caper, the 45f. value shows the desert scabious but is labelled "Wattle", while the 15f. value depicts wattle but is labelled "Caper". A 1z.65 Polish stamp of 1972 features the shrub Sweet Nakai (*Chaenomelos speciosa*), but misnames it "*Chaenomelos lagnaria*". Bulgaria issued a 2s. stamp in 1968 showing the gentian *Gentiana clusii,* misnamed "*Gentiana acaulis*". A Rumanian issue of 1964 portraying garden flowers (NOT Rumanian flowers as some catalogues aver) shows *Dahlia pinnata* on the 75b. value (not "*Dahlia hybrida*" as labelled) and *Hosta ventricosa* (not "*Hosta ovata*") on the 1l.25 value. A 5f. 1955 stamp of Somalia depicts *Ammocharis tinneana* but wrongly names it "*Haemanthus multiflorus*", while a 50k. Laotian stamp of 1971 shows the orchid *Ascocentrum curieifolium* but misidentifies it as "*Ascocentrum miniatur*" (which is in any case a misspelling for ' *miniatum* ').

Illustration of plants which are not native to the stamp-issuing country is frequent. It is obviously justified for crop plants which have become widely grown locally, acknowledged horticultural species, and species which have become extensively naturalised, but it does seem a pity when countries with interesting indigenous plants of their own show exotic introductions, such as Night-flowering Cereus on a 5s. 1961 stamp of St. Helena and the Cereus on the 9d. 1960 stamp of Norfolk Island (all cacti came from the Americas originally), that Great Britain in 1974 produced a 10p. stamp in a series supposedly illustrating ' British Trees ' depicting the Horse Chestnut (introduced in the 17th century and uncommon in the wild anywhere in Britain) (fig. 24). However the wooden spoon must go to the Pitcairn Islands for their floral offering of 1970: the 1c. depicts *Lantana camara* and the 2c. depicts *Canna indica* (Indian shot), both plants of tropical American origin, the 25c. shows the Wild Gladiolus, a garden escape, and only the 5c., featuring *Hibiscus tiliaceus,* shows a truly native plant.

Turning to animals, we find that some of the islands of the South Pacific do not always identify their molluscs correctly. In the 1974 issue of Aitutaki featuring seashells the 3c. value shows *Phalium bandatum* but labels it "*Phalium strigatum*", the shell on the 20c. value is not "*Oliva sericea*" as labelled but a fossil form of *Oliva miniacea*, and the 25c. value depicts *Bursa bubo* var. *zissostoma* but labels it "*Tritonalia rubeta*". The Cook Islands do no better, for on their seashell issue of 1974 the 3c. value does NOT show "*Aulica vespertilio*" (which does not occur around the islands) but *Aulica antica*, the 10c. value features *Terebra aerolata,* not "*Tenebra muscaria*" as labelled, and the 4c. is labelled "*Strombus gibberulus*" but depicts *Strombus gibbosus*. A 1½d. stamp of the British Solomon Islands of 1965 shows a shell labelled "Scorpion shell", but the true Scorpion shell (*Pterocera scorpio*), shown on a 20s. 1971 stamp of Kenya and a 20f. 1962 stamp of the Comoro Islands, has seven projections, and this one, which has only six projections, is a Chiragra spider shell (*Lambis chiragra*), shown on a 10f. 1973 stamp of the Malagasy Republic. A Kenyan 50c. 1971 stamp depicting *Janthina janthina* first appeared labelled "*Janthina globosa*", but this was subsequently corrected. A 75f. Mauritanian stamp of 1972 features what is described as "COQUILLAGE FOSSILE" (fossil shell), but is in fact a fossil trilobite, a crustacean not a mollusc.

This leads us to crustaceans. Iceland in 1971 produced a 20k. stamp showing a shrimp claimed to be "*Pandalus borealis*" but in fact a warm-water species *Penaeus setiferus* not found in Icelandic waters (fig. 25). Morocco has misnamed (on the tab) the shrimp *Plesiopenaeus edwardsianus* as "*Aristeomorpha foliacea*" (itself a spelling error) on a 1965 1d. stamp, and Algeria made the same mistake on a 25c. stamp of 1970. The shrimp can be seen under its own name on a 50c. 1968 stamp of the Cameroons. However a 10f. stamp in this issue shows the European freshwater crayfish *Astacus astacus* (under the outdated name "*Astacus fluviatilis*") which does not occur in Africa at all. Similarly stamps in a 1963 issue of Dubai portray a European hermit crab (1n.p. value) and an edible crab (4n.p. value), copied from a French educational booklet "*Histoire Naturelle VI. Poissons, Crustaces,* neither of which occurs anywhere near Dubai.

Coming to insects, a 3d. Nigerian stamp of 1962 backing a Malaria eradication campaign shows mosquitoes as adults, larvae and pupae, but the larva of the *Anopheles* mosquito which carries the malarial parasite has a short air siphon and lies parallel to the water surface, whereas the mosquito larva shown has a long siphon and an obliquely hanging position, and is clearly of a relatively inoffensive *Culex* mosquito (fig. 26). Malawi in 1973 produced a handsome set of butterfly stamps and a miniature sheet, but the butterfly on the 30t. value was wrongly named "EUPHAEDRA ZADDACHI", corrected to "AMAURIS ANSORGEI" in less than one month on the stamp, but the sheet was not re-issued.

A curious case of piscine misidentification occurs on a 1969 6c. stamp of St. Christopher, Nevis and Anguilla, for the stamp claims to feature a Tarpon (*Megalopa atlantica*), a well-known game fish figured on a 25c. 1967 stamp of British Honduras, but instead features an accurate illustration of a species of *Centropomus*, a quite different kind of fish. A 5s.50 1970 Peruvian stamp illustrates the Wolf-fish *Anarhichas lupus,* but misnames it "*Otaria flavescens*". A 12a. Israeli stamp of 1962 shows the Peacock Kingfish *Pygoplites diacanthus,* not the Imperial Angelfish "*Holacanthus imperator*" as on the stamp. Both fish figure on stamps of the Maldive Islands, *Pygoplites diacanthus* on a 2l. 1963 stamp and *Holacanthus imperator* on a 1r. 1970 stamp, the latter, curiously enough, having been designed by M. Shamir, the same Israeli artist who in collaboration with G. Shamir was responsible for the 1963 Israeli issue.

Turning to reptiles we find that misidentifications and mislocations seem rare. It has been claimed that the definitive 1933 and 1938 issues of Basutoland were in error in depicting a crocodile, which did not occur in the country, but as the crocodile is the family emblem of the House of Moshesh, a minor chief of the immigrant Bakoena tribe who founded the Basuto race, it clearly has a legitimate place on the stamps of the country. A 2l. 1965 stamp of San Marino shows a dinosaur labelled as "*Brachiosaurus*", but comparison with the *Brachiosaurus* on a 1z.15 Polish stamp of 1965 clearly shows that its forelegs ought to be shorter than its hindlegs, and the head also is incorrect. Indeed it is probably intended to be a *Diplodocus* such as the one featured on a 25l. 1972 stamp of the Maldive Islands. However the 7l. stamp of this Maldivian issue shows a *Dimetrodon* but names it "EDAPHOSAURUS". A true *Edaphosaurus* is shown on the 20g. value of the Polish series already mentioned.

Birds feature frequently on stamps, often very erroneously. The Great Black Cockatoo (*Probosciger aterrimus*) on the 12c. value of a 1909 issue of North Borneo and the 2c. value of a 1939 issue is a native of Papua and New Guinea, not found in North Borneo. The 24c. value of this 1909 issue was probably intended to show a Mound bird (Megapod), as figured on a 2/6d. 1939 stamp of the British Solomon Islands, and is so described in early catalogues, but in fact shows the common Cassowary, which does not occur in North Borneo. The Hornbill on the $2 Liberian stamp of 1921 is even further from home, for it occurs in south-east Asia and not in Africa at all, though native Hornbills do feature on later Liberian issues. The 1fo. value of a 1962 Hungarian issue featuring birds of prey depicts the shrieking sea eagle but misnames it "*Haliaëtus leucocephalus*" (the American bald eagle) which is in any case misspelt. A 5c. Canadian stamp of 1968 shows the Gray Jay (*Perisoreus obscurus griseus*), but this bird occurs mainly in the United States, just getting into British Columbia, and the bird clearly intended to be illustrated is the Canada Jay (*Perisoreus canadensis*), widely distributed in Canada from Alberta eastwards, and indeed the bird on the stamp is given the name "*Perisoreus canadensis*".

The bird shown on the 1963 5c. Audubon commemorative issue of the United States and also on a 20c. air stamp of 1967 was unfortunately selected, for it is Collie's Magpie Jay, a native of S.W. Mexico which does not occur in the U.S.A., and the birds are portrayed perched on a plant of Poison Ivy, which does not occur within their range. They had been painted by Audubon from a stuffed bird procured for him by a friend who mistakenly told him it had come from the Columbia River Region, hence the errors. A 1s. 1964 stamp from the Pitcairn Islands shows the Chicken Bird, which occurs on Henderson Island, not in Pitcairn, but this is quite in order for the islands of Henderson, Ducie and Oeno were annexed to Pitcairn in 1902 (hence the plural "Islands" in the name of the group). The well-known 1d. 1860 stamp of Western Australia which shows the Black Swan, the State symbol, is a somewhat dubious case, for it has been suggested that the stamp designer simply shaded in an illustration of the Mute Swan for this design. Certainly the bird depicted lacks the white underwing of the true Black Swan (shown on some of the later issues), but this does not always show, and it is difficult to be categorical about this design. Black swans are also illustrated on a 10b. Rumanian stamp of 1964. The Bee-eater shown on a 30a. 1963 stamp of Israel is not the Blue-cheeked Bee-eater (*Merops superciliosus*) as claimed on the stamp, but *Merops apiaster*, figured on an Albanian 40q. stamp of 1965, a beautiful bird which occasionally visits the British Isles, and indeed visited the garden of one of us in the summer of 1975. The Paradise Whydah shown on a 35f. 1971 stamp of the Niger is the type subspecies *Steganura paradisea paradisea*, not the Broad-tailed Whydah *Steganura paradisea orientalis* as labelled. West Germany in 1976 issued a 50pf. stamp showing a Golden Plover, in support of Bird Protection, but illustrated the Northern Golden Plover (*Pluvialis apricarius altifrons*), with very black throat and breast, which is very common in Northern Europe and in relatively little need of special protection, in place of the Southern Golden Plover (*Pluvialis apricarius apricarius*) with lighter throat and breast, which is highly endangered in Central Europe, with only 30-40 pairs in West Germany. One might also perhaps cavil at the inclusion of the Starling (*Sturnus vulgaris*) on the 50c. value of a 1962 issue of Monaco for the Protection of Birds Useful to Agriculture; although the Starling does destroy immense numbers of harmful grubs and beetles, it can also be very destructive to fruit crops. It seems in little need of protection, and indeed in this country is one of the few species excluded from protection by our various Wild Bird Protection Acts.

Two cases of symbolic birds may also appropriately be dealt with here. The dove (actually a cruel and belligerent bird towards its own kind) has long been selected as an international symbol of peace, but the birds figured on Polish and Chinese 1950 issues marking an International Peace Conference are apparently Trumpeter pigeons, not doves. The 1s. 1898 pigeongram stamp of the New Zealand-Great Barrier Island service shows a bird with a letter, not as one might expect a pigeon, but a swift. In this case the expediency of being able to use a modified cliché which had previously been used to print Valentines overcame considerations of inappropriateness of the avian messenger.

As to mammals, we find a 21.55+45c. 1930 semipostal of Tripolitania featuring the Indian Blackbuck *Antilopa cervicapra*, clearly identifiable by the black back, white underparts and spiral horns of the male, as shown on a 2a. 1945 stamp of Bahawalpur, which does not occur in Africa. Possibly the designer meant to portray the somewhat similar Addax (*Addax nasimaculatus*) shown on a 10f. 1965 stamp of Tchad, which is native to Tripolitania. It has been claimed that a 25m. Finnish stamp of 1953 features a Canadian moose rather than the intended elk, but this is probably a case of inaccurate drawing rather than of mis-identification. The Reindeer which appear on the ½d. 1963 issue of South Georgia are strictly speaking in the wrong hemisphere, but they were indeed introduced into South Georgia, and the stamp design is after a photograph of Reindeer in Jason Valley, South Georgia. The Sloth shown on a 5c. Colombian stamp of 1960 is obviously the Three-toed Sloth *Bradypus tridactylus* (the three claws of the right forefoot are clearly visible) but it is wrongly labelled "Unau", which is the Two-toed Sloth *Choloepus didactylus*. The Palmroller *Hemigalus derbiganus* is wrongly labelled "*Chrotogale owstoni*" on a 12x. 1965 stamp of North Vietnam. The Malay Tapir *Tapirus indicus* appears on a 1c. 1909 stamp of North Borneo, but although fossil Tapir bones have been found in Sarawak, there is no authentic evidence of its occurrence in Borneo within historic times. The Elephant on the 1925, 1938 and 1953 general issues of Northern Rhodesia is very small-eared for an African Elephant, and it has been suggested that it is an Asian Elephant. The Hare shown on a 60fi. Hungarian stamp of 1964 is the common Brown Hare, *Lepus europaeus*, not the Mountain (or Blue) Hare (*Lepus timidus*), a species of northern Europe, as labelled here (with the misspelling "*timides*" at that!). The otter featured on a 15m. Mongolian stamp of 1966 is not the old world otter (*Lutra lutra*) as labelled but the sea otter of Pacific North America, copied from a photograph in Brehm's *Animal Life* (vol. 4, p. 225) lightened in colour and given a fish. The Afghan Hound on a 7a. stamp in a 1973 Afghan issue labelled "SERIE ANIMAUX SAUVAGES" certainly has no place there, for it is not a wild animal, having originated in Egypt at least 5,000 years ago, though it has been bred in Afghanistan for many centuries. The Leopard on a 2ch. 1966 Bhutanese stamp is *Panthera pardus*, not the Snow Leopard "PANTHERA UNCIA" as labelled. The monkey on a 2c. 1963 stamp of El Salvador is *Ateles geoffroyi*, not "*Ateles neglectus*" as labelled on the stamp. Finally in this section we come to Man. A 1973 issue of Gibraltar marks the 125th anniversary of the discovery of the famous ' Gibraltar skull ', a Neanderthal type skull as illustrated on the 4p. value. The suggested appearance of its owner is shown on the 6p., clearly a male, but anthropologists concur that the relatively small size, cranial capacity and light build by Neanderthal standards indicate that its owner was a female.

Passing from works of nature to works of art, we may note that the $1 U.S.A. stamp of 1898 labelled "Western cattle in a storm" is no such thing, but is reproduced from an engraving after a picture by J. MacWhirter R.A., entitled "The Vanguard", and shows Scots Highland cattle. A 2½c. 1968 Christmas stamp of New Zealand shows the painting "Adoration" by van Honthurst but labels it "Adoration of the Shepherds", a similar work by the same artist but with shepherds replacing the angels depicted here. The 40c. value of the Spanish 1961 issue commemorating El Greco is not as labelled "The Holy Family", a painting now in the

Prado which was shown on the 1955 Christmas stamp of Spain, but a detail from the painting "Virgin of the Good Milk" in the Hospital of San Juan Bautista, Toledo. A 15p. 1972 Christmas stamp of Ghana is labelled as "Madonna and Child" by Andrea Rico, but is in fact after a Byzantine-Greek ikon of the 16th century, an Eastern grieving Madonna that has no connection with Christmas. The Belgian 50c.+2f.50 semi-postal of 1944 entitled "The Good Samaritan" is also out of place, for it was painted by Jacob Jordsen, yet this Red Cross Relief Fund issue was intended to present only paintings by Van Dyck. The painting by Palma Le Vieux in the Manama Mothers' Day issue of 1968 seems even more inappropriate than the other paintings in this issue (none of which bears any obvious connection with motherhood) as it shows a resolute figure in armour!

Also out of place in their issue are the 5ore and 10ore values of a Swedish 1970 set meant to illustrate Swedish forgings, for these values portray a gilded bronze standard formerly used to decorate a mast top or the bow of a Viking ship, later the weathervane of Soderala Church. Bronze is of course cast, not forged. The porcelain and cut-glass on a 40f. French stamp of 1954 have raised some controversy, for although the issue was supposed to feature national industries and literary figures, and an official French description claimed that the crystal portrayed was from Baccarat, Nancy and St. Louis, it has also been claimed to be from Vale St. Lambert in Belgium, which would be most embarrassing for the French if true. A 1968 2e. stamp of Portuguese Guinea showing a cow-headed statuette from Bijago was wrongly inscribed "TOCADOR DE BOMBOLON". It was only issued surcharged, with heavy obliterations over the offending inscription, and only a version corrected to "VACA BRUTO—ARTE BIJAGO" was issued unsurcharged.

Heraldry is a very precise art, and stamp designers frequently take improper liberties with it, but it is relatively rare for coats-of-arms to be ascribed to the wrong armiger altogether. A general issue for the French Zone of occupied Germany in 1946 shows the arms of the incorporated states, but the 15pf. and 24pf. values show the arms of the town of Saarbrücken instead of the Saar territory. The latter are depicted on a 15f. 1957 stamp of the Saar. A 5p. Spanish stamp of 1965 purports to show the arms of Tarragona, but the wavy blue vertical stripes on a silver shield shown on this stamp are not correct although the error is a longstanding one, perpetuated in various works and even on official buildings—the true arms should have wavy red and gold stripes. The official first day cover is discreetly ornamented by the arms of the province of Tarragona, thus avoiding either repeating the error in the arms of the provincial capital or drawing undue attention to it. A 1964 issue for Paraguay which marks the World Eucharistic Congress, Bombay, includes the papal badge of the wrong Pope—not Pope Paul VI who participated in the Congress but his predecessor Pope John XXIII. The 2½d. South African stamp of 1910 shows the arms of Cape Colony in the upper left corner, wrongly labelled as those of the province of The Cape of Good Hope, which are quite different. A set reproducing the heraldic arms of famous men was prepared by Portuguese India for issue in 1957, but although copies were distributed to the press, when the issue was finally put on sale in 1958 there were considerable differences in colours and crests from the issue as first prepared. Presumably errors had been found in the depiction of the heraldic arms, but we do not know the details.

Scottish, Irish and Welsh Nationalists might well protest about stamps which represent the participation of England in international football events by portraying the flag of the United Kingdom in place of the St. George's Cross of England. Examples of this include Fujeira (1970, 10d.), Hungary (1962, 2fo.), Nicaragua (1970, 5cor.), Ras Al Khaima (1966 issue) and Togo (1970, 10f.). Australians might also protest at their champion motor-cyclist Kel Carruthers being assigned a Union Jack on a 2b. 1969 stamp of Yemen (Royalist). An 8c. Canadian stamp of 1973 commemorates the arrival of Scottish settlers in Nova Scotia, and shows them wading ashore waving the Royal Scottish standard, but this is personal to the Scottish monarch, and only to be flown when the monarch is personally present.

Other straying emblems include the Red Cross emblem which appeared in the Charity Tax overprint applied to a Greek 50l. stamp in 1937—although the Red Cross Society was not one of the beneficiaries of the tax. The Greek Red Cross Society then complained, so the Post Office subsequently used a green overprint. Conversely a Liberian issue of 1941 was surcharged in aid of the Red Cross fund but with a cross patée overprint instead of the Greek cross symbolic of the Red Cross organisation.

However the symbols which have been involved in the greatest confusion in the minds of stamp designers have been the Rod of Aesculapius, knobbed with a single twining serpent, a symbol for medicine, and the Caduceus of Hermes, a slender wand, winged, with two entwined snakes, a symbol of commerce and communications. Aesculapius himself is shown with the former on a 50m. 1968 Cypriot stamp, and Hermes (Mercury) with the latter on numerous issues, such as the 3s. 1961 Austrian stamp marking the World Bank Congress. The Caduceus is shown without its wings but in its proper context on a Belgian definitive issue of 1932 and on a closely similar series of French issues from 1938 to 1944. The Rod of Aesculapius is featured with two serpents instead of one on a number of issues—Afghanistan (1952, 1953 issues) (figs. 3 and 4), Brazil (1952, 3cr.80), Chad (1969, 100f.), India (1955, 6a.), Iran (1962 issue), Jamaica (1923 issue), Syria (1965, 60p.), Tunisia (1958, 30f.) and doubtless others which we have missed. The full Caduceus is mistakenly used as a medical symbol on stamps of Australia (1957, 7c.), Ceylon (1970 issue), Dominican Republic (1950, 12c.), South Korea (1963, 4w.), Liberia (1954, 25c.+5c.), Pakistan (1960 issue) (fig. 27) and U.S.A. (1940, 5c. Dr. Walter Reed).

Finally we may close this chapter with a group of miscellaneous errors which belong here but were brought to our notice too late for inclusion in their proper contexts within the chapter. The eagle shown flying over the Pyrenees on an Andorran Spanish Post Offices 20c. stamp of 1929 is found in Africa and the U.S.A. but not in Europe. A 1961 Angolan issue features Angolan women, but there is a stranger in their midst, for the lady on the 30c. value belongs to Mozambique. The Flower labelled "Orquida" (orchid) on 1956 5c.+5c. and 20c. stamps of Spanish Guinea is not an orchid, and the plant labelled *Anabasis articulata* on 50c., 1p.50 and 10p. stamps of Spanish Sahara of 1962 is not this species. The fleet of

Columbus has little relevance to Cocos Island, with which it is figured on a Costa Rican issue of 1936, for the island is in the Pacific, which Columbus never saw.

A New Zealand issue of 1936 commemorates the 21st anniversary of the ill-fated landing of Australian and New Zealand troops at 'Anzac Cove', Gallipoli, during the First World War. The stamps purport to show a New Zealand soldier of 1915 against a background of 'Anzac Cove', but the soldier is from a photograph of a 1936 soldier in old uniform, specially posed, and the beach is actually Karaka Bay, in Wellington harbour. The choice of the 50l. stamp of 1852 for the Vatican City issue of 1952 marking the centenary of the first stamps of the Roman States was singularly unfortunate, for almost all the other values of this issue had appeared more than six months earlier. Both the Bahamas (in 1959) and British Honduras (in 1966) produced issues to commemorate the centenary of their first issues of postage stamps, but in each case wrongly labelled the event as "POSTAL CENTENARY"—postal services had been operating for considerably longer. A 10c. Venezuelan stamp of 1940 purports to show the bed on which Bolivar was born, but although the bed figured is probably of the correct period it is not the correct bed. In the same issue a 37½c. value claims to show the pomegranate courtyard of the house in which he was born, but actually depicts the site of the family chapel.

72

73

74

75

76

77

79

80

81

83

82

78

CHAPTER 3

Denomination Errors

In contrast with most other categories of design errors those embodying denomination errors are far less numerous, perhaps because issuing authorities are most conscious of the values for which they sell their products. Nevertheless some very interesting, almost unbelievable errors have been perpetrated in this category.

One of the most common types of error involves confusion between singular and plural words for the currency. The early Sudanese issues from 1898 to 1941 used the old Turkish word ‘ Gersh ’ (piastre) regardless of number: this was changed to the correct Arabic equivalent for the 1948 issue 1p. value, and the appropriate Arabic plurals for the various other values. Egypt had trouble with the 1 piastre value of the 1867 issue, for the printer in error inserted the letter ‘ wow ’ in the lower label, effectively changing ‘ piastre ’ into ‘ piastres ’. This was discovered and removed at an early stage, but traces can still be seen on stamps from early sheets. The word ‘ thema ’ (value) was also altered by removal of one dot from the three in the first syllable, thus changing ‘ thah ’ to ‘ tah ’ (giving the correct pronunciation but the wrong spelling). The record for errors in this category must go to the Palestinian postage due set of 1923, printed at the Greek Orthodox Convent in Jerusalem. The Arabic on both the 1 and 2 milliemes values was incorrect, showing plural instead of singular on the 1m. and plural instead of dual on the 2m. (text. figs. 1, 2 & 3). This was compounded on the 1m. with an English plural “milliemes” and the Hebrew on the 2m., 4m., 8m. and 13m. to compensate showed singular instead of plural (text. figs. 4 & 5).

مليمات	مليم	مليمان	מילים	מילימים
1	2	3	4	5
1. as is	2. should be 1	3. should be 2	4. as is	5. should be

The 1928 Iranian fiscals surcharged and overprinted for air mail use have the singular for all values except the “2Krs.”, while a Turkish set of 1923 has the plural except for the “100 piastre” value. In a Turkish set of 1880 the 1 piastre value was given as “PIASTRES”. The final ‘ S ’ was deleted from the plate very inexpertly, leaving a number of varieties with part of the ‘ S ’ still present or part of the ‘ E ’ removed. The 1c. 1892 stamp of Paraguay featuring Rivarola has “centavos”, corrected to “centavo” on the chalk-surfaced issue of 1896. Dominican Republic issues of 1904 are surcharged “1 CENTAVOS”, corrected to “UN CENTAVO” on 1906 surcharges. The Indian state of Kishangarh has “2 anna” or “TWO ANNA” on issues of 1899 and 1912 respectively, the latter corrected to “TWO ANNAS” in 1913. Shanghai in its issues of 1865 seemed undecided, for all values of the wove paper issue had “CANDAREEN”, while all values of the pelure paper issue (except of course the 1c. value) had “CANDAREENS”. In July 1894 a 64 att value for Siam (Thailand) was surcharged “1 Atts”. This was corrected to “1 Att” the following month. Nevertheless the same mistake was made in 1895 in surcharging the 12a., and once again this was corrected. The corrected 1894 surcharge was itself amended by the addition of a reversed capital ' S ' to read " 1 Att Ƨ", an unusual case of compounding an original error.

A complicated story involves the 1858 issue for the Argentine province of Buenos Aires, where a change of tariff necessitated an immediate supply of 4 reales and 1 peso values. Pending arrival of new plates from Paris these were supplied by partial erasure of the ' P ' of the "CUATO Ps" (4 pesos) value to convert it to "CUATO rs" and parts of the "CINCO Ps" (5 pesos) to convert it to "IN Ps" (for 1 peso). The raised ' s ' was left, however, so that ' pesos ' remained in the plural. For some reason the amended 4 reales plate was further altered by erasure of "CUA" and "O", leaving "T rs" to stand for 1 peso, the value the issue represented.

Confusion between singular and plural has also occurred for European countries. A Greek 1 drachma stamp of 1933 portraying the Temple of Neptune, originally intended as a 3 drachmai value, was altered to 1 drachma at the last moment. Unfortunately the engraver changed the numeral value but left the written plural. Gibbons catalogue illustrations of the 1906 1 drachma value of the Second Olympic Games issue wrongly portray what appears to be a similar error, for in this case the issued stamp was quite correct. An 1893 Rumanian issue has a 1 ban stamp incorrectly in the plural as "1 bani"—this was corrected for the 1902 issue. Spanish 1 peseta air and definitive stamps of 1939 wrongly had the plural "1 Pts", corrected for the 1940 issue (without imprint), wrong again for the 1943 definitive issue, corrected for the 1951 definitive issue (figs. 28-30). Italy likewise had a period of confusion between singular and plural. Here there were two acceptable alternatives, ' Lire una ' (or ' Lire 1 ') as on the 1924 Victory 1l. stamp and the Monte Cassino stamp of 1944 respectively, or ' Una lira ' (or ' 1 lira ') as on the 1889 King Umberto definitive or the 1932 1l. value of the Dante commemorative issue respectively. However, the 1923 1l. Fascist commemorative stamp wrongly has "Lira una", as does the 1l. Royal Jubilee stamp of 1925. The postage due issue of 1870 was printed initially without figures, so the 1 centesimo value became wrongly "1 centesimi" and the 1 lira became "1 lire". In German nouns employed as denominations of measure have the plural like the singular, hence the 1861 Bergedorf issue was wrong to have the plural "SCHILLINGE" on the 3s. and 4s. values. The 1½s. likewise had been wrong as far as the proof stage, but here the lithographer erased the final ' E ' from each design, thus leaving a clear gap in the design of the issued stamp. There was, however, some disagreement on this point amongst linguists, and the 1875 German definitive issue was allowed to have "PFENNIGE" instead of ' PFENNIG '. By 1880 opinion had hardened, and the issue of that year has "PFENNIG" for all values. A surcharged 1923 issue of Danzig also wrongly had the plural "pfennige" throughout. The 5f. Belgian stamp of 1915 showing King Albert at Furnes likewise wrongly had "FRANKEN" in the Flemish inscription, corrected to the singular "FRANK" for the 1919 issue. The designation of the 1f.10 "FRANCS/FRANKEN" value Belgian Railway Parcel stamp of 1916 was changed to the more correct "FRANC/FRANK" in 1919. The plural ' Marken ' was wrongly included in the design of a 5g. stamp prepared for the 1856-63 issue of Bremen, but not issued, and was replaced by a stamp bearing the correct 'Marke'. The Saar, however, in 1921 had a stamp surcharged "5 FRANKEN" and a 5f. stamp of 1927 showing the Burbach Steelworks likewise gives the value as "5 FRANKEN".

In 1885 Bulgaria produced 1st. and 2st. stamps on which the values were given in the wrong gender—masculine instead of feminine—no doubt because the issue was printed and produced by the Russian Government Printing Office, St Petersburg (now Leningrad); these were corrected in 1886. However the written Bulgarian language was less rigidly structured at this period. The 1922 Egyptian stamp featuring the statue of Rameses II was first issued with the noun for the value printed in the nominative instead of the accusative singular in the Arabic inscription. This was speedily corrected. The postal authorities intended to use up fiscally the large stock of stamps with the error, but in the event considerable numbers were used up postally.

In 1960 Cambodia marked the inauguration of Sihanoukville Port by issuing 2r., 5r. and 20r. values, correctly inscribed with western values but unfortunately uniformly valued at 20r. in Cambodian. Several thousand copies were sold prior to receipt of corrected supplies (figs. 31-35). The 1964 Afghan stamp commemorating the Human Rights Seminar, Kabul, similarly has the correct value (3a.75) in western figures, but 3a.25 in the Arabic inscription. The 15c. 1890 stamp for Shanghai has the Chinese figure of value as 5 instead of 15—very confusing for the local population! Lebanon very nearly made a similar error, for a 40p. value was prepared for a 1963 issue marking the Baalbek Festival, but just in time was noticed to have the Arabic value as 45p. and it was promptly withdrawn and destroyed. The 1970 5c. value of New Zealand had the sheet value wrongly given as $12 in the marginal inscription, obliterated and corrected to $10.

For the Afghan 20p. stamp of 1921 marking the Royal Star of the Order of Independence there are two types. The commoner (17 out of 25 stamps per sheet) in fact has an error in the value in the upper-left lozenge, three dots instead of one, converting the 'b' into a 'p', while in the central lozenge the converse error changes the 'p' of 'Paisa' into a 'b'. Misspelling of the currency unit has also occurred on a 1974 issue of Thailand marking the centenary of the National Museum, where the 'baht' values are given in "bath", and on a 40m. 1961 Tunisian stamp commemorating Dag Hammarskjöld, which misspells MILLIEMES as "MILLIMES". When in 1927 Afghanistan first deigned to translate the currency on the stamps for the benefit of Occidentals, there seemed to be some confusion in the spelling adopted, for on the 15p. value it is "POUL" and on the 60p. it is "POOL". In 1932 a 10p. value has "POL" while a 20p. has "PUL". Afghanistan then discovered plurals, and a 1933 50p. value has "POOLS", a 1936 50p. value has "PULS" and a 1946 15p. value has "POULS". By 1952 the Afghans appeared to have given up trying, for a 10p. value simply has "P". Kishangarh on a 1913-16 issue gives the value in "RUPIES" instead of 'RUPEES' on the 2r. and 5r. values, while the Yemen in the 1930-1959 period alternates between "BOGCHA" and "BOGSHA" and "BOGCHAH" in the singular, "BOGACHES" and "BOGSHAS" in the plural. Egypt in 1915 omitted the grave accent from a 2 millièmes surcharge (it is present, for instance, on a 1905 3 millièmes surcharge), while Spain in 1937 produced a '1 CÉNTIMO' value both with and without the accent.

Abbreviations may or may not be marked by stops, but at least there should be consistency within an issue. In 1958 Kenya, Uganda and Tanganyika issued a 15c. stamp without a stop after the 'c', although other values of this set included a stop. This was considered sufficiently important an omission to warrant the issue in 1959 of a redrawn design including the stop, yet the stop was omitted for *all* values of the 1960 definitive issue. The 1929 Italian definitive issue had "CENT." with a stop to indicate abbreviation of 'CENTESIMI' on all values except the 20c., and this distinction was still maintained for the 1945 issue with the fasces removed. Similarly a surcharged issue of 1918 of the Mozambique Company has "Cent." with stop as abbreviation for 'Centavos' on the ½c. value, but omits the stop on the 2½c. value. The issues of Haiti from 1887 to 1898 all have 'centimes' abbreviated to "cent" with no stop, although the stop is present for earlier issues.

German occupation of Belgium stamps of 1914 were surcharged in "Centimes" (French) although Belgium is officially bilingual. Following objections this was shortened for the 1916-18 issue to "Cent.", which could equally represent the French 'Centimes' or the Flemish 'Centiemen'. The 1897-98 Canadian issue with the value in English only did not even bear numerals, and the 2c. and 10c. values were very similar in colour, which was hard on both illiterates and French-speaking Canadians. Objections were raised in Parliament, and in 1898 a corrected issue appeared with numerals in the lower corners (and a new colour for the 10c. value). The Jubilee Issue of 1897 likewise did not give the value in Arabic numerals (although U.P.U. regulations required this for stamps used on international mail), and the written value was in English only, as with most issues of Gibraltar to 1937 and indeed many British Colonial issues, too numerous to detail. The 1975 Christmas stamp of the U.S.A. was in even more flagrant violation of U.P.U. regulations in that it carries no value at all, for at the time of its production U.S. postal rates were about to be reviewed, and the value to be required for its function was not known. New Zealand was faced with a similar problem, for postal rates were increased in 1964 after the Christmas 2d. stamp had been prepared, and the authorities were unwilling to mar the stamp with a surcharge. In this case it was allowed, by special concession, to service First Day Covers and unsealed envelopes containing Christmas cards within New Zealand, without the additional stamps which the new rate would normally have required. A change in postal rate also caught Honduras on the hop, for the value of the 1866 issue, 2 reales, was altered to 1r. by decree of October 18th, 1865, although no surcharge was applied, so that the stamps were never sold for postal purposes at face value. Rose-coloured stamps were sold only in the Comayagua area, where a debased copper currency was valid, while the green-coloured stamps were sold in Gracias, Ymo and other areas which accepted only silver currency. Issue of a stamp of the wrong postal value for the function which it was intended to perform is also shown by the 10c. 1928 air stamp of the Dominican Republic, for the minimum air fee at that date was 12c. The 6b. and 8b. Air Mail stamps of a 1951 issue of the Yemen were not issued until 1957, and then only to serve as ordinary postage stamps.

The Yemen produced 5b. stamps in issues of 1940, 1947 and 1951 which were not released at the time because they served no postal use, but that of the 1951 issue was released in 1956 to serve as a 4b. stamp, and again with the other 5b. stamps in 1957 as 4b. values, all without any surcharge to indicate the changed values.

Semipostal issues can also cause confusion regarding their cost and postal value. A 1956 issue of Afghanistan marking an International Exhibition in Kabul is just marked "50p.", with no indication that the postal validity is only 35p., the remaining 15p. representing premium. A Brazilian issue of 1931 commemorating the 3rd October Revolution was intended to be a semipostal, and carries additions, but in fact was sold at face postal value without premium. Conversely a 1956 semipostal issue of Ceylon (Sri Lanka) marking the 2,000th anniversary of the birth of The Lord Buddha was intended to raise funds for the Lanka Buddha Mandalaya, but the Rs. 21,068 thus raised could not be handed over, because the provision of the Special Stamps Act had not been met (that approval for such a levy on a special stamp issue should be given by a special vote in the House of Representatives). Hence the Post Office retained its windfall, and the remaining stock had the premium obliterated and was issued at postal value in 1958.

Changes in currency are usually met by appropriate surcharges, but not always. An issue of 5r. and 10r. stamps was prepared for Paraguay in 1879 but not accepted, because in the previous year the currency had been changed from reales to centavos: instead they were returned to the printer, who was permitted to sell them to stamp collectors. A few were returned to Paraguay and used postally, but were not valid for this purpose, and surcharged stamps of this value are purely bogus. The same printer, Señor Roberto Large, produced the centavos issue of 1879 which was accepted and used. On 15th November, 1894, Macao produced a definitive issue with the values in reis, despite the fact that a decree of 5th July, 1894, had changed the currency to avos and patacas (with a very awkward exchange rate of 1 avo $=6\frac{1}{2}$ reis) and that on 1st November, 1894, the then current definitives had been provisionally surcharged in the new currency. Sharjah in 1966 produced an issue commemorating the F.I.P. and A.I.J.P. Congress in Munich: this issue was valued in naye paise and rupees, although the currency had been previously changed to piastres and rials. In the event the three values were printed se-tenant and sold as a single unit for 4 rials. Their actual postal status would seem somewhat uncertain, but nevertheless they have been honoured with recognition and catalogue status by Gibbons. It has been reported that the 1966 issue for Muscat and Oman was issued *before* the currency change which its values represented, but we would be grateful for more information about this. The 1955 Swedish issue marking the centenary of Swedish postage stamps was intended to be a reprint of the original 'Skilling Bancos' of 1855, but with a 'Crown and 1955' watermark; just in time someone realised that skilling currency had been obsolete for 98 years, so the stamps were produced with two parallel bars through the skilling values in the bottom panel, leaving the upper panel numerals to be treated as öre values. The British Military Administration of Tripolitania produced an issue in 1948 surcharged in Military Administration Lire; when Tripolitania was transferred to British Administration the overprint was altered accordingly from "B.M.A. Tripolitania" to "B.A. Tripolitania", but values were still given in Military Administration Lire. A rather different case of wrong currency occurs on 6f. French Marianne postage stamps and French consular stamps overprinted in dubious circumstances in 1948 by the French Consul in Jerusalem for use in Palestine/Israel with surcharges of "20 millièmes" (Egyptian currency) instead of 'mils' (the Palestinian/Israeli currency) (figs. 36 & 37). The first 1957 definitive issue for the Saar gives value numerals with no mention of currency (an increasing modern practice), amplified by a corresponding issue later in the year which includes "F" (for 'Frank') after the figure of value. The higher values of the Austrian stamps overprinted "LEI" in 1917 for use during the Austrian occupation of Rumania still also retained the 'K' (kreuzer) of the original value, so appear to be in both currencies.

Errors in the numerical part of the denomination also occur. A Rumanian 50b. stamp of 1948 was wrongly inscribed "BANI 0.50", which of course means '½ ban', speedily corrected to "LEI 0.50" (figs. 38 & 39). A Colombian 1921 3c. provisional stamp (misspelt "PROVICIONAL" in the overprint) has "$003" instead of '$0.03', corrected on both points later in the year. The 1965 International Co-operation Year issue of Gibraltar has two values, ½d. and 4d. Even back in 1965 ½d. was a low and rather useless denomination, it is here in the colours used for higher values of the corresponding issue of other Crown Colonies, and the numeral value is given as "1/2" not '½'. Clearly this was intended to be a 1/2d. value (*cf.* the Australian 1/2d. definitive of 1962), as that is what the numerals actually represent (fig. 40). The figure of value is reversed on the right side of a 1c. 1897 stamp of Newfoundland marking the sixtieth year of the reign of Queen Victoria (a year late!). It is similarly reversed on a 1d. 1961 Kuwaiti stamp, while the native numeral '2' is reversed on a 12k. 1958 stamp of Laos marking the third anniversary of the Laotian Red Cross (the 20k. of the same issue shows it correctly). An Egyptian 5p. issue of 1874 has the side panels transposed and inverted, so the '5's are upside-down. In 1948 Mozambique issued a 3$50 value showing the Nhanhangare Waterfall with the sign for 'escudos' (the same as the dollar sign) reversed. The 10s. and £1 British stamps of 1955 for some peculiar reason give the figure '1' as an upper-case letter "I" and this practice is now regularised on the Machin definitives.

In German the figure '7' when written is given a cross-bar to make it clearly distinct from the figure '1'. This should not appear on the printed '7', but does so in the dates on a West German 7pf. stamp of 1955 featuring the Arms of Baden-Württemberg, and the 7pf. definitive of 1954 featuring Heuss. This was corrected for the corresponding 7pf. value of the 1959 definitive issue. The 4c. Nicaraguan stamps of 1898 had 'CUATRO' misspelled "CUARTRO". However the spelling "DIWI RUBLI" in the surcharges on some 1920 Latvian issues instead of 'DIVI' as appears on other issues is not wrong, for it was only later that Latvian spelling reform banned the letter 'w' from the Latvian alphabet. A 1s. 1903 stamp of Niue should have been surcharged 'Taha e Sileni' (One shilling) but in error was printed "Tahae Sileni". This looks a trivial error, but unfortunately 'Tahae' means 'thief'. The authorities were most distressed and tried desperately to recover all the erroneous stamps; only 96 were sold in all.

Until 1956 Pakistan was apparently uncertain whether it is correct in Arabic to place a fraction to the right or to the left of an integer. Although Arabic, like Hebrew, is written from right to left, numerals are written left to right. An exception can be made with the date (as in postmarks), which frequently is written from right to left. As far as we are aware all issues inscribed in Arabic for other countries have the fraction to the right of the integer. Not so for Pakistan, which with splendid impartiality alternated from issue to issue until 1956, when on instructions from the Pakistani Government the printers (De La Rue) changed the position on the then current 2½a. and 3½a. stamps from left to right of the integer. Still apparently unsure, in the 1957 versions they cut the Gordian knot by omitting Arabic script numerals altogether, and since then only western numerals have been used. Between 1959 (2½p. and 7½p.) and 1961 (12½p.), Syria issuing stamps as the U.A.R. placed the currency denomination between the integer and the fraction as, for example "7p½". This practice appears to have ceased with the reversion to the name of Syria.

A 1920-21 issue for Memel is surcharged in pfennig or mark, but without the first letter being capitalized, as it should be in German. Subsequent surcharges of 1921 have the denominations capitalized. India in 1911 issued a "One and half anna" value, corrected in 1921 to "One and a half annas" to meet the criticisms of grammatical purists. Tranvancore managed to resist such criticisms and retained a "THREE QUARTER CHUCKRAM" issue from 1889 to 1939. A 21c. 1943 stamp of Honduras has the value written out in full wrongly as "VIENTE Y UNA", which should be ' VIENTIUN ' or ' VIENTE Y UN '. New Brunswick was saved in 1868 by the union with Canada from altering her "TWELVE & HALF CENTS" issue of 1860. The 1860-63 issue of Nova Scotia includes "EIGHT & ½ CENTS" and "TWELVE & ½ CENTS" values, a curious mixture of words and figures. The British stamps of 1862 and 1865 wrongly hyphenated the word ' SIXPENCE ', the hyphen being removed at the express request of Rowland Hill's brother Ormond, and 2d. and 4½d. 1886 values of the British Consular Mail of Madagascar are likewise wrongly hyphenated as "TWO-PENCE" and "FOUR-PENCE HALF-PENNY", while Victoria in 1884 and 1886 issued denominations with hyphens which should have been omitted. Various issues with the value in words omit a hyphen which *should* be present, *e.g.* Newfoundland 1897 (24c., 35c.), 1924 (24c.), 1928 (28c.), 1932 (25c.), 1932-8 (24c., 48c.), 1937 (24c., 25c., 48c.), U.S.A. 1857-70 (24c.) and Ceylon for various issues of 1872 and 1899.

CHAPTER 4

Mis-statements

The errors in this category merge into errors of identification on the one hand and false claims on the other, but we may first consider a group of errors which belong unequivocally in this category—those concerned with dating events. Many stamps commemorate the lives of celebrated men and women and surprisingly often get their birth or death dates, or indeed both, wrong. In the International Education Year series of Grenada of 1970 the 50c. shows Maimonides and gives his dates as 1139-1208. They are correctly given as 1135-1204 on the tabs of the Israeli 110pr. of 1953. The 1948 issue of Monaco commemorating the sculptor F. J. Bosio (1768-1845) on which, as mentioned earlier, his birth date is given as 1769, was corrected in the 1968 issue. In 1961 Jordan overprinted 15f. and 35f. World Refugee Year stamps to mark the tragic death of the U.N. Secretary-General Dag Hammarskjöld (1905-1961) but gave his birth date as 1904. A miniature sheet of Mali in 1965 gives the date of birth of Albert Schweitzer as 11th January, 1875, but he was born on the 14th of January of that year. Russia commemorated the composer Glinka on two issues (1954 and 1957), in each case giving the date of his birth (correctly) as 1804, but a Rumanian 55b. stamp of 1958 wrongly gives it as 1803. Russia also commemorated the American William Foster (1881-1961) with a 10k. stamp of 1971 which gave the date of his death as 1964. This was speedily withdrawn and a corrected version issued only a month later. On the other hand the author Maxim Gorky—pen-name of Alexei Maximovich Pyeshkov (1868-1936) is given his correct birth date on a Russian 4k. stamp of 1968 but the birth date 1869 on a Rumanian 55b. stamp of 1956 and a Hungarian 40fi. stamp of 1948. The Belgian writer Jules Destrée was born at Marcinelle on 21st August, 1863, but the Belgian 1f. commemorative stamp of 1963 gives his birth year as 1864. Czechoslovakia honoured Stodola on a 40h. stamp of 1959, but gave his death date as 1924 instead of the correct 1942. West Germany commemorated the authoress Annette Kolb (1870-1967) on a stamp in 1975 giving her birth date as 1875: in this case the postal authorities were hardly to blame, for she had assumed her sister's date of birth, never admitted her real age, and ' 1875 ' had been accepted by all major reference books. Nevertheless she had been christened Anna Mathilde Kolb on 13th February, 1870, in the diocese of St. Bonifazius in Munich by the Benedictine Pater Odilo Rottmanner. The great German poet Goethe (1749-1832) has his birth date given incorrectly as 1742 on a Hungarian 4fi. stamp of 1948—it is given correctly on numerous issues, for instance a 1m. 1945 stamp of the French Zone of occupied Germany. Hungary appears to have been somewhat negligent in checking birth and death dates of several of the many celebrities honoured on Hungarian stamps; the chemist Janos Iringi (30fi., 1954) has his birth date wrongly given as 1819 instead of 1817, the chemist Karoly Than (60fi., 1954) died in 1908, not 1904 as on this stamp, and the physician Endre Högyes

(2fo., 1954) died in 1906, not in 1921 as given here. On the other hand a Hungarian issue of 1950 marking the centenary of the death of General Bem does give the date of his birth correctly as 1794, whereas a Polish 30z. stamp of 1948 wrongly gives it as 1795. The same Polish stamp also features General Henryk Dembinski, who died in 1864, not 1866 as on the stamp (fig. 40). Poland has also erred on a 20g. stamp of 1957 honouring the Polish physician Dr. Wojciech Ocyko (1545-1608) in giving his dates as "1537-1599".

Italy commemorated the pioneers of the Italian wool industry, G. Marzotto and A. Rossi, with a 20l. stamp of 1950, but gave the dates of the latter as "1819-1918", making him nearly a centenarian; in fact he died in 1898. The Italian 10c. and 1l.75 commemoratives of 1937 inscribed "CENTENARIO DI SPONTINI" would also seem to be in error, for the composer Gasparo Spontini was born in 1774 and died in 1851. Still with Italy a 25l. stamp of 1958 commemorating the actress Eleonora Duse gives the date of her birth as 1858, but she was born on 3rd October, 1859, and a 30l. stamp of 1964 commemorating the Italian type designer and printer Giambattista Bodoni (1740-1813) does get the date of his death correct, but was a year late in being issued to mark its 150th anniversary.

Austria honoured Prince Eugene of Savoy on a 12gr. semipostal of 1935, but wrongly gave his year of birth as 1667 instead of 1663. A 1s.50 Austrian stamp of 1960 marked the 300th anniversary of the birth of the architect Jacob Prandtauer, but he was in fact born in 1658, as correctly given on a 30g. semipostal of 1934. The pioneer balloonist Pilâtre de Rozier (1756-1785) was commemorated on a 75c. French stamp of 1936, but with his year of birth given as 1754. François-Nicolas Appert, inventor of food-canning, was born in 1750, not 1749 as given on a French 12f. stamp of 1955.

Turning outside Europe we find that India in 1963 issued a 15n.p. stamp in honour of the formidable Mrs. Annie Besant (1847-1933), but enlarged her life span by giving her year of birth as 1837. A 1s. 1959 Ecuadorian stamp honours Dr. A. B. Moreno, President of Ecuador from 1919 to 1920, but gives the year of his birth as 1859 instead of the correct 1861. Colombia likewise commemorated a former President, Laureano Gomez (1888-1956) on a 1p.30 stamp of 1972, but gave his year of birth as 1898. Nicaragua in 1957 produced an issue to mark the centenary of the birth of the founder of the Boy Scout movement, Sir Robert Baden-Powell (1857-1941), but through some surprising aberration gave the date of his birth as 1856. A more complex case occurs on a 70f. 1971 stamp of Dahomey and on a 3p. 1972 Ghanaian stamp, both showing a detail from the Adoration of the Magi, a panel of the Keisheimer altarpiece by Hans Holbein the Elder (c.1460-1520), but here attributed to Hans Holbein (1497-1543), who was of course the son of the painter of this work. Strictly speaking, therefore, this error should perhaps be placed in chapter two rather than here in chapter four.

With many famous people of long ago or of obscure origin, the dates of birth and death may not be known with great certainty. Thus the date of the martyrdom of St. Wenceslas is given on the Czech issue of 1929 as "929", yet most authorities accept that he was slain by his brother Boleslaw in 935. The great Arab philosopher and physician Avicenna

(979-1037, according to the *Encyclopaedia Britannica*) is given the vital dates "980-1037" by Pakistan (1966, 15p.) and "952-1037" by East Germany (1952, 35pf.). Afghanistan commemorated the millenary of his death by an issue of 1952 which wisely did not bear any dates, although Iran calculated the millenary as occurring in 1951, the millenary issue of 1954 again wisely giving no precise dates for his life. The French scholar Guillaume A. Budé is given the dates "1467-1540" on a 12f. semipostal French stamp of 1956, and these dates are confirmed by the *Encyclopaedia Britannica*, but other authorities consider he was born in 1468. Similarly, modern research indicates that the generally accepted date of birth of Jonathan Swift (1667-1745) may be wrong, in which case the Irish commemorative issue of 1967 is in error, though one can scarcely blame the stamp designer here. The same applies to the 1957 3c. stamp of the U.S.A. and issues of St. Christopher, Nevis and Anguilla (1957, 24c., 1963, 60c.), which give the year of birth of Alexander Hamilton as 1757, for recently unearthed evidence indicates that he may have been born in 1755, which certainly would make his early political pamphleteering seem not quite so precocious.

The birth date of Sukhe Bator, founder of the Mongolian People's Republic, is given as 1894 on a Mongolian 40m. stamp of 1932 and a 45m. stamp of 1943, yet as 1893 on an issue of 1963, this latter being the generally accepted date. A Hungarian 1fi. stamp of 1948 honours the printer Gutenberg. His dates are not precisely known, but are given by the *Encyclopaedia Britannica* as c.1398-c.1468, but on the stamp as "1393-1468". President Gomez of Cuba likewise has an uncertain birth date, given categorically as "1833" on the 2c. stamp of 1954, replaced with a question mark on 2c. stamps of 1961 and 1969. The Gomez commemorative issue of 1936 carries the date "18th November 1935" but does not specifically assert that this is the precise centenary of his birth.

The date of the death of the Christian King Olaf Haroldsson, defeated and killed in the Battle of Stiklestad, can be very precisely dated, for an eclipse occurred during the battle, which places the event on 31st August, 1030, not on 29th July as given on a 30ore Norwegian stamp of 1930 depicting the battle (fig. 41).

Misdating is sometimes due to difficulties in conversion of dates based on calendars other than Gregorian. Thus Libya marked the centenary of the death of the Imam Essayed Mohamed Ali by an issue in 1956, and gave the dates "1856-1956" on the stamps, but the Imam in fact died in 1859, the centenary commemorated being based on the Moslem calendar (1273-1373 A.H.). A similar situation appears to apply to the Egyptian issue marking the millenary of Al-Azhar University, which bears the Muslim dates "361-1361" and was intended for issues in 1942. It was actually issued in 1957, bearing the correct Muslim year as a red overprint, but even that was not a millenium by the Gregorian calendar, which dates the foundation of this ancient seat of learning as 970. The tabs of the 3pr., 5pr. and 10pr. of the 1949 (second) coin issue of Israel gives the Jewish dates for the First Revolt against the Romans as 3824-3830 (text. fig. 6), the Common Era dates in western numerals being correct. The correct Jewish dates (given on the tabs of the same three values of the 1950 coin issue) are 3826-3830 (text. fig. 7).

גיתתכ״ד - גיתת״ל

6

ג.תתכ״ו - ג.תת״ל

7

A 1972 set from ever-prolific Manama features British royalty in a series of miniature sheets. The name of the monarch and dates of reign are given, not on the stamps but above the top centre stamp of each sheet. For William III (50d.) they are given as "1688-1689", whereas he was proclaimed joint sovereign (with his wife Mary II) in January, 1689 (James having fled the country in December, 1688), and died in 1702. Mary II died in 1694, so the superscription of her sheet (75d.), which reads "1689-1702", is also wrong. Correct dates are given on 35c. stamps of Barbuda of 1971. As Queen Victoria came to the throne in 1837 a Newfoundland 1c. stamp is in error in proclaiming the sixtieth year of her reign when it was in fact issued in 1897, the sixty-first year.

A Rumanian 6l. stamp of 1932 commemorating the fifth death centenary of Alexander I (Alexander the Good) gives the date of his accession as 1406 instead of 1400—hence the comparatively small number (100,000) of these stamps issued. Nicaragua in 1953 produced an issue commemorating its many (often short-lived) presidents, making several mistakes in dating their respective presidencies. Solórzano (4c.) was President from 1st January, 1925, not from 1924 as given, General Somoza (15c., 30c.) was President from 1937 to 1947 and from 1950 to 1956, not "1937-1939" and "1951-1957" as on the stamps, General Martinez (35c.) was President from 1857, not from 1859 as stated, and R. Sacasa (1cor.20) was President from 1889, not from 1891.

Some events have rather indefinite starting points, which may lead to apparent conflicts in dating them. The centenary of the telephone, for instance, was celebrated by Canada with a 1974 issue, since Alexander Graham Bell conceived the principal idea of his telephone while staying with his parents in Brantford, Ontario, in 1874, but a 13c. 1976 stamp of the U.S.A. marked the centennial of the registration of his patent with the U.S. Patent Office at Boston, Massachusetts, in 1876. Italy in 1965 issued a 70l. stamp honouring Antonio Meucci as the inventor of the telephone, and he did indeed obtain a U.S. patent in 1871, but he lacked funds to develop it, the patent lapsed in 1873 and Meucci died in poverty. In any case, the telephone was not a practical instrument for general use until later modifications due to Thomas Edison. Similarly the choice of 1944 for the issue of a 3c. U.S.A. stamp to mark the 50th anniversary of motion pictures appears to have been somewhat arbitrary (indeed the Postal Department issued this stamp with considerable reluctance, under heavy pressure from lobbyists). Although a Canadian named Holland did open a "kinetoscope parlour" in April, 1894, on Broadway, the first kinetoscope had been completed by Edison and Dickson in 1889, followed shortly by further manufacture in England and Germany as well as in the U.S.A. The origin of baseball is much less clear than the 3c. 1939 centennial stamp produced by the U.S.A. would have us believe. On rather slender grounds it is assigned to General Abner Doubleday, who is credited with laying out the diamond-shaped field with four bases 60ft. apart in 1839 in Cooperstown, New York State, but at that date Doubleday was a West Point cadet, and he never made this claim for himself. Furthermore baseball was named and briefly described in "A little pretty book" published in London in 1744, the Rochester Baseball Club in the U.S.A. had 50 members in 1820, and the origins of the game go back at least to 11th century Europe. The Rev. Thomas Wilson, a Puritan divine, of Maidstone, wrote of "baseball" in 1700. The centenary of County Cricket commemorated by a British issue of 1973 is likewise a somewhat dubious sporting anniversary. Certainly the M.C.C. laid down the rules governing county qualifications in 1873, but the first recorded inter-county cricket match was ' Middlesex ' v. ' Kent ', when ' the Londoners ' met ' the Kentish men ' in 1719! (The first game for which rules are known was between the Duke of Richmond's XI and the Gentlemen of Peper Harow in 1727). Inter-county championships go back to 1864, when Surrey were champions, so the 1973 centenary ought at least to be much more precisely defined than it is on this issue.

An 8c. U.S.A. stamp of 1972 marks the centennial of mail order services, marking in fact the origin of that of Montgomery Ward, but mail ordering can be traced back to Harriet B. Shaw of Alfred, Maine, who sold a variety of items by mail in the 1850s to 1870s; the extent of her mail order business may be gauged from the present-day existence of over 133,000 known postal covers from her business! A 5c. Canadian stamp of 1963 places the commencement of the Quebec-Trois Rivières-Montreal postal route in 1763, but Pedro da Silva, a Portuguese Canadian, commenced mail-carrying on this route in 1693 and was appointed official letter carrier in 1705 by Jacques Raudot, Intendant of New France, augmenting his official salary by carrying private mail for fees based on the distance travelled. One might question if the British issue of 1960 marking the Tercentenary of the General Letter Office was really marking the most significant anniversary, for the Act of 1660 was based very largely on a similar Act of 1657 promulgated by Cromwell, which had been declared void by Charles II, then very largely reproduced in his own ' new Act '. In 1963 Costa Rica produced an issue to mark the centenary of Costa Rican postage stamps, but of the stamps illustrated two (4r. and 1p. values) were issued in 1864 and there appears to be some doubt as to whether the first stamps appeared in 1862 or in 1863. It has been general to accept the foundation date for the Universal Postal Union as 1874 and to give the main credit to the Prussian postal official Heinrich von Stephan, as on the German issues of 1924-28 which marked the 50th anniversary. However, the general idea of an international postal union originated with the American Postmaster-General Montgomery Blair, and was proposed by him at the First International Postal Conference in Paris in 1863 (commemorated by a U.S. 15c. stamp in 1963). Its ratification was delayed by the American Civil War and the Franco-Prussian War, but though the inaugural meeting was held on 9th October, 1874, the Union did not formally come into being until January of 1875, so the Swiss commemorative issue of 1900 is the only one to date which is commemorating the technically correct anniversary!

In 1965 East Germany produced an issue to mark the 800th anniversary of the Leipzig Spring Fair, but although Leipzig itself was founded in 1165, the Fair privileges were given to the State of Leipzig by Maximilian I in 1497, so this commemoration was considerably premature. In 1958 East Germany issued a 20pf. stamp honouring the 200th anniversary of the "Systema Naturae" of Linnaeus (Carl von Linné), but the work was first published in 1735, though Vol. I of the 10th edition, which *was* published in 1758, is the starting point of zoological nomenclature.

Russia and France both produced issues in 1975 to mark the 50th anniversary of Franco-Soviet relations, but the 6k. Russian stamp has it set in 1974, the 1f.20 French stamp in 1975. As diplomatic relations were established following the Treaty of Locarno in 1925, the French celebration would seem better timed. Canada commemorated the 50th anniversary of the Royal Canadian Legion by an issue of 1975; the Unity Conference in Winnipeg at which the decision to found the Legion was taken was indeed in 1925, but Dominion and Provincial charters were not granted until 1926. Hence Dominion Command decided that the jubilee would be officially celebrated from November, 1975, to November, 1976, so the date for this issue is perfectly acceptable.

The U.S.A. commemorated the tercentenary of Connecticut with a 3c. issue of 1935, but the first European settlement made in Connecticut appears to have been the setting up of a trading post by Capt. William Holmes in 1633. In 1634 some Watertown (near Boston) inhabitants set up huts at Wetherfield, and in 1635 many of the residents of Dorchester (Massachusetts) moved to the neighbourhood of Capt. Holmes's post. The chief early migration into Connecticut was in 1636, led by Thomas Hooker into Hartford, and the demand by General Andros for the charter (hidden in the oak depicted on the stamp) did not occur until 1687, so the choice of 1635 as the foundation date for the state appears rather arbitrary.

Anniversaries can be wrong for dubious or various reasons. An Italian issue of 1934 commemorates the alleged 75th anniversary of the invention of the dynamo by Antonio Pacinotti, *i.e.* in 1859. It is true that Pacinotti discovered the principles of the continuous current dynamo, though 1861 is a more usually accepted date for this, but it was the Belgian Gramme who made the dynamo a practicable proposition and displayed it as such at the Vienna Exhibition of 1873. Niger marks the 150th anniversary of the invention of the bicycle with a 100f. stamp of 1968, thus dating the invention from 1818, but there were earlier forerunners, such as the 1809 bicycle of Drais commemorated on a 2f. 1968 stamp of the Mali Republic. A 3c. 1939 stamp of the U.S.A. marks the 300th anniversary of printing in Colonial America, featuring what purports to be the " Stephen Daye Press" and bearing the dates "1639" and "1939". Many authorities believe the first printing was done by Stephen's son Matthew in the autumn of 1638, his name may have been preferentially spelt ' Day ' (though this is by no means certain), and the press figured on the stamp is *not* the so-called "Stephen Daye Press", which still exists in Cambridge, Massachusetts, but an early press belonging to the Vermont Historical Society of Montpelier, Vermont, which was shipped to New York, sketched for the stamp, and then exhibited at the Fifth Educational Graphic Arts Exposition in New York at which the stamp was issued (fig. 42). A 6c. U.S.A. stamp of 1953 marks the 50th anniversary of the great achievement of the Wright Brothers in making a powered flight in a machine heavier than air, but mistakenly labels the occasion as the "50th anniversary of powered flight", thus ignoring the many earlier airship flights, *e.g.* of Gifford using a steam engine in Paris, 1852, Haenlein, with a gas engine, in 1872, the Tisandier Brothers in 1884 and Renard and Krebs in 1884, in both cases with an electric motor. The 3c. U.S.A. stamp of 1944 commemorating the 125th anniversary of the transatlantic crossing made by the S.S.

Savannah is technically correct in captioning this as "FIRST STEAMSHIP TO CROSS THE ATLANTIC", but the *Savannah* also had sails, and in fact steamed for only eight hours and sailed for the rest. The first transatlantic crossing to be made virtually entirely under steam was by the *Royal William* in 1833, as commemorated on a 5c. Canadian stamp of 1933. A 1977 issue of Mali commemorates the first solo non-stop crossing of the Atlantic by a heavier than air aircraft, made by Charles Lindbergh in 1927, but mislabels this great achievement as "1ere TRAVERSEE DE L'ATLANTIQUE". Even discounting the sailors, the U.S. Navy flying boat NC4, the British aviators Alcock and Brown and the dirigible R-34 all made the crossing before Lindbergh.

Dating of events is sometimes just unequivocally wrong. On a 1972 issue of the British Solomon Islands the 4c. value features Louis de Bougainville (1729-1811) and his ship *La Boudeuse*, in which he discovered the three northern islands of the group in 1768, *not* 1776 as on the stamp. On the 15c. value of the same issue is shown Philip Carteret and the *Swallow*, which he commanded when he visited Gower Island in 1767 *not* 1707 as on the stamp: the correct date is given on the 1s. stamp of 1956. On the other hand the 1968 issue marking the quatercentenary of the discovery of the islands by Alvara Mendana in 1568 is correctly dated—it is the *Encyclopaedia Britannica* which is wrong in placing the event in 1567 on St. Isobel's Day (19th November), in fact the date on which the expedition set out from Peru. 30c. and 50c. Spanish stamps of 1930 wrongly give the date of the departure of Christopher Columbus from Palos as 2nd August, 1492, instead of 3rd August. A 1948 issue for the Bahamas marks the tercentenary of settlement of the island of Eleuthera, placing this in 1647, when the island was explored by William Sayle. The date of actual settlement is less easily fixed, but is given as 1646 in the *Encyclopaedia Britannica*. The se-tenant 40c. and 70c. values of the 1976 issue of Montserrat which marks the American bicentenary form a composite picture inscribed "Raleigh attacks H.M.S. *Druid* 1776", but this event in fact occurred in 1777. The foundation of San Domingo is dated as occurring in 1502 on a 1902 issue of the Dominican Republic, but San Domingo was founded by Bartolomeo Columbus in 1496, as marked by an issue of 1946 which is not, however, specifically so captioned. A 1937 set of Honduras gives the date for the founding of Comayagua (then named Valladolid la Nueva) as 1537, whereas the *Encyclopaedia Britannica* gives 1540. An apparent error concerns the founding of São Paulo in Brazil by José de Anchieta in 1554. This event was duly commemorated in 1954 by a stamp issue. However, in 1934 Brazil issued a set of stamps to commemorate the missionary work of José de Anchieta with the dates "1534-1934", wrongly described in Gibbons catalogues as marking the 400th anniversary of the founding of São Paulo by Anchieta. The proclamation of British sovereignty over New Zealand made by Governor Hobson at Akaroa took place on 21st May, 1840, not 11th August as seems to be implied on a 5d. New Zealand stamp of 1940.

East Germany marked the 40th anniversary of the November Revolution which began on 7th November, 1918, with a singularly ugly 20pf. stamp which was withdrawn for 'technical reasons' on the afternoon of the day of issue, the 'technical reason' being that the stamp wrongly gives a starting date of 9th November for the Revolution. A 12f. French stamp of 1954 purports to mark the 150th anniversary of the establishment of the French Legion of Honour, and carries the dates "1804" and "1954", but the French Legion of Honour was in fact founded on 19th May, 1802. Similarly the French National Academy of Medicine was founded in 1820, so the French 45c. stamp issued in 1971 to mark the 150th anniversary, and inscribed "POSTES 1971", is a year late. The correct foundation date appears in Roman numerals on an arch of the Assembly building portrayed on the stamp. The 1974 stamp to mark the tercentenary of the Hôtel des Invalides wrongly bears the date "1675", for it was founded by decree of Louis XIV in April, 1674. An 8c. 1928 stamp of Newfoundland wrongly places the first transatlantic cable as being landed in Newfoundland in 1866: a 1958 4c. stamp of the U.S.A. correctly places the event as occurring in 1858. A 10pf. West German stamp of 1964 marks the 100th anniversary of the publication by Kekulé of the formula of Benzole, a most significant advance in the science of organic chemistry, but Kekulé's theory was in fact formulated and published in 1865, and indeed the 25th anniversary of this discovery had been marked with considerable ceremony in Berlin on 11th May, 1890. A 1966 stamp of Ecuador claims that Albert Schweitzer was awarded the Nobel Peace Prize in 1954, but he was in fact nominated for it in 1952, and it was awarded in 1953.

Postal events can also be misdated, as we have already seen. A 3c. Jamaican stamp of 1971 in a postal tercentenary issue features a letter labelled "Dummer packet, 1705" but the correct date should have been ' 1708 '. A 1973 issue of Papua and New Guinea marks the 75th anniversary of the first stamps, featuring several early stamps with their purported dates of issue, but several of these latter are wrong. For instance the 1c. bears the legend "FIRST ISSUED 1897", but includes a 3pf. value first issued in July, 1898. The 2m. stamp featured on the 6c. value was not "FIRST ISSUED IN 1900" as claimed, but in January, 1901. Lastly the overprinted and surcharged registration label featured on the 7c. stamp was not "FIRST ISSUED IN 1914" as claimed, but in 1916. A more complex case is that of an 18c. stamp of the British Solomon Islands, issued in 1970 and part of a set commemorating a new post office, which features the 5s. ' small canoe ' stamp of 1910-14 and a Tulagi postmark. This latter is listed on the stamp as having been in use from 1911 to 1919: the original postmark of this period is not known to have been used before 1913 and was certainly used later than 1919, but also differs from the illustrated postmark by including lazy eights above and below the date, which had the year in full, not abbreviated as on the stamp. The I£1 value of an Israeli set issued in 1966 marking various postal services from Turkish to modern times has on the tab a reproduction of what is supposed to be the first definitive postmark used in Israeli Jerusalem and bears the No. 1 handstamp, which is incorrect as No. 1 was not ready on July 4th 1948. The first handstamp used on that day was No. 4. The 10p. British stamp of 1974 in the U.P.U. centenary series shows a postmark which is at variance with the special postmark for mail carried on the inaugural flight of the flying boat service to South Africa. The letters forming "SOUTHAMPTON AIR PORT" should have had narrower ' O 's, the month should have been abbreviated in capitals of uniform size (not upper and lower case), and there should not be an apostrophe before the digits for the year.

Details of some important events are unfortunately historically very vague, but nevertheless are often given an unwarranted precision on commemorative stamps. The date of printing of the so-called ' Gutenberg Bible ' is one of these. A 3c. 1952 stamp of the U.S.A. shows Gutenberg presenting his bible to Duke Adolf of Nassau, Elector and Archbishop of Mainz, after the mural by Edward Laring. The Archbishop is not in his clerical robes, as he surely would have been for such an occasion. Furthermore, it is unlikely that the Bible was completed by 1452: a West German issue of 1954 dates the event in 1454, but it is more probable that it was not completed until 1456. Finally, it seems probable that this Bible was not printed by Gutenberg at all, but by Peter Schöffer, perhaps partnered by Johann Fust. In 1971 Tanzania, Kenya and Uganda commemorated the celebrated meeting of Stanley and Livingstone with a 5s. stamp which placed the date of this meeting very precisely as 28th October, 1874. Although this date is accepted by some authorities as at least very likely, we shall probably never know with certainty. Livingstone himself recorded it for 24th October and Stanley for 10th November, and all three dates can be found cited in reference books.

Railway events seem curiously prone to error, and this applies to dating as well as other features. Paraguay on a 20g. stamp of 1972 dates Stephenson's Locomotive No. 1 as 1925 instead of 1825. The locomotive on the 50c. value of this issue labelled "Badenia 1863" is not the *Badenia*, which was built as a 1-A-1 locomotive by Ernst Kessler, Karlsruhe, before 1841, but a German locomotive of the Rampton design built between 1846 and 1864. The locomotive on the 15g. value labelled "BLENKINSOPS 1812" should more properly be entitled ' MURRAY-BLENKINSOP 1812 ' as on a 1l. 1964 stamp of San Marino. A 30h. 1966 stamp of Czechoslovakia shows a locomotive labelled "Karlštejn 1865": this was No. 427 (not 408 as on the stamp) of the Österreichische Staats Eisenbahn Gesellschaft built in 1872, the date "1865" on the stamp referring to the date when production of this *class* of locomotive commenced. The American 4-4-0 locomotive on a 1975 stamp of Cuba is an early Rogers type of about 1860, with the outside framed bogie, not of 1895 as stated on the stamp. Finally, a 35c. Peruvian stamp of 1936 and a 1954 Chilean issue are in dispute as to whether the Peruvian railway from Lima to Callao (inaugurated 1851) or Chile's Copiapó to Caldera line (also inaugurated in 1851) was the first in South America. Although Peru led by about three months, neither claim is correct, for British Guiana had an operational railway by 1848.

The Space Age has bought a flood of stamps featuring rockets, satellites and astronauts, surprisingly often linked to misdated events. The sets produced in 1966 to honour American astronauts by both Ras al Khaima and Qatar have wrong dates for Lovell's launch (which was 4.12.1965), Schirra's launch (which was 3.10.1962) and Cooper's launch (which was 15.5.1963). A 20f. Jordanian stamp from a space issue of rather dubious status likewise misdates Schirra's launch to 3.9.1962 instead of 3.10.1962. The Maldive Islands on their 1966 set marking the space rendezvous of Gemini 6 and Gemini 7 gets the date a week late (22nd December instead of 15th December, 1965). Even Hungary errs—the timing of the landing

84

85

86

87

88

89

90

91

92

93

of the Russian moon rocket on a 1959 60fi. stamp is ten seconds later than the official time (given correctly on a 60h. 1959 Czechoslovakian stamp); on a 3fo. stamp of 1966 the launch date for Conrad and Gordon is a whole year out—1965 instead of 1966. A 1967 issue of Qu'aiti State honouring the American astronauts Grissom, White and Chaffee who died in a fire during a ground checkout at Cape Kennedy gives the date of the accident as 21st January, 1967, whereas it occurred on the 27th, as correctly given on a 1967 memorial issue of Ras al Khaima. The airmail stamps of Paraguay for 1964 featuring the Saturn Apollo 5 give the wrong launching date—30th January instead of the 29th, 1964. There may have been confusion with the Russian Electron I and II satellites which *were* launched on 30th January, 1964. An 11c. space research stamp of Panama of 1965 claims that the Ranger 7 satellite was launched by a Titan 2 rocket on 29th July, 1964, whereas an Atlas-Agena rocket was used and the launch occurred on 28th July; a 1964 1c. stamp featuring the Transit 2A satellite claims it to be a meteorological satellite, which it was not—it carried Canadian built instruments to measure radio interference in space. A 1965 5f. stamp of Guinea marks the flights of Luna 2 and Luna 3, with the dates 14th September, 1959, and 8th October, 1959, respectively. Luna 2 was launched on 12 September and hit the Moon on the 13th, 33 hours 32 minutes later: Luna 3 was launched on 4th October, 1959, and photographed the far side of the Moon (the event to which the second date appears meant to apply) on the 7th. A 1959 60h. Czechoslovakian stamp gives the correct date for the Luna 2 moon-strike. An Albanian 50l. stamp of 1962 gives the launching date of Sputnik I as 11th October, 1957, instead of the correct 4th and a 5l. 1963 stamp gives the launching date of Lunik 3 as 4.11.1959 instead of 4.10.1959, while a 2p. 1975 stamp of Ascension shows a photograph of Ascension Isle taken from Skylab 3 but dated 11th January, 1973, although Skylab 3 was not launched until July, 1973. (For many of these and other Space errors we are indebted to a very comprehensive "Space Variety Checklist" published by Les Winick in 1969.)

In many cases dating errors on stamps are due to postponement of events after a commemorative issue has already been prepared. The first flight of the Anglo-French Concorde was expected to occur in 1968, but did not in fact occur until 2nd March, 1969. The New Hebrides got tired of waiting and in 1968 produced an undated issue commemorating the project, originally intended to mark the first flight. The French Southern and Antarctic Territories prepared an 87f. stamp inscribed "Concorde Premier Vol 1968", but during the delay a change of postal rate made a new engraving necessary. The original printing was destroyed (although about 20 copies are known to have survived) and a correctly dated 85f. value was issued in 1969. The Niger Republic issued a 100f. commemorative in 1972, but wrongly dated the first flight as "2 Mai 1969". A Liberian issue was prepared for a projected first flight to the U.S.A. by overprinting an issue "First Flight LIBERIA-U.S. 1941" with or without a surcharged value. However, this flight was cancelled and covers sent by ordinary mail. The date was cancelled with a bar and the stamps re-issued in 1942, when the flight did take place. The Lithuanian air set of 1922 was originally prepared to mark the founding of the air postal service but the stamps were not issued at that time, so the word

‘ISTEIGIMAS’ (=founding) was overprinted “ZENKLAS” (=value) and the date “1921.VI.25” was obliterated. Similarly the Russian air stamps of 1924 were meant for use on the air service inaugurated in 1923 and were so dated: because of delays in delivery the air service had been suspended for the winter, and changes in the currency which had been made in the interval necessitated a surcharge. Stamps of Newfoundland were overprinted “FIRST TRANS-ATLANTIC AIRPOST April, 1919” for use on mail carried by Hawker, but the flight was not actually commenced until 18th May. Railway services can also suffer inaugural delays. A 1930 issue of Guatemala marks the opening of the Los Altos electric railway from San Felipe to Quetzaltenango: the surcharge claims “Inaugurado en 1929” but the opening in fact occurred in 1930, as shown correctly on a specially produced set issued concurrently. The 11th Inter-American Conference was due to be opened in Quito on 1st February, 1960, and a commemorative issue was prepared by Ecuador which included the date “FEBRERO” in the design. The Conference was postponed until August, but the original stamps were nevertheless issued in February and a new issue of different design produced in August for the Conference.

A rather amusing example, though perhaps not a fair error, is the Sudanese issue commemorating the establishment of Self-Government. This was long awaited, and anticipated by production of three lots of stamps, dated progressively “1952”, “1953” and “1954”. When the New Constitution finally came into force on 9th January, 1954, the appropriately dated stamps were duly released in the Sudan, but through an error the Agent in London released stocks dated “1953” to dealers. These were never valid for postage, so do not strictly count as an issue. Stamps commemorating the Arab Postal Union and bearing the date “1-7-1954” were prepared for the Yemen but not issued until 1957-58, with date unaltered. The 25m. Finnish 1956 stamp marking the return of Porkkala territory from Russia carries the date ‘1955”, but the event took place on 26th January, 1956. A 140p. Afghan stamp illustrating Royal Buzkashi bears the date “1956” in the margin, but was not actually issued until late in 1957. Rumania produced in 1966 an issue to mark the World Chess Championships in Cuba. The 20b. and 11.60 values were inscribed “OLIMPIADA DE SAH-CUBA. SEPTEMBRIE—OCTOBRIE 1966”, but the event actually took place from 25th October to 20th November. A 1d. war charity semipostal of the Bahamas was to have been issued on 1st January, 1917, and was duly overprinted “1.1.17”, but owing to delay in shipment was not issued until May, 1917. A similar 1d. war charity semipostal was to have been issued on 3rd June, 1918, the bicentenary of the appointment of the first Royal Governor, and was likewise overprinted “3.6.18”, but the issue was held up by unavoidable production delays and did not occur until 1919. Israel produced a stamp issue and also miniature sheets to mark an International Philatelic Exhibition due to be held in Jerusalem in December, 1973, and the stamps were accordingly inscribed “Jerusalem 73”. However, the Yom Kippur War intervened and the Exhibition was postponed until March/April, 1974. The stamps were issued unaltered in December, 1973, though First Day Covers bore a cachet explaining the change of date, while the miniature sheets were not issued until the opening of the Exhibition.

Royal occasions can also suffer postponement. France produced a 1f.75 stamp in 1938 to commemorate the visit to Paris by King George VI and Queen Elizabeth, projected for 28th June, and this date was incorporated in the design. Due to the death of Queen Elizabeth's mother the Royal Visit had to be postponed until 19th July. Issue of the stamps was also delayed until this date, but they still bore the original date unaltered (fig. 43). Similarly Italy prepared an issue for a projected visit of the Shah of Persia in October, 1958, and incorporated the date in the design. The visit was postponed until November due to the death of the Pope, and issue of the stamps should likewise have been postponed, but they were issued in error from some offices on the originally authorised date, so were placed on release with date unaltered. On October 11th, 1976, King Shah Khalid of Saudi Arabia was due to open the Faisal Mosque in Islamabad and Pakistan printed a 65p. stamp for release on that day to commemorate the event. The ceremony had to be postponed until October 12th and it was intended to withdraw the stamps, but not all post offices were notified in time, so some were issued and used. Perhaps we should refer in passing to the British 13p. stamp of June, 1977, issued on the occasion of the meeting of the Commonwealth Heads of Government. The design incorporates 36 devices encircling a five-sided figure, each device representing the attendance of a state representative or Head of State. However, events in Uganda and the Seychelles precluded their attendance at the Conference, leaving only 34 representatives.

In many cases, of course, a dated issue prepared for an event which is then delayed is corrected by a suitable overprint or obliteration. The 1974 issue of Zaïre to mark the boxing championship match between Mohamed Ali and George Foreman had the original date blacked out and the revised date (24-9-74) substituted in the 1975 issue. An issue prepared by Singapore to mark the 2nd Afro-Asian Housing Congress was intended for issue in 1966 and was so inscribed. Issue was postponed until 1967, so the original date was blacked out and "1967" substituted, but in this case some of the 10c. values escaped without the overprint. The laying of the foundation stone of Calavi University is correctly dated by an overprint on a 100f. stamp of Dahomey of 1970, reading "CALAVI 6.11.1970". A 1962 issue of Saudi Arabia supporting the campaign for eradication of malaria was put on sale one month late, by which time the Islamic year 1381 had passed. Exception to the common era date being put first had already been taken, so the set was issued overprinted "1382 1962", with bars over the original dates.

Sometimes it is the date of issue of the stamps and not the dating of the event which is at fault. The West German 40pf. stamp issued in 1974 to mark the 125th year of the Diaconate was issued a year late, as was the Czechoslovakian issue of 1957 marking the 250th anniversary of the Polytechnic Engineering School, Prague. An issue of Honduras to mark the 150th anniversary of independence is correctly dated "1970" but was not issued until 1972. A Cuban 8c. stamp marks the 50th anniversary of the beginning of the War of Independence in 1895, and is so inscribed, but was actually issued in 1948, the 50th anniversary of the *end* of the War. Anniversary issues of Central American countries which appear to time are perhaps the exception rather than the rule, but it was not the fault of Guatemala that the issue marking the centenary of the first adhesive postage stamps was released in 1946, over six years late: the stamps had been ordered from the Netherlands in 1940, but owing to the Second World War were not delivered until 1946. The Seychelles produced an issue to mark the bicentenary of the first settlement of St. Anne Island, but as the true bicentennial date was 27th August, 1970, which clashed with the British Red Cross centenary, the settlement commemorative issue was released on April 27th, and as commemorative issues must not be on issue for more than three months it was withdrawn before the event commemorated—though the post office did produce an official bicentennial cachet for the appropriate date! Korea in 1902 produced a 3ch. stamp to commemorate the 40th anniversary of the accession of the Emperor (as King), but rashly issued it fifteen months in advance! He did in fact reign for over 43 years, but this issue certainly did seem to be taking chances! In 1977 Nicaragua issued three more stamps, 35c., 1cor. and 10 cor. in their series commemorating Women's Year of 1975.

Rumania in 1956 marked the fifth anniversary of collective farming with a 55b. stamp bearing the dates "1951-56". However, the stamp was withdrawn from circulation two days later, when it was pointed out to the postal authorities that collective farming had in fact been in existence for seven years! A new issue bearing the dates "1949-56" duly appeared about three months later. The Malagasy Republic produced an issue in 1976 to mark the 75th anniversary of the first zeppelin flight, and the accompanying miniature sheet was dated "1901-1976", but in fact the first zeppelin flight was made by the LZ1 on 2nd July, 1900. The correct year is given on a 120f. 1977 stamp of the Mali Republic, but the 130f. value of this set shows the *Graf Zeppelin* dated 1924, although it was not built until 1927 and first flew on 18th September, 1928. A 1971 issue of Guyana features the Guyana National Co-operative Bank, and should have borne the legend 'ESTABLISHED 24 FEB. 1970 TO SERVE A GROWING GUYANA'. During production it was noticed that "1971" had been put in place of '1970', the issue was duly amended and no stamps with the incorrect date were in fact released. The Ryukyu Islands in 1969 produced a 3c. stamp marking the 70th anniversary of Toyama's Ryukyu-Hawaii Emigration Project bearing the date "1970", but this was cancelled by bars and "1969" substituted, which would seem to indicate a dating error narrowly averted. Surinam on a 15c. semi-postal of 1970 and Ajman on a 5d. value of 1972 both reproduced the Horneman miniature Beethoven portrait of 1802, in both cases misdating it as of 1804. A 1977 issue of the Maldives commemorating Beethoven misdates the 1800 Neidl portrait as 1801 (2l.), the 1824 Decker portrait as 1825 (5r.) and the meeting at Taplitz of Beethoven and Goethe on 19th July, 1812, as occurring in 1811. The Great Seal of the Admiralty, which was granted to Barbados in 1663, appears on $2.40 stamps of 1950 and 1957, in each case wrongly dated "1660" on the stamp and wrongly described in many catalogues as representing the Arms of Barbados (not granted until 1965). Russia in 1973 produced an issue featuring automobiles, including a Russo-Balt car misleadingly dated as of 1909, for the model shown existed as far back as 1901—the prototype was made in Riga by Leutner-Werk.

We may round off this section on dating errors with three somewhat anomalous cases. Canada produced a postage due issue from 1935-65 which included ' secret ' dates of issue appearing in the scrolls flanking the central tablet, two figures on either side, but on the 3c. value the figures ' 6 ' and ' 5 ' are missing from the right-hand scroll. Gibraltar in 1973 issued a series showing military uniforms of different periods, the date being given on all values except the 6p., which shows a Royal Northumberland Fusilier in the uniform of 1736. Finally, a Hungarian issue of 1962 featuring aquarium fish includes the date of issue, but on several sheets of the 1fo.50 value for some reason an extra date was included below the value, as well as the date given after the name of the fish. This is presumably better classed as a production error, but it is a somewhat mystifying one.

Leaving dating errors, we may turn to those involving names of people. An interesting case is that of the literary critic Nikolai Alexandrovich Dobrolyubov, who features on a 10k. Russian stamp of 1936 with his initials transposed "A.H." instead of "H.A." This was not corrected, but for a long time the Russians were apparently very sensitive regarding the error (possibly because there was a mystic poet Alexandrei Dubrolyubov, by no means favoured by the Communists, whom the stamp might have been thought to commemorate)—so much so that the issue was omitted from official Soviet catalogues for many years. The Slovak patriot Josef Miloslav Hurban had his initials transposed on a 1k.50 Czechoslovakian stamp of 1948. Another case is that of the 20c. Argentinian stamp of 1935 which features General Martin Miguel Juan de Mata Güemes yet named him "JUAN MARTIN GÜEMES". This was corrected in the issues of 1936 and subsequently to simply "MARTIN GÜEMES". One might also, perhaps, question the propriety of the Argentinian 10c.+5c. semipostal of 1944 which familiarly names Alexander Graham Bell simply as "GRAHAM BELL", although he was known as Graham only to his family and intimates. His name was also reduced to "Graham Bell" by other countries, such as the Congo (Brazzaville) (1976, 35f.), Niger Republic (1972, 100f.) and Pakistan (1976, 3r.). His full name is given on many issues, for instance on a 4c. Canadian stamp of 1947. One might similarly cavil at the abbreviation of the name of François, Marquis de Barbe-Marbois to simply "Marbois" on a 3c. 1953 stamp of the U.S.A. in the issue commemorating the Louisiana Purchase. A Polish issue of 1960 features the magnificent wood carvings on the altar of St. Mary's Church, Cracow. These were executed by the German copperplate-engraver, wood-carver and painter Veit Stoss of Nuremberg, but on the stamps his name is given in Polish form as "Wita Stwosza", thus implying quite improperly that he was a Pole. The authority for the name of Canadian Pondweed, *Elodea canadensis,* is Michx., not Rich as given on a 1l. Rumanian stamp of 1966.

Titles can also cause trouble on stamps. A well-known case is that of the 5d. Greek stamp of 1927 honouring the English admiral, Sir Edward Codrington, who commanded the combined British, French and Russian fleets at the Battle of Navarino. The Greeks did not appreciate that the given name is a necessary part of a knight's title, and labelled him "Sir Codrington", corrected in a subsequent printing. A Canadian 3c. stamp of 1951 abbreviates Sir Robert Laird Borden's name to "Sir R. L. Borden", where properly the given name in which he was dubbed should have been given in full, as was done for other knights on Canadian stamps, such as Sir William Osler (1969, 6c.), Sir Isaac Brock (1969, 6c.) and Sir Donald Alexander Smith (1970, 6c.). A 6c. 1910 stamp of Newfoundland features Sir Francis Bacon, Baron Verulam, Viscount St. Albans, but wrongly labels him "Lord Bacon" (fig. 44). A 1933 semi-postal issue of Luxemburg (incidentally one of several that do not show a charity surcharge), features Count Henry IV of Luxemburg, later Emperor Henry VII of the Holy Roman Empire, but by confusing these two distinct titles mislabels him as "Le Compte Henri VII". A Zambian 25n. stamp of 1970 commemorates Edward Jenner, discoverer of vaccination, but wrongly entitles him "Sir Edward Jenner", for he was never knighted—possibly there was some confusion with Queen Victoria's physician, Sir William Jenner. A literally marginal error is that of the 1970 issue of the Virgin Islands commemorating the novelist Charles Dickens, for the printer's imprint on the sheet reads "Thomas de la Rue Limited"—strictly it should be 'Thomas de la Rue & Co., Limited'. The same mistake also occurs on a 1970 issue of Fiji featuring explorers. If printers do this to themselves, what further surprises can they offer us? One might also claim that a 7c. 1974 stamp of Australia marking the 150th anniversary of publication of the newspaper *The Australian* errs in illustrating the paper's co-founder, William Wentworth, but not naming him at all on the stamp, nor indicating his connection with the paper.

Extravagant claims can be a fruitful source of error. An issue of 1906 for Barbados commemorates Nelson and features the Nelson Monument in Barbados, proudly labelled "FIRST MONUMENT ERECTED TO NELSON'S MEMORY 1813". In fact, however, the first such monument was erected in Montreal, Canada, in 1808. A further inaccuracy lay in the palms around the statue, which were non-existent, added at the suggestion of Lady Carter, the Governor's wife, to relieve the rather stark appearance of the statue as depicted. A 7½p. 1971 stamp of Ascension features the Jodrell Bank radio telescope, and claims it as the world's largest radio telescope. It was indeed the largest *steerable* one at the date of issue, though now superseded by the 328ft. diameter assembly in the Effelsberger Valley, West Germany, but for instance the non-steerable radio telescope near Arecibo, Porto Rico, is four times the diameter (1,000ft. to 250ft.). The 1888 10c. special delivery stamp of the U.S.A. makes the remarkable claim "SECURES IMMEDIATE DELIVERY AT ANY POST OFFICE" modified in 1902 to " . . AT ANY UNITED STATES POST OFFICE". Guyana in 1967 issued 5c. and 25c. stamps featuring the famous British Guiana 1c. stamp of 1856, with the inscription "THE WORLDS RAREST STAMP", omitting the apostrophe of 'WORLD'S' but also making an obviously false claim. While this stamp may legitimately be termed the world's most highly valued stamp, it can obviously be no rarer than any other stamp of which only a single copy exists, *e.g.* the Swedish 3s. yellow stamp of 1855, while there are issues known to have been made of which no specimens at all are known to have survived, *e.g.* Chinese Communist issues of Shensi between 1935 and 1945. Ajman illustrated the same stamp on a 2r.50 value of 1971 and made the same untenable claim. A Yugoslavian issue of 1948 honours Laurence Kosir as creator of the idea of postage stamps, but he was clearly anticipated by the Swedish officer Curry Gabriel Treffenberg, who in 1823 suggested the introduction of stamps to his Parliament. A Polish 1z.50 1966 stamp shows the FR-1 satellite, wrongly labelled on the stamp as the first French satellite, for the A-1 had been launched 10 days earlier and really was first, as stated on the central label attached to a French issue of 1965. A Cuban 5c. stamp of 1914 acclaims the poetess, novelist and dramatist Gertrudis Gomez de Avellaneda as the greatest poetess of all times, an extravagant (though perhaps not easily refutable) claim which possibly has Sappho and other poetesses turning in their graves (fig. 45). El Salvador claims on a 10c. stamp of 1935 to produce the best cane-sugar. Since well-refined sugar is a virtually pure single chemical, it would seem unlikely that any one country refines it better than all others, but possibly this claim was not meant to be competitive. A more astonishing claim, made on a 20c. stamp of the 1924-26 definitive issues is that only El Salvador produces Peruvian balsam, which certainly sounds a contradiction in terms, though it may possibly have been true in terms of commercial production. The Virgin Islands produced an issue in 1972 displaying various game fish, together with a miniature sheet claiming world record weights for specimens caught off the Virgin Islands. However, the designs were all after photographs of fish caught elsewhere, apart from the Blue Marlin on the ½c. value, and the claim on the miniature sheet for the world record Allison Tuna for a fish caught off the Virgin Islands in May, 1969, had already been nullified by a fish caught off Mexico in 1971.

A marginal inscription for the 1961 definitive issue of the Maldive Islands makes the curious claim that this is the "Second Definitive Issue"—curious because there had been definitive issues in 1909, 1933, 1950, 1952, 1956 and 1960. Two rather improbable claims are those put forward by Russia on a 1956 issue featuring Mahmud Bagir Ogly Aivazov, said to be 148 years old, and a 1956 Colombian issue, perhaps a riposte to the preceding issue, featuring Javier Pereira, said to be 167 years old: gerontologists seem generally in agreement that there have been no modern authenticated cases of human beings reaching such advanced ages, and little likelihood that any such claims are based on fact, but one can always wonder.

Quotations on stamps are not always strictly accurate. The tabs of the 1967 Israeli stamps commemorating the 50th anniversary of the Balfour Declaration carry a biblical quotation ascribed to the wrong verse, Jeremiah 31:16, in Hebrew, though correctly Jeremiah 31:17 in the English. The 1950 issue marking the Jewish New Year carries a quotation from Nahum 1:15 ascribed to Nahum 2:1. The 1962 55a. stamp marking Heroes and Martyrs day and the 1968 60a. marking the 25th anniversary of the Warsaw Ghetto rising quote Psalms 42:5, and not Psalms 42:4, the 60pr. of the 1955 Festival issue quotes Psalms 81:4 in place of Psalms 81:3, the 120pr. value of the Tribes series issued in 1956, featuring Issachar quotes from Chronicles I. 12:33 in place of 12:32 and the 1972 I£1. stamp showing a symbolical ground station gives a Hebrew quotation from Psalms 19:5 and an English quotation of 19:4. All of these are on the tabs and none is incorrect, the discrepancy being due to differences between the Hebrew (original) and English (translated) versions of the Bible. The quotation from *La Poesia* (part 5, line 1) on the 1962 Italian stamps marking the 50th death anniversary of the poet Pascoli should in fact end with an exclamation mark, not a full stop as here. Similarly the 1923 30c. stamp showing a scene from *I Promessi Sposi* gives the first two words of a quotation "Addio, monti sorgenti, dall'acqua el elevate al cielo" (Farewell, mountains rising from the water and mounting to the sky), but omits the comma after "Addio". The Italian 30l. stamp of 1961 marking the centenary of the birth of Ippolito Nievo features his book "Le Confessioni de un Italiano", but on the stamp 'Le' is omitted from the title. The Greek 1954 'Enosis' issue carries an extract from the Hansard report of Parliamentary proceedings of 28th July, 1954, but omits a whole line from the English version (between the 8th and 9th lines from the foot).

A very well-known misquotation is that of the French 1937 90c. stamp marking the 300th anniversary of the *Discours de la Méthode* of Descartes, which as first prepared was inscribed "DISCOURS SUR LA MÉTHODE". Supplies had already been distributed to stamp sellers and post offices, for issue on 24th May, when the error was discovered. The stamp was immediately withdrawn without being issued, but a few sheets were not recovered and began to fetch rocketing prices, so the Minister of Posts had both erroneous and corrected stamps issued simultaneously on 10th June. Less well-known is the case of the Russian 1943 Turgenev commemorative issue carrying a quotation from one of his works which may be translated "O great, mighty, true and free Russian language", but with the wrong word for ' true ' (spravedleve instead of pravdeve), which alters the meaning somewhat. A misquotation of sorts occurs on a 10pf. West German stamp of 1959 commemorating the mathematician Adam Riese, who discovered the ' proof by nine ' method of checking multiplications and divisions, for it is claimed that the example given on the stamp is wrong—the figures ' 2 ' should be figures ' 7 '.

Translations may sometimes produce errors. Thus the 60c. value of the 1968 set of Mauritius illustrating Bernadin de St. Pierre's paintings of the legend of Paul and Virginia portrays the meeting in secret of the hapless lovers, but mistranslates the French ' en confiance ' (in secret) as "in confidence". A 1965 issue of Kuwait marking International Co-operation Year bears the caption "INTERNATIONAL CO-OPERATIVE YEAR". The campaign for the peaceful use of atomic energy had the rather meaningless slogan "Atoms for Peace", but when the pacifist atoms are reduced to one as on an Afghan issue of 1958 inscribed "ATOME POUR LA PAIX" it becomes plainly ridiculous. However, countries can produce sloppy phrasing in their own languages. An 1897 issue of Newfoundland labels mining, logging and fishing as ' resources" on the 5c., 6c. and 8c. values respectively, whereas they are, of course, industries based on resources. The 12c. value of the same issue is inscribed "PTARMIGAN. NEWFOUNDLAND SPORT", but the sport is, of course, ptarmigan shooting. A 3c. 1948 stamp of the U.S.A. commemorates Moira Michael, labelled "FOUNDER OF MEMORIAL POPPY", another example of telegraphese, for a poppy can scarcely be founded. The credit for associating the poppy with remembrance of the dead of the First World War strictly belongs to the Canadian Col. John McCrae—previously it had been associated rather with forgetfulness. Jamaican 1d. stamps of 1921 and 1922 purport to show an Arawak Indian "making" Cassava. In fact Cassava is the meal prepared from the roots of the manioc plant by grating and pounding

—it is not ‘ made ’, therefore, but ‘ prepared ’. The inscription on a 1936 airmail issue of Macao is, however, intentionally nonsensical, a mixture of Greek letters, some invented and some on their sides, intended only to make forgery more difficult.

We can hardly omit some discussion of the famous “Post Office” Mauritius stamps of 1847. Popular legend has it that the local watchmaker, J. Barnard, who produced the dies, was given a verbal brief to engrave ‘ POST PAID ’ on the stamps, was reminded of this by seeing the words ‘ POST OFFICE ’ on the facade of the local post office, and engraved these in error. However, there is absolutely no evidence for this, and as various pre-adhesive postal markings were inscribed “Post Office, Mauritius” there is no reason to suppose the words were not intentional. For those who prefer the legend and cannot quite afford the genuine stamps, they are featured on the Mauritian centenary issue of 1948 (one year late), a 1966 issue of Umm al Qiwain and a Nicaraguan 1c. of 1976.

Distinction of postage, revenue and dual purpose stamps appears to have exercised postal authorities considerably. The 18c. and 24c. 1894 stamps of North Borneo carefully indicated that they belonged to this last category, but on the 1897 issue this was converted to the misleading “POSTAL REVENUE” on the 18c. and omitted entirely from the 24c., though hurriedly restored to both on a later issue of the same year. The 1949 Canadian definitive issue was duly labelled “POSTES—POSTAGE”, yet three months later a new issue appeared without these words. It has been suggested that the latter issue was prepared first in error, then put in store and replaced by a corrected version, and only issued to counter speculation following leakage of ‘ defective ’ stamps from store to the philatelic public. A 1975 Canadian 8c. stamp commemorating Lucy Maud Montgomery (authoress of “Anne of Green Gables”) omits ‘ postes/postage ’ although the se-tenant stamp commemorating Louis Hémon does bear them. Rather more oddly, a 20c. Canadian special delivery stamp of 1927 is simply labelled “special”, with no promise of delivery at all! The Jamaican 1d. definitive of 1921, alone in its set, did not bear the words ‘ POSTAGE & REVENUE ’, an omission corrected in 1922. The Rumanian definitive issue of 1934 similarly omitted the word ‘POSTA’, included in the definitive issue of 1935. Conversely Paraguay produced Red Cross charity labels in 1929, sold at 1p.50 each, cancelled in blocks of 4 with the seal of the Inspector General of Posts, which were allowed to be affixed on postal matter alongside ordinary postage stamps and which were inscribed “Correos del Paraguay” (Paraguay postage), yet had no postal validity whatsoever.

The 1c. and 2c. stamps ordered by El Salvador from the American Bank Note Co. in 1889 were supposed to be labelled ‘SERVICIO POSTAL DEL SALVADOR’, but due to faulty instructions were labelled “UNION POSTAL DEL SALVADOR”. This was considered so serious that they were not issued in this state, a shortage of 1c. stamps being met by surcharge of the 3c. The offending inscription was obliterated with a bar, but owing to the destruction of the chief post office by fire only the 1c. was actually issued in this state, though copies of both are available, with and without the obliteration. Incidentally, it was suddenly decided that “DEL SALVADOR” was incorrect, and in 1896 a new set was issued labelled "CORREOS DE EL SALVADOR", concurrently with an issue inscribed in the old fashion. Since these were both Seebeck issues the motive for the change may be suspect, but El Salvador has stuck to this decision meticulously ever since.

Stamps issued for one function are not unusually utilised for a different function. Normally in such cases they are appropriately overprinted, but this is not always so. British Guiana produced an issue in 1882 with stamps perforated "SPECIMEN", but this was purely a security measure, and the stamps were always intended for postal use. Issues of 1888-1890 were overprinted "INLAND REVENUE" but again were valid for postage, while Guyana kept the tradition going by producing in 1975 a set overprinted "REVENUE ONLY" which nevertheless as "an act of grace" was allowed by the postal authorities to function as postage stamps until 30th June, 1976. A 10r. stamp of Ceylon inscribed "REVENUE" was nevertheless used and on sale for postal use from December 1952 to March 1954, with no alteration to mark its change in function. Spain in 1930 produced a 5c. postage due stamp, properly labelled "DERECHO DE ENTREGA" which was nevertheless released and used for ordinary inland postal use without any modifying overprint. Similarly the 5c. Stamp Duty adhesive of Hong Kong was authorised for postal use from its issue on January 11th 1938 for ten days, and a Bulgarian issue of 1950 inscribed for use on official mail was issued for regular postal use. A rather different case is that of the 1964 issue commemorating the United Republic of Tanganyika and Zanzibar and inscribed accordingly, as if for use in the United Republic, yet which nevertheless had no postal validity in Zanzibar!

Changes in place names can sometimes catch stamp designers napping. One such case involved the 5s. stamp of Nyasaland of 1964, which featured Lake Nyasa. On achieving independence both land and lake were renamed Malawi, but the corresponding stamp for Malawi of 1964 still featured "Lake Nyasa" and this was not renamed "Lake Malawi" on the stamp until 1965. Syria and Egypt merged on 1st February, 1958, to form the United Arab Republic, yet the next Syrian issue (the Five Years Plan issue), admittedly of only a few days later, still bore the name "Syrie". The International Children's Day issue for that year took the form of a simple overprint "RAU" on the stamps of the previous year, but though this was presumably a contraction for the French 'République Arabe Unie' it was not considered an acceptable alternative for 'UAR' and the issue was withdrawn. Ceylon changed its name to Sri Lanka in 1972 yet subsequently produced an issue marking the 10th Conference of the World Fellowship of Buddhists which was still inscribed "Ceylon"—in this case the issue had been prepared prior to the change, as it had been intended for release in 1971, and indeed is dated "May 1971". However Sri Lanka did not seem in a particular hurry to suppress its former name, for as late as 1973 it was still to be found on metered mail cachets, even from government establishments. The Khmer Republic was proclaimed on 9th October, 1970, and its constitution ratified on 1st November, 1970, yet the issues marking the 25th anniversary of the U.N.O. (24/10/70), International Education Year (9/11/70) and even the Chuon-Nath anniversary (27/1/71) were still labelled 'CAMBODIA'. The Yugoslavian issue of 1929 marking the Millenary of the Croatian Kingdom (four years late) was labelled as the Kingdom of the Serbs, Croats and Slovenes, although the name 'Yugoslavia' had already been officially adopted: this was corrected by overprint in 1931. In 1916 Tanganyika produced an issue overprinted for use of the Nyasaland Field Force, but with "N.F." instead of 'N.F.F.', apparently due to an operator's error in repeating the telegram from General Northey to the Governor of Nyasaland authorising this issue. It has been claimed that the compositor who set up the overprint did not have enough 'F's and hence got round the problem by abbreviating the overprint, a charming but probably apocryphal story. Another possible explanation is that as the force contained Rhodesian troops as well as troops from Nyasaland the "N.F." could stand for 'Northey Force', which was an accepted name at that time. Various stamps of Western Australia produced between 1902 and 1912 were incorrectly labelled "WEST AUSTRALIA"; this was because basic designs of Victoria were being used and the designer had obviously felt unable to get the full correct name into the space available.

A wrong name which cannot really be termed an error is that of the migrant schooner featured on the 1s. 1961 stamp of the Pitcairn Islands. This vessel carried Pitcairn Islanders back from Norfolk Island, to which they had migrated, and was known to them as the *Mary Ann,* the name which appears on the stamp. It was, however, the *Louisa,* a smuggling vessel fleeing the Australian authorities under a false name. The building labelled "Technische Hochschule" on 20pf., 80pf. and 90pf. stamps of West Berlin issued in 1949 had on re-opening in 1946 been renamed "Technische Universität". The aircraft labelled a "seaplane" on a $1 1941 stamp of Hong Kong would be more precisely described as a flying boat. The British 4d. stamp of 1968 showing the Tarr Steps in Somerset labels them "prehistoric". Although this is somewhat controversial, it is now generally held that they are mediaeval and that previously the River Barle was forded at Three Waters, about a mile to the south. A 6d. 1906 stamp of New Zealand purports to show the annexation of New Zealand, but technically the ceremony depicted—Captain Cook at Motuara Island—was a proclamation of British sovereignty, not an annexation, the first of five such occasions. A 35pf. East German stamp of 1953 commemorates the architect Balthasar Neumann, showing one of his works, grandly labelled "Wurȝburger Schloss": however it is far from being a castle, or even a palace as some catalogues label it, and would have been better described as a residence (Residenz). A 2k. Panamanian stamp of 1964 features the great Mosque of St. Sophia, Istanbul, wrongly calling it a Cathedral, which it has not been since Constantinople fell to the Turks in the 15th century. An Austrian 2s. stamp of 1968 marking the 150th anniversary of the Christmas carol "Silent Night" depicts the hand-carved wood relief altar of the Memorial Chapel, Oberndorf, Salzburg, but wrongly calls it a crib, for a Christmas crib (first assembled by St. Francis of Assisi at Greccio in 1224) is a nativity portrayal made up with free-standing figures (fig. 46). The Jagra lily, *Lilium jagra,* on a 55b. Rumanian stamp of 1971 is named "Life Jagra", a mixture of common and scientific names, on the stamp, though all others of this issue are given their proper scientific names only.

A curious error occurs on a 1k. 1967 Czechoslovakian stamp. which shows a star map with Lepus (the Hare) and Lupus (the Wolf) interchanged. 15c. and 2s. stamps of Kenya, Uganda and Tanganyika of the 1935 (George V) and 1938 (George VI) definitives portray "Mount Kilimanjaro"; since Kilima-Njaro means ' Mount Njaro ' this inscription is tautological, and the 65c. and 2s. stamps of the 1954 (Queen Elizabeth) definitive issue dropped the redundant ' Mount ', but East Africa reintroduced it on a 1s.30 stamp of 1968. Can the fact that popular speech refers to it as "Mount Kilimanjaro" excuse this error? The tab of the 2m. 1948 Israeli definitive (first coin issue) reads "Bronze coin from the period of the Maccabaeans or the First Revolt...", but by the time of the issue of the 3pr. 1949 definitive (second coin issue) this doubt had been cleared up, for it was then correctly assigned to the period of the First Revolt (66-70 A.D.) and not of the Maccabaeans (142-135 B.C.). A Chinese issue of 1953 marking the 35th anniversary of the Russian Revolution inadvertently included two characters meaning "SOVIET UNION" in the inscription. The stamps, which had already been distributed to post offices, were hastily withdrawn before issue, but were mistakenly released at one post office in Hunan before notice of withdrawal was received! Corrected stamps in different colours were released later in the year. A similar error occurred in 1958, when a Chinese issue marking the Fifth International Students' Union Congress was inscribed rather vaguely as "5th Congress of World Students' Representatives". The stamps were withdrawn before issue and replaced with ones bearing a more precise inscription "International Students' Union, 5th Congr.", but some 8f. stamps were on sale for one day only in Liaoning Province (North-East China). A 1951 issue of French Morocco showing the General Leclerc Monument as first prepared was inscribed "Leclerc-Témara" but on a last minute decision the statue was erected in Casablanca, not Témara. A new corrected set was accordingly prepared and issued, and the original was destroyed, apart from a few sets presented to a few high-ranking officials (but these were never valid for postage). The United Nations decided to produce a set inscribed ' Peace, Progress and Justice ' to mark the 25th anniversary of the U.N. Charter, but due to a secretarial error, when the issue appeared in 1970 it bore the words "Peace and Progress" only. On the insistence of Jamil Barody, the Saudi Arabian delegate, a new issue was made in 1971 bearing the agreed slogan "Peace, Justice and Progress"; indeed the importance of Justice was stressed by the symbolic scales which formed the principal features of the new design. It is therefore rather surprising that the 1971 issue of the Yemen Arab Republic which also commemorates this 25th anniversary (a year late) likewise omits ' JUSTICE ' from the U.N. slogan. The Bahamas in 1969 produced a 12c. stamp marking the 50th anniversary of Bahamas Airmail Services with an illustrated postcard addressed to San Francisco/California; however the inscription reads "FIRST AIRMAIL FLIGHT MIAMI NASSAU 1919", which is the reverse direction to that taken by the illustrated postcard.

Numerical errors can occur in various ways. The little *Lundy Gannet* featured on the 2d. local stamp of Lundy of 1969 is correctly named but bears the wrong registration number—"H37" instead of ' H57 '. A Cuban issue of 1965 featuring railway locomotives shows on the 7c. value a French type BB-63,000 given on the stamp as "BB 69,000". Incidentally, the diesel locomotive on the 13c. value of a 1975 issue is Hungarian, not

French as stated on the stamp. The marginal inscription of the British 2d. blue of 1841 originally read "Price 2d. per label 2/– per row of 12 £2 per sheet", but after plate 4 had been in use for some time this was altered to "...£1 Per Sheet"; this was intended to avoid confusion, as stamps were to be issued to post offices in half sheets, but was nevertheless factually wrong, as an entire sheet consisted of 240 stamps. The German 2m. air stamps of 1922-23 were issued in sheets which bore along the top selvedge the total value of vertical rows to that point, but the figures above the 5th and 6th rows (100m. and 120m.) were accidentally transposed and were corrected by small tabs stuck over the erroneous figures bearing the correct ones. A Bavarian issue of 1919 was surcharged in aid of war-wounded, but accounting figures in sheet margins were not altered accordingly, which led to considerable confusion of postal accounts. Plate 2A of the 1938 2c. perf. $13\frac{3}{4} \times 13\frac{1}{4}$ issue of Ceylon was wrongly engraved as "1A" (bottom margin below second stamp from right), corrected by engraving a ' 2 ' over the "1". Plate No. 1 of a 15m. 1932 Palestinian stamp had the figure ' 1 ' printed in reverse. A 45a. Israeli stamp of 1973 featuring Mt. Hermon and a 95a. stamp featuring the "Fjord" at Hamifratz Hane'elam both carry the same plate number (367) which properly belongs to the former. The correct plate number for the 95a. should have been 368.

Afghanistan produced an issue in 1962 to honour the 4th Asian Games, Djakarta, but wrongly called them "Olympic Games" and included the 5-ring Olympic Games symbol. Similarly the 11th Balkan Games were called the Balkan Olympics on a Turkish issue of 1940; a Nicaraguan issue of obligatory tax stamps in 1937 bore the inscription "SELLO OLIMPICO", and supported the so-called ' Central American Olympic Games ', but these Games did not, of course, have any connection with the true Olympic Games. This also applies to the 1939 issue of Ecuador commemorating Ecuadorian victories in "South American Olympic Games". The Liberian issue of 1956 to mark the Olympic Games in Melbourne, and the 1972 Olympic Games issue of Equatorial Guinea refer to the "16th Olympic Games" and "20th Olympic Games" respectively, but although these were the 16th and 20th modern *Olympiads*, the Games themselves had not been held in 1916, 1940 and 1944 due to world wars, so that the count of the Games themselves is perhaps debatable.

Paintings on stamps can be erroneously inscribed in various ways. A 5c. Costa Rican stamp of 1959 features El Greco's "Boy blowing on charcoal", which is in the National Museum of Naples, though the stamp claims that it is in the Prado Gallery in Madrid. (fig. 47). Another 5c. stamp of the same issue shows Modigliani's "Girl with Braids", locating this one in the National Museum of Naples, though it was in fact in a private collection. A 70c. 1972 stamp of Gabon shows a painting by Canaletto of the Rialto Bridge, Venice, but wrongly ascribes it to Caffi, and 30f. and 60f. 1972 Christmas stamps of Togo show a "Nativity" by the Masters of Hohenfuhrt (Vyssi Brod), wrongly attributed to Master Theodor of Prague on the stamps. Ribera's painting "The Club-footed Boy" (which appears on a Jordanian 5f. stamp of 1975) features (truncated) on a $\frac{1}{3}$b. 1967 stamp of the Yemen Arab Republic as "The Knock-Kneed Man". A 50c. Dominican stamp of 1969 illustrates the painting "Pilate washing his hands", formerly wrongly ascribed to Rembrandt, as it is on this stamp; it is by an unknown artist. A 10c. Liberian stamp of 1970 shows a portrait of Napoleon Bonaparte ascribed on the stamp to Gerard but apparently from a painting by Isabey. The sculpture "St. John the Baptist" shown on the 50c. value of a set produced in 1975 by Grenada to mark the quincentenary of the birth of Michelangelo was formerly attributed to Donatello, has more recently been credited to Francesco Sangallo, but has certainly never been attributed to Michelangelo. The titles of paintings and statues are also somewhat freely translated or altered. A 2r. 1968 stamp of Ajman shows a Van Dyck painting of the three eldest children of Charles I—Prince Charles, Princess Mary and Prince James, but on the stamp it is entitled "Les fils de Charles I" (the sons of Charles I), apparently disregarding Princess Mary altogether. The painting ' The Assumption ' by Botticelli appears on a 30f. 1969 stamp of Togo, wrongly labelled "The Annunciation", and the Fragonard painting on a 1939 40c.+60c. French semipostal is not entitled "LA LETTRE" as on the stamp but 'l'inspiration favorable'. A 10c. 1975 United States stamp features the painting ' Birth of Liberty ' but labels it "Lexington & Concord 1775 by Sandham". Since that is the subject, though not Sandham's actual title, it is perhaps overly pedantic to call this an error. However a $5 U.S.A. stamp of 1923 shows the head and shoulders of the statue surmounting the U.S. Capitol, Washington, which was named ' Armed Freedom ' but on the stamp is labelled "America", which does seem an unjustifiable change. The statue is shown in full (but unnamed) on 1c.—10c. newspaper stamps of 1896.

Music on stamps is often given wrongly. A notorious case is that of the 1956 East German issue commemorating the composer Robert Schumann, which featured the composer against a background of the music for the song "Wanderers Nachtlied" by Schubert! A corrected version with a background of authentic Schumann music ("Mondnacht") was hastily prepared and issued a few months later. More frequently the errors occur simply in the notation, as in the few bars from a regimental march which feature on the 2m.75 1941 President Kallio memorial stamp of Finland. Here merely a dot is missing, after the third note. In 1941 Bohemia and Moravia commemorated the 150th death anniversary of Mozart with an issue of four stamps which were printed alternately with labels throughout the sheet. The extract from "Don Giovanni" printed on the labels attached to the 30h. and 60h. values has a crotchet rest missing from the third beat in the treble, and the second and fourth beats in the bass should be composed of quavers (*i.e.* joined together by only one line at the top). The 10c. and 2f. stamps issued by Luxemburg in 1935 honouring ' The Arts ' show a quotation with the first two quavers marked staccato but nevertheless tied notes. A 2fo. Hungarian stamp of 1970 marking the birth centenary of Lehár includes a motif from Act I of his last operetta ' Giuditta ' with two triple brackets missing. A 3fo. Hungarian miniature sheet of 1959 honouring Haydn carries an excerpt from the Introduction to Symphony 104, but the flat in the treble clef is misplaced, on C instead of B. A 1974 issue of Dahomey honouring Chopin includes an excerpt from his Nocturne No. 9, op. 32, but in the first and third bars C sharps have been printed in place of the correct D sharps. A 50h. 1934 Czechoslovakian stamp honouring Smetana includes the opening four note motif from ' Libuse ', but a dot is missing from the second note. A Rumanian miniature sheet of 1946 (350l.+1650l. value) marks the 25th anniversary of the Bucharest Philharmonic Orchestra. It includes 12 stamps and four labels, with errors in musical notation. Sweden issued a se-tenant strip of five 95ore stamps in 1977 in honour of the Swedish poet Evert Taube and musical notation appears on each stamp. On the Seagull stamp a dot addition is missing on the 11th note. The Dance stamp has an unnecessary Natural because the waltz *is* in D-major (this is the third note second line). On the Boat stamp a line through C-sharp is missing (seventh note) and on the Tree stamp a C-sharp is missing (the *e* is only part of the chord!). In 1972 Dahomey issued a 65f. stamp marking the 75th death anniversary of Brahms in which the first six bars of ' Sommerabend ' (Op. 84, No. 1) were transposed from D minor to G minor. On the same occasion the Niger Republic issued a 100f. stamp in which the first half of melody of ' Wiegenlied ' (Op. 49, No. 4) was transposed from E♭ to F. The Egyptian 110m. stamp of 1971 marking the centenary of the first performance of Aida features a three-measure motif from the Triumphal March with the third note F instead of E♭. The Uruguayan 5p. stamp of 1971 honouring Eduardo Fabini features the first two bars of an oboe part with the fourth note C instead of B. The Hungarian 3fo. miniature sheet of 1959 commemorating Haydn has rhythmic errors in bars 1, 3 and 4 and the 60fi. stamp of 1961 featuring Liszt shows the right hand of measure 12 of the second Hungarian Rhapsody written an octave higher and transposed to C minor from C sharp minor. Stamps issued by Rwanda in 1976 and 1977 on the occasion of World Leprosy Day, honouring Schweitzer, an accomplished organist of J. S. Bach's works, show on some values opening notes of a piano arrangement of Bach's Toccata and Fugue for organ in D minor in which the G sharps should be G naturals. The Portuguese 7e.50 stamp of 1974 marking the 400th death anniversary of Damião de Gois repeats part of a line, making seven staves into eight of the cantus part of ' Ne laeteris ' from the 1547 edition of ' Dodecachordon '.

It is curious how often countries have honoured composers of their National Anthems with stamps quoting portions of the anthems—incorrectly! A 40c. 1947 stamp of Chile marks the centenary of the revised version of the National Anthem (the author of the first version, B. de Vera y Pintado, gets no mention on this stamp) but the musical fragment on the stamp (text fig. 8) is certainly not the opening bars of the anthem (text fig. 9), and indeed seems to be no part of it. The 1946 issue of the Dominican Republic honouring the National Anthem includes several errors in the second and third lines: on both lines clef signs and key signatures have been omitted, on the second line the first note should be a minim and on the third beat a crotchet, not a quaver rest. As the last bar is incomplete on the third line there should be a double bar line or no bar line at all. The Argentine Republic commemorated its National Anthem with two miniature sheets in 1944, and here again there are several mistakes in the music produced on the sheets (text fig. 10) as compared with the anthem itself (text fig. 11). Brazil marked the 150th anniversary of the birth of F. M. da Silva, composer of the National Anthem, by a 40c. stamp in 1945 with part of the music of the anthem in the background. Here again there are numerous errors: the second note

8

9

10

11

of bar three is a quaver on the note F—it should be a semiquaver on the note E; the second note of bar four is A instead of G; the fifth note in bar seven is an A instead of a B; the rest in bar four should be a crotchet rest; the clef sign and key signatures are missing in the second and third lines and the third note in bar three should be dotted. Quite a list! In 1973 South Africa marked the centenary of the birth of C. J. Langenhoven, author of the words of the National Anthem ‘ Die Stem van Suid-Afrika ’ with an issue, the 15c. value of which quotes a mysterious fragment of music which has only four lines instead of five to the stave and no key signature. However with a bottom line of staff added and a key signature of two sharps it becomes the closing line of “Die Stem”, composed by Marthinus L. de Villiers.

A 40c. 1976 stamp of Nicaragua features the singer Joan Sutherland with a musical excerpt from “La Figlia del Reggimento” but she has in fact never sung this in Italian, only in French. Lastly in this section we may consider some of the Gulf States’ productions. In 1969 Ajman issued a set to commemorate musicians. The 5d. features Bellini, with an excerpt from the chorus of the second act of the opera ‘ Norma ’, but

94

95

95

96

97

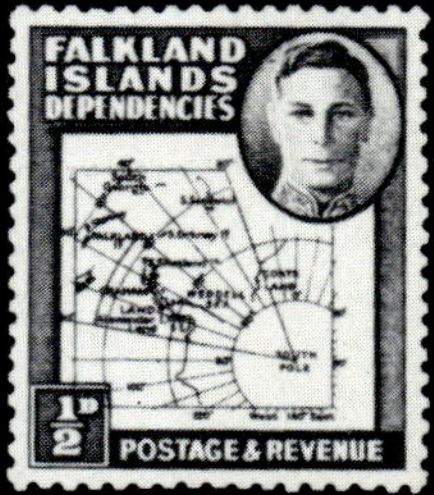

98

99

100

101

102

103

104

wrongly transposed from A minor to E minor. The 10d. value shows Liszt, with a quotation from his nocturne ' Liebestraum ', labelled on the stamp "Aus der Oper ' Liebestraum ' ", and with the melodic main note (C) missing. The 25d. value shows Bach, with a musical quotation captioned "Aus der Oper ' Der Choral ' ". Bach wrote no operas, and no opus called simply ' Der Choral '. The extract, (actually by Johan Crüger) was used by Bach (in B minor) in the St. Matthew Passion to the words ' O grosse Lieb ' (O Great Love), while there are also differences in note values. The 10r. value shows Bizet, with a quotation from the chorus of street boys in the first act of ' Carmen ', but for some reason transposed from the proper D minor to C minor. The accompanying miniature sheet includes a fragment from Papageno's aria ' Der Vogelfänger bin ich, ja! ' in the first act of ' The Magic Flute ' transposed from its proper G major to F major, but with the notation written in fact eight steps down.

We now come to map stamps, which lead to all sorts of trouble, and in more than one category. Like music they require so much detail in a limited space that it is scarcely surprising that errors occur. A well-known case is that of the 1c. 1928 stamp of Newfoundland in which Cape Bauld was wrongly marked to the north of Cape Norman instead of south of it. This was corrected on the 1929 issue, but the misspelling "Straits" (for ' Strait ') of Belle Isle was not corrected. A 1976 issue of the Seychelles commemorating rural posts has several misnamed townships marked in on the map of Mahé on the 1r. value: Victoria (the capital) is misnamed Belombre, Cascade is misnamed Victoria, and the real Belombre (which lies just where the first ' B ' of that name is placed on this map), is unmarked altogether. On a 6p. 1975 stamp of Argentina, Lapataia Bay is wrongly labelled "Lake Lapataia". Gotha, Vienna, Rome and Madrid are all misplaced on a 1c. 1964 stamp of Monaco, part of an issue marking an aerial rally.

Lines of latitude and longitude have produced many errors. The 1d. and 1/6d. Guernsey stamps of 1969 showed the Channel Islands as occurring at latitude 40°30′N, which would have placed them about Madrid: this was corrected the following year to 49°30′N. It has been wrongly claimed that the 2½d. 1952 map stamp of the Falkland Islands shows the western degree of latitude as 6° instead of 60°: however, comparison with the 1933 3d. map stamp indicates that this is the 61°W line of longitude, and careful examination of the stamp shows that the figure ' 1 ' is present but superimposed on the line itself. Stamp designers are sometimes more sinned against than sinning! The 12c. Mauritian stamp of 1950 shows a Dodo and a map of the island with its position given as 21°10′S and 57°30′E. This was altered on the 60c. stamp of 1964 to 20°10′S and 57°30′E, but this is still not precisely correct as maps show Mauritius to lie 20°10′S and 57°10′E. The 2d. and 6d. 1938 stamps of Fiji show a map of the islands with the very important 180° line of longitude unlabelled. This was corrected in the 1940 issue. However, in 1962 Fiji issued a 1/6d. stamp showing the International Date Line passing through Fiji which it deliberately avoids, detouring round it to the east (fig. 48). The lower value definitives of Réunion (1907-30) show, a map with longitude based on Paris as prime meridian, so that 53°E as marked on this map equals 55°20′E of the Greenwich prime meridian.

As the Greenwich prime meridian had been adopted for nautical and international calculations by the Washington Meridian Conference of 1884, it would seem reasonable to have expected it to be used here. This also applies to a 5c. 1956 stamp of Colombia bearing a map of the San Andrés Archipelago, with longitude lines based on Bogota, not on Greenwich. A rather different type of error occurs on the 1d. 1949 stamp of Cook Islands which shows a map of the Hervey Islands with each minute of latitude representing almost two miles instead of one mile. On a 1976 25c stamp of the New Hebrides showing a map of the islands, the 166°E line of longitude is wrongly given as 116°E, and the 1948 issue for the Tokelau Islands featuring Atafu village and a map bears the wrong lines of latitude and longitude, as shown by comparison with the inset map on stamps of the 1970 issue commemorating discovery of the islands.

The 1$20 1950 stamp of Barbados features a wireless mast against a map of the island divided into parishes, but omits the boundary line between the parishes of St. Michael and St. George. The Dominican Republic issue of 1900 shows the island of San Domingo, which it shares uneasily with Haiti, but on the stamps the Haitian share was so reduced that a war nearly ensued. Only an official and public admission of error by the engraver and withdrawal of the issue averted the threat of conflict. The 2c. value with island reversed and inverted and 5c. with seas (Mar Carib and Mar Atlantico) transposed are considered deliberately produced errors, and indeed could scarcely be otherwise. Ghana in 1958 produced an issue marking the First Conference of Independent African States, Accra, showing a map of Africa with the frontiers of the independent states marked. As first prepared Morocco included only the former French zone, excluding Spanish Morocco, but the mistake was noticed after printing but before release. The erroneous stamps were not issued, and a corrected version was released only a few days after schedule. Ethiopia made the same error with a corresponding issue, also in 1958, but this was not corrected. A 6c. 1975 stamp of Botswana marks the 90th anniversary of the establishment of the Bechuanaland Protectorate (which later became Botswana) with a map of the Protectorate. However the map includes in the Protectorate the former colony of British Bechuanaland (the territory between the Rivers Orange and Molopo). This was established on the same date (30th Sept., 1885) as the Protectorate, but was annexed to the Cape of Good Hope in 1895 and is now part of the Republic of South Africa. Furthermore, Bechuanaland Protectorate in 1885 extended north only to the 22°S line of latitude, only later taking in the additional territory to about 19°S which is shown as incorporated in Bechuanaland Protectorate on this stamp. The Canadian 2c. Xmas 1898 issue lays claim to a vaster empire than we had even then, for areas have been coloured in red which were not British at that time, such as S.W. Africa, The Orange Free State and Transvaal, and some areas which have never been British such as parts of Mozambique and the Dutch two-thirds of Borneo. South Africa does much the same on a 3d. 1959 stamp marking the South African National Antarctic Expedition, which features a globe with South Africa picked out in orange—including parts of Southern Rhodesia and the Protectorates of Bechuanaland and Basutoland. A French 30f. stamp of 1955 marking the 50th anniversary of Rotary International shows the boundary between France and Italy projecting sharply into Italy at the coast, where in fact it projects into France.

Maps are sometimes over-simplified by the stamp designer—for instance the map of Australia on a 5s. 1888 stamp of New South Wales omits Tasmania entirely and fails to indicate the Northern Territory, which admittedly had been annexed to South Australia (in 1863) for administration, but nevertheless remained a separate geographic entity. Several of the various 1969 Carifta issues with maps of Carifta countries, *e.g.* of Barbados, Guyana, Montserrat, St. Vincent and Trinidad & Tobago, bring Jamaica into the picture by placing it where San Domingo ought to be, that island, larger than the others put together, being completely omitted, while size and shape of the islands included is, to say the least of it, fanciful. A 16c. Bahamian stamp of 1976 shows the Turks and Caicos Islands incorporated in the Bahamas group. The map on the early issues of Panama is exceedingly crude, especially on the Pacific side, and the map of Newfoundland on its 2c. stamp of 1908 shows the Avalon Peninsula so badly malformed that it appears to be an island. The map on a Greek 2d. stamp of 1956 marking the 50th anniversary of Rotary International has Greece so enlarged that it borders on Egypt, and the Black Sea lies at the North Pole! The world globe on the 1/3d. British stamp of 1957 marking the World Scout Jubilee Jamboree manages to feature the British Isles yet omit Ceylon and all the East Indies. The map of the British Isles on the 3d. value of the National Productivity issue omits the Channel Islands and the Shetland Isles—in retrospect rather unfair considering the present importance of the Shetland-based oil industry. Conversely a 7b. 1970 stamp of the Yemen Arab Republic commemorating the victory of England in the 1966 World Football Championship gives an outline map of Great Britain, including Scotland and Wales which of course competed independently from England. A 6d. 1960 Gibraltarian stamp includes a map, but the coast from Ceuta to Tangier is shown cut away far more sharply than it is in reality, while the Spanish town of La Linea is wrongly shown as a single word. The 1961 6d. stamp of the Pitcairn Islands, showing Norfolk Island and Pitcairn Island together, has been condemned by Sir Dudley Stamp as being in his opinion the worst map stamp ever perpetrated, lacking any scale or guides to position, indeed with both islands drawn to different scales. Furthermore Norfolk Island is not oriented north and south but is arbitrarily twisted round to fit the frame better, the shape of Pitcairn is largely fictitious and the relief shown for both islands is entirely fanciful! (fig. 49). A 1969 issue of Norfolk Island marking the 125th anniversary of annexation to Van Diemen's Land (Tasmania) shows maps of both islands, but with no indication that Norfolk Island has been drawn to a scale some 25 times that used for Van Diemen's Land. Similarly St. Helena and Tristan da Cunha are shown on a 1968 issue of St. Helena, but with no indication that they are not drawn to the same scale, likewise the U.S.A. and Liberia on a 25c. Liberian stamp of 1976.

The general convention by which maps are oriented to show north at the top and south to the bottom is ignored by several map stamps. Thus the 20pf. 1969 stamp of West Germany marking the 350th anniversary of the Bad Reichenhall-Traunstein Brine pipeline shows a map of the pipeline, but here north is to the bottom and south to the top, with no indication on the stamp that conventional directions have been reversed. A 3c. 1955 stamp of the U.S.A. shows the Great Lakes, but they are tilted considerably from the conventional north/south axis, again with no indication of this on the stamp. Other maps which are not oriented with north to the top occur on stamps of Bermuda (1967, 1s.), Gilbert Islands (1976, 35c.), Gilbert & Ellice Islands (1969, 3c.), Maldive Islands (1961, 25l., 50l. and 1r.), St. Kitts-Nevis (1967, 10c.) and Oman (1975, 50b.). In this last case the detached part of the country to the north is also not sufficiently distant from the rest. The Ankara-Tehran route map of the 20f. value of a 1969 Mauritanian issue marking the London-Sydney Motor Rally is not on Mercator's Projection, so the direction rose incorporated can only apply to a very limited section of the map, even approximately. We must, perhaps, mention that many distinguished cartographers to as late as the early 19th century ignored convention, which originally had east set to the top out of deference to the holy places of the Orient, hence the term *Orientation.*

The portrayal of the South Sandwich Islands on the 1d. South Georgian definitive stamp of 1963 is far from exact as to relative size and shape of this remote group, strung out over some 130 miles of ocean. The islands of the Netherlands Antilles on a 1958 semipostal issue are to scale, but the distances between them should be about seven times greater. The islands are not in their correct positions on a 1973 issue marking cable and microwave telecommunications links. The issues produced by Egypt, Lebanon, Libya, Jordan and Syria (all 1955) and the Yemen (1957-8), to mark the Arab Postal Union, all omitted the Persian Gulf: that it could easily have been featured on a map of this scale is shown by the Iraqi set of 1956 marking the Third Arab Postal Union Congress. The map of the Suez Canal on a 10m. Egyptian stamp of 1956 shows the northern exit of the Canal touching on Lake Manzala, but it passes directly into the Mediterranean (fig. 50). The same design was used for a 100m. 1957 stamp. In 1961 a slightly different design but with a correct exit for the Canal appeared on a 10m. stamp. The 1953 1s. stamp of Tonga moves the small northern islands of the group, Toku and Fonualei, about 20 miles closer to Vava'u, as can be seen by comparison with the ½d. map stamp of 1951. They are likewise misplaced on the maps of the 1969 oil search issue. The map on the 35c. value of a 1969 issue of the Gilbert & Ellice Islands marking the end of the inaugural year of the South Pacific University wrongly shows the Ellice Islands lying east of the Gilbert Islands, whereas they actually lie south of them (they are also drawn to different scales), and Okinawa lies some 3,500 miles west of Hawaii, not just a few hundred miles south-east as shown on a 1969 3c. stamp of the Ryukyu Islands. A 1969 9d. stamp of Jersey shows a chart of the English Channel, but with the Channel Islands on a larger scale than the rest of the map, and on a 30p. map stamp of 1976 the scale is not constant—Guernsey should be further east and Sark further west.

The various 8c. (1939, 1950, 1954) and 10c. (1961, 1964) map stamps of North Borneo show many discrepancies—for instance the Sultan of Brunei has been presented with the 5th division of Sarawak and also part of Limbang. The Malayan 30c. map stamp of 1957 carefully includes all component states of the Federation but omits the large islands of Langkawi and Tioman, though the former is larger than Penang. The map forming the background on the 1927 United States 10c. stamp commemorating Lindberg's Transatlantic flight is full of inaccuracies—Nova Scotia appears to be attached to the Gaspé Peninsula, Newfoundland is badly misshapen, and Paris has been moved from well inland to the mouth of the Seine. The early map stamps of the Cayman Islands ($\frac{1}{4}$d. of 1935, 1d. of 1938, 2$\frac{1}{2}$d. of 1950) show startling inaccuracies in the alignment of the islands and in the enlargement of Grand Cayman by about 50%, when compared with the 2d. map stamp of 1962, itself copied from a survey map of 1957. Even here the islands are too large in relation to the lines of longitude. The 1966 issue marking the establishment of international telephone links still shows Grand Cayman enlarged and rotated relative to the two smaller islands. Cayman Brac and Little Brac appear on a 1969 6d. stamp, but not in their correct relative positions, while "South Town" on Little Cayman should be South Hole or alternatively Blossom Village. Similar aberrations of old maps are illustrated by comparing the 1s. 1958 and 6d. 1962 map stamps of Samoa (the former very inaccurate), and the 4$80 1952, 10c. 1964 and New Constitution 1967 map stamps of the Virgin Islands, which show considerable differences in the shape and position of the island Jost-van-Dyke, and in the position of the islands relative to the 18°30′N line of latitude. The map on Nepalese stamps of 1954 has many inaccuracies, as indicated by comparison with the more reliable map on a 1964 issue marking the inauguration of the East-West Highway. The 13c. Ottawa Conference Canadian stamp of 1932 shows Hudson Bay disproportionally small, while the 5c. Canadian Centennial stamp of 1967 shows it too large (correct proportions are shown on the 15c. U.P.U. Congress stamp of 1957). The globe on a 1955 2s.40 Austrian stamp marking the tenth anniversary of the U.N.O. shows land and water quite arbitrarily distributed. The 1951 air stamps of the United Nations show the U.N. emblem, but its world map is inconsistent, the 15c. having the Black Sea represented by a dot which is missing on the 25c. value. A 1970 United Nations issue marking the Lower Mekong Basin Development shows two small islands in the Mekong Delta (just above the value figures), but there are actually three. The franc values of the 1907 issue of Réunion include on the design a globe showing Africa and part of the Indian Ocean, together with a pointer which should presumably be indicating the position of Réunion but in fact points to inland Africa opposite the northern end of Madagascar. On a 1967 55m. Libyan stamp the eastern and southern boundaries are shown as irregular where they should be straight (*vide* the 1956 issue marking the anniversary of admission to the U.N.), and on an 8a. Afghan stamp of 1971 marking Red Crescent Day the long narrow eastern province of Wakhan, sandwiched between Kashmir and the U.S.S.R., is drawn much more elongated and narrower than it really is (*vide* the 2a. map stamp of 1970).

A 1961 issue of the Central African Republic bears a map of the country which omits the important River Kwango. An Austrian 1s.50 stamp of 1966 shows a map of Austria divided into its postal zones, but the boundary between postal zones two and three, on the map shown as the Danube, in fact lies north of the Danube. Furthermore the stamp shows the Krimmler Ache (which forms the famous Krimmler Wasserfälle) as the Salzach. The Salzach itself rises on the Salzachgeier, which is situated on the Gerlosplatte. A near error was the ¾a. map stamp of 1948 for Jaipur, part of the set marking the Silver Jubilee of the Maharajah. The printing plate had already been manufactured when it was noticed that the main railway line from Delhi to Ajmer had been omitted; this was hastily inserted by direct hand engraving onto the plate—producing numerous minor varieties in the process.

In 1937 the U.S.A. produced a 3c. stamp marking the 150th anniversary of the North West Territory Ordinance, bearing a map of the region concerned. However, on this map the country now comprising the states of Kentucky and Tennessee is designated "Territory Southwest of the Ohio", although its official designation was the ' Territory South of the Ohio '. In 1938 Iceland produced a miniature sheet marking Leifr Eiriksson's Day, bearing a map of the North Atlantic on which Vinland is identified as Newfoundland. At the time when this stamp was issued this was counter to generally accepted opinions, which considered Nova Scotia or the Cape Cod/Long Island region more probable sites. Nevertheless recent evidence would seem to support the hypothesis that it was indeed Newfoundland, vindicating the designer of this miniature sheet.

A 5c. 1975 stamp of the Cook Islands marks the route of Magellan's famous voyage on which his ship (but not Magellan himself) survived to circumnavigate the world. However, the route is over-simplified, failing to show, for instance, that he called at the River Plate and Rio de Janeiro. Similarly the routes of General Balbo's formation flights across the North Atlantic are over-simplified on the maps given on Paraguayan 20c. and 12g.45 stamps of 1966. The 2d. 1940 stamp of New Zealand inscribed "TASMAN'S DISCOVERY OF NEW ZEALAND 1642" raises the question of whether Tasman is not getting more credit than he really deserves, for William Bleau, who died in 1638, had already published a map showing a portion of coastline labelled "ZELANDIA NOVA". Another error which may suitably be dealt with here, though not strictly a map stamp, is the 8c. 1975 stamp of the U.S.A. which commemorates Sybil Ludington. The legend on the back of the stamp states "On the dark night of April 26, 1777, 16-year old Sybil Ludington rode her horse "Star" alone through the Connecticut countryside rallying her father's militia to repel a raid by the British on Danbury". However, the ride was in fact all within New York State, never coming within ten miles of the Connecticut border. On a lower plane, a 5pf. East German stamp of 1957 purports to show the route of the 10th International Cycle Race, but omits the Pilsen-Prague and Prague-Karlsberg stages by routing the race directly from Pilsen to Karlsberg, where the race terminated. The map on a 1961 Colombian issue marking the eighth Pan-American Highway Congress includes a major highway prominently marked by a thick blue line—with no indication that this highway was planned but had not at that time actually been built.

Frontiers, particularly when disputed, can cause difficulties: many examples of these are really political claims rather than genuine mistakes, and will be dealt with in a separate category, but the 1p. 1936 Argentinian map stamp featuring South America with the various frontiers marked comes into this category also, for it drew so many complaints from other South American countries that it was withdrawn and reissued with only the

Argentine Republic marked in—and reduced at that to give Chile rather more territory.

In two extraordinary cases, to which attention was drawn by Sir Dudley Stamp, countries refuted their own claims to disputed territories on their own map stamps. The 1946 Victory stamps of Burma show the entire region of the headwaters of the Irrawaddy, an area generally accepted as Burmese, as lying within China, and repeated this map on the 1948 Independence issue, though this generous gift of Burmese territory was rescinded on the map of the 1953 issue commemorating the Fifth Anniversary of Independence. Still more extraordinary is the case of the Indian definitive issue of 1957. On this map India has annexed the whole of Kashmir (including the Pakistani-occupied portion and the Tibetan portion disputed with China), Bhutan and Goa (the latter four years prematurely), but has ceded to China some 31,000 square miles of hotly disputed Himalayan territory between the McMahon Line along the Himalayan crests and the Assam plain just north of the Brahmaputra. Incredibly, this design was not replaced until 1965. The nearest parallel to this is the Egyptian 10m. stamp issued on June 22nd, 1967, *i.e.* after the Six Days War, inscribed "Arab solidarity for Palestine Defence", which shows a victorious and bellicose President Nasser superimposed on a map of Egypt and Israel but with the Gaza Strip as part of Israel, something no Arab state has acknowledged to date. Incidentally, the special pictorial postmark applied on the first day does not make the same error, here the Gaza Strip is obviously excluded from Israel. Iraq, on a 15f. stamp of 1969 and again in 1970 on 15f. and 35f. stamps, shows Israel in full post-1967 Six Days War boundaries. Somewhat comparable, perhaps, is the 8f. Chinese stamp of 1968 which bears a map with mainland China coloured red and entitled "the whole country is red", though Taiwan (Formosa) has been left white, thus postally relinquishing a claim which has certainly not been dropped politically. This stamp was on sale in Canton for only two days, then withdrawn.

We may conclude this section with one of the most notorious—and expensive—of modern design errors, the rose Gronchi. In 1961 Italy issued a set to commemorate the visit of President Gronchi of Italy to South America. The 205l. value, originally printed in rose, showed the boundaries of Peru with the ' Amazon triangle ' (an area in dispute with Ecuador) omitted. The Peruvian Ambassador lodged a formal protest immediately, the stamp was withdrawn and invalidated on the day of issue, and a ' corrected ' version in slate-violet, with the disputed territory firmly incorporated in Peru, was hastily issued. A few covers bearing the withdrawn stamp did get through the post and mint copies are available, but both are scarce and very much sought after.

CHAPTER 5

Errors in Portrayal of Subject

We now turn to the category of factual errors in portrayal of the subject of the stamp design—by far the largest and most heterogeneous of our categories. It is also, perhaps, the most controversial, since it involves subjective judgments as to when artistic licence has gone beyond the permissible bounds in modifying the appearance of the subject to fit artistic requirements, or when inexpert draughtsmanship can be considered downright error. Here we have tried to steer a middle course and to avoid criticising a design because it is not a precise photographic representation of its subject, but decisions in this field must necessarily often be controversial.

We may make a start by considering heraldic representations on stamps, as this is a common subject for stamp designs, also one governed by rigid rules of which many stamp designers appear to be little aware. For instance, colours (heraldically either tinctures or metals) can be indicated by appropriate shading, and conversely the wrong kind of shading is equivalent to using the wrong colour. Thus the Italian fascist arms, a fasces on a field divided vertically into a blue half and a red half, is shown on a 1927 issue marking the centenary of Volta, but with the field shaded with horizontal hatching only (*i.e.* blue). The 50c. 1928 stamp of the Italian issue marking the 4th centenary of Philibert has the arms of Savoy (white cross on red field) correctly, with the field shaded by vertical hatching, but the horizontal shading of the general background appears to convert this to cross hatching, representing black. The colour conventions are not followed on many stamps featuring the British coat-of-arms, for instance the British 5d. stamps of 1887 and 1902, the 2/6d. and 5s. stamps of 1939 and 1951 and the £1 of 1951. Furthermore, on all of these except the £1 stamp the tressure round the lion rampant of Scotland is single instead of double. This also applies to the Royal Arms shown on the Stamp Duty 6d. of 1879 and the 15s. Stamp Duty of 1879 and 1884 of Victoria, the Royal Standard shown on the special cachet and postmark for the Royal Train during the Royal tour of Canada in 1938 and to the Scottish arms shown on the Scottish regional 1/3d. (1958) and 1/6d. (1967) stamps. The Royal Arms which are incorporated in the seal of Antigua and Barbuda shown on Antiguan definitive issues of 1903-17 also have a single tressure, and in addition the harp of Ireland is without strings and the unicorn supporter without its chain. A 1s. Tongan stamp of 1951 has the arms almost correct but the double tressure is only counter flory, not flory counter flory, and an 80c. Belgian semi-postal commemorating the Anglo-Belgian Union has part of the outer tressure missing (1950).

The Isle of Man regionals of 1958-71 show the familiar three-legged emblem but with exaggerated spurs and without the armour which they should have. This was corrected with the 1971 decimal issue but recurred on the 1973 pictorials and on special commemorative issues. The

Canadian coat-of-arms shown on special delivery stamps of 1938, 1939 and 1942 indicates the wrong colours for the unicorn supporters, the scroll, flags which droop instead of being stiffly horizontal, and (1942 stamp only) the lining of the mantling. The 10c. special delivery stamp of 1946 shows the maple leaves as white instead of green.

Still on Canada, the colours are wrongly indicated for the arms of British Columbia on the 1958 Canadian centennial stamp (the bars should be blue, not black, and the sun gold, not silver). The 1959 5c. stamp marking the bicentenary of the battle of the Plains of Abraham shows a heraldic ' lion passant gardant ' to represent the British forces and two fleurs-de-lys to represent the French, but the British lion should properly be facing in the other direction and France would be better represented by three fleurs-de-lys than by merely two. The 1962 stamp marking the opening of the Trans-Canada Highway shows the arms of the Provinces, mostly correctly, but those of Saskatchewan (top centre) show the three garbs as silver instead of gold, the date of issue of the stamp has been incorporated in the arms of Prince Edward Island (second, bottom row), and on the arms of New Brunswick (bottom, centre) the lymphad is proceeding to the right instead of the heraldically correct left, though admittedly this last is an error of the official coat-of-arms as then accepted, not of the stamp designer. The 1964-66 set of Provincial emblems and badges contains a further selection of heraldic errors. Most include the date of issue of the stamp in the coat-of-arms, which is not permissible. The colours are wrong for the Canadian coat-of-arms (*e.g.* second quarter and lion supporter should be gold, not silver), the maple leaves of the arms of Quebec should be dark red (not green), the escutcheon and helmet of Nova Scotia, the garbs of Saskatchewan, the lions of Newfoundland and the bezants of the Yukon should all be gold (not silver). In addition, the arms shown for Quebec have three fleurs-de-lys, following the (improper) 1939 decree by Order in Council of the Quebec Government instead of the two assigned by Royal Warrant (and correctly shown on the 1962 stamp discussed above). The motto and crown were added in 1883, also without Royal Authority. Finally, the wreath of the Newfoundland arms has seven twists instead of the heraldically correct six. The arms shown on the 2c. 1910 stamp of Newfoundland as of the London & Bristol Company for Colonizing Newfoundland have aroused controversy. Technically they were first granted to Sir David Kirke and his associates on condition that they supervised the Colony's settlement, so can reasonably be held to be those of the Company, though later they were taken over for the Colony and since 1949 have been those of the Province. However, there are colour errors: the cross should be silver (not red), the lions gold (not silver), the ground colour red (not silver) and the unicorns with chains passing between their forelegs.

Continuing with Commonwealth issues we find that the Jamaican arms issues of 1903-11 err in that the alligator should surmount a plumed helmet, the woman supporter should have a single feather bound to her brow, and the man should have a stringed bow, not a staff, all shown correctly on the higher values of 1956. The postal fiscals of 1855-74 err in giving the female supporter no feathers at all in her headdress. The arms shown on the 1896 and 1905 5d. South Australian stamps and on the 1888-90 6d., 1890 5s., 1897 and 1899 1d. stamps of New South Wales were unauthorised at the time of issue. South Australia was granted arms (shown on a 4d. Australian stamp of 1957) on 20th November, 1936, while New South Wales was granted arms in 1912 (quite different from those depicted on the stamps of the state). The arms shown on various early issues of Mauritius were likewise unauthorised: those granted by Royal Warrant in 1906 were slightly different in all quarters from those depicted on the stamps and postal stationery, showing a lymphad instead of a barque, palm trees instead of sugar canes, the key facing east instead of west and a five-pointed star instead of six-pointed, yet stamps bearing the unauthorised arms continued to appear in 1907. The arms appear correctly in the 1910 issue and postal stationery, but the 3c. of 1968 has the palm trees coloured blue instead of green. An 18c. Australian stamp of 1976 depicts the modern arms of Australia but the border is silver (should be ermine), the wreath has only five twists (should have six) and the swan faces in the wrong direction. New Zealand features the ecclesiastical arms of Christchurch on a 1d. stamp of 1950, but instead of the correct three eight-pointed stars (with wavy arms) there are three six-pointed mullets (with straight-sided arms) on a field which is red (should be blue). The emblem of St. Vincent includes an ancient altar on the side of which is depicted a pair of clasped hands, but on the 5s. stamp of 1880 these are only indicated by a faint squiggle.

The arms of Transvaal include a veld-wagon, which has a single draught-pole (dissel-boom), the oxen being outspanned. The 1894 stamp and postal stationery, however, substituted two shafts: this was corrected in 1895. The 2½d. stamp of 1910 for the newly formed Union of South Africa showed the arms of Cape Colony, wrongly labelled as those of the Cape of Good Hope, which are quite different, while behind the shield of the arms of Transvaal are depicted two spears—these should be spades. These errors appear to be repeated on the 1960 6d. stamp marking the 50th anniversary of the Union. The coat-of-arms of the British South Africa Company on the 1892 issue of Rhodesia has a wreath of red and gold alternately instead of gold and red, and the field should be red, not silver. The die I issue of 1896 has the tusk clasped by the lion resting on the wreath (it should be clear of the wreath), and the lymphads, which should have black hulls, lack flagmasts and flags on poop and forecastle; these errors are corrected on the die II issue. The arms appear again on the ½d. value of a 1940 Southern Rhodesian issue marking the jubilee of the Company. Here the tusk once more rests on the wreath, the central lymphad has no flags or rigging, while the others have flags but no flagstaffs on poop and forecastle. Most of the stamps of Kishangarh portray a coat-of-arms, albeit rather crudely and variably. For instance, the 4a. stamp of 1899 and the 8a. of 1904 have four divisions of the upper chief whereas the others, *e.g.* the ¼a. of 1899, have five. The arms of Negri Sembilan are depicted on the issues of 1935-41 and are accompanied by seven pairs of palmettes and lotus flowers on each side of the shield, but correctly there should have been nine, to represent the nine sultanates in the league forming this state—its name means 'nine states'. The printers did not realise the significance of the number nine here, and had reduced it from the original design to get a better balance, causing a near riot in the state on the arrival of the stamps. Reluctantly the issue was accepted, but after the war the redrawn issue had palm trees at the sides.

Leaving the Commonwealth we turn first to Europe. The Austrian 10k. 1858 stamp shows a series of coats-of-arms. The second from the top on the left side bears the two impaled arms of ancient and modern Hungary: the ancient arms, with eight bars alternately red and silver, should properly be in the senior position on the left, but are here on the right. Furthermore, the top (red) bar appears to have got crowded out, leaving only seven. The 2s. Austrian stamp of 1970 marking the Carinthian Plebiscite shows the arms of Carinthia. The shield is surmounted by a jousting helmet with two bison horns, each bearing five twigs with three linden leaves apiece: these should be black on the dexter side, red on the sinister, but on the stamp the colours are interchanged. Andorra appears to have two coats-of-arms, a French version (shown on postage due stamps of 1937 and 1944) and a Spanish version (shown on the postage due issue of 1961), all, curiously enough, issued by the French post offices. However on the 1961 arms the two cows on the quarter which refers to the arms of the Compte de Béarn are facing in the wrong direction (dexter instead of sinister). A 3f. Belgian stamp of 1965, marking the 50th anniversary of the founding of Toc H, shows the arms of Poperinge, a hand holding a crozier on a red field. It is a right hand bearing the ring of a bishop and the maniple, but the ring is worn on the forefinger, not as here on the ring-finger, and a priest carries the maniple in his left hand. Presumably, however, these are errors inherent in the arms themselves and not in their reproduction. The arms of Appenzell and of St. Gall are shown incorrectly on Swiss 5c. 1924 and 20c. 1928 semipostals respectively. The bear on the arms of Appenzell should have tongue, male organ and claws red, but on the stamp the two former are white and the claws black. The bear on the arms of St. Gall should have collar, inside of ears, claws and eyebrows gold, the tongue and male organ red, but on the stamp only the collar is gold and only the tongue red.

The complexities of the history of the arms of Finland and of their portrayal on Finnish stamps and postal stationery could almost fill a chapter on their own. They are derived from the arms of Gustavus Vasa and go back to at least 1558. In the first issue, of 1856, the lion stands on a sabre instead of a scimitar, and wrongly has a forefoot on it as well as both hind feet, the tail is forked instead of just looped, the mouth shut instead of open with protruding tongue. it has no gauntlet on the dexter paw and is surrounded by seven stars instead of nine roses—just to mention some of the most obvious errors. There are similar errors in the arms issues of 1866, 1868, 1875-85 and 1889, and it was not until 1917 that the arms were correctly depicted on an issue. The U.S. 5c. issue of 1967 honouring 50 years of Finnish Independence is also correct.

The arms of Oldenburg, depicted on a 15pf.+15pf. German semipostal of 1928, should have in the second and third quarters a golden Greek cross pattée (with broadened but straight-sided truncate arms); instead on the stamp it is a cross moliné (with terminally notched arms). They are shown correctly on the 1g. 1859 stamp of Oldenburg. The arms of the Saar, portrayed on a 15f. stamp of the Saar and a 10pf. stamp of West Germany, both of 1957, are here portrayed in quite misleading colouring. The first quarter should show a silver lion on a blue field (here a dark lion on a white field); the third quarter should be the arms of the Duke of Lorraine (three silver eagles on a red diagonal band on a gold field), here given as three dark eagles on a dark-bordered white band; the lion of the fourth quarter should be on a black field, not white as here. Incidentally, the design on the stamps of Tuscany is NOT the arms of Tuscany, though generally so described, but a statue, the Marzocco, by Donatello, which stands in the Piazza della Signoria, Florence: the arms of Tuscany would be the Medici arms—six red discs on a gold field, one charged with three fleurs-de-lys. The Netherlands stamps of 1898 onwards featuring Queen Wilhelmina ran into trouble because they showed the arms tilted in the larger design (heraldically incorrect), gave them a bordure (which technically indicates a younger branch of the family) and gave the Queen two crowns at once, one on her head and one poised above it. These may seem minor points, but were considered serious enough to merit a special committee to investigate the charges against the design. A Rumanian issue of 1927 honouring the 50th anniversary of Rumanian Independence consisted of two basic designs, both including the Rumanian royal coat-of-arms, shown correctly on the vertical design but with the small central shield reversed on the horizontal design. Switzerland showed the arms of Zurich on twin shields, one a mirror image of the other, on a 5c.+5c. semipostal of 1951, and did the same for the arms of Berne on a 5c.+5c. semipostal of 1953, but it is heraldically improper to reverse a coat-of-arms in this way. The state emblem of East Germany is reversed on the first official issue of 1954, shown by the projection to the left of the compasses. This was corrected on a later issue of 1954. The hammer and sickle emblem of Russia is wrongly given on a 1f.20+1f.80 semipostal of Luxemburg of 1945 on which the sickle points to the right instead of to the left. The triskele emblem of the Isle of Man is reversed on the stamps of the authorised Manx service run by Mr. Gordon Quirk during the British postal strike of 1971.

In the Americas arms are often formulated under much less strict rules than those adhered to by European countries, but even so there is plenty of room for error. The Venezuelan arms shown on issues of 1861 and 1912 have the horses facing the wrong way, and on the 1865 arms issue the charges of the quarters in chief are transposed; they are shown correctly on official stamps of 1898. The 3c. 1920 Colombian provisional arms stamp has only six stars above the eagle's head, instead of one for each of the nine confederated states as shown on the contemporaneous 3c. stamp produced by Perkins Bacon & Co. The arms of the Argentine Republic are reproduced extremely crudely on the first issue (1858), and with a human head in place of the sun, a horizontal in place of a vertical ellipse, and with no laurel wreath. Stamps of 1868 (10c.) and 1878 (16c.) featuring General Belgrano, and of 1888 (10c.) featuring Avellanida, include small coats-of-arms, but here the arms of the clasping hands are clothed (they should be bare), the background of the lower half is shaded as red (it should be silver) and the sun and laurel branches are omitted. However, admittedly the precise format of the arms was not fixed until a decree of 24th April, 1944 (they are shown on a 5c. stamp of 1944 marking the first anniversary of the Revolutionary Government), so perhaps some latitude is allowable for these early stamps. The 50c. Argentinian stamp of 1973 showing the inauguration of President Campora errs in depicting the Presidential sash of office (to the right) with the full arms of the country on it—it bears only the sun. The arms of Bolivia, adopted by law of 14th July, 1888, are so crowded and complex that it would perhaps be unfair to expect any designer to squeeze everything in correctly on a stamp of normal size. However, there should be nine stars (for the nine departments forming the country), as on issues of 1868, 1890, 1894 and later issues, whereas issues of 1871, 1878, 1887 and 1893 wrongly show 11 stars. The arms of Ecuador, adopted in 1845, are similarly complex, reproduced with variable accuracy on numerous issues. Those of 1865-72 are very crude, but omit only the four zodiacal symbols for the months (March to June) during which Ecuador fought for its independence. These are also omitted from issues of 1881, 1887, 1896, and 1897 (Liberal Party overprint), but present in other arms issues from 1897 onwards; the banners wrongly bear stars on the issues of 1881, 1887 and 1896, a caduceus is wrongly included (above the fasces) on issues of 1881, 1887, 1896, 1897 (regular issue) and 1920 (overprinted fiscal stamps). The arms of Panama were adopted in 1904 and modified to their present form in 1946. The arms issues of 1906, 1909 and 1924 show only seven stars above the eagle's head, whereas there should be nine, as on the 1942 issue which features the arms of Panama and Costa Rica, and on the 1952 issue. Note that the arms on the ½c. 1921 stamp of the set marking the centenary of independence are those of Panama City, not of Panama as often suggested in catalogues. Haiti also has a complex state emblem, designed by President Pétion in 1807, which varies considerably on different issues. On the issues of 1891-95 the central palm tree bears stiffly projecting leaves, rendered more naturally drooping on the issue of 1896. All these have two cannon but no cannonballs, and two anchors. An 1896 issue has two designs, differing in details of the emblem, one with two piles of nine and six cannonballs respectively, the other (correctly) with both piles of six. A shako and a cap of liberty appear on the cannon and disappear in different issues—they seem to be unwarranted additions, like the trumpet which appears in the 1898 A.B.N.Co. issue (second design), becoming two trumpets on the 1961 parcel post issue.

The emblems of the Tribes of Israel provide some interesting and sometimes controversial features, reflected on various Israeli postage issues. Although one generally talks about the 'Twelve Tribes of Israel', Joseph was not recognised as a tribe, his sons Ephraim and Manasseh being each recognised as half a tribe, so we properly have eleven and two half tribes. The 1,000pr. stamp of 1952 omits the bullock emblem of Manasseh. The tribes issue of 1955 includes Joseph as a tribe (here represented by a sheaf of wheat on the 200pr. value). On the 30pr. of this set the High Priest's breastplate, the emblem of Levi, is shown on its side, for this should have four rows of three jewels (see Exodus 28:17), not three rows of four as depicted here. The 1973 issue reproduces the Chagall windows of the Hadassah-Hebrew University Medical Centre Synagogue in Ein Karem; these represent the 12 sons of Jacob, but the tabs mistakenly claim that these represent 12 tribes.

The swastika emblem of the Nazis is shown reversed on the rudder of the Arado AR196 seaplane on a German 20pf. stamp of 1944. The formalised sun emblem on the 1931 issue bearing Sun Yat Sen's portrait was first produced by De La Rue with a double disc: this was rejected as ridiculous by the Chinese Government, the master die was altered to a single line disc and a corrected issue produced, but the faulty stamps were also put on issue. A 2s. Austrian stamp of 1934 showed the double eagle with only five feathers per wing instead of the correct seven. It was withdrawn and a corrected version in a different shade was issued the following year.

The Condominium of the New Hebrides is run by France and the United Kingdom, each producing stamps in its own language and currency. Conventionally the French issues have "RF" to the right of or above the Royal Cypher, while the positions are reversed on the British issues. However in the 1963 definitive issue the 10c., 20c., 40c. and 3f. values were produced for the French by the British firm of Harrison & Sons, Ltd., who inadvertently reversed these positions. Corrected versions of the 10c., 20c. and 3f. were finally produced in 1967 (figs. 51 & 52) and the 40c. was replaced by a correct 60c. of the same design in 1968. Another error involving a royal monogram occurred in the Belgian semipostal set of 1962 portraying Belgian queens, where the 40c.+10c. value showing Queen Louise-Marie should have borne an ' L ' monogram, as shown in advance publicity illustrations, but in error the printing cylinder bore an ' ML ' monogram. The error was spotted at the proof stage and a correct cylinder prepared, but unfortunately the wrong cylinder was used for the first printing and some 24,000 stamps with the error were sold in Brussels before the mistake was noticed. Although efforts were at first made to suppress the "ML" stamps, they were soon reprinted and distributed to discourage speculation.

The Esperanto emblem is a plain green five-pointed star, but on the Hungarian 1957 set marking the 70th anniversary of Esperanto the star is white, and on the green 6cr.50 stamp of Brazil issued in 1960 to mark the centenary of the birth of Zamenhof (inventor of Esperanto—actually born in 1859) it is also white. It is shown correctly on numerous issues, *e.g.* on a 1s. Austrian stamp of 1954. The signs of the zodiac have formalised symbols as shown on an I£1 1961 Israeli stamp, but several of them are grossly distorted on 1968 issues of Fernando Poo, Ifni, Rio Muni and Spanish Sahara, notably those representing Gemini, Capricornus and Pisces. In 1960 the CEPT emblem was a wagon wheel with 19 spokes to represent the 19 participant countries, but by mistake the Portuguese post office was sent a design with 22 spokes, and although a correct 19-spoked design was sent later, the damage had been done and the original 22-spoke design was reproduced on the Portuguese Europa stamps of 1960.

The badge of the boy scout movement is a fleur-de-lys with a mullet on each side petal, but these five-pointed mullets (straight-armed stars) are often omitted, as on stamps of Austria (1s.50, 1962), Dominica (set, 1971), Mahra (set, 1967), Nigeria (set, 1965), Paraguay (set, 1962) and South Korea (7w., 1968). A scouting symbol of a different kind is the left-handed handshake, demonstrated on a 20y. Japanese stamp of 1972, but right-handed handshakes are shown on 2c. and 75c. 1972 stamps and miniature sheet of Grenada, also on a 3c. Nicaraguan stamp of 1957 in the set marking the centenary of the birth of Lord Baden-Powell. Furthermore, the emblem shown on Saudi Arabian stamps marking 3rd Rover Moot (1969) and 6th Rover Moot (1974) likewise shows a right-handed handshake.

The Olympic Games symbol of five linked rings, symbolic of the five continents, has been widely misapplied and misrepresented. It has frequently been associated with non-Olympic events, such as the "Coupe des Tropiques" Games, Bangui (Central African Republic, 100f., 1962, where the rings are also wrongly positioned), the First Mediterranean Games, Alexandria (Egypt, 1951 set), where it was inverted on the 30m. value, Fourth Pan-Arab Games (Egypt, 1965 set), Long-distance Swimming Championships (Egypt, 10m., 1965), First Asian Games, New Delhi (correctly commemorated on an Indian set of 1951, but wrongly labelled "Asiatic Olympic Games" and marked with the Olympic rings on an Indonesian set of 1951), Fourth Asian Games, Djakarta (wrongly called ' Olympic Games ' and bearing the Olympic rings on a 1962 set of Afghanistan), Indonesian Youth Conference, Bandung (Indonesia, two values of a 1960 issue, with rings wrongly arranged), First African/U.S. Sports Meeting (Mali, 1973 set), 53rd "Cross des Nations" cross-country race (Morocco, 25f., 1966), Pan-Arab Games, Cairo (Ras Al Khaima, 1966 set), South African Games (South Africa, 1969 set, also including the Olympic torch), local sports (Yemen, 1964 set, with deformed emblem and including non-Olympic events such as darts, table-tennis and horse-racing). They are legitimately present but upside down, on end or otherwise distorted on stamps of Egypt (1960 set), Germany, West Berlin (1952 set), Great Britain (2½d., 1948), Germany (1935 and 1936 sets), Guatemala (1964 set), Lebanon (20p., 1968), Mauritania (1964 set), Monaco (1953 set), Monaco (only the 30f. 1956), Peru (1948 set), Qatar (1964 set) and Yugoslavia (1952 set). The 1976 Czechoslovakian set marking the Winter Olympic Games gets the special emblem of these Games wrong by printing "INNSBRUCK 1976" under it instead of around it, while an Albanian issue of 1976 changed the spelling to "INSBRUK". Haiti gets the symbol of the Winter Olympic Games, Grenoble, wrong on a set of 1968 (it is shown correctly on a French 60c. stamp of 1967) by converting the six-armed symbolic snowflake into an impossible eight-armed one.

Snowflakes by their nature must always show hexagonal symmetry, but this has not always been appreciated by artists. The motif of the University Winter Games shown on a 1966 Italian set represents an eight-armed snowflake, as does the background to 3b. and 4b. 1971 stamps of the Yemen Arab Republic, also marking Winter Olympic Games, while two Russian issues of 1964 marking the Winter Olympic Games and Soviet Medal-winners respectively, have a background of five-armed snowflakes. A 1926 2c.+2c. semipostal stamp of the Netherlands bearing the arms of Utrecht also shows an ice crystal—a reference to the supposed origin of the name from the ancient German snow god Ultr—but impossibly eight-sided, and an eight-armed symbol of a snowflake appears on a 3c. 1971 Christmas stamp of the Bahamas.

The emblem of the Apollo Soyuz link-up in space, which is correctly featured on the U.S. commemorative 10c. stamps of 1975, is variously transformed on many of the issues which commemorated this event, though it is questionable if these variations can really be termed errors. They include issues of Bolivia (1975,) Congo (Brazzaville) (1975), Malagasy Republic (1974), Mauritania (1975), Niger (1975) and Poland (1975). A very different kind of symbol is the Royal Orb, signifying the triumph of spiritual over temporal power: on the 1935 Silver Jubilee issue of India and the 1937 1½d. Coronation issue of Great Britain the orb is shown with the vertical plane of the jewelled band at right angles to the plane of the surmounting cross, but in both King's orb and Queen's orb it is in the same plane, as shown correctly on the 1953 2½d. Coronation stamp of Great Britain (figs. 53 & 54).

Medals seem on the whole to be faithfully represented on stamps, but the ribbon of the 'Academic Palms' decoration, honoured on a 20f. French stamp of 1959, is shown streaked instead of plain violet, too long by a good third, and with the two twigs interchanged on the medal—the laurel twig should be on the right.

The 10p. and 13p. values of the British issue of 1977 marking the centenary of the Royal Institute of Chemistry show the formulae of vitamin C (ascorbic acid) and a crystal of common salt respectively, with atoms symbolised by coloured balls, but the designer has not followed the accepted British colour code for such representations, and here hydrogen (which should be white) is red, oxygen (which should be red) is blue, carbon (which should be black) is dark blue in the vitamin C formula, while the salt crystal correctly has green for chlorine, but sodium (which should be gold) here has the blue proper to nitrogen. The 1s. 1965 stamp commemorating the surgeon Lister has his portrait enclosed in a hexagon meant to represent the formula of the antiseptic carbolic acid (of which he pioneered the use), C_6H_5OH, but alternate sides of the Carbon hexagon should be doubled to represent double bonds between carbon atoms.

Flags can be in error in many different ways. Our own flag, the Union Jack, probably causes more difficulties than any other. A frequent error is to place the red saltire of St. Patrick exactly central in the white background, which thus technically eliminates the white saltire of St. Andrew, as, for instance, on the 1d. (1s.) semipostal of Queensland of 1900 in aid of the Patriotic Fund, the 1974 Cook Islands miniature sheet marking the British Commonwealth Games, the 10d. 1970 stamp of Fujeira in the issue marking the World Football Championships, Mexico, the 1k.50 Czechoslovakian stamp of 1945 showing flags of the victorious allies, and the corresponding 3,000l. Rumanian stamp of 1947. This latter also has the white border of the vertical arms of the cross of St. George continued over the horizontal arms without interruption. On the 2½d. Jamaican stamp of 1921 the flanking Union Jack of the left is technically inverted, as the broader white band is below the red saltire in the lower quarter next to the flagpole, instead of above. This was corrected the same year on differently watermarked paper. The Scottish flag appears on a 4d. British stamp of 1966 commemorating the Scottish poet Robert Burns, but here the white cross should be about five times as broad.

In 1958 the Russians produced a 40k. stamp to commemorate the Communist Postal Conference in Moscow, and attempted to show the flags of the countries concerned, in colour. However, they unfortunately inverted the Czechoslovakian flag by putting the horizontal white stripe below instead of above the red stripe: this was corrected later in the year. In the second issue of Olympic Games commemoratives produced by the Dominican Republic in 1957 there was included a miniature sheet on

Postkarte
Deutsches Reich
6
BERLIN NW 40
20.4. 1940
Werbeschau der
KdF. Betriebssammlergruppe AEG
AEG
Abgabepreis 20 Rpf.
100 Jahre
Briefmarke
70 JAHRE POSTKARTE
K.D.F.-SAMMLERGRUPPEN
RUDI HOPPE

which the Dominican Republic flag had its colours transposed. This was withdrawn on the day of issue when the error was pointed out, and is now a very rare item. The red and blue colours are likewise transposed on the Venezuelan flag portrayed on a 45c. 1969 Venezuelan stamp, though as this issue features children's art one must make some allowances for the juvenile artist. The flag of the Council of Europe is shown upside down on a 3s.50 Austrian stamp of 1969—the stars should have one point upwards, not two as here. It is shown correctly on, for instance, the 1963 France Council of Europe issues.

Turning to less obvious types of flag error, a 1971 West German stamp shows the red and white flag of Nürnberg flying from the Heidentower, which, however, flies only the white and blue Bavarian flag. A 10c. 1976 stamp of South West Africa shows a fortress flying the German military flag, with a cross in the upper hoist corner from the tower on the left: however, during the period of German occupation it was the trade flag (with black, white and red stripes) which was flown from here. The flag at the bows of a Fascist coastguard vessel on a 15c. Italian stamp of 1932 is one which was not flown at sea. A 1938 Ecuadorian issue bears the flags of the U.S.A. and Ecuador: the latter is the mercantile flag, but should in this context more properly be the national flag, while the American flag has the blue field out of proportion and the stars incorrectly arranged.

The relatively complex flag of the U.S.A. is frequently misrepresented. A 1940 issue of the Dominican Republic shows it with only 28 stars in place of the then correct 48, while a 10c. 1956 stamp of Surinam and a similar 15c. stamp of the Netherlands Antilles show it with only 20 stars. A French 25f. stamp of 1949 marking Franco-American Amity shows an emblem of the U.S.A. with eight rows of six stars instead of the proper six rows of eight stars, while a Rumanian issue of 1964 showing U.S. astronauts and their flag has a star arrangement which, although partly obscured, is obviously incorrect. Honduras in 1959 produced an issue marking the 150th anniversary of the birth of Lincoln: here the red stripes are thick and the white stripes very thin, though properly they should be of equal width. A 75c. Dutch stamp of 1976 marking the bicentennial of the U.S.A. shows a flag with only nine stripes instead of 13, while a 5r. 1972 stamp of Umm Al Qiwain marking a U.S. victory in speed-skating has a flag with only eight stripes. A Chinese 1945 issue has the stripes of unequal width. The 2c. 1926 American stamp marking the 150th anniversary of the Battle of White Plains shows on the right the White Plains Flag, but this was red, not white as indicated on the stamp. In 1976 an issue was produced featuring the flags of all the States, but at least three of these are in error. The Iowa flag is shown with three vertical stripes of the same width, but the white central one should be double the width of the others, as shown correctly on the 1946 issue marking the centenary of the statehood of Iowa. The New Jersey State flag includes two female figures, that on the hoist side (left) with a gold blouse, that on the fly side with a red blouse, but as figured on this stamp both have red blouses. The Tennessee State flag has been a source of controversy, for the U.S. postal authorities insist they have got it right, although the General Assembly of the State passed a resolution (HJR 399, passed 16th March, 1976) insisting that it was upside down, that the offending stamps should be recalled and a corrected version issued. This, however, was not done, not surprisingly perhaps, as all designs appeared on each sheet, so that this would have meant recall of the entire issue.

The 1972 issue for the Gilbert and Ellice Islands to mark the 25th anniversary of the South Pacific Commission shows seven stars on the Commission flag instead of the correct eight (one for each member country), and on the 35c. value, which shows the flags of the individual members, that of Tonga, not then a member, was wrongly included. Furthermore, the Fijian flag was shown as deep blue instead of the correct light blue. All these features are shown correctly on the 3s. 1972 stamp of the Western Samoan issue marking the same event.

The Samoan issue of 1921 shows a flag which presumably ought to be that of New Zealand (of which Samoa at that time was a mandated territory), but no stars are visible on what appears to be a plain red ensign. The 1946 Mexican air stamps commemorating the U.N.O. err by including the Swiss flag amongst those of member states, for Switzerland was not then a member of the U.N.O. The Australian flag features the Southern Cross constellation, and the Flag Act of 1953 specified that the four major stars should be seven-pointed, the fifth five-pointed as shown on the 1970 30c. stamp marking the Royal Visit. It would be logical to expect these conventions to be also adhered to when the Southern Cross is used as a symbol for Australia on its own, but on the 4c. stamp of 1967 marking the 50th anniversary of Lions International the stars have five, six, seven, eight and nine points respectively, and on the 20c. Expo stamp of 1970 have five, six, seven, seven and eight points respectively, apparently through confusion with the Victoria State Crest. The flag of the Central African Republic bears a golden star, as shown rather muddily on a 1959 issue, due to rather inexpert use of a new colour printing system, but it is wrongly left white on the 1961 issue marking admission to the U.N.O.

Flag colours are often not very accurately reproduced on stamps. A Russian issue of 1950 showing national flags of Communist countries appeared in two printings with distinctly different colours, but each time wrong for at least one country's flag, notably that of East Germany. The East German flag, of black, red and gold horizontal stripes, should be shaded according to heraldic convention (crosshatched, vertically hatched and dotted stripes respectively) when colours are being represented rather than used, but on a 1951 East German issue marking German-Soviet Friendship the top stripe is wrongly in solid colour. Similarly a 5s. Jamaican stamp of 1945 marking the New Constitution shows a Jamaican flag which ought to have had a blue background, but with vertical shading which would indicate red. A Czechoslovakian 1945 issue featuring clasped hands above a map of Czechoslovakia, with Czechoslovakian and Russian flags at the side, has the former shaded to indicate white and black horizontal stripes with a red triangle at the hoist, instead of the proper white and red stripes with mauve triangle.

The Korean flag is more complex than at first appears, consisting of a central Monad (the combined Yang and Yin) surrounded by four combinations of broken and unbroken lines (the Trigrams) representing amongst other things Heaven, Earth, Fire and Water. Three different versions appear on Korean stamps, type (I) on issues of 1895-98, type (II) which is the reverse of type (I), on issues of South Korea of 1948 and also on a

United States stamp of 1944, type (III), which appears to be the correct version, on issues of South Korea in 1950 and subsequently. It is said that the South Koreans forebore to point out the error on the U.S. stamp because of gratitude to the Americans for issuing the stamp at all, and it is even possible that the errors were deliberately repeated on the 1948 issues by the South Koreans to avoid embarrassing their benefactors!

An East German 70pf. stamp of 1965 shows a bilateral demonstration of Communist and Socialist parties, prominently featuring a banner inscribed "Sozialistische Einheitspartei Deutschlands" (Socialist Unity Party of Germany), but the original banner, which also features (correctly) on a 5pf. stamp of 1966 (marking the 20th anniversary of the Socialist Unity Party) did not bear the word ' Deutschlands ', which in any case incorrectly has a short ' s ' instead of a long ' s ' in the middle of the word. The demonstrators on a 20m. Egyptian stamp of 1969 bear a variety of flags, including one with a crescent and a four-pointed star very like a Christian cross and hence unlikely to have been carried in the 1919 revolution being commemorated.

The 9d. British stamp of 1969 marking the first flight of Concorde shows the flags of Great Britain and France in the top left-hand corner. Where flags are illustrated unattached, as here, they should be shown as with hoist to left, fly to right, so that on this stamp the blue, white and red tricolour of France technically is reversed. The same rule applies to the 3d. 1927 Greek stamp featuring the cruiser *Averoff*, where the frame on either side of the name of the country is formed by Greek naval ensigns, so that in this case the ensign on the left technically is reversed.

Reversals are not, of course, confined to flags. The 8d. Greek stamp of 1934 illustrating the entrance to the Athens Stadium includes a 2,500 year old frieze shown correctly at the bottom right but reversed at bottom left. The design of the 28d. Yugoslavian stamp of 1952 commemorating Navy Day is taken from a relief sculpture entitled *The Fisherman*, but is a mirror image of it. The statue shown on the 20l. Italian stamp marking the 10th International Textile Exhibition in 1951 is a reversed image of a fourth century B.C. Greek statue of Diana. A 1a. Indian stamp of 1949 portrayed a mediaeval sculptured image of the Bodhisattva Simanda Lokesvava (now in Lucknow Museum), once again as a reversed image, but in this case a corrected version was issued in 1950.

Reversed paintings are not uncommon, *e.g.* the *Head of a Child* by Rubens, from the gallery at Vaduz, shown reversed on a 20r. 1949 stamp of Liechtenstein, and Goya's *Doña Isabel Cobos de Porcel* (now in the National Gallery, London), reversed on a Spanish 70c. stamp of 1958—it is shown correctly on a 1r. 1967 stamp of Dubai. Her name, incidentally, should be Doña Isabel Lobo y Mendita de Porcel. Piazetta's *A Young Standard-Bearer* (in the Dresden Art Gallery) is reversed on a 40pf. East German stamp of 1957. A painting of *The Nativity* by Lucas Ch'en is reversed on a 1961 Christmas issue of the Vatican City. Carracci's *Christ appearing to St. Peter* is reversed on a 3c. 1970 stamp of Jamaica (but correct on a 15c. 1971 stamp of Anguilla). (figs. 55 & 56). Chardin's painting *The Letter-sealer* is reversed on a 1946 2f.+3f. French semipostal (correct on a 75d. 1968 stamp of Fujeira). The legend of Paul and Virginia is illustrated on the 20c. value of 1950 and 25c. of 1953 for Mauritius by reversed reproductions from an old print now in the Historical Museum of Mahébourg. The post rider featured on the 3c. 1869 stamp of the U.S.A. is a reversed version of the original work, and on the 3p. 1973 British stamp showing Court Masque costumes designed by Inigo Jones, the figure on the left is reversed from the original sketch. The 1861 postmaster's stamp of Mount Lebanon, Louisiana, of which only a single copy is known, was printed from a positive design cut on a wood block, so is therefore reversed, and the 6p. 1966 Spanish stamp showing an Inca postal runner reverses the design of a 10c. Peruvian stamp of 1936 (figs 57 & 58). An interesting reversal occurs on Dürer's *The Nativity,* from *The Small Passion,* a woodcut of 1511, featured on 3c. and 35c. Antiguan stamps of 1970, for Dürer forgot to reverse the ' D ' of his monogram on the woodblock, so that it appears reversed on the print, as faithfully shown in part on the stamps.

A rather complex case is the treatment of the scenes from the Bayeux Tapestry shown on the British stamps issued in 1966 to commemorate the Battle of Hastings, where on the first stamp the prostrate Norman and severed hand have been brought from the edge of the tapestry into the main scene, while the archers at the top, also from the edging, have been reversed. The scene shown on the third stamp, the death of Harold, is out of sequence, its rightful place being between the fifth and sixth stamps.

The only issue of Icaria shows a portrait, commonly mistakenly thought to be that of Hermes. It is in fact of Dionysus, indicated by the wreath of vine leaves, is adapted from a coin design, and is a reversed image. Various Greek stamps (1000d. of 1954, 2d. of 1955 and 2d.50 of 1959) show a portrait of Alexander the Great taken from a quartz gem of the fourth century B.C., but again a reversed image.

Reversed portraits are indeed much commoner than is generally realised, as stamp designers frequently reverse them to obtain a better balance in the design. Nevertheless, as faces are never precisely bilaterally symmetrical these must to some extent be faulty representations of the original. For instance Queen Victoria's portrait on the 1960 issue of Bechuanaland marking the 75th anniversay of the Protectorate is reversed from a photograph by Bassano, though in this case the sash and jewellery were carefully transposed in the finished design to keep them correctly positioned. The 3c. stamps of Newfoundland for 1870-96 and the 6c. of 1894 also show a reversed portrait of Queen Victoria, in this case from an 1869 photograph by Hughes and Mullins, as does the 1c. stamp of 1897, marking the 60th year of her reign (though issued in the 61st) from a painting by John Thomson. As previously noted, the right-hand figure of value is also reversed. A mirror image of the ' small fillet ' head of Queen Victoria, based on the Wyon medal, appears on various Canadian issues of 1868-97, and on a 4c. value of 1948 marking the centenary of Responsible Government, though shown correctly facing left on the 8c. value of 1893. The beautiful Chalon portrait, shown correctly on the 12½c. value of 1859, is reversed on the 1897 Jubilee issue. The Queen, in fact, never allowed her right-side profile to be painted or photographed.

There is only one colonial issue showing King George V facing east—that of Nyasaland of 1934—on which he was thus portrayed to face his eastern possessions, but this appears to be a reversed portrait, as indicated by the hair parting. The portrait of Queen Elizabeth II on the 1969 Dominican issue is reversed, while that of James I on a 1c. 1910 stamp of

Newfoundland is reversed from a portrait by Muytens (now in the National Portrait Gallery, London).

Looking further afield we have the Danish monarchs Christian IV and Christian X, each facing both left and right in a Danish issue of 1924. As the portraits are otherwise identical, one of each must be a mirror image. This also applies to the 1940 and 1945 issues of the Vatican in which the same portrait of Pope Pius XII faces left on some values, right on others. President Bogran's portrait is reversed on the higher values of an 1891 issue of Honduras (shown by the coat fastenings on the wrong side). The portrait of Prince Francis Joseph II is reversed on the 5f. 1963 stamp of Liechtenstein marking the 25th anniversary of his reign, though correct on other issues, such as the 1f. stamp of 1966 marking his 60th birthday.

The 5c. U.S. stamp of 1847 shows a reversed portrait of Benjamin Franklin, after a painting by J. B. Longacre, repeated on the 5c. stamp of the Centennial miniature sheet of 1947. President Truman had his portrait reversed on a 40c. Brazilian stamp of 1947—compare with that on the 8c. U.S. stamp of 1973. A 2c. 1941 issue of the Philippine Islands shows a reversed portrait of President José Rizal—correct on the 2c. stamp of 1946. Nelson's portrait on the 20c. and 30c. Antiguan stamps of 1961 is a reversed version of the painting by L. F. Abbott, now in the National Portrait Gallery, London. A reversed portrait of the Duc de Choiseul (after a painting by Louis van Loo) appears on a 15f.+5f. 1949 semipostal of France. The portrait of Dr. Luis D. Beauperthuy is reversed on a 1b. Venezuelan stamp of 1971, while a 40c. Chilean stamp of 1948 honouring Admiral Arturo Prat Chacon (given simply as "Arturo Prat" on the stamp), has the background scene, after a painting by Sommerscales of the naval Battle of Iquique, reversed.

Turning to men of letters, the portrait of Shakespeare on the 1964 British issue is a reversal of the engraving which appeared in the First Folio of his Plays (1623), though if the original copper plate from which this was printed bore a true portrait then it is the Folio portrait which is reversed—a confusing thought! The portrait appears unreversed on a 12c. Antiguan stamp of 1964. In comparable fashion the self-portrait by J. Louis David, shown on a 100f. 1967 stamp of the Niger Republic, was probably literally a mirror image, so that the reversed version on a French 5f.+2f. semipostal of 1950 is probably thereby more accurate as a portrait. The Nasmyth portrait of Robert Burns (now in the Scottish National Portrait Gallery, Edinburgh) is copied in reverse on 40k. Russian stamps of 1956 and 1957 and also on the 1/3d. British stamp of 1966. An East German 20pf. stamp of 1956 shows a mirror image of Thomas Mann (correct on the 20pf. West German stamp of the same year). (figs. 59 & 60). The portrait of Cervantes on a 1949 issue of Ecuador, after a painting in the Rischgitz Collection, is correct on 3s. and 10s. values, reversed on others of the issue. A 5c. 1947 stamp of the Argentine Republic also shows a portrait of Cervantes, reversed from a painting by Juan de Jaurequi (now in the Académie de la Langue, Madrid). The portrait of Descartes on French 90c. stamps of 1937 is a reversal of a Frans Hals portrait in the Louvre. A West German 90pf. stamp of 1974 shows a portrait of Kant, after a copper engraving, but reversed. Emile Gentil's portrait on the Oubangui Chari postage due issue of 1930 and a 1937 issue of French Equatorial Africa is a mirror image of the frontispiece portrait of the 1902 edition of his book *La Chute de l'Empire de Rabah.*

Taking musicians next, the portrait of Chopin on a 1951 issue of Poland is reversed, as is the portrait of Beethoven (after a Klöber drawing of 1818) on a 150f. 1974 stamp of Dahomey and a 60fi. 1960 Hungarian stamp, the same portrait appearing correctly on a West German miniature sheet of 1959. J. S. Bach's portrait (after a painting by Haussmann in 1746) appears reversed on a 12pf. 1935 stamp of Germany and 20pf. 1961 stamps of West Germany and West Berlin, but is correct on a 1969 stamp of Ajman.

A reversed design is not necessarily an error, of course, if an actual portrait is not intended, *e.g.* the farmer planting a mango on Jamaican 1d. and 8d. stamps of 1963, a reversed version of a photograph. The four blacksmiths of the German 60pf. and 80pf. stamps of 1921 are all left-handed, improbable though not impossible, though for all four to work on one anvil is stretching credibility rather far. The miners on the 100pf. and 120pf. stamps of the same issue are likewise all left-handed, though in this case the design was reversed for the 1922-23 issue. The fisherman on the $1 Canadian stamp of 1951 has the buttons of his waterproof fastening on the wrong side—again evidence of a reversed design.

Reversed buildings also occur, *e.g.* Westminster Abbey on a 5r. stamp from Ajman of 1966 to commemorate the death of Sir Winston Churchill (it is shown correctly on the 3d. British stamp of 1966). The Town Hall of Thorn is shown reversed on a 4pf.+3pf. German semipostal of 1940. The Collegiate Church of St. Peter and St. Stephen, Bellinzona, is shown as it was originally (before removal of the bell-tower) but reversed on a 70c. Swiss definitive of 1960, redrawn the correct way round and without the bell-tower on a 2f.80 definitive of 1963. (figs. 61 & 62). Turning to natural features, the 2s. New Zealand stamp of 1898 showing Milford Sound is said to show the whole range of mountains—Mitre Peak, Mount Pembroke and Lion Rock—reversed. The view of El Santuario on 1943 air stamps of Ifni is reversed, also the "Almirante Brown" Base on a 25c. 1972 Argentinian stamp marking the 10th anniversary of the Antarctic Treaty. On a grander scale still, the Southern Cross constellation, shown very compressed on the 300r. Brazilian stamp of 1887 and reasonably accurately on the 1890-91 definitives, is reversed on Newspaper stamps of 1890 and on the 400r.+200r. semipostal of 1939, on the Italian 71.70 1930 stamps marking "Transatlantic Mass Formation Flight", and on a 6e.50 1969 Portuguese stamp marking the 500th birth anniversary of Cabral. On a 5y. Japanese stamp of 1952 marking the 75th anniversary of Japan's membership of the U.P.U. the Southern Cross is shown as a symmetrically cruciform arrangement of four stars, whereas it actually consists of a rather irregular cross formed by five stars.

Turning next to vehicles, the reversal of the Express Service Messenger on the Mexican 20c. Express Delivery stamp of 1919 is indicated by the reversal of the letters ' RM ' on the sidecar, while the Pierce-Arrow truck on the U.S. 20c. Special Delivery stamp of 1925 is possibly reversed, since it wrongly has a right-hand drive on the stamp. Conversely the Brougham of the U.S. 4c. 1901 stamps should have a right-hand drive (not left-hand as on the stamp), as should the 1902 vehicle shown on the U.S. 4c. 1952 stamp marking the 50th anniversary of the American Automobile Industry.

Looking now at other types of error involving vehicles, the Indian motorcycle shown on various U.S. Special Delivery stamps from 1922-25 lacks the spring fork over the front wheel, and the cyclist postman on a 10c. U.S. Express delivery stamp of 1902 has a cycle without brakes. The modern postal bus shown on a 15pf. West German stamp of 1965 shows the doors on the left side, where they should be on the right, while a 40pf. 1973 stamp of West Berlin shows a bus of 1923 with the left front wheel apparently missing (it should be visible from this angle). A 20pf. East German stamp of 1960 shows a Trabant car with the two windscreen wipers in different positions, but in fact they work in parallel.

Railways and railway engines feature frequently on stamps, often remarkably inaccurately. A Yugoslavian 2d. stamp of 1949 shows a class 151 0-6-0T engine of Yugoslavian Railways, but the artist has added two extra wheels at the rear. Stephenson's *Rocket* as featured on a 15d. 1969 stamp of Fujeira is a hybrid between the original locomotive and the rebuilt version with, for instance, the cylindrical chimney of the original type (not bell-mouthed like the rebuilt version), but with the almost horizontal cylinders of the latter in place of the vertical cylinders of the original. A 15c. Jamaican stamp of 1970 shows the engine 54-1944, copied from a photograph but with the airhose at the front apparently misinterpreted as a rigid yoke. The illustration of Trevethick's locomotive on a 50gr. Polish stamp of 1976 has been reversed, so that its mechanisms are on the wrong side. The locomotive featured on a 25ore Swedish stamp of 1956, the *Fryckstad*, was built for 1093mm. gauge and was never used on passenger trains, but nevertheless is here shown coupled to a German-built carriage which was built to standard gauge, and without its heavy sheet-iron cab. The lumber train of the Caile Ferate Forestiere shown on a 55b. Rumanian stamp of 1956 is doubtfully authentic, as the engine lacks the spark arrester essential for forestry work. The first Paraguayan locomotive, featured on 5c. and 20c. Paraguayan stamps of 1944, could not have operated very efficiently, as it lacks connecting rods between cylinders and driving wheel, and has no safety valve. It also features on a 75c. stamp of 1972, here with connecting rods in place but also with both buffers and cowcatcher added, although usually engines with a large cowcatcher dispensed with buffers. The *Prince of Wales*, No. 12 locomotive on the 1c. 1860 stamp of New Brunswick should have 15″×22″ outside cylinders, absent on the stamp. A Czechoslovakian issue of 1956 includes a number of poorly produced locomotives: the 1846 *Zbraslav* locomotive on the 10h. value has the back wheel of the tender missing, there appears to be no coupling rod for the 0-6-4 tank engine on the 30h. value, and the 4-8-4 tank engine on the 60h. value has a coupling rod which appears to connect with the trailing wheel of the bogie. The 1868 steam locomotive featured on a 5c. 1968 Brazilian stamp has the balance weight on the forward driving wheel incorrectly placed, while the locomotive on a 2f.50 1948 stamp of the Belgian Congo apparently has no wheels at all, for the whole of the rail surface is visible! The coupling rod which ought to be visible between the back and forward driving wheels on the locomotive *La Portena* on a 40c. 1957 stamp of the Argentine Republic is missing. A 1963 stamp of the Central African

Republic shows a Renault railcar with too many wheels, and the engine on the 50f. stamp should not have the side buffers which are here allocated to it. A 1971 locomotive issue of Sharjah includes various errors and omissions: the broad-gauge WR train on the 2d. value is running on mixed-gauge track, but the third rail has been suppressed, while the locomotive, an L.N.W.R. standard gauge Crewe-type 2-2-2 is given Caledonian livery! *The Flying Scotsman* on the 3d. value would be something of a lame duck with only a two-cylinder compound 4-4-0 F class locomotive (built in 1887)—not nearly powerful enough to pull a crack express. Furthermore, the train is rounding a left-hand curve, but the rails project in a straight line! Various 1944 10c. Obligatory Tax stamps of Bolivia show a curious 6-6-4 locomotive of a type unknown in Bolivia or indeed anywhere else. The hovertrain *Orleans* 1-80 shown on an 80c. French stamp of 1970 is depicted with eight blades on the turbine, but in reality has only seven.

Designers have sometimes not bothered to refer to photographs or to the actual locomotives themselves but have drawn their designs from models, themselves often simplified. This probably applies to the locomotive on a Chilean set of 1954, shown with a curiously formed and attached connecting rod, and a crosshead not apparently connected to anything. The High Speed Train on a 12p. British stamp of 1975 was likewise drawn from a model, which differed from the prototype in having an extra side window in the driving cab and no buffers. Fujeira's railway issue of 1971 was copied from a children's book on trains (*The story of Railways* in the Ladybird series), and incorporating numerous inaccuracies: the Surrey Iron Railway of 1801 (10d. value) had plate rails and plain wheels, not flanged as here, the tender of the *Rocket* on the 20d. value is back to front, the *Puffing Billy* (70d. value) has the water tank wrongly proportioned, and the perspective of coaches on 2r. and 3r. values has gone astray.

Electric trains on stamps have their own brands of error. The locomotive on a 25l. Italian stamp of 1970 has a single pantograph instead of the two which this type should have, and overhead feeder power lines are absent. On a 3s. Austrian stamp of 1962 the overhead wire has no catenary and no supports. A 1z.50 Polish stamp of 1976 shows an ET22 locomotive with both pantographs making contact with the overhead feeder power line. In the same way the power unit on the electric train shown on a 4c. 1973 South African stamp would only have one overhead pantograph up at a time and would not have any on main-line railway carriages. The Japanese 10y. stamp of 1962 marking the opening of Hokuriku Railway Tunnel just about establishes a record for the number of distinct errors on a single stamp: it shows old-fashioned power line brackets instead of the modern triangular brackets used for this tunnel, shows lights lined along the tunnel ceiling instead of on the sides, and has tracks with conventional sleepers, whereas in this tunnel the tracks lie in a concrete bed with intervening drain. No entrance is shown to the motorman's compartment, and in any case on this service a special high-efficiency electric locomotive is used, not a diesel engine such as is shown here. The Italian 25l. stamp of 1956 marking the 50th anniversary of the opening of the Simplon Tunnel is almost as bad. It shows a coach and horses (plagiarised from a painting by Rudolf Koller of ' The Gotthard Post ') on a road next to the tunnel mouth where no such road exists. The two tunnels are depicted, with two railway lines, but only a single railway line existed until 1921, while the route has been electrically operated from its inception, so that the steam engine puffing its way out of one of the tunnels on the stamp is ludicrously out of place. The trams shown in Collins Street, Melbourne, on an Australian 1s. stamp of 1956 have no overhead wires, which seems unlikely.

Track is often drawn in very cursorily. The Russian locomotive on a 1fo. Hungarian stamp of 1972 seems precariously balanced on a single rail with no ties, not extending beyond the locomotive itself. The train on 7c. and 15c. stamps of the Mozambique Company issued from 1918-34 is passing over rails which do not appear to be tied in any way, while the track arrangement ahead of the locomotive on a 45g.+20g. Austrian semipostal of 1948 would certainly lead to its derailment. Finally, in this section, a Swiss 10c.+10c. semipostal of 1947 shows Rorschach Railway Station, but the view is in fact obscured by a large goods shed which the artist has omitted altogether.

In reduction of designs to fit the small format of most stamps, omission of a vital part can easily occur. On the 5½d. Australian stamp marking the centennial of Newcastle in 1947, an essential jibstay is missing from both second and farthest coal carrier cranes, and both would collapse without it. On the 1½d. South African stamps of 1933-48 showing a goldmine, the winding rope has been omitted, and the engine room is on the wrong side of the headgear. Chilean 3p. stamps of 1941 show a telegraph post with four wires but only three insulators. The 3c. Swiss definitive of 1949 shows high tension pylons on either side of a river, four in all: each should be carrying six functional main wires and one additional protective main, so that 14 wires should be crossing the river, not just 11 as figured. Another missing wire is the support for the lamps on the 25f. French stamps of 1947-48 featuring Stanislas Place, Nancy. The 30c. and 5s. 1935 stamps of Kenya, Uganda and Tanganyika show the Jinja road and rail bridge by Ripon Falls, but with the road bridge unconnected to the bank on the left side. This was corrected on the corresponding 1938-54 stamps of King George VI (figs. 63 & 64). Engravers of ship designs very often merely sketch in rigging, leaving ropes suspended in mid-air. Examples of this can be found on ship stamps of Aden (35c., 1953), Falkland Islands Dependencies (set, 1954), Gambia (3d., 1953), Tonga (2d., 1953) and Turks and Caicos Islands (2s. 1957), although the best-known case is probably that of the dhow on the 5c. and 50c. 1935 stamps of Kenya, Uganda and Tanganyika, where the backstay did not reach the mast. This was corrected (rather clumsily) late in the life of the King George V issue for the 5c. and on all but stamp No. 15 for the King George VI 50c. plate (speedily corrected on a new plate). The guy ropes of the boom are missing from the sailing ship on the 1949 issue of British Honduras marking the 150th anniversary of the Battle of St. George's Cay, also from the Cayman schooner on the 1966 Cayman Islands issue marking the opening of the Cayman jet service. The trapeze wire is missing from the ' Fireball ' Class yacht on a 5c. 1969 stamp of Papua New Guinea which commemorates the Third South Pacific Games. It also lacks both rudder and tiller, while the crew are perilously perched on the side of the yacht—they should be either properly aboard or out on the trapeze. On the 1m. Finnish stamp of 1929 marking the 700th anniversary of Turku, the S.S. *Bore* is shown with wireless spreaders but no aerial.

A more complex error is that of the British 2½d. Victory stamp of 1946, on which a ship is shown with two hawse pipes for anchors near the bow on the port side, for though a large ship could have three anchors in the bows, the third (sheet) anchor should be just abaft the starboard bow anchor. It is possible, of course, that this is yet another case of a reversed design. The well-known key type for German colonies featuring the Kaiser's steam yacht *Hohenzollern* has seven davits for three lifeboats on the small design, but correctly six on the larger design of the high values. A ship-connected error which might be included here occurs on a $1 Canadian stamp of 1963 honouring the Export Trade, which shows a crate being loaded, but with the rope round the crate to the left doubled over the hook—and therefore not supported from it at all. Stamps of British Guiana of 1889-1910 issues show a sailing ship flying a flag from the halyards, but the redrawn design of the 1910 2c. value has it more properly flying from the main truck. The stern flag shown on the foreground ship of an 11c. 1964 I.M.C.O. commemorative stamp of the United Nations is missing on the 5c. value, although the designer claimed he had included it in both designs.

Ships in full sail with no apparent crew are not uncommon on stamps, *e.g.* the inter-colonial schooner on an 8c. 1950 stamp of Barbados, the sloop on a 5c. 1949 stamp of British Honduras, the Armed Vessel *Bounty* on a 6d. 1940 stamp of Pitcairn Islands and the native canoe on the 1½d. 1938 definitive of Fiji. This last is an interesting case, for on the original design (now in the Crown Agent's archives) the canoe held two natives, but these were omitted (perhaps to conform with the empty canoe in full sail on the Fijian crest). Nevertheless, following strong public criticism, a redesigned 1½d. value with a single native in the canoe was produced in 1940. The 1960 20c. stamp of Johore shows a fishing craft with no helmsman, although he is present for the corresponding value for the other Malay States. An Estonian issue of 1919 shows a Viking longship with billowing square sail but no mast! It is also historically somewhat inaccurate, for Viking longships appear to have been ' double-ended ', with bow and stern very similar, while this vessel has bow and stern very different—indeed more like a Roman galley. The Bullom canoe shown on a 5d. 1933 stamp of Sierra Leone also has an unsupported sail—it is depicted more accurately on a 1s. stamp of 1956. The outrigger of the sailing canoe on the ½d. 1938 definitive of Fiji is shown as blunt-ended, but in practice this would always be pointed to reduce wave resistance. The fishing village scene on 3d. and 2s. 1945 definitives of Nyasaland includes a native supposed to be resting his punting pole across the boat, but instead he has been given a double-ended Canadian-type canoe paddle—a type quite unknown in Nyasaland. The destroyer on a $1 1942 Canadian definitive has billowing black smoke pouring from the funnel far in excess of what such a ship should produce under proper control—smoke for a smokescreen does not emanate from the funnel in this manner!

The freighter depicted on a 3f. 1964 stamp of Luxemburg marking the inauguration of the Moselle Canal is about to run into serious trouble, for the bow wave shows that it is proceeding upstream to enter the sluice on the Grevenmach Lock, which is not open! The tugboat going upstream on the Rhine past Caub on 84pf. 1947 stamps of the Rhineland-Palatinate is breaking regulations by being on the left side instead of the right. The steamship and mail tender design of the 10c. 1912 Parcel Post stamp of the U.S.A. includes several errors, for the lower Manhattan skyline appears to have been put onto Staten Island and the ship must be heading directly for the Gowanus shore of Brooklyn, while if it is intended to be leaving New York a mailtender (which only met incoming ships) would not be in attendance. In fact the ship was copied from a postcard showing the arrival of the *Kronprinz Wilhelm* on her maiden voyage (23rd Feb., 1902), with the misleading Manhattan skyline added.

Turning to historical inaccuracies on ship design stamps, we may start with H.M.S. *Royalist*, shown on a 3c. 1967 stamp of the Gilbert and Ellice Islands as having eight gunports on the starboard side and a tall thin funnel, for an extant photograph (in the Mitchell Library, Sydney) clearly shows only five gunports and a low squat funnel. The Chandos Line steamship *Queen Frederika* is shown on a 6d. 1967 Greek stamp, but not in Chandos Line colours. The passenger and freight steamer S.S. *W. A. Scholten* is shown on a 30c.+10c. 1973 semipostal of the Netherlands with a sharp-pointed bow and a jib, but a poster of 1889 for the Holland-America Line shows clearly that the original ship did not have a sharply raked bow. The 5d. 1946 New Zealand stamp in the Peace issue shows the S.S. *Dominion Monarch* (on the right) with smoke pouring out of both funnels —unlikely, since the after one was a dummy! (fig. 65). A 2d. 1959 stamp also of New Zealand purports to show the careening of H.M. Bark *Endeavour* at Ship Cove, but has a full-rigged ship instead of a barque. The 15th century Mediterranean carrack on a 1z.15 1963 Polish stamp is shown with only three sails in place of the proper five, lacking the fore and mainmast topsails. The P. & O. Line M.S. *Chusan* on a 50c. 1955 stamp of Singapore has had its stern mast removed to make space for the Queen's head. A 1972 75c. stamp also of Singapore shows the *Maria Hickmers*, the first five-masted sailing ship to have an engine, but it had spars only on the first four masts, though being fully rigged on all five masts on the stamp.

The 1½d. South African stamp of 1949 marking the arrival of British settlers in Natal in 1849 shows the brig *Wanderer* which brought them—but by adding a third mast converts it into a barque. Furthermore the beacon shown on top of Durban Bluff must, in proportion to the Bluff, be at least 600 ft. high—quite an achievement for 1849! The 90-gun warship shown on a Danish issue of 1951 marking the 250th anniversary of the Naval Officers' College is out of place, for Denmark had no such warship in its navy in 1701. A 2c. 1909 stamp of the U.S.A. shows Fulton's steamboat on the Hudson River flying a pennant proclaiming it to be the *Clermont*. In fact, however, it was registered as simply the North River Steamboat *of Claremont*, and bore no name. Furthermore it is shown with a geared drive between engine and paddle wheels, whereas it should probably have been depicted with a direct drive, as on the 5c. 1965 stamp of the U.S.A. marking the bicentenary of Fulton's birth. A 3c. 1957 stamp also of the U.S.A. marking an international naval review shows the aircraft carrier *Forrestal* with deck number "88", which could not be correct.

Two cases which have been erroneously cited as design errors may be mentioned here. The Canadian 6c. air stamp of 1938 is labelled in various catalogues as showing a seaplane over S.S. *Discoverer* on the Mackenzie River, and it has been claimed that the stacked wood for fuel shown on the stamp is a mistake, as this ship was oil-fired. However the catalogues are wrong, for this ship is the *Distributor* (3rd), based on a 1932 photograph, and was not converted to an oil-burner until 1945. A 1947 3c. stamp of the U.S.A. features ' Old Ironsides ', the U.S. Frigate *Constitution,* and careful inspection reveals that the two flanking cannons bear the Royal Cypher ' GR ' beneath a Crown. This is NOT an error, as they were faithfully drawn according to Navy Department records of the 24-pounders originally mounted in the ship.

Aeroplanes also feature largely on stamps, particularly of course on air mail issues. The United States, anxious not to advertise any particular make of 'plane at the expense of others, produced a composite type on its air issue of 1941-44 which not only never existed but would never have flown. This also appears to apply to the aeroplane on the Chinese air mail issue of 1921 in which the undercarriage struts come from the leading edge of the wing, the upper wing has no connection with the fuselage and the propeller is at an impossible angle to the fuselage. The Fokker 'plane on the Cuban 1931 air stamps and the *Hercules* on the Indian 1929 air stamps both have disproportionately long fuselages, while the Liechtenstein air set of 1930 shows a fantastic aircraft with crenellated tailplane which certainly could never have flown. The Dornier flying boat on the Chilean 20p. and 30p. stamps of 1934 is even less airworthy, for it lacks propellers to its engines, as does the aeroplane on a German 40pf. stamp of 1919 and also the anonymous aeroplane on the 1949 Saudi Arabian air issue, while the Caudron Simoun aeroplane of the French air issue of February, 1936, lacks the tail fin though the July issue shows it correctly. An interesting case is that of the 3d. 1946 Peace stamp of New Zealand, for here the tail fin of the Short Sunderland is incomplete except for the retouched second stamp of the third row. The Santos Dumont ' grasshopper ' monoplane of 1909 shown on the 4f. Postage Due stamp of 1953 of Monaco and a 60l. 1962 San Marinese stamp in each case is wrongly given a tail wheel—a misinterpretation of a small flaw on the photograph copied in each case; in fact the real 'plane had only a tail skid. However the aeroplane flying over Santiago on 10c., 15c. and 20c. 1935 stamps of Chile should have a tail wheel but does not. 5f. and 10f. 1942 air stamps of Monaco feature a Caudron C530 Rafale aircraft, but from this angle the undercarriage should be visible. In the 1964 issue of Monaco to mark the 50th anniversary of the First Aerial Rally, Monte Carlo, the 2c. value shows Renaux's Farman with wheeled undercarriage, but for the final (maritime) lap of the race to Monaco floats were fitted. On the other hand a 12pf.+8pf. German semipostal of 1944 shows a Dornier Do.26 flying boat but wrongly adds seaplane floats—possibly from a misinterpretation of a shadow on a photograph. A 25p. 1973 stamp of British Antarctic Territory shows Hubert Wilkins' 'plane *San Francisco*, but wrongly gives it square-tipped wings of a type which did not come into use until World War II.

A 5s. 1968 Austrian stamp features a Douglas DC-8. It is doubtful, however, if Austria used DC-8s at that time, and although the 'plane has Austrian tail markings it has three lines around the nose (Italian markings) instead of the single (red) line of Austria, while the wing marking is A8021 but for Austria should commence with CE. A 5c. 1970 stamp of Papua and New Guinea shows a Fokker F27 Friendship in ANSETT livery, but the tail insignia is reversed (the smaller triangle of the two forming the central arrowhead should be to the left, not to the right as here). The 16c. and 17c. Canadian air mail stamps of 1942-43 feature a Lodestar, but the registration number shown here (CF-BAF) was never assigned to a Lodestar. The lettering on tail and fuselage of the Spad S33 biplane on a Rumanian issue of 1928 is not, as it should be, that of country and airline, but the name of the pilot Capt. A. G. Craiu.

A 1946 Czechoslovakian issue features aircraft captain Major F. Novák with a Westland-Lysander aircraft in the background, a slow reconnaissance 'plane quite inappropriate for this famous stunt and fighter pilot, for whom a Spitfire or Hurricane would have been more suitable. An 8p. 1974 stamp of the Falkland Islands commemorates the first U.K. aerial post, 1911, featuring a Farman biplane in flight with a Bleriot monoplane on the ground, but in fact the first mail was carried by a Bleriot, and the Farman did not participate until two days later. A 3c. stamp of the U.S.A. issued in 1945 honouring the army shows the Keystone Division marching through Paris after the liberation in 1944, with six B-29 aircraft flying overhead, but this type of aircraft was never used in the European theatre of operations, and was in any case much too large to be used for such low flying over marching men.

Taking lighter-than-air aircraft next, a 15-75s. Latvian air charity stamp of 1932 purports to show Charlière's Balloon, but includes an attached parachute, which he did not have. The 350f. 1977 stamp of Mali portraying the burning of the ill-fated zeppelin *Hindenburg* shows it coming down nose first, with fire at the rear (well clear of the gondola): in fact the *Hindenburg* came down tail first, the flames sweeping up through the nose and enveloping the gondola with its unfortunate occupants, as shown by photographs of the event (fig. 66). In the same issue the 120f. shows the LZ1, but with a number of extraneous attachments which the original airship did not have, and lacking the wire along which weights were slid to balance the dirigible. The hangar was a single large floating shed on Lake Constance, not cluttered with small buildings as shown on the stamp. The zeppelin commemoratives issued by the Niger Republic in 1977 include several design errors. The *Hindenburg* (40f.) is too spindle-shaped, too short in proportion to diameter, and the observation gondola is not near enough to the nose, while the 150f. value shows a remarkably hilly Friedrichshaven in the background—it is mainly flat with a small hill close to the promontory. Similarly, on the 50f. value the zeppelin is NOT over Würzburg—the River Main is much narrower and Würzburg lies on both banks, while the Marienburg is missing. The 100f. value of a 1977 issue of Chad goes even further in this respect, providing Friedrichshaven with an unmerited background of mountains. The 125f. value of this issue of Chad marks the zeppelin flight of 1931, showing Esquimaux (not encountered on the flight) with skis (which they do not use). The *Graf Zeppelin* depicted on a 200f. 1977 stamp of the

Congo (Brazzaville) and also on a 500f. miniature sheet should have the name painted on the fuselage in black, not red as here, and the *Graf Zeppelin II* shown on the 200f. value of this issue had swastikas prominently displayed on the tailfins—absent here.

The technicalities of the Space Age often defeat stamp designers. For instance the 1fo. and 3fo. values of the 1962 Hungarian set marking the Astronautical Congress, Paris of that year, show escape towers still attached to capsules while in flight over the Earth, and the same applies to the Mercury capsule shown on an 80h. Czechoslovakian stamp of 1964 and the 50p. and 100p. 1962 stamps of Afghanistan marking World Meteorology Day. A 12x. 1966 North Vietnamese stamp and a 1l.60 Rumanian stamp of 1966 show Luna 9 apparently circling the Moon, but with panels outspread as they would be only following landing. It is shown correctly on a 2fo. Hungarian stamp of 1966. The 5l. value of this Rumanian issue shows the launching of Gemini 6 and 7, but in such a way that they appear to have been launched from Texas instead of Florida.

A 1d. 1970 stamp of Ajman purports to show the launching of Gemini 4, but in fact features an Atlas rocket with warhead, while 3n.p. and 50n.p. 1965 stamps of Sharjah claiming to show the launching of Telstar satellites replace the Thor Delta rocket actually used by a much more powerful Atlas-Agena. A 1966 space issue of Fujeira shows Pioneer 5 and Explorer 8 near the Moon, whereas one went to Venus and the other was put on Earth orbit. The 200f. 1965 Guinea stamp featuring the launching of Ranger 7 wrongly shows a Saturn 5 rocket as the launch vehicle instead of the Atlas-Agena actually used. In the Hungarian 1966 set commemorating twin space flights the 20fi. shows Vostok 3 and Vostok 4 side by side, whereas their nearest approach was 11 kilometres; on the 1fo. the target vehicle is shown as an Agena instead of an ADTA Angry Alligator, while the 1fo.50 shows the exterior hatch opening directly into the interior instead of into an airlock, as it did. A 3f. Jordanian stamp of 1966 shows Borman and Gemini 7, but Borman did not rendezvous with Gemini 7 as shown here.

The Copernican planetary system featured on a 40pf. West German commemorative of 1973 is sadly awry, for Mercury is missing from its orbit, Earth and Venus are on the same orbit and the orbits of Jupiter and Saturn are also incorrect. A 10c. 1975 stamp of the U.S.A. commemorating the Pioneer-Jupiter space probe shows Jupiter with its Red Spot in the upper part, but since this well-known feature is in Jupiter's Southern Tropical Zone, which should conventionally be depicted towards the bottom, Jupiter is technically inverted here. Similarly on the 20pf. East German stamp of 1959 marking the landing of a Russian probe on the Moon, the Moon map is upside-down, the time when the rocket's pay-load (small metal plates bearing the Soviet emblem and date) reached the Moon's surface is given precisely as "$22^h02^m24^s$ UHR MEZ", but as the "h" denotes ' hours ' the "UHR" (hour) is superfluous. Finally, the Moon is shown two days after full moon, but should have been depicted as two days before full moon (fig. 67). The flight of Lunik III, which first photographed the back of the Moon, is depicted on a 20l. Albanian stamp of 1962 and a 1l.25 Bulgarian stamp of 1960, but in each case the back of the Moon is shown fancifully, not as revealed by the probe's cameras. The orbits of Lunik III are represented quite incorrectly on stamps of Poland (1964, 60gr.), Rumania (1959, 11.75) and even Russia itself (1959, 40k.). The 40fi. 1969 Hungarian stamp illustrating Jules Verne's story *Flight to the Moon* shows the manned projectile over the Moon with a trail behind it as if rocket-propelled, but in the story it is fired from a cannon and is not self-propelled. A 6c. 1969 stamp of the U.S.A. marks the Apollo 8 Moon Landing, which was near the Moon's equator, but the angle of shadow of the Earth as depicted would imply that the landing had been close to the Moon's North Pole. Two Russian stamps (16k., 1967 and 4k., 1967) show Earth as seen from space, but highly unrealistically, with all land masses clearly contoured and not a cloud in sight! This also applies to a Chinese 8f. stamp of 1958 showing Sputnik 3 circling the Earth, and a Rumanian 1l. stamp of 1971. A 35c. 1973 stamp of the Gilbert & Ellice Islands features the constellation Orion but omits the three stars which form the sword. A 1977 Libyan miniature sheet shows the eight planets on their orbits, but the Earth and its moon are wrongly shown on the second instead of the third orbit.

Designers do often deliberately simplify or distort a scene for artistic reasons, and it is a matter of opinion how far such artistic licence is allowable. The 1946 British colonial Victory issue (of Aden, for example) portrayed the Houses of Parliament from across the river, but omitted the portion of Westminster Bridge which should be visible between the medallion and the right border, as shown on the British 1963 aerogramme depicting the same scene. A 65c. French stamp of 1961 shows Dinan, but the design is a condensed picture of a much wider view, the bridge is re-aligned across the river and most of the lower town has been completely omitted. An 80pf. 1921 stamp of the Saar illustrates the Alte Brücke (Old Bridge), Saarbrücken, but (perhaps diplomatically) omits the Kaiser Wilhelm Memorial. A Swiss semipostal 40c.+10c. of 1955 features Lake Bienne, but on the stamp the tip of the spire of Ligery church shows above St. Peter's Island, and from this angle nothing of the lake ought to be visible beyond the island. A 1c. 1935 stamp of Trinidad and Tobago shows First Boca, but from this position another island should also be visible. Various issues for the Turks and Caicos Islands from 1900 onwards show salt-raking (the principal industry is salt production) in progress, with a sailing ship alongside the shore, to which a gangplank is extended: in fact there was no place on the islands where a ship of this size could have come so close to the shore. The Acadian Memorial Church shown on a 50c. Canadian stamp of 1930 should have two chimneys, one at each side of the steeple, but only one appears in the stamp. The Memorial to the Fathers of the Convention, Charlottetown, has had liberties taken with it on a 5c. Canadian stamp of 1964—for instance the doors shown to the right (above 'NA' of "CANADA") should be in the centre under the triangular glass-domed roof, and the entrance to this part should be much wider than illustrated.

A Swiss 10c.+10c. semipostal of 1939 shows a much simplified and distorted view of Laupen Castle, making it look much more romantic and impressive than it really is, while the two unequal steeples of St. Peter's Cathedral, Geneva, have been transposed by the designer of a 40c. Swiss stamp of 1960. A 40pf.+20pf. East German semipostal of 1959 features Leipzig Stadium with a large tower in the stadium, apparently blocking the public's view; in actuality this tower is outside the stadium. The roof of the Kultur Palast, Dresden, featured on an East German 10pf. stamp of 1969, has a rugged outer rim which on the stamp is drawn as flat, while the castle tower in the background has been moved. The high values of the 1948 issue for the British and American zones in Germany feature the Holstentor at Lübeck with two straight towers instead of them leaning towards each other as they do. The 70pf. 1966 stamp of West Berlin illustrating the Technical University, Charlottenburg, has a storey missing above the annexe to the left. Tegel Castle, shown on 15pf. and 1m.30 1965 stamps of West Berlin and West Germany has pointed ornaments on top which were omitted on the stamps to leave room for the inscription. The television tower on the left of the 40pf. 1973 West German stamp honouring Hamburg is shown with only five platforms for the parabolic antennae, but in fact has six. A 70l. Greek stamp of 1961 shows the Parthenon, Athens, with only seven pillars in the front—there should be eight, as shown, ironically enough, on a Russian 40k. stamp of 1959 honouring the Greek communist editor Maniolis Glezos. On a 35a. Israeli stamp of 1970 showing the 'Portuguese Synagogue', Amsterdam, the low buildings in the front have been greatly shortened on the left side to fit into the framewoık of the design. The turrets shown on the two square towers of Lisbon Cathedral on a 40c. Portuguese stamp of 1931 were not there at the date of issue of this stamp.

A Russian 7k. stamp of 1925 shows an orator haranguing the crowd from the base of a lamp-post in the 1905 rebellion, but Russian lamp-posts of that period did not have such projecting bases. Another Russian stamp, a 5k. of 1932, features the storming of the Winter Palace, Petrograd, but the inner archway shown has much broader supporting columns than the real one, and the trumpeting angels depicted on the spandrels belong to the courtyard face of the arch, not the outer one. A 5c. 1963 stamp of the U.S.A. shows the White House, but completely omits a large magnolia tree which stands to the left front of the White House, as shown on a 3c. 1950 stamp marking the sesquicentennial of the National Capital. Conversely the palm trees in the background of scenes on ½d., 1½d., 2/6d. and 5s. 1953 stamps of Nigeria are disproportionately huge. A 5c. South African stamp of 1974 marking the restoration of Church Street, Tulbagh, shows a row of houses with a central staircase appearing to lead to a blank wall below a window: however this is NOT an error, for the staircase actually leads to a raised sidewalk which is not visible from this angle, although the view appears to be composite rather than actual.

The Australian 1936 issue marking the centennial of South Australia shows King William Street and the General Post Office, Adelaide, with a man riding a bicycle on the right side of the street instead of on the left—a very clearly printed stamp is necessary for this to be made out. It has been claimed that the 25c. Swiss stamp of 1949 which shows the Melide Causeway at Lake Lugano wrongly features four arches where there are but three (*G.S.M.* November, 1954: p. 36), but there are indeed four arches, though from some angles the fourth is hidden by a promontory. On the other hand the French 20f. stamp of 1929 featuring the Pont du Gard over the River Gardon near Nîmes shows 17 rather small flattened upper arches where there should be 24 semi-circular arches.

POST CARD.
THE ADDRESS ONLY TO BE WRITTEN ON THIS SIDE OF THE CARD.
For the UNITED KINGDOM, by the long Sea Route.
JUBILEE STAMP
2
2
1838
1888
IN COMMEMORATION OF THE FIFTIETH YEAR OF THE ISSUE OF POSTAGE STAMPS IN THE COLONY.
DESIGN OF THE FIRST POSTAGE STAMP
GENERAL POST OFFICE SYDNEY NEW SOUTH WALES
TWO PENCE.

Errors sometimes creep in where models are portrayed which differ from the actual building or other construction—often because lack of money has meant curtailment of plans. Thus the tower shown on the basilica of Chèvremont Basilica and Convent as featured on a 1f.35+1f.35 1948 Belgian semipostal has still not been built; nor has the 550ft. tower and retractable roof for the Olympic stadium shown on a Canadian $2 stamp of 1976 (as the original estimated cost of these was $2,000,000 they seem unlikely ever to materialise). The 1954 Belgian issue featuring the King Albert Memorial was apparently designed from a model, for the actual statue shows considerable differences in the positioning of the sword and the horse's tail, while the 2f. and 4f. designs differ sharply between themselves *re* sword, reins and horse's tail. The Belgian semipostal issue of 1938 to support the completion fund for the Koekelberg Basilica showed the building as planned, with a dome not present at the date of issue.

Statues are often rendered rather inaccurately in stamp designs. The 60c.+10c. 1947 semipostal of Luxemburg showing the statue of Abbot Engels has the wall behind smooth-surfaced, whereas it is of hewn stone blocks with very distinct lines of juncture. The 1928 18pi. Cypriot stamp showing the statue of Richard I which stands before the Palace of Westminster has the inscription "COEUR DE LION" on the right hand side of the plinth, but the actual inscription is much fuller and very different. The positioning of the Fountain of Neptune on a 1929 issue of Danzig has been slightly changed in relation to the Artushof behind, the windows of which have been much simplified, but this appears within reasonable bounds of artistic licence. The Peter Pan statue in Kensington Gardens has been simplified on the New Zealand Health stamps of 1945 with, for instance, the omission of the fairy head which occupies the angle between Peter Pan's left foot and the base. Many issues show the lost statue of the discus-thrower (Discobolus) by Myron, drawn from restored copies. Several, for instance a Greek 5l. stamp of 1896 and a Peruvian issue of 1968, show the head looking forward, whereas according to Lucian the original had the head looking back towards the hand holding the discus. A better restoration is shown on a 1920 5c.+5c. semipostal of Belgium. The 1867 Egyptian stamps featuring the Sphinx and a pyramid do not appear to have them in correct positions relative to each other. A 1933 airmail issue shows the Sphinx and the three large pyramids, but omits the three smaller pyramids in front of the Great Pyramid and the three to the side of the third large pyramid. The French stamps of 1936 showing the Canadian War Memorial, Vimy, have the mourning figure of Canada moved to the left—it should be in front of the right pylon looking down at the tomb of the Unknown Warrior below. The Canadian 2c. stamp of 1939 showing the National War Memorial has the shadow inside the arch inconsistent with the shaded front (south) and the sunlit west side: the Memorial itself is in error in showing a kilted machine-gunner, as the Machine Gun Corps of World War I wore slacks and puttees. A 25l. Italian stamp of 1952 shows the Lion of St. Mark, Venice, but from this angle both wings should show, not just one as on the stamp. The Colossus of Rhodes appears on several 1947/50 Greek stamps with legs apart astride the harbour mouth, but modern historians think the statue had its legs together.

The clock on the tower of the Vecchi Palace, Florence, on a 70l. 1961 Italian stamp is shown with two hands but has only one, a large hand with arrow-head pointer. The clock on the Peace Tower of the Parliament buildings, Ottawa, is shown on the Inter-Parliamentary Conference Canadian stamp of 1965 with a figure IV on its dial, where in fact it has IIII. There are two VIIs and no VIII shown, and the figures read outwards on the stamp but inwards on the clock face itself. A 60gr. Polish stamp of 1963 features a painting *A Love Letter* by Czachorsky, and includes a clock with XII on its dial where XI should be, but this is true also of the original painting.

There are numerous cases in which design errors are present in a work of art faithfully copied by the stamp designer, who can therefore hardly be at fault. The painter David portrayed Napoleon crossing the St. Bernard Pass on a spirited white charger, although he actually travelled more safely but with less panache on a mule. This painting is copied on numerous issues, *e.g.* Grenada (1971, 35c.), Cameroun (1969, 1000f.), Rwanda (1969, 20c.), St. Helena (1971, 2p.) and Upper Volta (1969, 50c.). David also painted *The Coronation of Napoleon,* including Napoleon's mother as present, although she was not. This painting appears on stamps of Cameroun (1969, 30f.), France (1973, 1f.) and Liberia (1970, 50c. Miniature sheet). Canadian stamps of 1917 (3c.) and 1927 (2c.) show the painting *The Fathers of Confederation* by Robert Harris. In this the light is coming through arched windows (which is wrong, as the Conference Room did not have arched windows) behind the Fathers, yet their faces are clearly seen. Furthermore, most of the Fathers are portrayed as they appeared in later life, not as at the time of the Confederation meetings. Note, incidentally, that eight of the Fathers were omitted from the 1917 design; one at the left and seven at the right.

Stamp designers do sometimes amend works of art which they are reproducing. The self-portrait by Van Gogh (in the Louvre) shown on a 200f. 1968 stamp of the Niger Republic should have a deep mignonette background, not blue as on the stamp. The pen and ink sketches by Cook's companions shown in a 1968 issue of the Cook Islands have been reproduced in full colour by the designer (J. Berry). The two paintings 'Adam' and 'Eve' by Lukas Cranach (Uffizi Gallery, Florence) are joined together to form a single painting on a 10g. Paraguayan stamp of 1973, while El Greco's *The Holy Trinity* has been reduced to a duo on a 2p.50 Spanish stamp of 1961 which omits the Dove representing the Holy Ghost. An interesting near-error occurred in the preparation of an Israeli I£1 stamp of 1970 illustrating Anski's play *The Dybbuk*. A Dybbuk is traditionally an evil spirit which takes possession of a person, hence the stamp designer initially portrayed the possessed bride with an evil expression (as shown on the relevant Philatelic brochure), but the Dybbuk in this play is not an evil spirit so the bride's features were altered appropriately for the stamp as issued.

An interesting type of error involved the Sirmoor 1p. stamp of 1892. The stamps of 1879-80 had a design with small sprigs at top and bottom, but an early catalogue illustration left the lower sprig out. A dealer asking for the earlier stamps in 1891 was told that if he ordered enough they would be printed for him. He ordered 50 rupees' worth (to be cancelled) and sent the printers the catalogue illustration, which they faithfully copied, perforations and all! The stamps not required by dealers and collectors were put into postal use, so this is an unorthodox but legitimate issue. About the same date (1893-1902) stamps with printed perforations were issued for Djibouti and Obock, and we wonder if there is another story behind these. The stamp centenary issue of Antigua (1962) features the 6d. stamp of 1862, but inadvertently the illustration was prepared from a photograph illustrating the Iremonger's No. 70 re-entry. While the engraver did not reproduce the most obvious faults several are clearly there on the illustrated stamp, *e.g.* the elongated dot below the ' U ' of "ANTIGUA". The modern issue stamp featured on the 1942 Bolivian issue marking the First Students' Philatelic Exhibition should be perforated 13½, but is shown much more finely perforated than that. On the other hand the 1k. 1967 Czechoslovakian stamp marking Stamp Day has the perforations of the central and right-hand stamps depicted with far too wide a gauge. The 25c. 1960 stamp of Monaco commemorating the 75th anniversary of Monaco's first postage stamp features on the left a 20c. Sardinian stamp of 1860, but with "BOLLO" printed from bottom to top instead of from top to bottom as on the original. The Communist republic of Hungary commemorated the 80th anniversary of the first Hungarian stamp with a 1951 issue, getting round the problem of having to portray a portrait of King Francis Joseph I by substituting a mock first-day cancellation and obliterating the monarchist coat-of-arms and crown of St. Stephen of the design by superimposing modern arms and a laurel twig. However the mock cancellation gave year, month and day in that order (modern Hungarian style) whereas all contemporary cancellers gave day, month and year in that order (German style) (fig. 68). Several designs purporting to show postmarked postal material bear similarly fictitious postmarks, *e.g.* the Cuban Stamp Day issue of 1961 and the 1956 issue of Jordan marking the First Arab Postal Congress.

A rather peripheral category of error is that in which the colours used for stamps or for overprints have proved unsuitable and have had to be changed—a surprisingly large category of which we can include only a few representative examples. The long New Zealand Arms issue of 1931-39 included several different values of the same or similar colour, and in 1939 a clerk mixed up his stock of 35s. and 1/3d. values, both orange-yellow—a costly mistake. The 35s. value was withdrawn and surcharged with its value in black, and various new values issued at this time had their values repeated as a black surcharge, to avoid further errors of this kind. A black 10c. stamp of New Caledonia was overprinted in 1903—in black—to mark the 50th anniversary of French annexation. Not surprisingly the overprint was practically invisible, so the black overprint was itself overprinted in gold, while later printings carried a scarlet overprint. The first stamp of all, the 1840 1d. black of Great Britain, might also be placed in this category, for cancellations were not always easy to see, so the Post Office, ever fearful that lightly cancelled stamps might be re-used, changed the colour to red-brown the following year.

Sport has produced many errors of design. The 150f. 1971 airmail stamp of Mali purporting to show the Epsom Derby, a flat race, in fact features a steeplechase (fig. 69), while the yacht shown on the 200f. value would surely have its spinnaker hoisted if competing for the America Cup under the conditions shown. The gentleman engaged in a game of bowls on a 7c. Australian stamp of 1974 would NOT have heels on his shoes, for bowling shoes are without heels to avoid damaging the turf of the bowling green. The runner on a 3c. 1963 Nicaraguan stamp improperly has spikes on the heels of his running shoes.

The 15c. value of this same issue shows a racing cycle with no spokes to the wheel and no footrest to the pedal, while a 15z. Polish stamp of 1948 marking the Warsaw-Prague Cycle Race has spokes missing from the wheel. There are no spokes to the cycle wheels on a 40c. 1949 stamp of Nicaragua (rather incongruously marking the 10th World Amateur Baseball Championships), and they are also missing on a 1l. Bulgarian stamp of 1960 marking the Tour of Bulgaria Cycle Race, though here their absence could reasonably be held to represent motion of the wheel.

A Rumanian 11l. stamp of 1950 shows runners all bunched in the middle of the track, instead of in separate lanes or on the inside lane as they would be in an actual race. A Polish 5z. stamp of 1966 shows a long distance race, but the arm movements of second and last runners are clearly quite inappropriate to such a race. A 20pf.+5pf. East German semipostal of 1970 shows hurdlers, the second from the front quite wrongly with both arms forward, while the runner on the right must have both arms back and hurdlers on a 20f. 1962 stamp of the Central African Republic also have faulty arm positions. Similarly on the 80h. Czechoslovakian stamp of 1956 featuring a marathon race, it is clear that the second runner from the left is in fact sprinting. The baton exchange is shown very peculiarly in the race featured on a 2cr.50 1956 Brazilian stamp, and it is difficult to decide whether a sprint or relay race is meant to be depicted on a 2k.+2k. Slovakian semipostal of 1944, while the hurdlers on a 15pf. East German stamp of 1956 wear one-piece garments which appear to be gymnastic clothes! On a 2cr.50 Brazilian stamp of 1957 the young gymnast appears to be holding an untenable position even for a gymnast, though this is perhaps arguable. The Yugoslavian 1938 1d.50+1d.50 semipostal of the IXth Balkan Games issue shows a pole vaulter going over the bar in a most unorthodox position, as does a 3c. 1949 Nicaraguan stamp, while the boy on a Brazilian 2cr.50 stamp of 1958 appears to be tackling a high jump, but with the position of a long jumper, with both feet together. The high jumper on a 10l. 1963 stamp of San Marino also has a most unorthodox body position, while on a 100f. 1964 stamp of Chad his arms are impossibly far back for this stage of his jump. The high jumper on a 50f. 1962 stamp also of Chad also has his arms behind him in a scarcely less awkward position. The shot-putter on an 8c.+4c. semipostal of Surinam of 1960 has disqualified himself by stepping outside the circle while the shot-putter on a 2cr.50 Brazilian stamp of 1959 should have the right foot forward as the shot is released. It has also been claimed that the Indian shooting fish on a 2c. 1931 stamp of British Guiana should have his left foot forward instead of his right, but this appears arguable. The 3c. Nicaraguan stamp of 1949 shows a pole-vaulter sitting on the bar. Javelin throwers with faulty stance appear on an 8pf. German stamp of 1936 (summer Olympic Games), with incorrect positioning of his left foot, a 1l.+50b. Rumanian semipostal of 1937 (he wrongly bends the throwing arm), in the same year another 2l.+1l. semipostal has him wrongly raising his left leg and the javelin is too short on a 50f. 1964 stamp of Chad. The discus-thrower on a 6f.50+3f.50 1960 semipostal of the Belgian Congo and a similar issue for Ruanda Urundi has an incorrect stance, with his weight apparently on his right foot instead of on his left, while the discus-thrower on a 100f. 1962 stamp of Chad has such an incredibly awkward stance that it is difficult to see how he can throw his discus at all. The torch-bearer on a 2d.+2d. Yugoslavian semipostal of 1938 looks as if he is making his run-up for the high jump, while the torch-bearer on a 12pf. German stamp of 1936 is portrayed as a sprinter.

The 15pf. stamp of this same issue shows a fencer with a faulty stance—his left foot ought to be in line with the direction of his fencing. The leg and left arm positions of the fencer on a 2c.+1c. 1928 semipostal of the Netherlands is also faulty: this Olympic Games issue carries many errors, for the shot-putter on the 7½c.+2½c. has faulty positioning of head and arm, the runner on the 10c.+2c. value has his arms too extended, the sculler on the 1½c.+1c. value also adopts a very unorthodox attitude, and the horseman on the 15c.+2c. value appears to be braking his mount rather than encouraging it to jump. Finally, the 5c.+1c. value shows a cutter, a type of boat not represented in any Olympic event. The horseman on a 55b. Rumanian stamp of 1964 is taking a jump too shortly and too steeply, and appears liable to somersault. The basketball player on a 4l. Bulgarian stamp of 1947 appears to be tipping the ball into the basket from its own level—he must indeed be a giant! On a 15c. 1949 Nicaraguan stamp the basketball players appear to be using a medicine ball. The table tennis player on a 30fi. Hungarian stamp of 1958 has his forefinger far extended across the playing surface of his bat—a very unlikely hold indeed.

The two fencers shown on a 50c. Bolivian stamp of 1951 should be wearing protective face masks, as should Dr. Rizal and his opponent fencer on a 30c.+5c. semipostal of the Philippines of 1962. A Spanish 2p. 1976 stamp, a 1cor. Nicaraguan stamp of 1968, a 30f. stamp of 1968 of Cameroun, a 25f. 1960 stamp of Togo, a 40f. 1960 Moroccan stamp, a Lebanese 2p.50+2p.50 of 1961 and a 30c. 1972 stamp of the Cook Islands all show boxing events of the Olympic Games, but the boxers are without the vests which are habitually worn for amateur contests such as these. Furthermore, on the stamp from Togo one of the boxers is clearly hitting below the belt. Vestless boxers appear in other non-Olympic amateur events on a 50f. 1963 stamp of Dahomey and a 1b.25 1966 stamp of Thailand. The boxing gloves illustrated on a 3d. Nigerian stamp of 1964 lack the mandatory 6cm. broad lacings. The 60h. Czechoslovakian stamp of 1957 showing a young lady archer fitting an arrow to her bow has no bowstring, so it is not surprising that the bow is unbent. The Swiss issue of 1908-09 showed Tell's son with his crossbow cord on the wrong side of the stock—this was corrected for the 1910 issue.

A 1e. 1962 stamp of Mozambique illustrates wrestling, but no doubt inadvertently shows a foul being committed. It has been claimed that all three stamps of the British 1966 issue to mark the World Football Cup Competition show fouls being committed—perhaps an inadvertent comment on modern football practices. Brazilian 10c. stamps (1969) and 75c. miniature sheets (1970) show Pelé scoring his 1000th goal, but in Brazilian international strip, though this goal was scored while he was playing for his own team, Santos. The two footballers struggling for the ball on a 1952 15m.+2m. semipostal of Finland appear from their strips to be on the same side, while an 80c. 1974 stamp of Rwanda purporting to show the match between Haiti and Argentina in the World Cup Football Championships of that year show the Argentinian player in a shirt horizontally striped white and blue instead of the pale blue shirt with broad white vertical stripes which his team actually wore for this match. A 5st. Bulgarian stamp of 1964 shows a footballer apparently tying himself in knots over the top of the ball, while the attitude of the footballer on a Sudanese Olympic issue of 1960 would seem more appropriate for boxing—or perhaps even skiing. A Liberian 50c. miniature sheet of 1966 marking the World Cup Championships shows a goal with the uprights only a quarter the length of the horizontal bar instead of a third (a goal measures 8ft. × 8yds.). Incidentally the cup shown on the 25c. stamp of this issue is certainly not the Jules Rimet trophy presented to the winning team, which is shown on a Bermudian 10d. 1966 stamp. A 25f. 1964 stamp of Chad also shows a goal with the horizontal bar proportionately far too long.

In the East German 1966 issue to mark the World Canoeing Championships, the 10pf. value shows a canoeist in red shorts who would be braking the boat by his paddle action, while on the 15pf. stamp the lady in the black boat somehow holds the paddle behind her neck! A 50f. French stamp of 1953 shows the French team of coxed pairs in the 1952 Olympics, but in the background boat the cox is clearly not in time with his oarsmen. The water polo player on a 1fo. 1958 Hungarian stamp is bare-headed, but caps are compulsory to mark clearly the team to which each player belongs. The 5k. Russian diving stamp of 1938 and a Bulgarian 3st. stamp of 1964 show the diver's toes well short of the end of the diving board or block respectively, while the Icelandic swallow diver on 1k.25 (1955) and 1k.75 (1957) stamps is flattened out too close to the water and is about to make a disastrous belly flop. The diver on a 2k. 1935 Russian stamp has similarly taken up too flat a position, with the head held too far back. The diver on a 4f. 1948 stamp of Monaco appears to be in a position for a racing dive, but is poised on a diving board, not a starting block, and, although this is part of an issue marking the 1948 Olympic Games, is diving into open water with a yacht in the background —certainly not into an Olympic Games standard pool. The discus-thrower on the 2f. value of the same issue will perhaps join her, for he appears to be clad in swimming trunks.

Turning to winter sports, the 1932 2c. stamp of the U.S.A. marking the 3rd Olympic Winter Games, Lake Placid, shows a downhill skier: this event was not represented in those Olympic Games, the skier has his skis crossed, his body posture is quite wrong, and he is liable to choke himself with his loose cravat, which no Olympic Games skier would wear (fig. 70). The 12pf. East German stamp of 1952 marking the 3rd Winter Sports Meeting, Oberhof, shows a skier with his ski-stick quite wrongly between his legs. Ski-jumpers lean forward with arms tightly pressed to their sides to minimise air resistance, but not so the jumpers on stamps of Albania (1l., 1967), Austria (1s.50, 1963) and Russia (20k. 1949), while the ski-jumper on a French 1f.50 stamp of 1937 actually has his skis crossed. The two-man bobsleigh on a 1r. 1968 stamp of Sharjah commemorating the Winter Olympic Games, Grenoble, has a steering wheel, but since the 1950s only steering ropes have been allowed. The 80fi. 1963 Hungarian stamp showing the rifle-shooting on skis event of the Winter Olympic Games biathlon has the competitor shooting from the kneeling position, whereas he ought to be shooting from an erect position. Competitors are correctly erect on the 20pf. 1967 East German stamp showing this event in an issue marking the World Biathlon Championships, Altenberg, but the rifleman on the right does not have his ski-stick close to hand as he would in competition, and appears to lack the distinguishing number on his chest. On the 10pf. value of this issue the left hand fingers of the rifleman in the foreground are in a quite impossible position, looking indeed like a second right hand. The No. 6 ice hockey player on a 50pf. 1975 West German stamp is without an ice hockey stick, while on a 6c. 1969 Canadian stamp commemorating curling, the proportions of curling stone and circles are quite incorrect (a curling stone is 1ft. diameter, while circles are of 1ft., 4ft., 8ft. and 12 ft. diameter respectively).

Finishing on a more sedentary game, a 5d. Yugoslavian 1950 stamp from an issue marking the World Chess Championships, Dubrovnik, shows a stage in an actual game between Capablanca and Lasker played in New York in 1924, but the black bishop should be on KN1, not KB1 as here. The land-masses on the globe in the background appear fanciful, with no relation to actual contours.

Distortions of the human figure are quite common. A 6g. 1934 Austrian stamp shows a peasant of Lower Austria with his ears back to front (corrected in 1935). There is also something wrong with the 80c. 1964 Mexican stamp showing President Kennedy shaking hands with an equally tall President Mateos of Mexico, for Kennedy was in fact much the taller. Egine (being carried off by Jupiter) on a 1947 100f. French air stamp has only four toes on her right foot. A 10pf.+5pf. 1961 East German semipostal shows Pioneers playing volley-ball: the player in the red and white jersey has only four fingers on his left hand (no thumb). The peasant girl on a Uruguayan 10c. stamp of 1901 has only three fingers on her raised right hand (corrected for the 1905 design), and the witch on the 20pf.+10pf. West German semipostal of the Hansel and Gretel issue of 1961 has only four fingers on her raised right hand. The ' Canadian citizen ' on a 4c. 1947 Canadian stamp has only three fingers on his raised right hand. However President Roosevelt on a 50c. 1947 stamp of Monaco has five fingers and a thumb on his right hand. The Chagall portrait on the Israeli I£3 1969 stamp shows King David with two left hands, but that is Chagall's doing, not the stamp designer's. Chagall, as an orthodox Jew, deliberately avoided representing a perfect human figure. In this connection it should be noted that orthodox Jews and Moslems would regard accurate representations of the human figure on stamps (or any other medium) as an error, as it runs contrary to religious belief. A 6pf. East German stamp of 1953 shows two workmen shaking hands, one with his right hand and the other with his left—hardly likely to be correct, while a 24pf. East German stamp, also of 1953, shows an obviously right-handed postman delivering letters from a postbag on his right side—he would surely have had it on his left. A

3f.50+1f.50 semipostal of 1930 of the Belgian Congo showing a nurse bathing a baby has the child drawn so out of proportion to the bath that it appears to have no lower half, while the heads of Mother and Child on a 1939 90c.+35c. French semipostal are relatively quite out of proportion. Turning to not quite human figures, we have a 5c. Canadian air stamp of 1928 showing two winged messengers with but one wing apiece. A 5c. 1965 Christmas stamp of the U.S.A. shows a figure supposed to represent the Archangel Gabriel (though not so labelled on the stamp) after a painting of a weather vane by L. Chabot, but it clearly has a female body. A 1950 Icelandic issue commemorates Bishop Jón Arason, the last Roman Catholic Bishop of Iceland, but quite improperly gives him a halo, for he has never been canonized.

A 2½d. Australian stamp of 1948 shows a Rover Scout, and this design has aroused considerable controversy. Although the model, as mentioned in an earlier section, was an English scout, it is claimed that he does wear the badge of an Australian unit, that of the Essenden (Victoria) Scouts—two aboriginal scouts making smoke signals with a tube of rolled bark and a grass fire, all on a background of gum leaf. It has been claimed to be in error because Rover Scouts should carry thumb-sticks, not staves, but it has also been claimed that this could be a thumb-stick turned round, and that the shadow running perpendicular to the scout's thumb is from the other branch of the thumb-stick's fork. The design was repeated on a 1952 3½d. stamp. The sea scout shown on a 1963 20m. stamp of Cyprus should not have a staff, scouts should not salute as shown on a 1948 issue of the Philippine Islands and a 30l. Greek stamp of 1960 without hats on, and on the 2d. value of this latter issue the hat of the Chief Greek Scout should come to a point, not a ridge.

An Egyptian 10m. stamp of 1956 showing symbolic Egyptian resistance to the Anglo-French invasion shows an Egyptian soldier with a helmet curiously intermediate between British and American styles and certainly not typically Egyptian. The machine pistol worn by soldiers on a 20pf. 1960 East German stamp and a 60fi. 1953 Hungarian stamp should be pointing towards the left, not to the right as here. The ammunition drum and lid casing are the wrong shape on the former, while the trigger (which could NOT be completely covered by the soldier's hand) appears to be missing on the latter. The Italian soldier on the left in the background of the Italian 1941 issue marking Italo-German Friendship wrongly has his rifle on the right shoulder instead of the left. The 1946 Victory stamp of Hyderabad shows a native soldier returning home to his family after the war, in full kit with rifle, but in practice under British rule sepoys were never allowed to take weapons home on leave—experience had shown that soldier and weapon often failed to return. The Black Prince, so-named following the Battle of Crecy, in which he wore a suit of black armour, is disconcertingly pictured in silver armour on a 10p. British stamp of 1974. The 7½p. British stamp of 1971 marking York's 1900th anniversary has both won a European award and been fiercely attacked for its design, which shows a centurion on horseback carrying an eagle standard. The standard itself is much too short and should in any case have been borne by a special standard-bearer (the aquilifer) who went on foot and wore a bearskin cap. The native chief Te Po shown on 2½d. 1927 stamps of Rarotonga and of Niue has had the barbed head of his spear removed in this adaptation of the original portrait, converting it into a meaningless stick.

The peasant from the Traunkreis district on a 12g. Austrian stamp of 1934 is smoking a typical pipe with a hinged lid, but the hinge should be on the side nearest the smoker, not furthest from him as here. President Schärff's suit on an Austrian 1s.50 stamp of 1960 has a lapel on the right side only and not on the left. The clerk on a 3pf.+2pf. 1934 German semipostal wears a jacket with revers on the left side but none on the right. He also holds a telephone receiver with no cord attached. These errors were noted, but too late for the stamp to be withdrawn. The girl with the little jacket on a 70pf. East German stamp of 1964 (marking the East German Women's Congress) has the jacket buttoning towards the right, the male way. A Brazilian 20c. stamp of 1969 shows Gandhi and a treadle spinning-wheel, but Gandhi used a hand spinning-wheel, and his own wheel is shown on an Indian 15n.p. stamp of 1963, with Eleanor Roosevelt. A 20r. 1957 stamp of Liechtenstein portrays Lord Baden-Powell (very badly) with a floppy hat at a rakish angle, whereas he always wore a stiff-brimmed hat squarely on top of his head. The 1974 stamp of Mali marking the centenary of the birth of Churchill is also, incidentally, an extremely poor likeness of its subject. Where double portraits appear on a stamp the person of prime importance should be on the left of the stamp, as on the Canadian 3c. stamp of 1935 featuring King George V and Queen Mary, but this rule is violated on the Canadian 1908 issue, both on the ½c. value (King George V and Queen Mary when Prince and Princess of Wales) and the 2c. value (King Edward VII and Queen Alexandra).

The open newspaper held by the journalist on 15c. and 5f. 1935 stamps of Luxemburg has what obviously should be the front page on the back page. On a Polish issue of 1947, the harvester (10z.) is using a scythe, but would be completely off balance as he has the wrong leg forward; the fisherman (15z.) is holding up a large fish which appears to have its tail dorsiventrally flattened like that of a cetacean; the miner (20z.) is working at the coal face in bare feet, which must be most uncomfortable. The very long ' palanquin ' series of Madagascar (1908-22) portrays the first pair of bearers with the poles on their left shoulders, the back pair with the poles on their right shoulders, but invariably all bearers use the same shoulder, left or right. The elephant-borne royal courier on a 1k. 1962 stamp of Laos is scattering enormous letters in his wake in a singularly careless manner. Postal employees are prohibited from dragging mail sacks over the ground in the manner shown on a 1951 12f.+3f. French semipostal. The native priest on 10c.+5c. and 50c. 1955 stamps of Spanish Guinea wears the violet ribbon, the maniple, on his lower right arm on the stamp, but it is ritually correct to wear it on the left arm. A 1946 5c. stamp of the Argentine Republic marking the installation of Juan Peron as President wrongly shows ' Argentina ' taking the oath with left hand raised instead of the right hand. The labourer on a Venezuelan 5c. stamp of 1964 has his maul raised above his head in a quite unorthodox and unworkmanlike manner. The National Reconstruction Fund semipostal East German issue of 1952 also portrays quite unworkmanlike workers. On the 24pf.+6pf. value one worker holds a stone as if it is an accordion, while his co-worker appears to be demolishing the wall rather than constructing it. On the 30pf.+10pf. value the carpenter is taking hold of the beam in the wrong way, and violates safety regulations by lifting it over the head of his kneeling companion, while on the 50pf.+10pf. value the builder's head is held at a very unnatural angle. The man on a 10r. 1951 stamp of Liechtenstein who is supposed to be whetting his scythe seems rather to be hammering its edge, and the farmer on a 12pf. German stamp of 1934 is likewise sharpening his scythe in a very unorthodox way. There has been controversy over the Irish reaper's scythe shown on a 2d. stamp of 1931, as to whether the handles are accurately drawn—the final verdict appears to have been that they are. It has also been claimed that the lumberjacks on a 50c. Canadian stamp of 1946 are violating safety precautions, but this too may be arguable; it does seem odd, however, that the cut tree on the left has not been clear-felled and that the worker on the left does not wear a safety helmet.

The man being X-rayed on a 12f. French stamp of 1957 commemorating Béclère has his arms in the wrong position for a chest X-ray. This also applies to the patients on a 1956 4f.+2f. Belgian semipostal and a 1951 30fi. Hungarian stamp—the arms should be akimbo. A 40n.p. 1970 stamp of Ghana and a 1/9d. 1970 St. Helenan stamp both show first aid being very inexpertly given, for the bandage has been allowed to form a ' long tail ', *i.e.* to become too far unrolled for efficient bandaging to be carried out. Bandaging of a limb should be from below upwards, but on a 2/6d. 1966 Nigerian stamp it is being done in the reverse direction. The loading of a casualty onto a stretcher is being performed very inexpertly on a 30c. 1970 stamp of Turks and Caicos. Armpit crutches should be used in parallel, but on a 15c. 1970 stamp of Montserrat are wrongly shown being used alternately.

Blacksmiths roll their sleeves up with the cuffs on the inside to avoid the risk of trapping sparks, but the blacksmith on 1922-23 Estonian stamps has his cuffs on the outside. The ' peasant ' on a 1m. 1953 Egyptian stamp was posed by the doorman at the "Survey of Egypt", and holds his hoe in his left hand over his shoulder in an awkward and rather dangerous position: this was corrected in the 1954 design, modelled on a genuine fellah. Ploughing designs seem rarely to be accurate in detail. The ploughman shown on the 3c. Alaskan commemorative of the U.S.A. (1937) has a plough throwing soil to the left instead of to the right, and he is wrongly walking in the new furrow, while on the Canadian 8c. ' Reconversion to Peace ' 1946 stamp the higher shaft of the plough should be on the farmer's right. The Bavarian 1920 ploughman drives his horse without reins, as does the ploughman on the Mecklenburg-Vorpommern issue of 1945 (who is in any case ploughing across the furrow), while the plough-horse on a 10c. Swiss stamp of 1941 has no bridle. The plough-horse on the Australian 6c. 1971 R.S.P.C.A. centennial stamp has at least six separate errors in harnessing—for example it has a bridle but no blinkers. (Incidentally, the cat on this stamp has whiskers differing in length and position on the two sides of the head) (fig. 71). The harness of the horse ridden by a scout on a 20l. 1960 Greek stamp is incomplete, while on a 200f. French air stamp of 1946 Apollo drives the four horses of the sun chariot with only three reins. St. Martin rides on his horse facing the tail on a 1943 5f.+25f. Belgian semipostal.

Among other design errors involving animals, the 42pf.+108pf. German ' Brown Ribbon ' semipostal of 1944 shows a racehorse and foal, but the foal is shown with a light coat, though the dark first coat is not lost for some time. The foal on the Swedish 1946 Agricultural Show Centennial issue is portrayed feeding from behind, but it is claimed that foals always feed from in front. The 1940 3c. U.S.A. stamp commemorating the Pony Express shows a pony in an apparently impossible posture with only one hoof touching the ground. The two horses pulling the mail wagon on a 40h. 1906 stamp of Bosnia & Herzegovina have only six legs between them while on 50c. and 2col. 1948 stamps of El Salvador showing Roosevelt's funeral, the horse at the right has only three legs, the gun carriage has three wheels and the men on the left of the gun carriage have no legs at all! (fig. 72). On a 3c. 1946 issue of the U.S.A. commemorating General Kearney's capture of Santa Fe, the horse of the second horseman from the right has only three legs. Many of the stamps of Jaipur figure Surya, the Hindu sun god from whom the Jaipur maharajas claimed descent, in his one-wheeled chariot drawn by seven white horses, but on the 1904 issue he wrongly has only a single horse, while on later issues, *e.g.* 1905-08, there appears to be a seven-headed horse with but four legs. This also appears on postal stationery of this period. On a 1946 5f. stamp of Cameroun the camel above the word "TCHAD" has only two legs. The cattle on a 1c. 1900 stamp of Uruguay appear to have hind legs like those of a horse—the 1c. of 1904 shows much more realistic animals.

Elephants are often badly drawn in stamp designs. Those on the 1912 and 1921 series for Sierra Leone, the Sirmoor series of 1895-99 and the Gambia for 1922-27 and 1938-46 all seem to have their hind legs bending backwards, as a horse does but an elephant does not. In addition the elephant on the 1938 Gambian issue has small rounded ears, reminiscent of Asian rather than African elephants, and somewhat misplaced tusks—a much improved depiction of an African elephant was produced for the Elizabethan £1 stamp of 1953. As pointed out on page 41 the elephant on the Northern Rhodesian issues of 1925, 1938 and 1953 is more akin to Asian than African elephants, though this is perhaps debatable. Similarly the elephant on a 1963 5c. stamp of Ceylon marking National Conservation Week would indeed be worth conserving, for it has the large floppy ears of an African elephant allied to the high forehead of the Asian elephant.

The ox team on a 6c. 1897 stamp of Newfoundland stands properly lined up to pull the sled—except that the animals are unharnessed! The caribou on the 1919 Newfoundland Contingent issue has the large palmate and projecting antlers of a moose and the very hairy neck of a wapiti—a more typical caribou is shown on a stamp of 1932. A 10c. 1950 Canadian stamp featuring drying furs was issued with a post office department handout that these were beaver pelts, but they are obviously far too large for this in proportion to the woman illustrated with them (maximum length of a stretched beaver skin is 36″). The silkworm on a Rumanian 40b. stamp of 1963 is shown on a lime tree leaf, but it only eats mulberry leaves. The giraffe on various 1901-23 issues of Nyassa appears to be munching the leathery leaves of a date palm, which are too tough for even the hungriest giraffe. A near relative of the giraffe, the okapi, a creature of densest forest, is shown on stamps of the Belgian Congo (3f.25, 1932; 2f.50, 1937 and 20f. 1942) in open country, though admittedly when featured in its typical forest environment, as on a 5f. stamp of 1959, it is not easy to see at all. A 1971 wild-life issue of Trinidad and Tobago ran into considerable criticism. The brocket deer (3c.) was alleged to be in an unnatural position and the wrong colour, the lappe (6c.) to have its white stripes grossly exaggerated, the ocelot (40c.) to be poorly represented, and the background environment to be atypical of the habitats of the respective animals. A 10c. 1950 stamp of Sarawak shows a scaly anteater with an enormous tail and apparently no hind legs—or perhaps an enormous portion of hind leg and no tail, it is difficult to be sure. The posture—in a vertical position on its two hind legs—was also held to be unnatural, and in 1952 the design was replaced by one showing a map of Sarawak. A curious case is that of the lion on the 1d. British stamp of 1911, designed in part by King George V himself. The lion is a mangy looking animal (referred to contemptuously in Parliament as 'the starved lion'). A modified design with a plumper looking animal was released in 1912, but the design was not popular and was soon replaced by something completely different—and without the lion! The pair of lynxes shown on a 40pf. East German stamp of 1959 are quite well drawn, but the lynx is a solitary animal, pairing only very briefly and so better represented by a single animal. A 3d. 1929 airmail stamp of Australia shows a flock of sheep, on the original die accompanied by a well-horned ram. This was spotted on trial pulls and the die retouched to remove the horns, as rams are NOT joined to sheep in the wool.

The 2/6d. 1954 definitive for Tristan da Cunha shows an elephant seal basking on a rock to the south of Snug Harbour. In fact, at this point any rocks lie under about 20 fathoms of water, but in any case the seal is wrongly shown with its hind flippers tucked forward underneath it—an anatomical impossibility for the elephant seal, though not for sea lions. The seal on the 5c. Newfoundland stamps of 1866-76 has been considerably criticised because the front flippers are shown clawed. This was redrawn with more conventional flippers for the 1880 issue. It has been suggested that the animal first depicted was a sea otter, an animal which never occurred in or near Newfoundland, but this in any case has quite different hindquarters and tail. In fact it appears to have been a quite reasonable representation of the Ringed Seal (*Phoca hispida*), locally abundant and much more appropriate than the indeterminate species which supplanted it on the later issue. Another source of controversy has been the whale featured on the 1929 issue for the Falkland Islands. This is shown well above the surface and spouting, but whales spout from a position almost fully submerged and only float high in the water when dead. Local authorities requested that it should be redrawn, but the Colonial Office refused. The whale on the 1933 6d. stamp is also controversial, for it is highly unlikely that any large whale could leap so far out of the water. The sperm whale about to be harpooned on a 2d, 1956 stamp of New Zealand should stand a good chance of getting away, for there is no rope attached to the harpoon!

Turning to birds, the kingfisher on a 10c. Swiss stamp of 1966 should have greenish blue plumage, not deep blue as here. The same species (*Alcedo atthis*) is shown on a 2d. 1972 stamp of Qatar, but here the breast is coloured scarlet where it should be brown-red and the tail is purple instead of blue. The bullfinch on a 1k. Czechoslovakian stamp of 1959 wrongly has a white beak—it should be black as on a 1l. 1959 Rumanian stamp. The serin on a 10q. Albanian stamp of 1971 is shown as predominantly dark green, but it ought to be brown with typical yellow streaking. The grey wagtail on a 4f. 1970 stamp of Burundi lacks the characteristic black spot on the throat. The Troupial on a 1961 5c. Venezuelan stamp has the hind toe of its left foot too large, while the back of the Tropical Mockingbird on the 15c. value of this issue should be grey, and the feet of the Snowy Egret (*Leucophoryx thula,* not *Leucophoyx* as here) on the 40c. value should be black. This issue has been ill-starred, for the Guanan Cock-of-the-Rock on the 10c. was misnamed "GALLITO DE ROCAS" instead of ' GALLITO DE LAS ROCAS ', and the Scarlet Ibis on the 50c. misnamed "COROCORO SIDRA" instead of ' COROCORO O SIDRA '. It has been reported that the birds shown on a 1969 issue of Cyprus are poorly coloured and far from lifelike in shape. A 28a. 1963 Israeli stamp shows a pied wheatear (*Oenanthe lucens*), but the black wings ought to be covering most of the white body plumage, since the bird is at rest. The Graceful Warbler on a 40a. of the same issue should be darker, and the tail should bear more dark stripes. It has been questioned whether the lyre bird shown on 1888-1906 8d. and 2/6d. stamps of New South Wales and on 1932-56 1s. stamps of Australia could in fact hold its tail stiffly erect in the fashion shown: the normal display position appears to be with tail swept forward to the ground in front of the bird. The goose on a 10pf.+5pf. 1958 semipostal of West Germany in the Berlin Students' Fund issue appears to have two ears, while the White Tern (*Gygis alba*) on a 3d. 1961 stamp of Norfolk Island is shown landing on rocks, which it never does: it lays its single egg on tree branches. A 10c. 1974 South West African stamp shows the Damara Rock-jumper nesting in a tree, copied from a diorama in Johannesburg Museum, but this bird is a ground-nesting species. The four species featured in this issue are not rare, although labelled so in some catalogues. The swan on which the god Brahma is seated in French Indian Settlements stamps of 1914-29 should not be there at all, for it is properly the *vahama* (carrier) of his wife Savaswati. The 1/9d. 1970 stamp of Jersey featuring ostriches in the ' Battle of Flowers ' series incorrectly enhances the popular misconception that ostriches bury their heads in the sand, a fact not yet observed anywhere. The collie birds of the Epiphany song are shown as bluebirds on a 7p. British Christmas stamp of 1977, but, as the accompanying Presentation Pack admits, these are generally accepted to mean blackbirds.

The iguana on a 1962 1s. stamp of the Cayman Islands is shown with a tail much too short, the only reptilian misrepresentation of which we are so far aware.

A Canadian 5c. stamp of 1961 commemorates natural resources, but the fish shown have heterocercal tails, making them look like dogfish (sharks), which far from being an important natural resource are a destructive nuisance. The codfish shown on the 1866 and 1880 2c. stamps of Newfoundland is very inaccurate in shape of tail, lack of distinct barbel and indistinct lateral line—the 1c. stamp of 1937 is a much better representation. A 5d. Turks and Caicos stamp of 1957 shows a

Permit, but the fish depicted has an extra fin about halfway between ventral and caudal fins. The illustration was made from a photograph of an angler and his catch, and the extra fin is a faulty interpretation of the shadowed edge of the angler's body. A 10f. 1974 stamp of Burundi shows the fish *Pantodon buchholzi* with dorsal fin missing, and *Synodontis angelicus,* on the 17f. stamp of the same issue, has its adipose fin missing.

Many countries issuing anti-cancer stamps have signified the disease by a crab (*Cancer* is the edible crab genus), but both the 100f. 1965 Mauritanian issue and the Kuwaiti 1970 W.H.O. issue show the crab with only three pairs of walking legs instead of the four pairs it ought to have, as, for instance, correctly shown on a 100f. 1965 stamp of the Niger Republic. The 80q. 1968 Albanian stamp featuring the Common Shore Crab (*Carcinus maenas*) gives it two extra small legs on its left side, while the other legs all seem short of a joint (fig. 73). The malaria-carrying mosquito *Anopheles gambiae* shown on a 1962 1e.50 stamp of St. Thomas & Prince Islands appears to have only four legs instead of the six it ought to have.

The principal error in portraying molluscs appears to be illustration of shells with left-handed spirals for species which normally have right-handed spirals (the more usual condition). If the shell has the apex to the top and the aperture to the right it has a right-handed (dextral) spiral. Left-handed (sinistral) spirals appear on a 30c. Cuban stamp of 1973 (*Liguus vittatus*), a 5f. 1970 stamp of the Malagasy Republic (*Volute delessertiana*), on a $5 1971 Taiwanese stamp (*Conus embrikena* misnamed *Conus stupa kuroda* on the stamp), on a 75c. Mauritian 1969 stamp (*Conus clytospira* wrongly labelled *Clytospira*), and on a 1968 issue of New Caledonia on the 39f. value (*Conus lienardi*), 40f. (*Conus cabriti*) and 70f. (*Conus coccineus*). On the other hand although all the stamps of Travancore show a stylised conch with a left-handed spiral, which only occurs in nature for about one shell in 3,000, this is perfectly appropriate here, for such shells are highly prized in India, being associated with the god Vishnu. Of the two Queen Conch shells shown on a 3c. 1977 stamp of Anguilla, that on the left has a left-handed spiral. It was copied quite correctly from a photograph of a shell in the collection of an Anguillan fisherman, but there is no indication whether this conch is the rare exception or if the print was reversed.

A 5c. Canadian stamp of 1964 publicising Canadian Unity shows the newly adopted emblem of three maple leaves arising from a single point, but maple leaves arise in opposite pairs, so this is botanically inaccurate. The same applies to the maple leaves on the arms of Ontario, Quebec and Canada on a 1964 Canadian issue: botanically accurate leaves are shown on the 1967 Canadian centennial issue of Ireland. The 'maple' leaves on a 15c. 1971 Canadian stamp commemorating Radio Canada International are certainly not the palmate maple leaves typically represented (although there are, of course, many different kinds of maple, with leaves of diverse shapes).

A 2c. 1935 stamp of Ceylon shows a native girl tapping rubber from a tree with large buttress roots (a rubber tree has no such roots). A very wide cut has been made, yet no latex is flowing, and background trees are very crudely and inaccurately drawn. All of these points were corrected on the redrawn design of 1938. It has been claimed that the bunches of bananas on the 2½d. 1932 Jamaican stamp are upside-down, but ripening bunches in fact hang down in this way. However when bunches have been cut they are never laid on their sides in full sun as shown on stamps of Dominica (5c., 1951) and Fiji (2s., 1956), but are carefully stacked on their big end against a support, as shown on a 5c. Costa Rican stamp of 1950. Fiji in 1938 produced a 5d. blue and scarlet stamp showing sugar cane. Following protests that blue is a most inappropriate colour for sugar cane this was issued in yellow-green and scarlet in 1940. A 25n. Zambian stamp of 1972 shows a native woman collecting light green maize cobs which are fully exposed. However the cobs while growing are tightly sheathed in leaves, and pass from white to golden or reddish as they mature, but are never green at any stage. The young breadfruit plants shown on 1d. and 2/6d. 1940 stamps of the Pitcairn Islands appear to have small feathery leaves, very unlike the large pinnate leaves of this plant, shown more accurately on a 5c. stamp of 1969.

Pakistan used a floral design for the Child Welfare Week issue of 1961: the catalogues list the flower as a narcissus, but a narcissus has six perianth segments, not five as shown in this design. The rather crudely drawn Bermuda Easter lilies on a ½d. 1953 stamp of Bermuda are shown with two-ranked leaves, but they should be radially arranged, as shown more accurately on the 1½d. stamp of the same issue. These lilies are not native to Bermuda but were introduced from the Far East in 1853: the species on these stamps, *Lilium longiflorum,* is shown on 10s. and 40s. 1948 stamps of Ryukyu Islands, to which it *is* native. The Bermudiana (*Sisyrinchium bermudiana*), which is the emblem of Bermuda, is shown on the 1949 stamp centenary issue of Bermuda as having five rounded or very slightly notched petals, but should have six deeply notched petals with prominent protruding filaments (as shown on the 4c. definitive of 1970); the 7½d. stamp of 1938 also shows a Bermudiana flower with only five petals. A 1972 25c. stamp of Guyana shows the Marabunta orchid (*Gongora quinquinervis*), but upside-down! This was corrected in 1973 (figs 74 & 75). A 10m. Mongolian stamp of 1960 shows a tulip with several more stamens than the six it ought to have, while the Jersey fern on a 1972 3p. stamp of Jersey has circular sori instead of linear ones. The stamp designer had shown these correctly, but apparently the engraver thought this incorrect for a fern and reduced their length accordingly. The flowers flanking Mount Cook on the right side of the ½d. 1898 stamp of New Zealand are specified in the official description (though not named on the stamp) as *Ranunculus,* in which case they ought to have 6-9 rounded petals, not five pointed petals as here. The palm tree in the foreground of the English Harbour scene on ½d. and 2d. 1938 stamps of Antigua ought, it is claimed, to be an agave. The Water Violet (*Hottonia palustris*) on a 5l. 1966 stamp of Rumania is shown with red flowers with white throat, but ought to be lilac with yellow throat. The heraldic flowers on the 1857 issue of Newfoundland are very crudely drawn: the rose, for instance, is given simple leaves whereas nearly all species have pinnate leaves, the shamrock is trilobed instead of trifoliate and the thistle bracts are not imbricate as they ought to be. It has been suggested that the mushrooms on a 1961 Bulgarian issue are so misleadingly coloured that they could easily be confused with poisonous toadstools.

Turning from organisms to artifacts, we may look first at musical instruments. A 1971 issue of Fujeira marking the birth bicentenary of Beethoven embodies numerous errors; those pertaining to this section include a reversed grand piano (70d.) and the inappropriate inclusion of a harp (3r.), for Beethoven never used a harp in his orchestral compositions, and the only music he wrote for the harp was an unimportant accompaniment to a Romanza for soprano voice in 1814. The angels of the British Christmas issue of 1972 must indeed have superhuman powers to extract music from their instruments, for the cittern (3p.) is unfretted, with tuning pegs halfway down the neck, the pipe (2½p.) is without reed or mouthpiece and the harp (7½p.) hangs unsupported in the air. The Scottish piper on a 100f. 1956 stamp of Monaco (marking the 26th Monte Carlo Rally) has a drone missing from his pipes and has the bag in front, Continental fashion, instead of tucked under his arm like a true Scot. The buglers on a 2cr.50 1958 Brazilian stamp and 70d. and 3r. 1967 stamps of Ajman are blowing their bugles upside-down—possible, but not done in the best musical circles. The Scout bugler on a 15y. 1971 Japanese stamp shows how it ought to be done. This last stamp is interesting, for in the original design the Scout emblem had been omitted, and 28 million stamps had been printed before the omission was noted. Nevertheless these were pulped, the design was changed to include the emblem, and the corrected issue appeared on schedule—a remarkable feat.

A Canadian Education Year 5c. stamp of 1962 shows a violin with no finger board and with strings extending past the pegs, meshed gear wheels which would interlock, and a microscope with no substage condenser. Microscopes are often very poorly detailed; thus the 1966 set of Lesotho marking the 20th anniversary of U.N.E.S.C.O. has a microscope with no mirror or other light source, a 4d. 1968 Gibraltarian stamp marking the 20th anniversary of the W.H.O. shows a microscope with disconnected mirror and optical tube, both tilted at very improbable angles, an East African (Kenya, Uganda & Tanzania) 1s.30 stamp of 1968, also commemorating the W.H.O. anniversary, has a vignette labelled "RESEARCH" yet showing a very simple microscope with no substage condenser, and this is also missing from the microscope on the Canadian 5c. 1958 stamp marking the International Geophysical Year. The microscope shown on the Ethiopian 1967 issue marking the Second International Conference on Global Impact of Applied Microbiology has a very flimsy base, and no mirror, condenser or other substage apparatus. The coarse adjustment knob appears to be missing from the Koristka (Milan) microscope depicted on the 25l. 1955 Italian stamp commemorating the biologist Grassi. Dr. Janot's microscope on a 15f. 1954 stamp of Cameroun has the objective protruding at right angles to the axis of the body tube—a rather improbable arrangement. Pasteur's microscope on a 65f. 1972 stamp of the Comoro Islands has the mirror so adjusted that it would completely cover the opening of the condenser, thus blocking out all light. The highly stylised depiction of a microscope on a 70f. 1973 Moroccan stamp (marking the 25th anniversary of the W.H.O.) has a barrel which is not cylindrical, nose-piece and objectives represented only by a small wedge-shaped block, a curiously tapered eyepiece, and no obvious method of viewing by transmitted light. A 6k. 1966 Russian stamp (fig. 76)

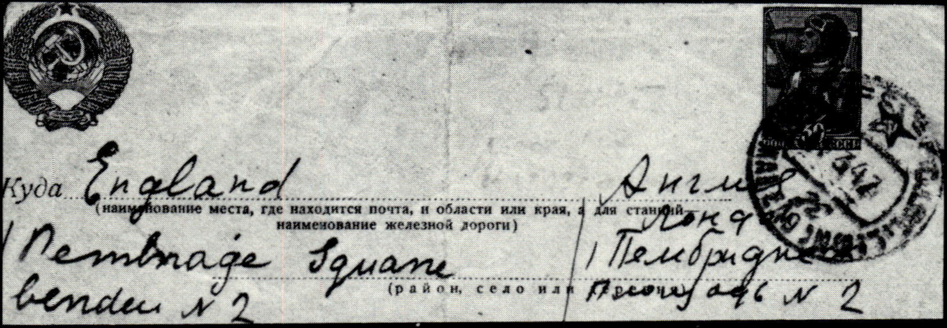
Куда England

107

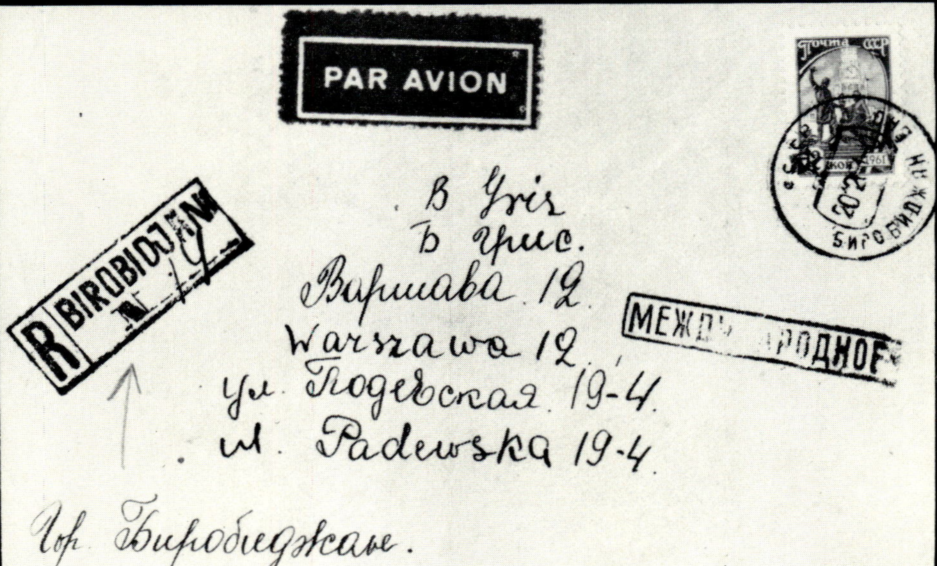
PAR AVION
R BIROBIDJAN
Варшава 12
Warszawa 12
Z.S.R.R.

108

marking an International Congress of Microbiology has the microscope's objective out of line with the centre of the mirror, while the mirror itself has insufficient room in which to pivot. The microscope of the Material-testing Laboratory, Berlin, on a 30pf. 1971 issue of Berlin, quite appropriately lacks a substage condenser, but it should still have a vertical illuminator, which is missing. The microscope on a 100f. 1970 stamp of the Niger Republic marking World Telecommunications Day is a curious instrument, for it appears to be focussed on its own mirror and to have attached to its body tube a finder telescope such as would be found on an astronomical telescope! The armillary sphere shown on a 1945 Portuguese issue marking the Naval School centenary has the zodiac belt placed so that it reaches the polar circles, which is incorrect.

Telephones without attached flex appear on stamps of Ethiopia (issue, 1976) and Switzerland (80c. 1976) and with dials with fewer than the normal ten holes on stamps of Kenya, Uganda and Tanzania (3s. 1976, also on miniature sheets), with a separate issue from each country. The tension spring of the morse key shown on a 3½d. 1954 Australian stamp should be screwed down onto the key bar, but here is ' floating '. A 30pf. 1966 stamp of West Germany marks the centenary of the discovery by Werner von Siemens of the principles of the electric dynamo, but the machine illustrated is wrongly poled, amongst other minor inaccuracies. A 1964 issue of East Germany shows characters from children's T.V. programmes, but the aerial included in the designs is not a T.V. aerial but an upside-down UKW aerial which could only receive T.V. pictures at very short range. In addition the character Master Nadelöhr on the 10pf. value is depicted with a left shoe on his right foot. A West German issue of 1965 shows the Radio Tower, Stuttgart, with a representation of radio waves, but these are shown apparently coming from the broadcasting and restaurant rooms, and not from the transmitting tower itself. A 3d. Maltese stamp of 1958, from a set commemorating Technical Education, shows two large octagonal nuts, but with very few exceptions nuts are always hexagonal. The Kentucky rifle shown on a 6c. 1968 stamp of the U.S.A. commemorating Daniel Boone has the patch box on the left side of the stock, but it should be on the right—the same side as the lock. The traffic lights on a 25l. 1957 Road Safety Campaign stamp of Italy are in reverse colour order—an extraordinary error considering the purpose of the issue. The colours of the rainbow are in reverse order on a 1p.60 Mexican stamp of 1960 marking a U.N. Conference on Human Settlements.

A 5c. Canadian stamp of 1955 marking the 50th anniversary of Alberta and Saskatchewan has wheat associated with Alberta and oil with Saskatchewan, but it should have been the other way round—the 1955 edition of the Canada Year Book showed that Alberta was producing more than 25 times as much crude oil as Saskatchewan, while the field crops of Saskatchewan were more than double those of Alberta!

Stamps featuring historical occasions can err in many ways. An almost unavoidable historical inaccuracy occurs on the 3c. 1951 stamp of the U.S.A. marking the 175th anniversary of the Battle of Brooklyn. The stamp shows General Washington on his white charger directing the crossing of the mile-wide East River, a remarkable operation in which his army of 10,000 men successfully escaped, complete with artillery and wounded, from a greatly superior British army, without losing a man. The actual crossing, however, took place under cover of darkness and in dense fog, not in broad daylight as shown, but perhaps some artistic licence can be forgiven in this case! Another deliberate error involving George Washington occurs on a 4c. 1960 stamp of the U.S.A. (in the Credo series) in which his almost illegible signature has been replaced by a clear but bogus one. The Wilderness Battle scene on a 5c. 1964 stamp of the U.S.A. has also departed somewhat from historical accuracy, for it shows an artillery crew in the midst of blasted trees: in the battle itself the brush and undergrowth proved too dense for cannon to be taken through (fig. 77). The transatlantic Gunpowder Plot, by which sympathisers with the American revolutionaries daringly supplied the hard-pressed Americans with much-needed gunpowder from the Royal Magazine at St. Georges, Bermuda, is commemorated on a 1975 issue of Bermuda. However, as the miniature sheet of this issue freely admits, the magazine is illustrated as being much closer to the sea, and the waiting American ships as much closer to the shore—"but complete accuracy would spoil a stirring picture".

The United States has had some tricky decisions to make in the matter of commemorating Confederate successes and heroes of its own Civil War. In the 1937 Army and Navy Heroes series a 4c. value commemorates Confederate generals Lee and Jackson, but gives Lee only the badges of rank of a U.S. colonel, the highest rank he attained before turning 'rebel'. 'Stonewall' Jackson, however, is raised to a full general, though in fact even in the Confederate army his highest rank was Lieutenant General. Similarly Marshal de Lattre de Tassigny is portrayed on a 15f. French stamp of 1952 (also on a 12f. stamp of 1954) with only five stars on his uniform instead of the seven proper to his rank.

The New Zealand 2s. stamp of 1935 showing Captain Cook at Poverty Bay has the *Endeavour* very close to land (in his journal he states that it was anchored half a league from the shore) and omits the civilian botanists Banks and Solander who landed with him, while the men attending to the boats appear to be pushing and pulling in opposite directions! The 3d. 1906 stamp also depicting the landing of Cook may not, in fact, be intended to represent the same landing (on which he met with a very hostile reception) but his later reception at Tolaga Bay by the Paramount Chief: however it is rather unlikely that the Chief would have shaken hands—not a Maori custom—on this occasion. A 2½d. New Zealand stamp of 1940 shows the signing of the Treaty of Waitangi, with Captain Hobson seated, in full uniform, near Maori Chief Kowhite, yet the only extant eye-witness account of this occasion (by William Collenso) affirms that Captain Hobson "came in civilian clothes, having not time to don more of his uniform than a cocked hat". Ironically, on a 4c. stamp of 1974 picturing the same occasion he is shown in full naval uniform except for his cocked hat! An 8c. 1933 stamp of Newfoundland correctly shows the departure of Sir Humphrey Gilbert's little fleet from Plymouth: one ship, the *Raleigh,* turned back shortly after leaving, yet on the 9c. value of the same issue all five are shown entering the harbour of St. John's in Newfoundland. A 1d. 1931 stamp of South West Africa shows Cape Cross with the ship of Bartholomew Diaz, and on the land a cross of the type Portuguese explorers erected to mark annexation of newly discovered land. However there is no evidence that Diaz landed here, and indeed his landfall is now generally accepted as having been Luderitz Bay (shown on the 6d. value of this issue). 4p. and 10p. values of a 1930 Spanish issue show the arrival of Columbus in America, but with a priest present although no priest or friar travelled with Columbus (fig. 78). On a Paraguayan 1943 issue Christopher Columbus is portrayed with dark hair and a neat goatee beard, but contemporary accounts and the one known authentic portrait indicate that he was white-haired and clean-shaven. Emperor Dom Pedro II appears on various Brazilian stamps between 1866 and 1883, his beard changing in colour from black to white and back again in apparently arbitrary fashion. A 20cr. Brazilian stamp of 1964 depicts Pope John XXIII, but gives him only the vestments of a cardinal, not of a pope.

A 30c. Swiss stamp of 1931 features Alexander Vinet, an early 19th century theologian, founder of the Swiss Free Church. He lived and died in Clarens, but as it was inconvenient for the designer to illustrate Clarens he arbitrarily chose as a background for the portrait an illustration of the island of Salagnon in Lake Geneva, which had no association whatever with Vinet.

The Hoechle drawing of the death of Beethoven reproduced on a 4r. 1977 stamp of the Maldives wrongly places this in his studio, but he died in his bedroom. The portrait on the 1l. stamp in this series, is spurious, incidentally, and he was assistant, not court organist, and not at 15 as claimed here.

A 1s. 1968 Gibraltarian stamp purports to show King John signing Magna Carta with an enormous quill pen: in the first place the nib is far too broad to have been cut from the quill, and in any case King John was illiterate and did not sign but appended his seal (fig 79). In the Fairy Tale ' Frau Holle ' the golden rain falling on Gold Marie should adhere to her, but does not on the 30pf. West German stamp in the 1967 issue illustrating the tale, though the pitch sticks firmly enough to Pitch Marie on the 50pf. value. In a 1964 semipostal issue of East Germany supporting a Concentration Camp Victims Memorial Fund, the 5pf.+5pf., 10pf.+5pf. and 15pf.+5pf. values show anti-fascists pursuing illegal activities near brightly-lit windows—in spite of wartime blackout regulations. Finally in this section we may take the rather gruesome case of a 50c. Mexican stamp of 1957 honouring Jesus Garcia Corona, a shunter on the Nacozari Railway. He heroically reversed his train of two coaches loaded with dynamite, one of them smoking ominously, out of Nacozari into a cutting, where it exploded, killing Garcia and twelve others. The stamp shows the dying Garcia in the arms of his wife, but in fact no part of his body was recovered.

CHAPTER 6

Anachronisms

With the popularity of historical subjects for stamp design it is scarcely surprising that anachronisms abound. Probably the most notorious is that of various issues for St. Kitts-Nevis from 1903 onwards which show Columbus looking through a telescope, an instrument not invented until about a century after his death (probably in 1608). Unfortunately this scene was adopted for the arms of St. Christopher, as shown on the $5 stamp of 1963, hence the islands were stuck with it until a new coat-of-arms was adopted for the Associated State of St. Christopher-Nevis-Anguilla, as shown on the 25c. stamp of the 1967 issue commemorating statehood. Here of course, as with several other errors, the designer can hardly be blamed for reproducing an existing error. Renaissance religious paintings, for example, appear frequently on stamps and show many anachronisms, especially of dress. 'The Nativity' by Piero della Francesca, for instance, shown on a 4d. 1968 Christmas issue of Malawi, shows angels plucking stringed instruments of a period at least 1,000 years after the Nativity. Incidentally the stamp designer has cut off both top and bottom of the original painting. A 7p. 1974 Xmas stamp of Ghana shows the Magi approaching a town, presumably Bethlehem, the silhouette of which includes a large domed building and a minaret—unlikely architecture for Bethlehem at the beginning of the Christian era.

Returning to Columbus, we can find other anachronistic issues. In 1973 St. Vincent issued a set to mark the 475th anniversary of the supposed discovery and naming of St. Vincent by Columbus—on St. Vincent's Day of course. However none of the accepted routes of any of his four voyages comes close to St. Vincent, and his known whereabouts in 1498 on the days of any of the five St. Vincents of his time (with the just possible exception of 30th September, the day of St. Vincent Medelgarius) rule out discovery of the island at that time. In any case the *Santa Maria*, shown on the 50c. value, had in fact been wrecked on his first voyage and its timbers used to construct Fort Nativity in what is now Haiti, so it certainly was not available for his third voyage as implied here. 2l. and 25l. 1952 stamps of San Marino show Columbus standing by a terrestrial globe featuring the Americas in some detail—well beyond what was known in his lifetime—and on a stand of a type not used at that time, while of the three caravels in the background the middle one is rigged in 18th century fashion. The fleet of Columbus shown on an 1892 issue of Argentina is likewise equipped with sails and other gear of a much later period.

A 1s. Samoan stamp of 1970 purports to show Captain Cook's sextant, but the instrument illustrated, although donated by a descendant of a member of Cook's crew, was actually made in Belfast in 1850, while Cook was killed in 1779. A Fijian 3c. stamp of 1970 commemorates Cook's visit to the islands in 1774 on his second voyage, when he commanded the *Resolution,* but illustrates the *Endeavour,* which he commanded on his first voyage, ending in 1771. A 10c. 1970 stamp of Norfolk Island features H.M. Barque (or Bark) *Endeavour* but wrongly entitles it "H.M.S.", a designation then used only for ships of the line. This type of error is extremely common, applying also to H.M. Sloop *Resolution* (St. Helena, 5p., 1975; Norfolk Island, 1c., 1967; Niue, 1d., 1950): H.M. Armed Vessel *Bounty* (Aitutaki, 1c., 1974; Sharjah, 5d., 1969): H.M. Brig *Britomart* (New Zealand, 5d., 1940).

New Zealand has been peculiarly prolific in the production of design errors, and as we have already seen, the Centennial issue of 1940 had more than its share. The 3d. value of this issue shows the landing of immigrants from the barques *Tory* and *Cuba* and the ship *Aurora* in 1839-40, but illustrates the ships with double topsail yards, which did not come into use until 1855. Epaulettes were not adopted for naval officer uniform by the Royal Navy until June 1795, but nevertheless are worn by Captain Cook in 1769 (New Zealand 2s., 1935), by Captain George Phillip in 1788 (Australian issue of 1937) and by an unnamed British naval officer in 1794 (Seychelles, 1r., 1969). The Australian design was reproduced from a painting "The Discovery of the Site of Sydney by Governor Phillip" by John Allcot, who made the error in the first place.

The 8p. value of the 1974 Falkland Islands issue marking the Battle of the River Plate illustrates the *Admiral Graf Spee,* but shows the ship as it appeared before its 1939 refit, not as it was at the time of the battle commemorated. The searchlights shown on either side of the mast superstructure had been removed and replaced by a single searchlight on the forward side of the superstructure (fig. 80). The train ferry *Ahegweit* shown plying between Prince Edward Island and New Brunswick on a $1 1946 Canadian stamp was only launched several days after the stamp was issued, and not taken into service until 16th August, 1947, nearly a year later. The fishing boat with it, incidentally, appears headed for imminent collision with the *Ahegweit.* The 8c. Canadian stamp of 1973 commemorating the arrival of Scottish settlers at Pictou, Nova Scotia, in 1773, shows in the background a four-masted vessel which is certainly not the *Hector* which transported them, but a ship typical of the late 19th century. The Mississippi riverboat shown on a 4c. U.S. stamp of 1962 marking the 150th anniversary of Louisiana statehood is of a type which did not come into use until some 30 years after the establishment of the State in 1812. The 5c. value of the U.S. issue of 1925 marking the arrival of Norwegian immigrants in the sloop *Restaurationen* is not as anachronistic as at first appears, even although the Viking galley depicted flies modern Norwegian and U.S. flags, for in this case the design is taken from a photo-engraving of a ' Viking barque ' built in Norway, modelled on the ancient preserved Gokstad ship, which sailed to the World Fair in Chicago in 1883, manned by 12 rowers, and which did indeed fly both flags. Had this been intended for a genuine longship, the double instead of single row of shields, the jib-sail (not used until centuries later) and the placing of the steering oar would all have been further anachronisms. The South African 1d. stamps from 1926 onwards which are meant to show Van Riebeeck's ship *Drommedaris* in fact illustrate the model of a 24-gun Dutch man-of-war (now in the New Museum, Pretoria), of a much later date. Since Cape Town faces North to North East, the sun in this design should be at the opposite end of Table Mountain if setting and not on the design at all if rising! The South African 1s. stamp of 1952 featuring Van Riebeeck's arrival at the Cape in 1652 embodies several anachronisms. The hat and collar he wears did not come into fashion in Holland until 1658 at earliest, the lower half of his coat is in the fashion of Cromwellian England, he carries a long cane, not the short Commander's Staff of Authority which he should have borne, the two soldiers to his left are in uniforms of half a century earlier and the flag they bear is much larger than the usual Dutch flags of the period.

Other forms of transport than ships can also be involved in anachronisms. A West German 10pf. stamp of 1952 purports to show "letter post despatch Thurn & Taxis 1852", but the postillion is wearing Bavarian uniform, although there was no Thurn & Taxis post in Bavaria after 1808: in reality the stamp shows postal traffic between Neu-Ulm and Günsberg around 1846 (fig. 81). The well-known Arab camel postman on the Sudanese issues from March 1898 onwards carries mailbags inscribed "KHARTOUM" and "BERBER", but at the time they were first issued this was wishful thinking, for Berber had only recently been captured and Khartoum was not recaptured from the Dervishes until September 1898. The postal bus on the 20pf. West German stamp in the 1955 issue marking the 50th anniversary of Postal Motor Transport does not correspond to the type of 1906 as specified. A ½d. 1936 stamp of New Zealand shows a wool-laden lorry with registration 11-957, but in 1935 new regulations had been enacted governing number plates on motor vehicles, and a heavy lorry such as this should have carried the letter ' H ' before the number. However the designer was not to blame for this, as the stamp had been designed prior to the change although issued subsequent to it. One might also accuse New Zealand of perpetrating anachronisms in commemorating the 13th International Vintage Car Rally in 1972 with an issue which includes an 1895 Benz (3c.) and 1904 Oldsmobile (4c.), for these are technically *veteran* cars, *i.e.* built before 1905, of a period older than *vintage* (which is 1917-1933).

The tremendous crop of railway centennial stamps has predictably produced many anachronisms, several of which were pointed out by A. M. Goodbody in a letter to Stamp Magazine of 1973. The Italian 1939 issue marking the centenary of the Naples-Portici line opened in 1839 shows a later period locomotive built by Stephenson for the Royal Neapolitan Railways. A 15l. 1964 stamp of San Marino shows *Bayard*, one of the original locomotives which should have been depicted on the Italian stamp. Similarly the "train of 1849" on the 1949 Yugoslavian 2d. centennial stamp is a class 151 locomotive of the Yugoslavian State Railways, originally built as class 32d of the Austrian Südbahn in 1885. The 20ore Norwegian centennial stamp of 1954 shows an engine with a cab—probably one of 1861, as the earliest types had no cabs. The camel on a 30k. 1936 stamp of Tanna Touva might well take fright on seeing a train, if the report that no railways existed in the country at that time is indeed correct. However the report that the engine *Baronesa* shown on a 40c. Brazilian stamp of 1954 marking the centenary of Brazilian Railways had been built by Robert Stephenson in 1857 and could therefore not have been one of the first engines (A. M. Goodbody, 1973) appears to have been incorrect; the *Baronesa* would seem to have been built by William Fairborn of Manchester in 1852, and to have indeed been one of the pioneer engines.

Anachronisms also abound on stamps featuring aircraft. An interesting one involves the *Southern Cross,* the Fokker monoplane in which Kingsford Smith made trans-Pacific and world flights commemorated on Australian issues of 1931 and 1958, New Zealand 1958 and Fiji 1968. At that time it still bore the British registration letters G-AUSU, although records show that the Australian registration letters VH-USU had already been allocated to it before the trans-Tasman flight to New Zealand of 1928. Nevertheless the Australian registration letters were substituted on the 'plane as illustrated on the stamps to emphasise that this was an Australian 'plane—a deliberate official anachronism! At the time of the flights it had two-bladed propellers only, but the 1958 issues of Australia and New Zealand clearly show the central propeller in its later state with three blades (fig. 82). A 1967 Bhutanese issue commemorating Churchill shows 'planes associated with the Battle of Britain, but the Hurricane featured on the 4n. value is a Mark 2c, not the Mark I used at that time. A more controversial case is that of the 8d. and 9d. stamps of 1956 for the British Solomon Islands showing Henderson Airfield, Guadalcanal. This airfield was re-captured from the Japanese and used as an advanced air base in 1942. In 1949 a QANTAS service was operated from it, later transferred to Kukum, but although it was later re-established as a QANTAS terminal for Honiara, it has been claimed that at the time of issue of these stamps it was not operational at all. The aircraft on the British 10p. stamp of 1974 labelled "Imperial Airways flying boat 1937" should have been a ' C ' class flying boat, but in fact was the *Maia*, a later adaptation with special superstructure on its wings to which the small *Mercury* 'plane could be attached, not delivered to Imperial Airways until June 1938. The 5½p. stamp of this issue commemorates the first U.K. air mail flight (9th September, 1911). It shows a Farman biplane, but the inaugural flight was made by Gustav Hamel in a Bleriot, the first flight by Farman being on 11th September. A 300f. 1977 stamp of the Niger Republic shows the zeppelin LZ130 above the modern post-war railway station of Essen (the earlier station having been destroyed during the War), yet the LZ130's flights were all pre-war. A 5c. Canadian stamp of 1959 marks the 50th anniversary of Canadian Aviation, and features the *Silver Dart*, the first 'plane to fly in Canada, with a background of modern delta-winged aircraft, but in fact the only Canadian delta-wing aircraft in 1959 was the Avro *Arrow*, which did not get beyond the test-flight stage, further development being cancelled by the Government, ironically, on the day of issue of this stamp.

It has been suggested that the field gun shown on the Chilean 3c. stamp of 1910 commemorating the Battle of Roble is of a much later period than the battle, and also that a general officer would not make his headquarters in a battery position so close to the gun as shown on the stamp. A 1p. 1971 stamp of Gibraltar claims to show a soldier of the Black Watch of 1845, but his doublet was not authorised until 1855 (in 1845 he would have worn a coatee), while gauntlet cuffs were not introduced until 1868 (fig. 83). Indeed the Black Watch Regimental H.Q. have dated this uniform as post-1900. The ½d. New Zealand stamp of the 1940 centennial issue shows the arrival of the Maoris, but two of them sport walrus moustaches, although until the arrival of the British it was the invariable custom of Maoris to remove all facial hair except eyebrows, eyelashes and that of the top of the head. The 7d. and 8d. values of this issue show a Maori Council, but the ladder leaning against the Maori building in the background is of European type, not the notched pole used by the Maoris themselves.

In 1964 Andorra issued a 1f. stamp in the Andorran History series purporting to show the Confirmation of the Co-Government in 1288, but showing the bishop in modern rather than 13th century robes. The triple crown which Pope Sylvester II is shown wearing on a French 30c.+10c. semipostal of 1964 did not exist during the lifetime of this pope; in his time Popes used to wear a peaked white cap, with one gold band added in the 12th century and two further bands much later, eventually developing into the triple crown. Likewise the famous Hungarian crown of St. Stephen, a Byzantine circlet converted into an Emperor's crown in the early 12th century, could not have been worn by St. Stephen himself as shown on various Hungarian issues of 1928, 1929, 1938 and 1970. One might also argue that a quotation from the *Internationale,* composed by Degeyter and Pottier in 1888, should not be associated with the Paris Commune of 1871, as it is on the label accompanying a 1k. Czechoslovakian centennial commemorative of 1971. It might also be said that the 2c. Canadian stamp of 1934 commemorating the establishment of the Province of New Brunswick in 1784 should not feature the seal of New Brunswick, which was not granted by letters patent until 21st February, 1785, but perhaps that is just hairsplitting. The 3l.70 Italian definitive stamp of 1930 featuring Romulus, Remus and the wolf which suckled them shows the Royal Arms and the Fascist emblem side by side, although by then it had been decreed that these should be figured intertwined, as on the 1930 Virgil bimillenary issue.

Emblems and flags have indeed provided numerous anachronistic pitfalls for designers. The badge of St. Helena includes a ship flying the Cross of St. George, which went out of use in 1606, although the colony was first settled in 1659, so that various issues of 1922, 1934, 1938, 1949, 1953, 1959 and 1967 all perpetuate this anachronism. A 6c. U.S. stamp of 1970 commemorates the arrival of the Pilgrim Fathers in America in 1620, but instead of the 1605 Union flag, the *Mayflower* is flying the Union Jack, although the Cross of St. Patrick was not added until 1801. The British 1/6d. stamp of 1970 showing the departure of the *Mayflower* has the correct flag, but a 5t. Bangladeshi stamp of the issue marking the Bicentenary of American Independence also falls into this trap of depicting the *Mayflower* flying the modern Union Jack. The 2c. U.S. stamp of 1926 marking the 150th anniversary of the Battle of White Plains shows a flag which did not come into use until 14th June, 1777, almost eight months after the battle took place. American flags have often been a source of trouble, for a Polish 1z. stamp of 1938 commemorating the U.S. Constitution shows Washington grasping a Stars and Stripes banner complete with 48 stars, though this was not adopted until 1912, and there were never more than 15 stars on the flag in his lifetime (fig. 84). A U.S.A. bicentennial souvenir sheet of 1976 shows Washington crossing the Delaware River (after a painting by Emanuel Leutze and Eastman Johnson) on 25th December, 1776, but with the 13-star flag only adopted by resolution of the Continental Congress on 14th June, 1777. A more controversial case is the U.S. 3c. stamp of 1952 marking the 175th anniversary of the arrival of Lafayette in America which includes his portrait, sailing ship and cannon of the period, and *modern* flags of France and the U.S.A., since it could be argued that these signify a continuing bond with France at the time of issue, but it did arouse contemporary criticism. The flag shown with Diego de Losada, founder of Caracas in 1567, on a 55c. Venezuelan stamp of 1967, originated with Charles III in 1785.

Liberia has a flag anachronism on the 5c. 1949 stamp showing the stockade defence by Jehudi Ashmun and Matilda Newport in 1822, for the lone star banner they are flying was not adopted until 1847. South Korea in 1951 produced a long issue showing flags of the nations which participated in the Korean War on the side of the South (plus Sweden, which provided Red Cross teams), but represented Italy by the former royal flag, which includes a crown, This did not please republican Italy, so it was speedily replaced by the republican flag. In 1966 the United States of America issued a 5c. stamp to mark the Polish millenium and featured the Polish eagle surmounted with a crown thus symbolising the pre-communist state, but as 1,000 years were being represented one cannot be too dogmatic about which is or is not a correct representation. The Italian flag shown on a 1952 3cr.80 Brazilian stamp marking U.N. Day bears the shield of Savoy, not the emblem of the Republic.

Musical themes have also supplied anachronisms. The 40a. value of an Israeli "Purim" Festival issue of 1976 shows an instrument resembling a kamanja (spike fiddle) not known before 900 A.D., although the tab refers to Ahasuerus (Xerxes), whose reign commenced in 485 B.C. A 1971 issue of Fujeira commemorating Beethoven includes on the 30d. value a modern rotary French horn, whereas even the piston valve French horn was only invented 10 years before his death, and the modern timpani on the 4r. value is also an anachronism. The type of metronome figured on the French 30c.+10c. semipostal of 1968 commemorating Couperin (who died in 1733) was only patented by Mailzel in 1814, although the first suggestion of a time marker in the form of a pendulum appeared in 1676. Wagner's opera *Mastersingers* was set in the 16th century, but a German 6pf.+4pf. semipostal of 1933 portrays Hans Sachs (1494-1576) with an oil lamp of a type not invented until 1855 (by the American chemist Silliman). (fig 85). An Italian 25l. stamp of 1951 marking the 50th anniversary of the death of Verdi shows Roncale Church and its organ, but the organ is shown with its pipes symmetrically arranged whereas in the time of Verdi they were asymmetrically arranged. The 20m. Egyptian stamp of 1969 commemorating the centenary of the Opera House, Cairo, shows a performance of *Aida*, which had not been completed in 1869, and indeed the first performance was in this Opera House in 1871, as commemorated on an issue of 1971.

The German stamp of 1924 featuring Cologne includes a bridge which had been demolished before the First World War, while the 10pf. 1962 stamp of West Berlin featuring the Waisenbrücke (Orphan's Bridge) in a view dated "1783" (an adaptation of an etching by Johann Georg Rosenberg) includes a tower demolished in 1782. The 20pf. of this same issue shows a view of Berlin Castle dated "1703" on the stamp, yet including four carrier figures with the equestrian statue of Elector Frederick William which were only added to the statue in 1709. A 1c. stamp of 1963 from Monaco shows Wembley Stadium in a view clearly taken from an old picture, for it shows only half of the spectator accommodation as under cover, whereas by 1963 it was fully covered. A 1958 4d. stamp of Western Samoa shows the House of Assembly of the Samoan Parliament, the same design as on the 1d. 1952 stamp, but in the meantime the large Samoan ' fali ' (house) had been considerably enlarged, while the smaller house (beneath the two flags) had been entirely removed. A 4½d. 1974 stamp of the Isle of Man shows King Magnus Haraldson crewing a rowing boat ' coxed ' by King Edgar (959-975), but the City of Chester in the background is shown as a walled mediaeval city with architecture typical of the 14th to 15th century. A 5c. Canadian stamp of 1965 marks the centenary of Ottawa as capital of Canada, and is intended to show the Parliament Buildings as they were in 1865 (though this is not specifically stated on the stamp). However it actually illustrates an anachronistic period, for it shows the old Peace Tower (burned down in 1916) and also the circular Library of Parliament (of which only the foundations had been laid by 1866).

A 3c. U.S. stamp of 1948 marks the centennial of the discovery of gold by James W. Marshall at Sutton's Field, Coloma, in California: it shows the site but includes a large double-trunked tree of a species not even found in the area at that date. A further historical inaccuracy is involved in the 3c. U.S. stamp of 1954 marking the 150th anniversary of the Lewis and Clark Expedition, for this shows the landing of Lewis and Clark on the banks of the Mississippi preparatory to going into winter quarters, which occurred in October 1804. Behind stand their guide, the Shoshone Indian girl Sacagawea and her husband Charbonneau, a French-Canadian trapper, but these did not join Lewis and Clark until the following month (fig. 86). The unconstructed highway, prominently marked as if already in functional existence, on a 1961 Colombian issue as recorded earlier (on page 82) might equally well have been considered an anachronism and included here.

Turning to more miscellaneous anachronisms, the 13p. British stamp of 1976 in the issue marking the 500th anniversary of Caxton's press shows two printers operating a primitive press of 1516, although Caxton died in 1491. The Australian 18c. stamp of 1976 marking the centenary of the first telephone transmission shows Bell making a telephone call, but does not indicate that he is using the ' Williams ' coffin telephone of 1878. The 60c. Australian stamp of the 1972 issue commemorating pioneer days shows Morse tape and a Morse key, but the former arrived long after the latter and does not belong to pioneer days. Incidentally, the message on the Morse tape mysteriously reads "Darn MLB end of message"—who or what this signifies we have no idea. A French 50c. stamp of 1970 honours Pelletier and Caventou, who isolated quinine from cinchona bark and showed that it was the anti-febrile constituent. The stamp shows quinine (represented by its structural formula) attacking the malarial plasmodium, and it has been alleged that this is an anachronism, as the full structural formula was not known until about half a century later, but this seems uncalled for hair-splitting. An apparent anachronism occurs on a 50pf. West German stamp of 1974 marking the U.P.U. centenary and showing, on the left, a 19th century Swiss mail box with collection times given on a 24hr. time-table, whereas in the last century a 12hr. time-table with a.m. or p.m. would have been used. However the post box concerned is in fact still in use to this day, in Spalentor Street, Basle, and does carry the modern time-table. The 1948 ½d. Springbok issue of South Africa was an economy print from plates of the 1926 issue, made to use up old stocks of cut paper. However, in the interval the accepted spelling of the name of the country in Afrikaans had changed from SUIDAFRIKA to SUID-AFRIKA, so that it was no longer correct on the stamp.

Sports have produced at least two anachronisms. The discus-thrower on a 1935 issue of El Salvador is obviously based on the Discobolus statue of Myron, for the throwing style is clearly classical, yet he is dressed, presumably for modesty's sake, in modern sportswear. A 1fo. Hungarian stamp of 1963, part of an issue marking the Winter Olympic Games of 1964, shows a figure-skating pair wearing old-fashioned skates of a type popular before the First World War, highly unlikely for modern championship contestants.

One rather special category of anachronisms concerns the scientific names of organisms. These are intended to remain constant, but from time to time may have to be changed for taxonomic or nomenclatural reasons. Stamp designers ought to use the scientific name generally accepted at the time of issue of the stamp, but often when they copy an old illustration they copy with it an out-of-date name. Thus the fungus on a 60h. Czechoslovakian stamp of 1958 is named "*Krombholzia rufescens*", but '*Krombholzia*' had earlier been used for a genus of flowering plant so could not be used here, and the correct name would have been *Leccinum testaceo-scabrum*. It could be argued that the hawthorn labelled "*Mespilus oxyacantha*" on a 1st. Bulgarian stamp of 1969 should have been named *Crataegus oxyacantha*, the generally accepted name, but in this case there is a taxonomic decision to be made, and the boundaries between these two genera are very ill-defined. The flower named "*Clappertonia ficifolia*" on a 1967 1f. stamp of Dahomey ought more properly to have been named *Honckenya ficifolia*.

Molluscs, which feature surprisingly frequently on stamps, seem to be particularly subject to being labelled with names which have been long out-of-date. A Kenyan 1971 20s. stamp shows *Lambis* (*Lambis*) *scorpio*, but under the out-of-date name "*Pterocera scorpio*", which is also used on a 20f. 1962 stamp of the Comoro Islands. It is correct on a 15c. 1968 stamp of Papua New Guinea. The French Somali Coast 60f. airmail stamp of 1962 shows *Tibia insulaechorab* subsp. *curta* under the archaic name of "*Rostellaria magna*". The Red Volute *Voluta* (*Antica*) *norcisi,* is shown on a 10c. stamp of Papua New Guinea under an our-of-date synonym ("*Voluta ruckeri*"), while on the $1 value of the same issue *Papuina pulcherrima* is wrongly named "*Papustyla pulcherrima*". In a 1975 issue of the Maldive Islands the 1l. value shows *Cyprocassus rufa* under the out-of-date name "*Cassia nana*" (it is correctly named on a 2f. 1962 stamp of the Wallis and Futuna Islands), while on the 2l. value *Murex* (*M.*) *pecten* is wrongly named "*Murex triremus*". A 1965 North Vietnamese issue uses several out-dated names: the crab on the 12x. value named "*Neptunus pelagicus*" ought to have been called *Portunus pelagicus*, "*Palinurus japonicus*" on the 20x. value should be *Panulirus japonicus* (this is a different genus, not a corrected spelling) and "*Uca marionis*" on the 50x. value should properly have been called *Uca vocans*.

Similarly the rock lobster named "*Palinurus vulgaris*" on a 20d. Yugoslavian stamp of 1956 should have been given its modern name *Palinurus elephas*. However the lobster on a 2c. 1965 stamp of Barbados is correctly named "*Panulirus argus*", although some catalogues have stated that this should be *Palinurus*.

The small tortoiseshell butterfly named "*Vanessa urticae*" on a 40g. Polish stamp of 1967 should properly have been called *Aglais urticae*. The correct name for the butterfly called "*Teria gundlachia*" on a 12c. 1958 Cuban stamp would have been *Eurema proterpia*, an earlier name which had been overlooked, and the butterfly on the 14c., "*Teria ebriola*" is only a seasonal form of *Eurema daira* and should have been so named. The scarce copper butterfly "*Lycaena virgaureae*" on a 1fo. Hungarian stamp of 1959 had earlier been assigned to a new genus and should have been called *Heodes virgaurea*. The name "*Danaus plexippus*" on a 19f. New Caledonian stamp of 1968 is wrong—it should be *Danaus genutia*.

The Zebra Firefish named "*Brachyrus zebra*" on a 1f. 1959 stamp of New Caledonia should properly have been named *Dendrochirus zebra*. The West Atlantic Sawfish named "*Pristis antiquorum*" on a 3cor. Nicaraguan stamp of 1969 should have been given the now accepted name *Pristis pectinatus*, and the name "*Phylipnus dormitor*" used for the fish on a 50c. stamp of the same issue is also out-of-date and should have been replaced by *Gobiomorus dormitor*. Similarly the guppy on a 40fi. Hungarian stamp of 1962 should not have been called "*Lebistes reticulatus*" but *Poecilia reticulata*. The Chinchilla on a 10s. Peruvian stamp of 1973 should be named *Chinchilla laniger*, not "*Eriomis chinchilla*", and the Sumatran Rhinoceros is properly named *Dicerorhinus sumatrensis*, not "*Rhinoceros bicornis*" as on a 30x. 1964 stamp of North Vietnam. Finally, the Fallow deer should now be named *Cervus dama*, not "*Dama dama*" as on an 80fi. Hungarian stamp of 1964 and a 12st. Bulgarian stamp of 1973.

We will close this section with anachronisms involving actual plants and animals and not just their names. A 10s. Maltese stamp of 1899 shows the shipwreck of St. Paul, adapted from a picture by Gustave Doré but with the substitution of a snake for one of the shipwrecked men scrambling ashore. However, in the Biblical narrative the snake does not appeaı until some time later. A 1967 1/6d. stamp of St. Helena shows settlers in 1667 clearing scrub which includes palm trees, but these were only introduced to the island about a century later (fig. 87). Aphrodite is shown associated with a hibiscus on a 1958 50l. Greek stamp, but as this flower was only brought to Greece in 1225 it is hardly an appropriate accompaniment for a Greek goddess. Finally we have breathtaking anachronisms on a 1972 issue of the Maldive Islands. The vegetation featured with the Stegosaurus on the 2l. value includes a Cycad (right), an *Araucaria* (centre) and a Liliaceous plant (left), none of them contemporary with the Stegosaurus. The 7l. stamp includes with the so-called Edaphosaurus (actually a Dimetrodon) a *Williamsonia* from the later Jurassic epoch. The 5r. stamp shows on the left a *Psilophyton*, one of the earliest known land plants, which flourished and apparently died out in the Devonian era, while the Tyrannosaurus featured with it lived perhaps some 250 million years later! (fig. 88).

CHAPTER 7

Impossible Compositions

The stamp designs which fall into this category embody certain features which are mutually contradictory. For example the 3c. U.S. stamp of 1944 marking the 75th anniversary of the completion of the first transcontinental railroad depicts the so-called ' Golden Spike Ceremony ' at which the last spike was ceremoniously hammered in to complete the railroad, at Promontory, Utah (the golden spike itself was straightway removed and replaced by an ordinary one). The stamp design (after a painting by John McQuarrie) shows a flag fluttering in a direction diametrically opposed to that in which smoke from the stationary engine is blowing. A similar error occurs in the various Peruvian stamps of 1925-28 which marked the Tacna-Arica Plebiscite, although in this case the locomotive is in motion, which makes the contradiction less clear. The ' War at Sea ' Greek issue of 1971 shows flags, pennants and sails blowing in quite different directions, and flags and sails blow in contrary directions also for the ships on a Liberian issue of 1972, the Arab dhow on a 1964 National Day issue of Kuwait, the ships on 2½d. and 1/3d. values of a ship set produced by Ghana in 1957, the *Hirondelle I* on a 2f. 1949 stamp of Monaco and on the ship featured on 1913-27 issues of British Guiana. Flags blow in wrong directions on a 70pf. West German stamp of 1965 showing an early steamship and a modern motorship, at the poop of a sailing ship on a 1949 4f. stamp of the Belgian Congo commemorating the 75th anniversary of the U.P.U., and the 1r. value of a 1976 issue of the Seychelles marking the U.S. bicentennial. The sails of the sailing ship and smoke of the steamer on the U.S. 20c. definitive stamp of 1923 featuring the Golden Gate appear to indicate contrary winds, and the winds propelling the yachts on an 8d. 1965 stamp of the Bahamas appear to be of differing strength and direction for each individual yacht. However one has to be careful not to jump too readily to the conclusion that the flag of a sailing ship must always stream towards the prow, for a sailing ship can sail to within about 45 degrees from the direction of the wind when beating close hauled to windward. Therefore the ½d. 1967 Gibraltarian stamp showing H.M.S. *Victory* on the starboard tack after a 1793 painting by Monamy Swaine is NOT in error. The local stamps of the St. Lucia Steam Conveyance Co., featured on a 1972 issue of St. Lucia, present a parallel case. The 1923 centennial issue for Liberia features the arrival of the first settlers, with the immigrants' vessel in full sail in quite rough seas, and here it seems rather unlikely that the two boatloads of immigrants could ever have landed under these conditions. The 1d. Otago Centennial New Zealand stamp of 1948 shows a sailing ship, the *John Wickliffe*, under full sail whilst at anchor, and it has been claimed that our own 1/9d. 1967 stamp commemorating Francis Chichester's world voyage shows *Gipsy Moth IV* in full sail under storm conditions and on the port tack in a wind which, as indicated by the waves, is on the starboard bow. Similarly 20g. and 45g. Polish stamps of 1925-26 show a full-rigged ship with directions of waves and sails at variance. The various sails on the sailing ship of the 1942 Free French issue of St. Pierre & Miquelon appear to be receiving wind from different directions, while the yacht on a 1965 60c. French stamp remains on even keel without heeling over even slightly, although the sail is bellied out in the wind.

Leaving ships, we have the 50c. Tanganyikan stamp of 1962 which shows the flag of the Republic being hoisted on the summit of Kilimanjaro. Here the flag blows bravely in a breeze which does not stir the steady flame of the Freedom Torch and which appears to leave the hoist rope quite slack (fig. 89). A 5y. Japanese stamp of 1949 shows the Japanese ladies' skating champion executing a graceful left back spiral, as indicated by her billowing skirt, yet the trace on the ice indicates a forward movement. A 24pf. East German stamp of 1950 appears to be a rather poor caricature of this, similarly having a tracing on the ice behind instead of in front of the skater. An aeroplane in flight with a stationary propeller appears on the 1931 Australian stamp marking Kingsford Smith's World Flights, and on the aeroplane on air mail issues of Costa Rica of 1934 and 1952. The Handley Page torpedo carrier shown on the 10d. 1931 stamp of South West Africa not only has a stationary propeller (although airborne) but also open wing slots, because the artist copied a photograph of the 'plane on the ground, from *All the World's Aircraft*. On the other hand da Vinci's flying machine, shown high in the sky on Italian stamps of 1932, was probably never ever constructed and certainly never could have flown.

A curious mistake occurs on a 30pf.+15pf. West German semipostal of 1969 featuring a pewter figurine ' Bird Salesman ', for here the cage held by the salesman has the bars behind the bird! This may, however, be true of the original figurine and hence no fault of the designer. This cannot be claimed for the U.S. ' Boston Tea Party ' stamps of 1973 which show part of the ship's rigging passing *behind* the moon! (fig. 90).

Shadows are another fruitful source of contradiction. A 4p. 1971 stamp from Tristan da Cunha shows the Presentation of a Scout troop flag, with almost every shadow falling in a different direction. We have earlier drawn attention to shadow inconsistencies on the Canadian 2c. National War Memorial stamp of 1939. A Belgian 10f. stamp of 1971 marking the Antarctic Pact shows penguins being photographed, the camera casting a strong shadow, the penguins apparently casting none. A 1930 35c.+15c. semipostal of the Belgian Congo shows a tent surgery, but the shadows of the table and on the tent do not match other shadows. Rising suns, a favourite symbol of stamp designers, create problems, for anything in the foreground ought to be poorly illuminated with long shadows to the front, which would usually spoil the effect, so we may reasonably excuse the lack of these as permissible artistic licence on, for instance, the 15c. 1972 stamp of Sri Lanka, the 15c. 1964 stamp of St. Lucia showing Pigeon Island, the 10c. 1921 Liberian stamp with the arms of Liberia, the 1945 and 1946 issues of Saxony (Allied Occupation, Russian Zone) featuring ploughing, and the various Nyasaland stamps featuring the symbol of the Protectorate, a leopard on a rock against the rising sun, though on the 1d. stamp of 1947 the existing shadow appears to be almost at right angles to where it ought to be. The long-lived

French Sower design, which first appeared in 1903, shows a lady in fluttering garments which indicate that she is sowing against the wind, and though the sun shines brightly she casts no shadow: later modifications of the design removed the sun, but the original design continued in use until 1936—a very long run for a design error. Current French coins carry the 1903 design, so obviously symbolism means a lot! A 3c. Ecuadorian stamp of 1936 shows a woodsman with both sun and shadow behind him, and a 1947 2pf. stamp of Germany (Allied Occupation) shows the sun's rays interrupted by a spade and changing direction to the left of the handle. A Turkish issue of 1931 marking the 2nd Balkan Conference includes a map of the Balkans with the sun rising in the north. Less obviously the sun is rising from the south, behind the roads of the Fort de France, on a 1908 issue of Martinique, and is likewise rising (or setting) to the north of the port of Rio de Janeiro on a 100r. Brazilian stamp of 1930, part of an issue marking the 4th Pan-American Architectural Congress. A 50c. Swiss stamp of 1963 marks the Swiss National Exposition, Lausanne, showing two spheres which appear to be illuminated from quite different directions.

As the sun's rays are effectively parallel the size of shadows cast is not affected by altitude, and it requires rather special atmospheric conditions to produce a greatly enlarged yet not distorted shadow (*e.g.* the celebrated Spectre of the Brocken). However stamp designers do not appear generally aware of this, and impossibly huge aircraft shadows appear on many issues, *e.g.* Cameroun (1941, 25c., 50c., 1f.), Egypt (1959, air issue), French Morocco (1939-40 air issue; 1947, 100f., 200f.), Monaco (1942, 5f., 10f.), New Caledonia (1938-40, air issue), New Zealand (1950, 1s., Centennial of Canterbury), Réunion (1947, 50f.).

Reflections do not seem to lead to as many errors as one might expect—designers appear to be on their guard here. However, the ½d. and 9d. Nyasaland stamps of 1945 show a fisherman on Lake Nyasa with his hands together, yet his reflection shows hands separated and arms outstretched, while the 70c. Ethiopian stamp of 1947 showing boating on Lake Tana has reflections of boat and crew bearing little relation in form or direction to their source.

Light plays curious tricks on some stamp designs. A 1955 Italian 100l. stamp commemorating G. Mazzini shows a lighthouse apparently producing a full circle of light, not a beam, uninterruptedly even through the roof. A 1967 Bulgarian 10st. stamp marking a Philatelic Congress shows a stamp, tweezers and magnifying glass, yet the tweezers, though partly under the glass, appear very little magnified. A similar 20st. stamp of 1971 removes the tweezers from under the glass, though here the magnified stamp has many fewer perforations than it ought to have (it should be perf. $14\frac{1}{2} \times 15$). This stamp portrayed, the first Bulgarian stamp (issued 1st May 1879) appears more correctly on a 1940 issue, though perhaps not very appropriately, as this issue marks the centenary of adhesive postage stamps—not, of course, of Bulgarian postage stamps.

Artistic licence may also be invoked for designs featuring activities on snow, sand or similar surfaces which remain magically unruffled. Thus the two climbers on Glittertind Peak on a 90ore 1968 Norwegian stamp have clearly just been dropped neatly into place by helicopter, as their progress has left no tracks. A 90ore 1961 Norwegian stamp showing

Amundsen's party and tent at the South Pole also shows no prints, unlike the photograph of the same scene taken later by Scott's ill-fated group.

The New Zealand Health stamps of 1939 show boys with a large beach-ball labelled "Health"—much too large for the cupped hands of the small central boy waiting to catch it. Here the design was adapted from three separate photographs, in one of which the two boys on the left were indeed playing with a much smaller ball, while the boy on the right, from a different photograph, played with a much larger ball, but the designer failed to notice this discrepancy, which was repeated in the 1940 issue. Bolivian stamps of 1942 and 1944 show clasped hands, but on close inspection it will be seen that the fingers of the hand on the right are curled round the hand clasped at an angle quite impossible if they are normally jointed. This also applies to the clasped hands on four values in the Czechoslovakian Kosice issue of 1945. The British 6d. World Cup stamp of 1966 shows the player to the left in back view but with feet pointing to the foreground, so his joints must be even more peculiar. The nurse on a 70pf.+35pf. 1974 semipostal of West Berlin seems to have her head set very peculiarly on her shoulders.

The 1927 5s. South African stamp featuring an outspanned ox wagon shows the yoke standing upright, although it is only loosely connected to the pole. Even more improbably, on a 60g. Polish stamp of 1959 a nurse is tilting a bottle and the level of the contained liquid is tilting with it; this also occurs with the milk in the feeding bottle of a 2z.50 Polish stamp of 1961 in an issue marking the 15th anniversary of UNICEF (fig. 91). A British 2½d. stamp of 1957 shows a Scout badge and a rolling hitch, but the rope of the latter becomes mysteriously double-stranded in the centre foreground, with the strands twisted in opposite directions—it would take a very gifted Scout to achieve this hitch! The watch on a 2p. Mexican Special Delivery stamp of 1976 shows the hour hand markedly not in conformity with the minute hand.

Finally for this section we may look at cases in which the inherent contradiction lies between the different stamps of a series. The most notorious of these occurs on the 1893 Columbus issue of the United States, where on the 1c. stamp a clean-shaven Columbus is in sight of land and on the 2c. he has just landed—by now with a magnificently full beard. The explanation here, of course, is that each design was adapted from a different painting, and while Powell visualised Columbus as beardless (historically correct), Vanderlyn thought of him as bearded. Other sequential errors where a single artist is responsible for the series have less excuse, *e.g.* the change of dress by the Sleeping Beauty between pricking her finger on the fateful spindle and being awakened by the kiss of her Prince on the West German semipostal issue of 1964, and the change of dress by Cinderella between feeding the birds and being brought a party dress by them in return, on the similar semipostal issue of 1965. In this same issue the colour of the sash of this party dress changes from gold to red and the Prince's crown changes in detail—perhaps he had two! Similarly in the corresponding semipostal issue of 1961, dealing with the story of Hansel and Gretel, Gretel's apron has a double red border on the 7pf.+3pf. value, a single border on 10pf.+5pf. and 20pf.+10pf. values, then back to a double red border on the 40pf.+20pf., while her green-striped dress of the first three stamps becomes blue-striped on the

Woodcut of the Knight from the second edition of Chaucer's Canterbury Tales (1484).
Reproduced from a stamp issued by the Post Office on 29 September 1976. The design has been developed from the winning entry made by Richard Gay in the Royal Society of Arts Industrial Design Student Bursary Competition for Postage Stamps in 1974, sponsored by the Post Office.

top value. Snow White and the Seven Dwarfs appear on the 1962 issue, but when poisoned (20pf.+10pf. value) she wears a short-sleeved blouse, an apron and a skirt with green dots, yet in her coffin (40pf.+20pf. value) wears a long-sleeved blouse, no apron and a skirt ornamented with short blue lines. The corresponding 1963 issue tells the story of the Wolf and the Seven Kids. Here the mother of the kids leaves the house wearing a green-striped blouse and a skirt with red crosses and a green patterned hem, but on her return all these colours have changed, while the colour of the collar of the youngest kid has changed from green to blue. East Germany has done little better, for the Puss in Boots issue of 1968 shows the rowels of the cat's spurs with six points on four values, but six on one and seven on the other for the 15pf. and 25pf. values. Our own Wenceslas issue of 1973 can also be faulted, for the old man is gathering his sticks in a treeless area, the moon appears to be cavorting about the sky in a most peculiar manner, and the dishes carried by king and page change ornamentation between the third and fourth stamps of the series. A 1963 Dutch issue marking the 150th anniversary of the Kingdom shows William, Prince of Orange, with a lapel to his coat on the 5c. value but without one on the 4c., with sideburns on the 30c. value but without them on the 4c. and 5c. stamps. Furthermore, the 'L' of "NEDERLAND" is not well formed, and except on the 5c. value appears more like an 'I'.

CHAPTER 8

Commemoration of Non-Events

This category of error is the commemoration or celebration of something which did not happen. We shall omit the vast number of issues which mark national or international events, such as the Olympic Games and the World Cup finals by countries which have absolutely no connection with the event in question—these are not errors but cynical money-making rackets carried out at the expense of stamp collectors. The commemoration of the Centenary of the Japanese Railways by Equatorial Guinea and of the First World Conference of Boy Scouts in Africa by the Maldive Islands are typical examples of this kind of philatelic malpractice. However, in a surprisingly large number of cases the issuing countries appear to be unaware of the nature of the events which they are marking, and in the case of the Olympic Games, for instance, include designs for sports which do not form part of the Games at all, for example table tennis (Yugoslavia, 1956, 70d.; Jordan, 1964, 4f.); lawn tennis—not an Olympic sport since 1924—(Costa Rica, 1960, 5c.; Laos, 1968, 80k.; Monaco, 1948, 10f.+15f.; Syria, 1965, 12½p.; Togo, 1964, 100f.; Tunisia, 1960, 15m.): badminton (Indonesia, 1972, 75r.): women's basketball (Bulgaria, 1956, 80st.): baseball (Costa Rica, 1960, 1col.): polo (Iran, 1964, 6r.; Syria, 1968, 50p.): American football (Mexico, 1966, 2p.25): horse-racing (Iran, 1972, 5r.; Mexico, 1968, 5p.): hunting (Iran, 1972, 2r.): an obstacle race (Mexico, 1966, 80c.): women's water polo (Yugoslavia, 1956, 50d.): silat—a type of unarmed combat—(Indonesia, 1972, 20r.): even chess (Iran, 1972, 1r.). A similar list can be produced for the Winter Olympic Games, *e.g.* tobogganing and curling (Sharjah, 1968, 1d. and 2d. respectively): three-man bobsleighing (Hungary, 1971, 3fo.; Liberia, 1967, 40c.; Spain, 1968, 3p.50; Yemen (Royalist), 1968, 1b.): the four-man bobsleigh event (Togo, 1960, 1f.) was not included in the 1960 Games. The baton exchange between Charles Jenkins and Thomas Courtney of the U.S.A. could not have occurred in the 4×400m. Olympic relay race as claimed on an 11c. 1958 stamp of the Dominican Republic, for Jenkins ran the first leg and Courtney ran the last leg.

The 1966 issue of Thailand marking the Fifth Asian Games, Bangkok, portrays tennis on the 25s. value, although this was not one of the events, and downhill skiing (Finland, 1938, 3m.50) was similarly not in the programme of the International Skiing Contest, Lahti, which this issue marks. Sports events heralded by stamp issues but which did not take place include the West African Football Championships (Ghana, 1959, issue), the Balkan Games of 1948 (Yugoslavia, 1948, issue), and the International Military Sports Festival of Socialist States, Prague (North Vietnam, 1962, 12x.), though to do North Vietnam justice the authorities did try to withdraw this stamp before issue but some post offices sold copies before they received the withdrawal instructions. One might also, perhaps, include here the Dutch semipostal issue of 1956 for the Melbourne

Olympic Games, for the premium here was intended to help to finance the Dutch Olympic team. In the event the Netherlands withdrew as a protest against the Russian invasion of Hungary, and the collected funds were given to Hungarian relief. The European Youth Athletics Competitions, Leipzig, marked by a 20pf. East German stamp of 1968, were in fact refused recognition as an official European contest because of irregularities concerning Russian participation. The World Judo Championships were scheduled to be held in Barcelona in September, 1977, but for political reasons connected with the Formosan team the event was cancelled. A 3p. stamp had been prepared and distributed and was withdrawn, but as some had been issued, in order to stop speculation the Spanish authorities released the remainder in late December, 1977.

Various sports issues feature the five linked rings of the familiar Olympic symbol, although not apparently intended to represent Olympic events, *e.g.* a 1963 Nicaraguan issue which includes not only tennis but also chess and angling, while a 1964 issue of the Yemen Arab Republic includes darts, table tennis and horse-racing (¼b., ½b. and 4b. values respectively). A 1965 issue for Ecuador actually explicitly marks the Fifth Bolivar, so the symbol for five continents linked in sport is hardly appropriate. One might also cavil at the contradiction in terms of National Olympic Games, supported by a Lithuanian issue of 1938 and Colombian issues of 1935 and 1937, with Olympic symbols on the 5c. stamp of the 1935 issue.

Projected events other than sport occasions may be commemorated in advance and then be cancelled. A 1960 issue of Togo marks a four-power ' Summit ' Conference which did not in fact take place. A 1958 Liberian issue marks places visited by President Tubman on his European tour, but the visit to Sweden anticipated on the 5c. value was called off at the last minute. Incidentally the grammar on the stamps is also inadequate (fig. 92). Similarly a 1965 North Korean issue marks the 2nd Afro-Asian Conference, Algiers, cancelled only a few days before it was due to take place, and the visit of the Mexican President to Bolivia marked by a Bolivian issue of 1960 also did not take place. A Lebanese issue was prepared to mark an intended Medical Congress of 1943 in Beyrouth; when this was postponed the issue was not made, but the stamps were overprinted and used to mark a quite different event, the Sixth Arab Medical Congress, held in 1944. A set was produced by Siam (Thailand) "To celebrate the King's reign equal to that of King Rama II, B.E. 2468" (*i.e.* 15 years) as the inscription puts it, but although King Rama VI did indeed reign for just over 15 years he died (in 1925) before the set could be issued. It was nevertheless issued, in 1926, as an ordinary postal issue, but of course Rama VI was then no longer King so the inscription was somewhat out-of-date. The issue of Europa stamps by Liechtenstein might be mentioned here, for Liechtenstein is not a member of CEPT, being represented in postal affairs by Switzerland, yet in the 1968 issue, for instance, uses the key design common to the true CEPT members, with the letters "CEPT" worked into the key design. Inadvertent commemoration of a real event, the converse situation, occurred with a 2k. 1939 stamp of Iceland which was intended for an ordinary definitive but by mistake was inscribed to mark the New York World's Fair. A corrected issue was made, but the leakage of 35 sheets of the faulty stock led the Icelanders to issue part of the remainder to squash speculation.

The U.S. 1952 3c. stamp commemorating the birth of Betsy Ross as designer of the first Stars and Stripes flag, and which shows her displaying it to the Flag Committee, marks another probable non-event, for historians now seem generally agreed that she played no part in its design—the claim was made by her grandson long after her death. Another rather dubious commemoration is the 225th anniversary of the first balloon ascent, by Kryakutni, marked by a Russian 40k. stamp of 1956 on which he is shown swaying perilously over the timbered roofs of old Moscow, presumably in 1731, for the credit for the first successful manned balloon flight is generally given to the hot-air balloon ascent of Jean Pilâtre de Rozier of Metz in 1785.

A great many countries issue air mail stamps with no pretensions of an air mail service for which to use them. Costa Rica, for instance, issued a 20c. air mail stamp in 1926 portraying an aeroplane which even had "Correo Aereo" inscribed on its fuselage, yet no air mail service existed in Costa Rica until 1930. The U.S. air issue of 1918 marked the inauguration of the first regular air service in the U.S.A., between Washington and New York, yet the Curtiss ' Jenny ' of that first flight, featured on the stamps, never made the maiden trip from Washington to New York, for due to a faulty compass it ended up near Waldorf, Maryland. Ethiopia marked the first flight of an aeroplane into Addis Ababa with an overprint which translates "16 Aug. 1929 Abyssinian Government Air Mail" on stamps which were available for five days and were presumably intended to service outgoing air mail, but in fact this 'plane departed without taking any mail at all. The 1959 issue marking the 30th anniversary of the air mail service presumably also refers to this non-event, thus doubly commemorating it (fig. 93). Stamps were issued by Honduras in 1929 to mark a planned flight from New York to Honduras, semipostals of a sort, though here the face value was to go to Garay (the pilot) and the premium to the Dept. of Public Health to finance a tuberculosis hospital—a dubious issue at best, particularly since the flight never took place. The projected Riga-Bathurst flight for which a Latvian issue of air charity stamps was overprinted in 1933 did at least start, but the 'plane crashed at Neustettin, Germany, and the mail it carried was forwarded by ordinary post. A Polish miniature sheet of 1938 shows a stratosphere balloon soaring above lofty mountains, but this also marks a non-event, for the flight never actually took place. It was delayed due to strong winds, and while the partially filled balloon was being emptied a strong gust of wind caused an explosion which destroyed the upper part of the cover and that was that. The flight covers were sent to Warsaw, given a special date cancellation and explanatory cachet, and then forwarded by ordinary mail.

Aircraft which never flew also occur on stamps, for instance the Boeing Supersonic ' 773 ' shown on 1968 stamps of the Maldive Islands (along with Concorde). The aeroplane on the Free French issues of 1942 has an interesting history. The stamp designer, the talented Edmund Dulac, produced a first sketch which was rejected as showing an out-of-date aircraft, so drew this design from a photograph of a model of the projected Fairey FC1, an aeroplane which never came into production.

The railways shown on 45c. and 5b. Bolivian stamps of 1938 are also largely imaginary, for the Sucre-Camiri line, shown on both stamps, had still not been completed by 1972, and was by then planned to link up with the Yacuiba-Santa Cruz line at Boyuibe instead of going to Camiri, while the Santa Cruz-Cochabamba line shown on the 5b. stamp was also still only partially completed by 1972. The Bangui-Douala Railway project marked by a 1963 issue of the Central African Republic was likewise subsequently abandoned. The air mail 10b. Bolivian stamp issued surcharged 1200b. in 1960 also relates to a railway non-event, for the original stamp was intended to mark the opening of the Corumba-Santa Cruz Railway in 1954, in the presence of the Presidents of Brazil and Bolivia: the railway was opened to schedule but in the absence of the Presidents, so the stamp was not issued unsurcharged.

Non-existent countries can appear on perfectly reputable stamps at times, as for instance the 1900 'Tablet' issue for French Sudan, for by Decree of 17th October, 1899, French Sudan had been officially abolished, its territories divided up amongst Senegal, French Guinea, the Ivory Coast, Dahomey and the territories of Senegambia and Niger. The issue had in fact been printed in error, but was allowed to be used in the colony as administratively re-distributed, though no further issues were produced under this name until 1921. Political events can of course destroy the justification for an issue before it can be produced, but it is rather surprising that the Germans produced 3pf. and 5m. stamps with lozenges watermark for the Marshall Islands in 1916, considering that they had been firmly in Japanese hands since 1914. A 1c. Cuban stamp of 1961 shows a revolutionary label of 1874 bearing a Cuba Mambisa postmark of 10th October, 1868, but actual postal use of this label is highly unlikely ever to have occurred, and this postmark seems a case of wishful thinking. The Mexican express mail issue of 1976 must be accounted somewhat belated, for this service had been discontinued in Mexico some years previously.

A curious near non-event is the Dilston Falls shown on a 6d. 1899 Tasmanian stamp, for these falls are only temporary, marking the outlet of a swamp which fills up at high tide and then empties by way of the falls at low tide. A fascinating story lies behind the frescoes on the walls of St. Mary's Church, Lübeck, shown on the West German issue marking the 700th anniversary of the church in 1951. The mediaeval frescoes had been vanishing under the wear and tear of centuries, and in 1938 Professor Ernst Fay was commissioned to retouch and restore them, but by accident he completely removed them. Horrified, he commissioned a minor artist, Lothar Malskat, to replace them, work which was completed in time for the 700th anniversary, and which was much admired. However, following a quarrel between Fay and Malskat the truth came out and it was discovered that the 'mediaeval' portraits as shown on the stamps included relatives of the artist and film stars such as Marlene Dietrich (whom the artist much admired). The frescoes were cleaned off, artist and professor imprisoned, the stamps remaining witness to their fraud (fig. 94).

Use of a stamp to commemorate a quite different event from that at first intended also occurs. Uruguay had stamps designed and authorised in 1937 to commemorate the 75th anniversary of the foundation of a Swiss Colony, with a picture of a monument to be erected to the event, but the monument was so long in being completed that the issue was shelved and finally issued in 1944 to mark the 50th anniversary of the legal creation of the township of Nueva Helvetia (which actually occurred in 1896)—with surcharges because postal rates had risen in the interim. Because the 1957 Dominican Republic's third issue to commemorate the 1956 Olympic Games didn't sell as well as hoped the stamps were overprinted in May 1958 with a 2c. surcharge and alternate Stars of David and Red Crescents, the surcharge to go to UNWRA. But the most sweeping change of function of an issue must surely rest with San Marino, which prepared an issue to celebrate the 20th anniversary of Fascism, presumably intended for issue on the 20th anniversary of the fascist march on Rome (22nd October, 1922). Events made such an issue somewhat inopportune, so San Marino, ever ready to earn an honest lira, philatelically, converted the issue with a simple overprint into a celebration of the fall of Fascism! (fig. 95).

CHAPTER 9

Diplomatic Errors

The errors included in this section concern designs which may in themselves be accurate enough (sometimes too accurate!) but which may in some way give offence to individuals, groups or even other nations. For instance the 1964 British issue which marked the Tenth International Botanical Congress shows four British flowering plants, a typically English rose, two rare species (Spring Gentian and Fringed Water Lily) which never grow wild in Scotland, and the Honeysuckle—all this for a Congress being held in Edinburgh! Small wonder the Scots were upset. The Scottish Nationalist Party also objected to the British 1965 issue commemorating the 700th anniversary of Simon de Montfort's Parliament, asking that these stamps should not be put on sale in Scotland, since they commemorated a purely English affair, but they were overruled. A Hungarian 1962 issue shows flags of competing World Cup football finalists in pairs, that of the winner above that of the loser, but it is a breach of flag etiquette to fly one national flag above that of an independent nation on the same hoist, even under these circumstances. Similar errors occur on a 1971 Brazilian 40c. issue showing flags of Central American Republics, a 1942 semipostal issue of Indo-China commemorating Hanoi University, a Bulgarian issue of 1963 marking Balkan Games, a Liberian issue of 1974 commemorating World Cup finalists, a Tunisian issue of 1953 marking the First International Fair, Tunis and a 1950 20l. Italian stamp marking the 32nd International Automobile Exhibition, Turin. This last was corrected on the corresponding 1951 issue for the 33rd Exhibition, on which the flags are on separate hoists on the same level. A 5c. 1964 stamp of the U.S.A. shows a flag with the words "REGISTER —VOTE" printed partially across it; this contravenes the Federal law governing use and presentation of the flag which provides that nothing must be placed over it or on it.

A 1977 issue of Trinidad and Tobago marks 50 years of airmail service in the islands, but the most modern aircraft featured, the Boeing 747 on the 50c. value, is in British Airways livery, and a British Airways aircraft is also prominently displayed on the accompanying miniature sheet. B.W.I.A., the national airline of Trinidad and Tobago, lodged a complaint, and the 50c. stamp was withdrawn by the Postal Authorities. It must have been rather a blow to Belgian national pride to find that the aeroplane flying over various Belgian cities on the 1930 air set in all cases bore the international markings of Italy (I-) not Belgium (OO-). Here the stamp designer had copied the illustration of the 'plane from a trade magazine, the *Fokker Bulletin*, not realising the national significance of the lettering, though he had in fact changed it from I-BBEC to I-BDEC. The Czechoslovakians found it similarly mortifying to have it pointed out that the first official issue of the new-born state in 1918 did not, as they fondly imagined, show the sun rising behind Hradschin Castle in Prague, a very suitable symbol, but as the stamp shows the eastern front of the Castle the sun must be setting! Consequently the following year the design was revised and the sun removed altogether. Perhaps prophetically the swastika-marked sun also sinks in the west on the German air mail issue of 1934. Pakistan's Independence issue of 1948 showed the crescent moon and star which form the country's emblem, but with the moon's horns pointing to the right, hence a waning moon, again not a very happy symbol; this was corrected to a waxing moon in the 1949 issue.

Religious taboos have provided many of the errors of this section. The Buddha of Bamian, an enormous statue carved out of the rock face, was portrayed on a 3a. Afghan stamp of 1932, no doubt to the dismay of a predominantly Moslem populace, for it was replaced by the National Assembly Building on the corresponding value of the 1934 issue. It was shown again on the 20p. value of a 1951 issue, but this was soon withdrawn following protests. A 1a. Indian stamp of 1911 was so poorly drawn that one of the Indian orders of chivalry worn by George V which was in the form of an elephant was alleged to be a pig—an unclean animal to Moslems—and quite a fuss was made. Nevertheless the design remained as it was until redrawn in 1934 (to change "POSTAGE & REVENUE" to "POSTAGE"), when the elephant was more clearly defined. The rosace watermark of the 1898 Sudanese issue also caused trouble, here because of its apparent resemblance to the Christian cross. In 1902 this was changed (at the order of Lord Kitchener) to multiple star and crescent, but perhaps that was felt to be favouring the Moslems too much, for from 1927 onwards a noncommittal multiple "SG" (Sudan Government) watermark was used. One objection made to the 1972 Irish Christmas stamps was that they showed a nimbus round Mary's head and none round that of the Christ Child, but here of course the designer was reproducing a portion of the Book of Kells, and the fault, if any, lies with the original. The first Christmas stamp produced by the U.S.A., a 4c. value in 1962, was attacked as being a violation of U.S. law on Church and State separation, but these protests were overruled. The 25c. Australian Christmas stamp of 1967 tried to be as undenominational as possible, even including the Star of David amongst the symbols represented, but this offended orthodox Jews, who do not, of course, recognise Jesus as the Christ, or Christmas. The 1977 15c. Australian Xmas offering also caused eyebrows to be raised as the design shows Santa Claus on a surfboard, and several religious orders conducted an unofficial boycott of it. The Protestant Federation protested against the choice of Sassoferato's painting 'Madonna in Prayer' for the 2½d. 1962 Christmas stamp of New Zealand, considering that this amounted to Mariolatry, but this design had been submitted in March by the Post Office to the interdenominational Christian Festivals Committee, and had gained unanimous approval. South African 1d. stamps of 1939 marking the 250th anniversary of the Huguenot Landing in South Africa showed a rising sun behind the darkness of night (symbolising the restoration of the Gospel after the false doctrines of the Middle Ages) surmounted by a brilliant cross commemorating the sacrifices made by the martyrs of the Reformed Churches of France. Understandably Roman Catholics of South Africa objected to this symbolism.

A 10pf. West German stamp of 1960 commemorates the Oberammergau Passion Play, featuring the Cross and other symbols of the Crucifixion, but inexplicably omits the highly significant Crown of Thorns. Various Turkish stamps were overprinted in 1915 with star and crescent, but inadvertently the star was six-pointed instead of the five-pointed star of Islam, and this was corrected for later overprints. Israel in 1970 produced a set of five values marking the Jewish New Year 5731 and showing various foreign synagogues. The 15a. value shows the Great Synagogue of Tunis which in its stained glass window shows God's name, the sacred tetragrammaton. Orthodox Jews objected to the unacceptable indignities which it might suffer during even normal treatment of a postage stamp, and the issue was withdrawn. As it would be equally profane to destroy the stamps they remain in the vaults of the Israeli Postal Authorities, probably for eventual burial in consecrated ground, as happens with disused prayer books.

Politics can also produce difficult situations. In 1967 Czechoslovakia produced a set commemorating the Millenary of the Jewish community in that country, but this was withdrawn a fortnight later to express disapproval of the Arab-Israeli Six-Day War. Not to write off their investment, however, the Czechs discreetly sold the stamps a couple of years later when the *brouhaha* had died down. In 1920 the E.E.F. stamps were overprinted for use in Palestine in three languages, English, Hebrew and Arabic. The Arabic overprint was only 8mm. long (much shorter than the Hebrew overprint), so the Arabs complained and later in the year had it slightly enlarged to be 10mm. long. Both of these overprints were produced at the Greek Orthodox Convent in Jerusalem. Late in 1921 the stamps and overprinting were produced in London, and from then until 1927, when the pictorial issue appeared, the Arabic overprint reverted to 8mm. There was also a Jewish objection to the overprints, and indeed to all the Hebrew inscriptions right until the termination of the Mandate, which was that the country was named ' Palestina ' in the Hebrew inscription, although followed with the letters ' EY ' (for *Eretz Yisrael*—Land of Israel), because the country had never been known as Palestina in Hebrew, the nearest approach being Philistina for ' Land of the Philistines '. The Arabs objected to the inclusion of the initials EY, and even took the case to the High Court to have either the EY removed from the Hebrew or ' SJ ' (*Souria Janoubia*—Southern Syria) added after the Arabic, but their case was rejected.

An amusing Arabic gaffe was the portrayal of an Israeli footballer on a 1r. 1968 stamp and miniature sheet issued by Dubai to commemorate the Olympic Games, although the Arab states did not officially recognise the existence of Israel (fig. 96). East China in 1949 produced a set marking the Seventh Anniversary of the Shantung Communist Postal Administration, showing a scene with a tower which on the $5 value flew a Japanese flag. This was intentional, to indicate the dangers besetting delivery of Communist letters during the war with Japan, but on second thoughts the inference that Japanese forces were in command of the area made it seem a less bright idea, and the flag was obliterated with a heavy overprinting character on the greater part of this issue, though unoverprinted copies do exist.

The 1894 issue of North Borneo by error carried inscriptions only in English, which would have been of little use to most of the inhabitants, and this issue was replaced in 1897 by a similar one which also included inscriptions in Malay and Chinese. On the other hand the 12pf. stamp produced in 1945 by South-Eastern Saxony whilst under Russian occupation erred in carrying an inscription in a language which it should NOT have borne—the single Russian word "ПОЧТА" (Posta), as this was contrary to Allied agreements. This appears to have been done without the official knowledge of the Russians, and the issue was withdrawn within a few hours of its release in Dresden and officially destroyed, a redesigned issue without the offending word being released only five days later. The use of the Afrikaans spelling "CALVYN" alone on the 2½c. 1964 stamp of the South African Republic commemorating the fourth centenary of the death of the Protestant reformer John Calvin and on a corresponding 1965 issue of South West Africa led to protests from the English-speaking people of these officially bilingual countries. Belgian railway issues of 1879 and 1882 had French inscriptions only: the Flemings objected and the issue of 1895 had inscriptions in both languages. A 30c. 1960 Dutch stamp marking World Mental Health Year bore a portrait of the Dutch 16th century physician Johannes Wier, but as first designed (and illustrated in publicity leaflets of the Netherlands Post Office) this had his name spelt "Johann Weyer", the German version. Indignant protests led to this being changed to the Dutch version by re-engraving. A 6c. 1930 Guatemalan air stamp bore the legend "Guatemala produces the best coffee in the world" in English only, which offended patriotic Guatemalans, and the 3c. stamp of 1932 which also bore this inscription carried it in both English and Spanish. El Salvador, incidentally, has an issue of 1940 which makes the same claim for the coffee of El Salvador—one at least must be in error, but we are not prepared to adjudicate here.

Italy in 1924 issued stamps with advertising labels attached, not even separated by perforations, though this had been intended. The U.P.U. protested because of the possible legal complications, almost immediately banning these from use on foreign mails, and the advertising concession was abrogated by Royal Decree in 1925—it had in any case been a financial failure. Stocks were not called in, but were gradually used up. The U.P.U. has indeed banned the use of stamps with non-postal labels attached since 1912, though this rule is widely flouted by postal use of, for instance, entire Australian booklet panes of the Famous Australians series with their non-postal labels still attached, and various British issues of similar nature. Presumably even the Israeli tabs offend this ruling, as probably did the pre-war Czechoslovakian and wartime Bohemia and Moravian and post-war Rumanian issues, to name but a few, although tabs are becoming almost *de rigeur* with many countries these days. This brings us to the vast field covered by the U.P.U. colour conventions for stamps covering different postal requirements. These are nowadays so widely flouted that there seems little point in listing offending issues, apart from a few special cases. The U.P.U. objected to the 200r. blue stamp produced by Brazil in 1909 to mark the Pan-American Congress held in Rio de Janeiro and this was withdrawn, but re-issued in May 1910 for postal use within Brazil only. The 1d.+1d. and 2d.+1d. 1931 Health semipostals of New Zealand, the 'Smiling Boy' issue, did not conform to U.P.U. requirements. New Zealand raised the universal inland postage rate from 1d. to 2d. and the commercial inland rate from ½d. to 1d. on 26th June, 1931, as an emergency measure to raise money, but the plate for a 1d.+1d. stamp had already been prepared. Rather than spoil the appearance of the stamp with a surcharge to enable it to cover entire inland postage, the 1d.+1d. stamp was printed and issued (but the Post Office forgot to change the colour from red to green) along with a 2d.+1d. stamp prepared by alteration of the old die (but in blue where it ought to have been red). Note the change in the size of the numeral and also in the full-stop. Germany was normally punctilious in conforming to the U.P.U. colour conventions, but transposed the required colours for the two 1942 semipostals marking the 10th anniversary of the National Goldsmith's Institution, though reverting to the correct colours for the corresponding issue of 1944.

U.P.U. regulations require that the stamps of member states used for foreign mail bear the currency value in Western style figures and with the name of the country in a European language (Great Britain excepted for historical reasons). The Canadian Jubilee issue of 1897 and definitive issue of 1897-8 wrongly gave the value in words only, while the two 10c. 1975 Christmas stamps of the U.S.A. bore no values at all. This was because a change in postal rates was pending at the time the stamps were being produced, but nevertheless U.P.U. regulations were broken by omission of the values. The 1966 150cr. Brazilian Xmas stamp omitted "BRAZIL CORREIO" from the design, and the Egyptian 1923-4 definitive issue used Arabic only in the inscriptions, replaced in 1927 by an issue with the addition of "EGYPTE" and written value in French. Honduras in 1926 overprinted a 6c. stamp with "1926", but forgot to send samples to the U.P.U. as required. A new batch was prepared in 1927 to make this good, but the printers, understandably confused, brought it up-to-date with an overprint of "1927". This was corrected for part of the supply by a further overprint of "1926" in larger figures. By this time supplies of 6c. stamps had not surprisingly run out, so the balance of these confused issues was placed on sale. The Great Barrier Island pigeongram service of New Zealand had its own adhesive stamp—the first distinctive air mail adhesive stamp, but the New Zealand postal authorities objected to the inscription "SPECIAL POST" and made the organisers overprint this with "PIGEONGRAM", substituted for SPECIAL POST in the redrawn design of 1899.

Portraits can cause trouble where the subject does not approve of the likeness and is in a position to have it suppressed or altered—indeed many issues have never appeared at all for this reason, *e.g.* the ' Narrow Head ' Swedish issue featuring King Oscar II which was prepared in 1885, withdrawn and destroyed without ever being officially issued on objections from the King, though a few sheets escaped destruction and some stamps were even used postally. A new issue with an acceptable portrait was prepared and issued in 1891. Similarly a stamp to mark the fourth anniversary of the accession of King Hassan II of Morocco was withdrawn on the intended day of issue in 1965 because the King did not like the portrait of himself. The Belgian issue of 1952 showing King Baudouin without the horn-rimmed spectacles he habitually wears, looking untypically close-cropped and accentuating his prominent nose, met with much criticism and displeased the King himself. It was replaced by a more typical (and flattering) portrait issue in 1953, although curiously enough a 100f. stamp in the old design appeared as late as 1958. King

George II of Tonga did not like his portrait on the issue prepared in 1895 and ordered it destroyed, but it had to be used because other stamps were in very short supply. The portrait was redrawn but was very little improved, and the redrawn design was never issued except with a surcharge which effectively masked the portrait: a pictorial issue followed in 1897 which at last included an acceptable portrait of the Monarch. Perhaps it might be appropriate to refer in passing to the notorious King Ferdinand II of Sicily, nicknamed ' Bomba ', whose vanity did not permit the defacing of his portrait by a postmark, so a special postmark had to be used that marked only the frames of the stamps and left the portrait unblemished.

Portraits may be unacceptable for other reasons. A 1939 Slovakian issue was prepared to mark the 20th anniversary of the death of General Stefanik (who became a brigadier-general in the French army in July 1918), but as he was shown in French uniform the Germans refused to allow the issue to be released. Nevertheless employees of the Bratislava post office cancelled a few on cover as a favour for friends, and a few, mostly from outlying villages, got through the Slovak postal system. There were objections to the portrait of the French Admiral de Rigny on the 5d. value of the Greek 1928 issue commemorating the Battle of Navarino, on the grounds that he was shown in civilian dress while the other Admirals were portrayed in naval uniform in this issue. The portrait of Marconi on an 8c. Canadian stamp of 1974 was objected to because for some curious reason he was given a green face. The children on a 1972 Japanese issue marking 100 years of state organised education were objected to as looking occidental rather than oriental. A 20g. stamp produced for German-occupied Poland in 1941 bore a portrait of the Nazi Governor Hans Frank, and similarly a German stamp bearing a portrait of Himmler appeared in 1943: in both cases these appear to have been Allied productions intended for secret circulation to get these Nazi leaders into trouble with Hitler. The choice of the portrait of Nelly O'Brien for a 1973 7½p. British stamp to represent the work of Sir Joshua Reynolds caused some raised eyebrows at the time, for the lady was an artist's model of rather questionable virtue. Ceylon (Sri Lanka) in 1961 produced a stamp featuring Prime Minister Bandaranaike, but this was objected to, particularly by Mrs. Bandaranaike, on the grounds that it showed him with greying hair apparently receding at the temples, so it was replaced later in the same year by a redrawn version showing darker hair at the temples. The Liberian 1c. stamp of 1949 as first issued showed President J. J. Roberts with a moustache, but most people were more familiar with him clean-shaven, so this version was withdrawn after only a month, stocks were destroyed, and it was replaced with a portrait showing him without the moustache. The portrait of the Shah of Persia on a 1965 120cr. Brazilian stamp was acceptable, but not the inscription, which omitted ' Pahlavi ', an essential part of the title of the occupant of the ' Peacock Throne '.

Perhaps the most notorious design blunder in philatelic history occurred on New Brunswick's 5c. stamp of 1860—part of an issue necessitated by a changeover of currency from the British system to dollars and cents, for this, when delivered, was found by a shocked Executive Council to bear the portrait, not of Queen Victoria, but of the Postmaster General,

Charles Connell. On the advice of the Council the Lieutenant-Governor on 12th May, 1860, approved and ordered the distribution of the other values, but ordered replacement of the 5c. stamp by one bearing the Queen's portrait: on the 19th May Connell resigned. He claimed not to have known that the stamp bore his own portrait until it arrived, paid for the rejected stamps himself, and ultimately burned them all in a garden bonfire, apart from a few previously given away. Ironically enough these few unissued copies remaining are now valued at much more than the annual income which Connell forfeited by resigning—£600 p.a. No doubt Queen Victoria was not amused.

The 1972 definitive 1c. stamp of Anguilla has a perhaps unfortunate juxtaposition, for the portrait of a very dark-skinned native in swimming trunks with spear and fish has an inconspicuous caption "spear fishing" tucked away to one side, and at first glance appears to be captioned "H.M. COMMISSIONER IN ANGUILLA"—not a very flattering portrait! The portrait of Söderberg on a 45ore Swedish stamp of 1969 marking the centenary of his birth is also not very flattering, for there is a distinct impression of a scantily dressed lady sitting in his lap! Perhaps the stamp which has caused more red faces than most is an Israeli 15pr. stamp of 1952 marking the Jewish New Year. It shows figs and fig-leaves, a design which, to some at least, has appeared to convey the pictorial equivalent of a *double entendre* in very questionable taste indeed!

In many countries there is a convention or law not to portray living people on postage stamps, but this is often broken. In the U.S.A. an Act of Congress of 1875 banned the engraving of likenesses of living people upon national stamps and securities—broken as early as 1898 on a 2c. stamp featuring "Farming in the West". Here the design was adapted from a photograph of ploughing teams at Amenia, North Dakota, and shows Even Nybakken (who died in 1934) on the nearer plough. A 4c. stamp of 1901 features a Brougham, after a photograph, and although the name of the driver is unknown, his passenger was a railway agent named Samuel Hege. The Red Cross nurse on a 2c. stamp of 1931 was adapted from a Red Cross poster of 1930 for which the model was Miss Marie Bard of New York—a professional model and not a nurse, which aroused some indignation. The most flagrant violation, perhaps, occurred on the Arbor Day 2c. stamp of 1932, for the two children shown planting a tree were the children of Alvin W. Hall, then Director of the Bureau of Engraving and Printing—the girl later became Mrs. James W. Neighbours, of Honolulu. The model for the 3c. stamp of 1932 marking the summer Olympic Games was the American schools champion sprinter, J. A. Le Coney, but here his face was deliberately altered in the design, to conform to the law. The design of the 3c. stamp of 1945 honouring the U.S. Army was adapted from a news picture photograph, and included recognisable living Americans. The 3c. stamp honouring the U.S. Navy was adapted from a photograph taken by Frank Alexander, again including living Americans, for instance on the lower right is Petty Officer Van Neil, who served on U.S.S. *Missouri*. The postman on the 15c. Certified Mail stamp of 1955 was also a living identifiable American, and the 'cripple' shown on the 4c. Cripples' Welfare Campaign stamp of 1960 was a non-handicapped professional model, which again raised some indignation.

Canada bars portrayal of all living persons other than members of the Royal Family, but a 6c. 1942 air stamp is from a photograph of an Air Training Camp, showing Flight Lieutenant Sprague climbing into an aircraft, with Corporals Massand and Corbin on the ground. The 5c. Mining Industry stamp of 1957 portrays Joe Kazur, of Yukon Territory, and the ' nurse ' on the 5c. National Health issue of 1958 was an Ottawan secretary, Florence Sullivan. The joggers on a Canadian 8c. stamp of 1974 are members of the Ottawa YM-YWCA Joggers' Club, after a 1973 photograph, while the cyclists in another 8c. stamp of the same issue are the family of Jacques Charron, of Hull, Quebec, after a 1972 photograph. Peru also had a law forbidding portrayal of a living person, but the 10c. value of a 1932 issue marking the First Anniversary of Constitutional Government carried the portrait of the then President, Col. Sanchez Cerro. When the illegality of this was pointed out the offending stamp was withdrawn, only 5,000 copies having been sold. Cerro was assassinated in 1933, whereupon the remaining stock of almost seven million stamps was overprinted "Defensa Nacional" and used as a tax stamp on all parcels going through the post. Chile had a decree which ordered that all Chilean postage stamps should bear the portrait of Columbus, yet during a stamp shortage in 1904, by Ministerial Decree telegraph stamps bearing either the Chilean coat-of-arms or a portrait of Pedro Valdivia were overprinted and used as postage stamps. Here there was an additional complication, as the American Banknote Company held the contract for sole supply of Chilean postage stamps, yet some of the overprinted telegraph stamps were produced by Bradbury Wilkinson, others by Waterlow. The American Banknote Company protested, whereupon a decree ordering new stamps bearing various portraits was rescinded and a new issue with various portraits of Columbus dutifully ordered from the Company.

A 1f.75+75c. semipostal issued by Belgium in 1949 to mark the 50th anniversary of the death of the Flemish poet Guido Gezelle bore a portrait adapted from a photograph of a painting by De Graer of Bruges, but the authorities neglected to get permission first to reproduce the portrait, and the De Graer family sued the Belgian State for a copyright fee of 75,000 francs. They eventually lost the case on the grounds that as the issue of postage stamps is a government monopoly the De Graer family had not lost any money through the Government's action, as no one else could have reproduced the portrait in this way. A 2c. Unemployment Fund Peruvian stamp of 1938 portrays the trademark of the Equitable Life Assurance Company, U.S.A. The original steel engraving for the trademark (' Protection ', by John Q. A. Ward) just happened to be in the files of the American Banknote Company which printed the Peruvian stamp, but we do not know if either the Peruvian Government or the Assurance Company were informed or consulted beforehand.

The U.P.U. rules forbid the use of designs which will be provocative or unacceptable to other member states, but this is widely flouted, and many issues are refused acceptance on political grounds by offended countries. The many issues unacceptable to East Germany have included the West Berlin issues of 1953 marking the East German Uprising and of 1959 marking the 10th anniversary of the Berlin airlift, also West German issues of 1958 for Humanitarian Relief, of 1963 and 1965 for German

Evangelical Church Day and for the Twentieth Anniversary of the influx of East German refugees in 1965, while West Germany has retaliated by blacking out the portrait of Stalin on the 1954 East German 20pf. stamp marking the first anniversary of Stalin's death. How much smaller this book would be without our German items! A rather childish retaliation to an unacceptable design is to produce an equally unacceptable one in return. Thus Russia in 1959 produced a 40k. commemorative stamp for Manolis Glezos, a Greek Communist editor imprisoned for five years by the Greek Government for alleged co-operation with spies, while Greece a few days later produced a stamp commemorating the third anniversary of the Hungarian revolution, with a portrait of the murdered Prime Minister Imre Nagy (incidentally misspelling his name "NAGHI"). Similarly Poland in 1938 produced an historical issue to commemorate the 20th anniversary of Independence, the 15gr. value of which included crossed swords above symbols of the Teutonic Knights, to symbolise their overthrow. At the same time the Polish Post Offices in Danzig produced an issue showing a 17th century scene from a time when Poland owned Danzig. These offended German susceptibilities, and Danzig requested the withdrawal of the offending issues. When Poland refused, Danzig in 1939 produced an issue commemorating the 125th anniversary of Danzig becoming a Prussian city, including an illustration of the defeat of the Polish King Stephen Batori by Danzigers in 1577 (although he won in the end!). Poland capitulated at least to the extent of replacing the 15gr. value by a similar design without the crossed swords and Teutonic Knight symbols. The 1910 10c. Colombian registration stamp showing Spanish troops executing insurgents at Cartajena on 24th February, 1816, by order of the Spanish Governor, brought complaints from Spain, resulting in the issue being withdrawn and remainders destroyed. The Eastern Bloc ' Peace loving nations ' objected to Israel winning the Six Day's War and commemorating it philatelically, so stamps of the 1967 issue marking the event were not acceptable. Similarly the 1960 World Refugee Year issue, the 1967 Independence Day issue, the 1968 Jewish New Year stamps (showing a unified Jerusalem) and the 1972 "Let my people go" issue were banned by the Eastern Bloc countries, and letters bearing them were returned with various cachets referring to what were considered to be the appropriate U.P.U. regulations justifying this ban. One might note, perhaps cynically, that Arabic issues commemorating organisations such as El Fatah are accepted without a quibble. The Austrian 3s. World Refugee Year stamp of 1960 shows refugees trudging from left to right (conventionally West to East), but the bow of the man's hat ribbon and the woman's coat buttons appear to be on the wrong sides, perhaps indicating that the design was reversed, to avoid too obvious reference to the stream of Hungarian refugees pouring into Austria near Morbisch during the repression of the 1956 revolution. Hungary took offence all the same, and lodged a formal objection to this issue. A Greek issue was prepared in 1957 portraying Archbishop Makarios and carrying a Churchill quotation commending the desire of Greek Cypriots to be united with Greece. The Turkish Government warned in advance that they would ban the stamps, returning any mail carrying them with the Makarios portrait obliterated. The Greek Government then had second thoughts, and the stamps were destroyed without ever being issued.

In spite of the ban on reproduction of the human form for orthodox Muslims and Jews, there appear to have been few formal protests to this practice by other countries, even in the case of nudes, though the ' Naked Maja ' in the Spanish Goya centenary issue of 1930 brought protests from the U.S.A., and the West German Post Office received an official complaint from the People's Republic of China concerning the 1974 Europa issue depicting statues of a naked man (30pf.) and woman (40pf.), with the polite request not to stick any more of these stamps on mail to the People's Republic in future.

Symbolism on stamps can backfire in various ways. In the British 1965 issue commemorating the 25th Anniversary of the Battle of Britain a 4d. value shows Hurricanes over a wrecked Dornier 17z2 bomber, but in such a way that the swastika on the tail of the Dornier is the most prominent part of the design. Many people objected violently to its representation at all on a British stamp; indeed questions were asked in the House of Commons, but the Postmaster-General stood his ground and refused to withdraw the stamp. The 1966 25c. stamp of the Netherlands Antilles marking the marriage of Crown Princess Beatrix and Herr Claus von Amsberg has a design of wedding rings and two lovebirds, but it has been claimed that both birds are male!

Use of inappropriately watermarked paper sometimes places symbols in the wrong country. Thus a 1946 issue for the Netherlands Indies was produced by the Netherlands Indies Government Printing Works, Melbourne, Australia, on paper watermarked Multiple Crown over ' C of A ', and the 1927 Liberation War Commemoration Fund stamps of Estonia are on paper watermarked with the Arms of Finland and ' Finland Suomi ', while the French 1911 definitive issue for the New Hebrides Condominium was at first produced on paper bearing the British Colonial watermark Multiple Crown CA, replaced in 1912 by paper more appropriately watermarked ' RF '. The first French issue for the Condominium was produced in 1908 by overprinting stamps of New Caledonia with "NOUVELLES HÉBRIDES", but the British Administration objected that this overprint omitted to mention that this was a Condominium, so the French met this objection by a further overprint of the stock remaining in Paris with the word "CONDOMINIUM", these stamps being issued in 1910. The United Nations Administration does not like to draw too much attention to which country is currently producing its stamps, so the sheets of stamps do not normally bear a printer's imprint, but the 8c. definitive stamp of 1958 bore the marginal imprint of Bradbury Wilkinson, and the 25c. 1965 stamp featuring the U.N. seal bore the imprint of BUNDESDRUCKEREI BERLIN. These sheets as originally produced lacked the four marginal inscriptions, which were added by hand operation in New York, often very badly placed, though a second printing (of 5th November, 1965) had the marginal inscriptions included and the printer's name deleted. Another printer's error which may be mentioned here concerns the 1d. black and carmine stamp of St.Helena issued in 1903. As supplies began to run low an order was placed with De La Rue for ' another consignment of the red penny '. The printers took this too literally as an order for an all-red stamp, and duly printed and shipped a consignment of these, which were, however, rejected and almost all destroyed, apart from ' SPECIMEN ' overprinted copies distributed to the U.P.U.

The Polish Government in Exile very nearly made a gaffe in the 1z. design of 1942 showing the Polish Underground Press at work producing an underground news-sheet *Polska Zyje* (Poland is alive) which was bitterly opposed to the Sikorski Government in London—this was changed in time to a pro-Government one. The 1929 1d.+1d. Health stamp of New Zealand figured a nurse, with the exhortation "HELP STAMP OUT TUBERCULOSIS". Offence was taken at this slogan, both because the subject was held to be too grave for this rather poor pun and because tuberculosis was at that time a virtually unmentionable disease. The Health stamp of the following year should have borne the 'Laughing Boy' design, but Perkins Bacon & Co. could not complete the die and plate in time because of pressure of other work, so the Government Printer hastily produced a typographic plate with the nurse design of the 1929 issue but the mild and acceptable slogan "HELP PROMOTE HEALTH" replacing the one held to be in questionable taste. New Zealand was again in trouble with the 1d.+1d. Health semipostal of 1932 picturing Hygeia, Goddess of Health, for to many straight-laced New Zealanders the half-naked young lady waving a wine-cup over her head looked more like a participant in a drunken orgy.

Designs and issues may sometimes err simply by being made or contemplated at inappropriate times. It would have been better had the French waited a little before featuring the Provence freight aeroplane on their stamps (1,000f., 1954), for in the event this was not a technical success, and was discreetly replaced for this value in 1957 by L'Alouette helicopter. Similarly a short wait before issuing in 1933 a 3c. stamp marking the National Recovery Act might have saved some red faces in the United States, for this Act was declared unconstitutional and thrown out by the Supreme Court in 1935. It is perhaps unintentionally symbolic that on the stamp the businessman is out of step. The 5c. Canadian stamp of 1956 commemorating ice hockey was most unfortunately timed, for Canada (which had won every Olympic championship from 1924 to 1952 apart from 1936, when Canada was second) came only third in 1956. A 6d. Jamaican stamp commemorating the proclamation of the abolition of slavery was prepared in 1921, but labour troubles and riots in May of that year made the subject appear liable to be used for inflammatory propaganda so the stamps were destroyed unissued, apart from three blocks in the Royal Collection, singles in the British Museum and Crown Agent's archives, and the copies overprinted SPECIMEN which had been distributed to U.P.U. members. The design was, however, used for the 6d. stamp of 1955. The 1965 Postal Ministers' Congress in Peking was marked by stamps of Albania (2l.50, 7l.50), Bulgaria (13st.), China (8f.), Czechoslovakia (60h.), East Germany (20pf.), Hungary (60fi.), Poland (60g.), Rumania (55b.), Russia (6k.), and various other communist countries, all bearing portraits of Marx and Lenin, but at the time relations between Peking and Moscow were distinctly strained, and neither Rumanian and Russian stamps nor the Soviet philatelic bulletins mentioned the event which the issue had been intended to mark. A Norwegian 30ore stamp of 1942, part of an issue marking the birth centenary of Rikard Nordraak, included two lines of the Norwegian National Anthem, which he composed. It was an error in psychology for the occupying Germans to allow this to be issued, for it helped to heighten

Norwegian patriotic feelings, and the whole issue was bought up within a week. However the issue which proved most costly to the issuing country was probably the Nicaraguan issue of 1900 featuring the volcano of Momotombo. The Panama Canal Company of France, which had a concession from Colombia, had gone bankrupt, and was trying to sell the concession to the Americans, through the agency of Philippe Bunau-Varilla, a young engineer. The U.S. Canal Commissioners favoured routing the canal through Nicaragua, which could provide a cheaper and easier route but was subject to volcanic activity. The Nicaraguan Government had denied that there had been any recent eruptions, but Bunau-Varilla sent to each of the 90 U.S. Senators a 1c. stamp of this issue, showing Momotombo with a great plume of smoke ascending from the crater, mounted above the caption "An official Witness of volcanic activity in Nicaragua". Ten days later the Americans settled for the Panama route, by the narrow margin of only eight votes (fig. 97).

CHAPTER 10

Intentional Errors

This last category of design error embraces those produced intentionally, sometimes a matter of wishful thinking, sometimes as an extension of artistic licence, sometimes for a variety of often bizarre other reasons, good or bad. For instance, map errors often fall into this category, where territorial claims are expressed as accomplished fact, as in the Argentinian claim to the Falkland Islands, first made philatelically on the 1936 1p. map stamp showing South America with the national boundaries drawn in and the Argentine Republic in solid colour—including the Islas Malvinas (Falkland Islands to us). This stamp was replaced in 1937 by one without boundaries and Argentinian mainland claims somewhat reduced, following protests from other South American countries, especially Chile, but the Islas Malvinas remained firmly marked as Argentinian, in spite of British protests. In 1951 a similar map stamp laid claim also to a large sector of Antarctica, overlapping Chilean claims made on various issues of 1947, 1958, 1959, 1967 and 1973, and the counter-claims of Britain made via the 1946 and 1947 issues of the Falkland Islands Dependencies. Argentina, undeterred, pressed these claims further on a 5p. map stamp of 1960 marking a National Census, and even more specifically in an issue of 1964 to mark, in the words of the official stamp bulletin "60th anniversary of the Take of Possession of the South Orkneys Islands by Argentine and Argentine Sovereignty in the Antarctic Zone", an issue which defiantly plants little Argentinian flags on all these disputed territories, and yet was accepted on incoming mail to this country by our own postal authorities. All this in spite of the fiat of the Antarctic Treaty Powers Conference, Canberra, 1961, which prohibited the use of maps depicting specific Antarctic claims and ordered all stamps showing such maps to be withdrawn during 1962 (figs. 98-103).

These are by no means the only claims to British possessions which have been pressed philatelically. For instance the Venezuelan Miranda issue of 1896, a set of 1965 and a 5c. stamp of 1970 all promote a Venezuelan claim to all of British Guiana (later Guyana) north of the Essequibo River. Britain protested and the dispute went to arbitration, being settled almost entirely in favour of Britain. Guatemala pressed a similar claim to British Honduras (Belize) on a series of stamps in 1936, 1939, 1948, 1950, 1956, 1959, 1967 and 1971. It is interesting that the 5c. stamp of 1950 did actually have ' British Honduras ' on the map as originally prepared, but it was not issued like this, being withdrawn and replaced by one without the offending name, although the original unaltered issue was released in 1959 defiantly overprinted "Belize es nuestra" —Belize is ours. It is only fair to admit that these claims do have some historical justification. The Republic of Ireland has from its first pictorial issue (1922) made plain its claims to the Six Counties, for this issue includes a map of Ireland undivided, also an amalgam of the arms of the four provinces, although the quarter representing Ulster includes a black hand dexter rather than the red hand sinister of the O'Neills which is the true emblem of Ulster. Incidentally, the plates for this 1922 issue were made by the British Royal Mint! The 1949 issue to mark international recognition of the Irish Republic and the 1937 issue to mark the new Irish Constitution also include the emblem of Ulster. However with the harp of Ireland still incorporated in the British Royal Standard we are perhaps not well placed to object to the heraldic practices of the Irish Republic. We may note in passing that the name of the country should have been Irish Free State (SAORSTAT ÉIREANN) on the early issues, for it only officially became ÉIRE on 29th December, 1937, with the adoption of the new Constitution.

Not all territorial disputes involve Britain, though it may sometimes seem like it. We have in an earlier chapter dealt with the 1900 issue of the Dominican Republic which laid claim to a large part of neighbouring Haiti, but there is also a 1924 Haitian 20c. stamp which goes even further with a map of the West Indies showing Hispaniola undivided and labelled "Haiti" only. The most notorious territorial dispute on map stamps was that between Paraguay and Bolivia triggered off by a Paraguayan map issue of 1924 which, though rather vague as to boundaries, clearly claimed a large part of the Gran Chaco territory also claimed by Bolivia. Map stamps of 1927 showed the claim still more clearly. The dispute led to a bitter and bloody ten-year war, won by Paraguay at great cost, during which both sides poured out philatelic propaganda—map stamps for Paraguay in 1932-1936 and Bolivia in 1930 and 1935, and Bolivian postmark slogans of *circa* 1935 announcing "El Chaco Boreal is and always will be Bolivian" in English, French, German and Spanish. The dispute was finally settled at a Peace Conference held in Buenos Aires in 1939: the agreed boundary lines are shown on a 500p. Paraguayan stamp of 1939.

A 1935 15c. map stamp of Honduras laid claim to an area disputed with Nicaragua, which replied with an air mail issue of 1937 'correcting' the boundaries. Honduras complained, but Nicaragua refused to withdraw the issue. Honduras produced a 3c. map stamp in 1939 and a 5l. map stamp in 1943, reasserting her claims to the disputed area. Eventually the dispute was settled in favour of Honduras by the International Court of Justice in 1960, and Honduras duly celebrated her triumph with a 1961 issue. A Chinese issue of 1939 showed a map of China which included Outer and Inner Mongolia as Chinese, which they certainly were not at that time, and there were many protests: because of these the stamps were put on restricted sale. The map issue produced by Pakistan in 1960 showed some provinces claimed by India as being firmly within Pakistan, which brought heated complaints from India.

War can produce many kinds of territorial readjustments which lead to designs falling into this category. Turkey prepared an issue for use in Sinai following anticipated conquest in the First World War. This did not happen, and following the War Turkey, too poor to afford wasting the prepared issue, used it up in 1920 with an overprint. Bulgaria had entered the War largely in the hope of gaining much of Macedonia, though by the time the first Bulgarian set commemorating the 'liberation' of Macedonia appeared in 1917 the Bulgars were already retreating from their newly conquered territories. By the time the second 'liberation' set appeared in 1918-1919 the Central European Powers had already lost the War, and the peace settlement gave Yugoslavia and Greece large parts of what had been Bulgarian Macedonia. When in 1921 Bulgaria attempted to use a set prepared in 1915 to commemorate Madedonian ' liberation ', complete with map of Macedonia, Macedonian views and portrait of Tsar Ferdinand (who had died in 1915) the Yugoslavs not unnaturally protested, and these stamps were withdrawn after three days.

Following a plebiscite in 1922 Vilna became Polish, but Lithuania never conceded this, and included Vilna as Lithuanian in an issue of 1932 and considered Vilna to be its capital! Vilna was restored to Lithuania by the U.S.S.R. on 10th October, 1939, and another issue produced to celebrate its recovery, but as Russia took over Lithuania itself less than a year later this rejoicing was rather premature. Indeed a 14k. Russian map stamp of 1927 already ominously included the Baltic States in Russian territory—the shape of things to come.

The Middle East, a perpetually troubled area, has also produced map stamps in this category. The 1964 Jordanian issue marking an Arab Summit Conference, shows a map of Jordan with no boundaries for Israel, thus perhaps inadvertently showing the original Mandated Territory of Palestine, as referred to in the Balfour Declaration. A 1972 issue for Qatar marking the Arab States Civil Aviation Council, Qatar, shows a map of Arab states which also ignores the very existence of Israel. In 1952 Egypt overprinted her current stamps with an inscription which translates ' King of Egypt and the Sudan '. This was quite unjustified, as the Sudan at that time was jointly administered by Britain and Egypt under a treaty of 1936. A further agreement of 1953 gave the Sudanese the right to determine their own future, and hence also the decision on sovereignty, and the Sudan became independent in 1956, but of course shortly after the issue of the overprinted stamps Egypt itself became a republic and Farouk was no longer king of anywhere. The union of Crete with Greece was prematurely signalled by overprints on Cretan stamps of 1908-10, for it was not formally recognised until the Treaty of London (1913). The Cretan 5d. stamp of 1900 was intended to show Bellerophon mounted on Pegasus fighting the Chimera, but instead showed St. George and the Dragon, as on the British sovereign as originally designed by Benedetto Pistrucci for George III's new coinage. The details of how this substitution came to be made are still obscure, but as St. George is also patron saint of Greece it is likely that this was also part of the Cretan ' Enosis ' campaign. The 1850 issue of stamps for the Australian State of Victoria were also premature, for at that date it was the Port Phillip District of New South Wales, not inaugurated as Victoria State until 1st July, 1851.

An interesting case of conflicting claims on stamps is that of 1959 issues of Brazil and Russia both claiming victory in the World Basketball Championship held in Chile. In fact the Russian team was unbeaten, but refused to play Nationalist China (Taiwan) in the final, was disqualified, and Brazil gained the championship, so the Russians are here really celebrating a ' moral ' victory.

Stamp designs can be deliberately misleading by what they omit as well as by what they include. Thus Cyprus commemorated the 400th anniversary of Shakespeare's birth in 1964 with a set which on the 100m.

value showed a scene from *Othello* in its actual Cypriot setting, the ancient fortress known as the Othello Tower. The scene shown is from Act IV Scene I showing Othello and Ludovico with the quotation "You are welcome, Sir, to Cyprus". However Othello is NOT in fact welcoming Ludovico as implied but is about to leave the stage angrily, having just been recalled from Cyprus, and the full quotation is ' You are welcome, Sir, to Cyprus—goats and monkeys! '—in other words ' You can keep Cyprus! ', a very different sentiment (fig. 104).

We have earlier dealt with stamp portraits which displeased by their inaccuracy, but sometimes they are deliberately falsified to please their subjects and others. Thus the 1891 Dutch issue and similar designs for Dutch colonies showed the young Queen Wilhelmina, from a photograph by Hottograf Kaneke, but the hair curling over her shoulders has been deliberately lengthened considerably at the instance of the Queen Regent, who thought Wilhelmina's short hair in the photograph altogether too boyish.

At first sight the use of English on the Belgian Express stamps of 1929, 1931 and 1932 might be considered an error, as the French ' Exprès ' could equally easily have been fitted into the available space in the design, but the Flemings would have been highly incensed if *their* rather cumbrous term ' Spoedbestellung ' had not also been included, so the designer chose a rather neat if unorthodox solution. Another apparent mistake which is not a mistake occurs on the 1957 Defence Fund semipostal issue of Israel, which has an inverted ' T ' instead of a + sign before the Defence Fund premium. It is general practice in Israel to avoid using symbols associated with Christianity. In the original design for the 18a. in the 1972 Educational Development series as depicted in the official handouts a + was also included, but was corrected before issue.

There are at least three cases in which a production error has been deliberately reproduced in a whole printing, thus becoming a design error. In 1907 a single sheet of stamps overprinted by Barbados to support the Kingston Relief Fund was inadvertently issued with the overprint inverted, whereupon the authorities deliberately inverted the overprint on another 20,000 stamps to prevent philatelic speculation. Likewise in 1937 a Greek 50l. stamp was overprinted as a Charity Tax stamp, but the overprint was accidentally inverted on a few sheets which were sold to the public before the error was discovered. The Postal Authorities then deliberately printed a supply with inverted overprint and put these on sale at the chief post offices to prevent speculation in the errors. A comparable production error, involving at least 400 stamps, occurred in the printing of the 1962 4c. Dag Hammarskjöld commemorative of the United States in which the yellow printing was inverted. Again the Postal Authorities reproduced the error and made it available to the public as ' philatelic curiosa '. A collector, Mr. Leonard Sherman, who owned a sheet of 50 of the original error brought a court action against the Post Office, but withdrew it on receipt of an official affidavit that his stamps were genuine and part of the original printing. The official reprint of the error was made to curb wild speculation in current stamps which had swept the country when the error, and its hypothetical market value, was publicised, with wholesale buying of entire sheets of stamps on a scale jeopardising supplies to the public. We suppose the moral is to keep quiet about misprints until the issue has been off-sale for a year or two, but in any case why should an administration complain if its sales exceed expectations in today's cynical society? In 1958 several sheets of the 10pf. 1957 ' Europa ' tree stamp of West Germany, which should have been on unwatermarked paper, were printed on paper carrying the multiple DPO quatrefoil watermark in error. When this mistake was discovered a further batch was printed on the same watermarked paper and issued, to prevent speculation, although by then the issue of the new Europa ' bird ' issue was imminent.

In 1962 the Canal Zone issued a 4c. stamp commemorating the opening of the Thatcher Ferry Bridge. One pane of 50 stamps included in a shipment to the Boston stamp dealer H. E. Harris & Co. lacked the silver printing (*i.e.* the bridge itself). A frenzied hunt by the Canal Zone postal authorities unearthed the other three panes of the sheet in their unissued stock. They then ordered an intentional reprinting of 100,000 stamps with missing silver, intending to make these available to stamp collectors at face value, whereupon H. E. Harris & Co. had an injunction served to prevent their sale. Judge George L. Hart in March, 1965, ruled that the Governor of the Canal Zone had no statutory authority to reprint the error solely for a philatelic purpose which would destroy the value of the existing sheet. Henry E. Harris was given the John E. Luff Award by the American Philatelic Society in 1966, largely on account of his firm stand for his rights in this case, and deliberate official reproduction of a production error in this way has not been perpetrated since.

An intriguing form of error is where the designer incorporates into a design, deliberately or accidentally, a feature which the authorities would certainly not wish to be there. The most notorious case of this is the Serbian ' Death Mask ' issue of 1904. King Alexander of Serbia and his wife Queen Draga had been brutally assassinated in Belgrade in 1903 and replaced by Prince Peter Karageorgević. This issue marked his coronation and also the centenary of the Karageorgević dynasty, showing profiles of the founder Karageorge and Prince Peter, but if the stamp is inverted a ghastly almost full-face portrait appears, bearing an uncanny resemblance to the murdered Alexander. It was claimed that this effect had been deliberately produced at the instigation of Alexander's mother, Queen Natalie, but the well-known and respected French engraver Mouchon who was responsible for the stamp indignantly denied that it was other than completely fortuitous. Nevertheless he got no further work from the Serbian Government! Apparent human faces which are almost certainly purely coincidental appear outlined in the view through Tasman's Arch on the 2½d. 1899 Tasmanian stamp, on the flank of the sheep above the word "sheep" on the MacArthur Centenary 1934 issue of Australia, and on the 2c. 1934 Grand Canyon stamp of the United States when viewed sideways from the left. The 1911 Bavarian issue marking the Prince Regent's 90th birthday seems a more suspicious case, for the garlanded pillars at the sides do appear to contain what could be a caricature of reigning German sovereigns of the day, *e.g.* Kaiser Wilhelm at the top right. However the claim that there are several caricatures in the garlands round the bust on the 1911 issue featuring King Ludwig III is more tenuous, and the alleged resemblance of Prince Rupert's beard on the former issue to a greyhound's head (when viewed from the side) is certainly fanciful. It is claimed that the last Austrian issue before the Anschluss in 1938, a Christmas issue of 1937 showing a vase of roses, has an inverted portrait of Hitler hidden among the roses. A Saar issue of 1947 showing steelworkers bears a more easily seen Hitler head, upside-down between the legs of the worker on the right. On the introduction of the saarmark a second printing was prepared on which the 'Hitler head' was removed by retouching: 15pf. and 24pf. values were issued briefly from a few post offices, becoming invalid when French currency was restored, but this second printing was also used for provisional surcharges. The 50pf. stamps with designs of the Castle Gateway, Ellwangen, produced in 1964 by West Germany and West Berlin, have an apparent likeness to Hitler wearing a top hat in the tree to the left of the gateway, though here the designer, Otto Rohse, indignantly denied any intention of producing this. At any rate the design was redrawn and the trees lopped to remove the 'portrait' for the 1967 issue. It is also claimed that a swastika appears on Titov's right hand (raised in salute) on a 40pf. East German stamp of 1961 on which he appears with Herr Ulbricht, but this is a wavering and uncertain crooked cross at best. The 50h. 1939 stamp of Bohemia and Moravia featuring Karlstein Castle has cloud formation, pine tree tops and rocks ingeniously arranged by designer B. Heinz to represent a map of the independent province of Bohemia before the Nazis invaded the Sudetenland, a dig at the Nazis which earned Heinz a place in a concentration camp and led to this stamp being replaced in 1940 by one showing the Castle of Neuhaus. Finally, coming nearer home, we have the occupation issues of Jersey. The 1941-1942 stamps have in their corners minute letters "AAAA" (1d.) and "AABB" (½d.) which the designer, Major N. V. L. Rybot, claimed stood for 'AD AVERNUM! ADOLPHE ATROX' (to Hell with you, atrocious Adolf!) and 'ATROCIOUS ADOLF' and 'BLOODY BENITO' respectively. More daringly E. Blampied on the 3d. design of 1943 cunningly worked the forbidden Royal Cypher into the design, adjacent to the value, and apparently got away with it!

CHAPTER 11

Other than Stamps

In this final section we intend to look at design errors occurring on postal stationery, postmarks, slogans and miscellaneous material published by postal services. This is a truly vast ocean of material into which we can but dip a tentative toe, and point the way for others to investigate more fully.

The Mulready 1d. and 2d. envelopes of 1840 provide an obvious starting point. The elaborately symbolic designs by William Mulready were generally ridiculed by the public, but particular scorn was poured on the one-legged winged messenger hovering over Britannia: indeed Mulready acknowledged this as an error implicitly by adding another leg to the original drawing before giving it to Thomas Baring, M.P. The envelopes were not popular, and gummed labels (' stamps ') won the day. A German postal stationery card of 1940 commemorates this centenary, but omits to mention that the stamps commemorated are British, not German: as our countries were at war at the time this is perhaps not surprising (fig. 105). New South Wales postal stationery cards of 1888 incorrectly commemorated the 50th anniversary of postage stamps: their design included the Royal coat-of-arms, but with the motto misspelt "Honi soit *uui* mal y pense" (fig. 106). It is of interest that the forgeries can be readily distinguished by their *correct* spelling of the motto! The Australian postal stationery cards of 1915 and 1917 (July) bore the coat-of-arms of the Commonwealth of Australia in its original form as granted by Royal Warrant of 7th May, 1908, with the motto "Advance Australia", but this had been superceded by new arms having only "Australia" below the shield, by Royal Warrant of 19th September, 1912. This later form does not appear on Australian postal stationery cards until late 1917. A Dutch postal stationery card of 1892 has the Royal coat-of-arms on the left, but Queen Wilhelmina is facing right on the ' stamp ', and so has her back to the arms, an offence against the usages of heraldry. This was met by interchanging positions of the ' stamp ' and the coat-of-arms, but the first (incorrect) printing of 20,000 cards was allowed to be circulated. Numerous other early postal stationery cards likewise had a Head of State turning his/her back on the national arms, *e.g.* for Italy, Spain, Austria, New Zealand, Portugal and various Portuguese colonies, but these states have not been as punctilious as the Dutch in putting right this impropriety.

The organisers of a Zurich Philatelic Exhibition of 1893 added a vignette to postcards on which the Swiss postal authorities had already printed a stamp, but put this on the same side as the stamp, contrary to U.P.U. rules. Nevertheless the Swiss postal authorities permitted the cards to be used, though pointing out that foreign countries might refuse to accept them—there is no evidence that any country was in fact such a stickler for the rules. A 5pf. German postal stationery card of 1896 likewise bears a vignette on the stamped side, contrary to U.P.U. regulations. Victoria went much further with the notorious ' Beer and Baccy '

1d. postal stationery card of 1895, which had advertisements printed on the address side of the postcard, in itself bad enough, but worse, advertisements for beer and tobacco. A perfect storm of criticism was aroused, and the offending cards were withdrawn (some 20,000 of them) after only two months of public issue. However the canny postal authorities then sent out notification that stamp collectors and others who desired to obtain the cards could still get them from the G.P.O. as ' curiosities ', at 2d. each, very obligingly cancelled without extra charge! In 1915 Australia produced 15 different designs of letter card with illustrations of war themes, but two were so topical that they were hastily withdrawn lest they gave the enemy useful information about troop movements. One of these, showing the AIF embarking, was subsequently re-issued but with the number of the troopship (A32) now obliterated with a white patch.

Austria in 1899 authorised a pictorial postal stationery card for ' the last Christmas of the 19th Century ', posted in Bethlehem with a special Christmas Eve cachet under the authority of the Austrian Minister of Commerce and forwarded *via* Jerusalem through the Austrian post. This was an exceedingly successful venture, but of course the 19th century ended a year later. Accordingly a similar card was produced in 1900, but although this was now factually correct it was financially much less successful. A German postal stationery card was likewise issued to greet the new century prematurely in 1900, and the whole issue of 1,500,000 cards sold out within 24 hours, but the cards, though they bear the magic figures "1900", do not actually claim specifically that the new century is beginning.

In 1973 Canada produced 8c. postal stationery cards with scenes from the different provinces. That for Manitoba shows Manitoba's Legislative Building but misspells it "Leglislative": that for Saskatchewan shows Downton Lake, misspelt "Downtown": that for New Brunswick portrays the Royal Kennebecasis Yacht Club, misspelt "Kennebeccasis". Misspellings are not infrequent in the instructions given on postal stationery cards, particularly those given in French, the international U.P.U. language. Thus a 3c. Liberian card of 1892 and an 80r. Brazilian card have "Union Postal Universelle", which should properly be ' Postale ': this was corrected for the Liberian card. A 3c. 1894 card of Ecuador is inscribed "REPUBLIQUE DU EQUATEUR" instead of ' DE L'EQUATEUR '. An 1892 reply-paid postcard of Montenegro has the instructions in French—"La carte ci-jointe..." printed in error on the second half instead of on the first, although the Montenegrin inscription is correctly placed. The 1875 5c. reply paid postcards of the Dutch East Indies had the Javanese inscription inverted and reversed, corrected in 1881. An 1895 postal stationery card of Holkar has the word ' Sirnámá ' (address) misspelt "Sirnágá". A German postal stationery card of 1945 with instructions in German and English bears English which is rather too literally translated from the German as "Correspondences only on the backside!" A South African ½d. postal stationery card of 1920 was withdrawn because instructions were given in English only, although South Africa was officially bilingual. The card was then overprinted for South West Africa, for which bilingual wording was not at that time obligatory. A South African registered envelope of 1967 bore the imprint of John Dickinson & Co. (Pty) Ltd., but misspelt as "Dickenson", subsequently corrected for both English and Afrikaans versions. A very minor error occurs on a 10pf. German postal stationery card of about 1887, inscribed "WELTPOSTVEREIN. (UNION POSTALE UNIVERSELLE)." However the final full stop clearly belongs within the parenthesis, and was so placed in a corrected version.

Various versions of the Forces Honour envelope, which carried mail uncensored at unit level, were labelled "GREEN ENVELOPE" yet had no trace of green colouring about them. The early envelopes were indeed wholly green and later types had at least green markings, but the term was retained even where it was clearly no longer literally correct. A South African "ON ACTIVE SERVICE" envelope of about 1941 has the South African Springbok emblem in a circle with the Union's motto round it, correctly in Afrikaans "EENDRAG MAAK MAG" incorrectly in English "UNION IS STRENGHT".

As we have already seen, German currency is expressed in the singular, but 3s., 4s. and 7s. postal stationery envelopes of Hamburg (5th April, 1866) bear the plural "SCHILLINGE" (the 2s. value is correct), later corrected to "SCHILLING". In 1952 the minimum registration fee went up from 4d. to 6d. in Great Britain. The embossed stamp of the registered envelope was accordingly changed to state "REGISTRATION SIX PENCE", but on the back of the envelope the information still read "...the registration fee of 4d. covers compensation up to £5...", until later corrected. A comparable error occurred in Palestine in 1943 when the charge for a registered letter was raised from 13m. to 15m. In this case the increased charge was duly given in English and consequently Hebrew, but the Arabic figures still read ' 13m.', though a correct version was issued later.

In 1892 Mexico produced a stamped wrapper with instructions that it was to be used for weights to 120gm., with a 1c. imprinted stamp, and a corresponding wrapper for weights up to 60gm. with a 2c. imprinted stamp. Each stamp should correctly have been on the other wrapper, and the former was rectified before issue by imprinting a further 1c. stamp on it. Brazilian stamped wrappers of 1889 had their values inscribed in Spanish—"Veinte Reis" (20r.), "Cuarenta Reis" (40r.) and "Sesenta Reis" (60r.), but the language of Brazil is Portuguese, so these were replaced hurriedly by the Portuguese versions (Vinte Reis, Quarenta Reis and Sessenta Reis respectively).

The 1893 Columbus issue envelope wrappers of the United States bore the U.S. arms, but the 13 stars which ought to form a nimbus above the eagle's head (as on the 1934-36 air special delivery stamps) are here wrongly placed in the upper part of the shield. The 1c. 1895 Mexican stamped wrapper in the transport series has the word ' FAJILLA ' misspelt "FAJILLLA". A 1927 1d. newspaper wrapper of Australia is inscribed "The postage value of this Wrapper will not be recognised, if the Wrapper is used for any Postal Article other than a Newspaper printed in Australia". The 1928 version has the unnecessary comma after ' recognised ' removed.

Aerogrammes are a comparatively modern but very important element in postal communication, and show many different kinds of design error. They ought, by U.P.U. regulation, to carry the word ' Aerogramme ' on them, but this was omitted from a U.S.A. aerogramme of May, 1971 (corrected 13th December, 1971) and a United Nations aerogramme of 29th August, 1952 (corrected later in 1952). A British aerogramme of 1971 threatens that if there is any inclusion it *will be* surcharged, but since at that time airmail letters to zone A countries (such as Iran, Iraq and Tunisia) allowed a weight of up to ½oz. for the 5p. rate, this would have permitted some inclusions without further charge in aerogrammes to these countries. Accordingly "WILL BE SURCHARGED" was changed to "MAY BE SURCHARGED". Fiji in 1949 produced a 7d. aerogramme imprinted with a keyplate style stamp inscribed "Postage and Revenue", although clearly not intended for revenue use. The South African 6d. overseas aerogramme of 1960 carried the instructions "Additional postage stamps must be affixed to this form if it is to be addressed to a destination outside the Union of South Africa and countries of the African Postal Union." This notice belonged properly to 3d. aerogrammes, and was soon replaced by a more accurate inscription. The 1973 15c. aerogrammes and 8c. domestogrammes of Canada all bore the word "Poste" in error for ' Postes ', and those for the Northwest Territories gave it wrongly as "North West Territories"—these errors were later corrected. The prairie lily which is the emblem of Saskatchewan is actually a subspecies *Lilium philadelphicum* subsp. *andinum,* but the subspecific epithet is omitted from the labelling on the Saskatchewan 'grammes.

Aerogrammes of British Guiana of 1952 featured the breathtaking Kaieteur Falls, but showed them reversed, finally corrected for the 6c. and 12c. aerogrammes of Queen Elizabeth II. A 50c. 1970 Mauritian aerogramme showed a view of Pamplemousse Gardens with the caption "Mauritius offers a variety of sceneries". This was corrected to ' scenery ' in 1971. 1963 aerogrammes of Togo bore the national flag, but with only two horizontal stripes in line with the square bearing a star, where there ought to have been three lines. The 1974 Australian Christmas aerogramme bears a Dürer angel, as do the official first day covers, but this is Dürer's representation of the Doomsday Angel, hardly appropriate for the Christmas season. The British Christmas aerogramme of 1967 also ran into criticism for portraying a decidedly feminine looking Jesus.

The British aerogramme of 1975 commemorating Robert Burns ran into several kinds of trouble. The Nasmyth portrait of Burns was reversed on it, the clock face has the figure 12 missing and no room for it in any case, Tam O'Shanter's witch ' Cuttie Sark ' (Nannie) is certainly not a ' winsome wench and waulie ' as depicted here, the mouse is disproportionally large for the vegetation it is holding, and "a-gley" should not have been hyphenated. Shakespeare got off comparatively lightly on the 6d. commemorative aerogramme of 1964. The ' stamp' purports to show the Globe Theatre, but the scene is adapted from Hollar's ' Long View ' etching of London, in which he interchanged the labels of the Globe Theatre and the Bear Garden, so this is the Bear Garden which is featured. The Shakespeare Theatre at Stratford-upon-Avon is here labelled " Shakespeare Memorial Theatre ", but its name had been altered to ' The Royal Shakespeare Theatre ' when it received the Royal Charter in 1962. About one million of these aerogrammes had been distributed before the error was pointed out, and a new printing made with the correct name. The 1977 aerogramme commemorating the Silver Jubilee of the

Queen's accession has the name of the photographer Peter Grugeon misspelt "Gruegon".

British railway stamps form a very specialised field of their own, and are really beyond the scope of this account, but they too have had their errors. For instance the Garstang and Knott Railway misspelt its own name as "Knot" on stamps issued pre-1908, corrected in 1909, and the Midland Railway (Northern Counties Committee) stamp issued some time before 1907 mislabelled itself as "Midland, Northern Counties of Ireland Railway" on its pre-1907 stamps, corrected in January, 1907.

The field of registration labels is similarly beyond our scope, but we can give a few examples from Australia to illustrate the kind of errors which do occur. Spelling errors are common, for instance Dirribandi for Dirranbandi (Queensland), Kooweerup for Koo-Wee-Rup (Victoria), Yoralla for Yooralla (E.8, Victoria). The district numbers may be wrong—for instance Chelsea (Victoria) given the number S.22 (which belongs to Carrum) in place of its proper S.15. A more unusual type of error occurred when the Postal District of Southern Riverina (New South Wales) was placed under the charge of the Postal Superintendent at Mildura (Victoria). The latter ordered new registration labels for the towns of the District—Euston, Palinyewah, Curlwaa, Cal Lai and Wentworth. The printer assumed that they were all in Victoria, since they had been ordered by a Victorian official, so the labels of these towns all bore the wrong state. A few examples from Israel prepared in haste after the Six Day War illustrate another aspect of errors, namely spelling in Hebrew of names of villages in some cases transliterated from Arabic. These were all spotted on the first day of issue and immediately corrected: Bet Gala with the letter ' aleph ' missing from ' Gala ', Bet Sahur with an aleph missing from ' Sahur ', Deir Dibwan with an aleph missing from ' Dibwan ', Deir el Gusun that should have a double yod in ' Deir ', an aleph missing in Tubas and Silat ed-Dahr appearing as "Silat Ezahr" in both Hebrew and English.

Stamp booklets are another fertile field for errors. Spelling mistakes are frequent, such as "Cannonsreach" (for Canonsreach) in 10p. and 30p. booklets of October, 1971, corrected for the December issues, "accommplish" (for accomplish) on the third interleaf of 2s. booklets issued in September, 1969 and January and March of 1970, and the Hop, *Humulus lupulus,* misspelt "*Humulus Lupus*" in the 50p. booklets of September and November, 1971.

A rather amusing gaffe occurred in the April 1971 edition of the 10p. booklet, which carried advertisements for Sun Life with a London address giving district numbers only—this at a time when the postal authorities were imploring the general public to use the postal codes on their correspondence! The June edition was converted from "S.W.1" to "S.W.1 Y5BH", an improvement, but the correct "SW1Y 5BH" did not appear until the August booklet. This mistake also occurred and was similarly corrected for the 30p. booklets.

Changes in postal rates also create problems. The 1s. ' E11 ' booklet of 1960 was inadvertently printed with the Overseas Postage Rates of the 1957 (' E8 ') edition, by then considerably out-of-date, and during December, 1960, an instruction was issued for the incorrect information to be struck through in stocks remaining on hand. Changes in the postal rates scheduled for June 24th, 1974, caught the Post Office with a 30p. booklet prepared for issue in June but bearing the information regarding postal charges about to become obsolete. It was decided that existing stocks of previous editions of the 30p. booklet would be sufficient to last until the change of rate had occurred, and that this booklet would therefore not be issued. However a supply was inadvertently sent on May 14th to Sheffield Head Post Office and put on sale. In view of this the booklet was put on sale as a philatelic issue at Philatelic Counters throughout the United Kingdom on 21st June, so the information about postal charges which it conveyed was good for only three days of official issue. Experimental booklets produced by Cyprus in 1971, containing advertisements for matches, in error carried out-of-date information about postal rates except for a very few copies which carried the new postal rates.

France in 1929 produced a booklet of 20 5c. stamps of the type showing Joan of Arc on horseback, with marginal advertisements. One page, however, carried advertisements for the dairy products of the firm ' La Vache qui Rit ' (the Laughing Cow), and the French public thought it exceedingly bad taste to have their national heroine setting off on her horse above the apparent caption "LA VACHE qui RIT en excursion" (the Laughing Cow on an excursion), so the booklet was speedily withdrawn.

British Presentation Packs have carried more than their fair share of errors. Spelling does not appear to be a strong point of our postal authorities. The 1964 pack for the Tenth International Botanical Congress has ' Depredations ' misspelt "Depradations". The 1970 pack for the Anniversaries issue has the name of the designer, Marjorie Saynor, misspelt "Majorie", also ' Descendants ' and ' descendant ' misspelt as "Decendants" and,"decendant" respectively. This was corrected in two stages, first the name of the designer only, then all three errors were put right. The 1971 pack for the Literary Anniversaries issue had Sir Walter Scott's publishers Ballantine misspelt as "Ballantyre", but this was noticed before issue and a correction slip duly introduced into the packs. The pack for the 1977 Christmas stamps has ' humorous ' misspelt "humerous". Other types of error also occur. The 1974 pack for the Horse Chestnut issue was listed on the reverse of the pack cover as "Pack no 58", whereas it was actually number 59, but this also was noticed before issue and a correction slip included in the pack. The 1971 pack for the low-value Machin definitives included an illustration of the 1841 ' White Lines ' 2d. blue stamp but with the date of issue of the ' No Lines ' 2d. blue of May 6th, 1840. A correct ' No Lines ' illustration was substituted later in the year. The British Ships pack of 1969 stated of the *Queen Elizabeth 2* that "she sailed on her maiden voyage to New York on 17th January 1969". This had indeed been the intended sailing date, but it was in fact delayed until the 2nd of May. The erroneous date is also given on the pack in German. The 1976 Social Reformers Presentation Pack asks concerning the Earl of Shaftesbury "Could there be a better monument for him than the God of Love aiming his shaft at the Avenue bearing his name—surely the only sculptural pun in the world?". However the winged figure on the memorial has his back turned to Shaftesbury Avenue and his arrow is aimed at Lower Regent Street. The stiffener for the Post Office First Day Cover for this issue twice misspells the name of the designer of these really very unattractive stamps, David Gentleman, as "Gentlemen". The stiffener for the Post Office F.D.C. for the 1976 issue marking the 500th anniversary of Caxton's press wrongly states that the design on the 8½p. stamp represents a woodcut of the Knight from the second edition of Chaucer's Canterbury Tales (1484), but in fact it represents the Squire, a sprightly young fellow as can be seen, very different from the grave and dignified Knight.

In passing, post office publicity hand-outs also err. For example the advance notice for the 1973 issue of British Explorers correctly refers to two 3p. se-tenant stamps featuring Livingstone and Stanley, a 5p. showing Drake, a 7½p. showing Raleigh and a 9p. featuring Sturt and then goes on to state that there are 100 stamps in a sheet but that the sheets of 5p. stamps are made up of 50 of each stamp arranged in horizontal se tenant pairs, obviously referring to the 3p. stamps. The Israeli Philatelic Service Bulletins are numbered consecutively, but Bulletin No. 242 of January, 1972 incorrectly gives No. 224 in English.

Meter franks are another specialised field for which we can give only a few representative examples. The Australian redesigned Flag type of 1954 showed only five-pointed stars in the Southern Cross whereas all but one should, on the Flag, have seven points. The special Royal Visit meter frank of 1954 likewise had only five-pointed stars in the flag. The meter frank used for one week of the Centenary Stamp Exhibition, Melbourne, Australia, bore the misspelt slogan "Sixth Australasion Philatelic Exhibition". An amusing British example is the meter franking slogan which the S.W. District Office of the G.P.O. granted permission for the Conservative Central Office, London H.Q. to use in December, 1946. This was "A Happy New Year and a NEW GOVERNMENT SOON", and it came into use on 30th December. However the postal authorities had second thoughts about the propriety of a Government Department authorising such a meter frank, and advised the Conservative Central Office that if the slogan were not withdrawn the words 'and a NEW GOVERNMENT SOON' would be obliterated. Indeed this was done in some cases. The Conservative Central Office capitulated, and the meter frank was withdrawn after only five days of use. Some 1,000 envelopes were franked with the slogan, but relatively few survived.

Postmarks frequently misspell the location of the post office, *e.g.* "MAURITUS" for Mauritius (1905-26) and within the island "MAPON" for Mapou, "CASE NOVALE" for Case Noyale and "RIVIERE DES ANGEILLES" for Rivière des Anguilles. Bathurst (Gambia) became "BATTHURST" (1938-39), Signy Island (Antarctic) became "SIGNY ISLANDS" and about 1887 stamps of Hong Kong used in Shanghai were postmarked "SHANGHAF". Nearly 40,000 of the 1957 first day covers issued at Philadelphia for the U.S. issue honouring Teachers carried a postmark with the misspelling "PHILADELPIA"—particularly unfortunate in view of the subject of the issue. In 1949 three offices in Tel Aviv in Israel misspelt the Arabic as "Yel Aviv". This was soon corrected.

Since dated cancellations are subject to the vagaries of the Postal clerk who sets the date stamp, errors here are numerous indeed. The catapult mail from the 'Bremen' posted on 28th May, 1930, and flown the following day all bore the date "28.4.29". First day covers from Port Moresby,

Papua, of the issue for the Coronation of George VI bore the date 2nd April, 1937, but as the stamp consignment did not arrive until 15th April and was only opened two days later, this indicates faulty change of date on one of the cancellers rather than premature issue. In the early days of the State of Israel the date stamps came as a complete plate from a central office, and on one day in 1950 every office in the country postmarked mail "1590". The arrangement terminated shortly after that event, and now local offices set their own dates.

More interesting is the 1888 cancel used at the Granville Post Office (Port Moresby, New Guinea) which had been established by the Queensland Government, consisting of the letters "N.G." (New Guinea) in an oval of eight bars. The proper name of the Territory was 'British New Guinea', and the British authorities who were nominally responsible for the Territory insisted on a new canceller being brought into use (in 1890) containing the letters "B.N.G.". The post office of the University of New England, Armidale (Australia) wrongly labelled its locale as "ARMIDALE UNIVERSITY" on its canceller of the 1960s, and the special postmark for the conference of the Economic Commission for Asia and the Far East in 1948 at the Lapstone Hotel, in the Blue Mountains, wrongly placed the conference in Sydney, some 40 miles away. The postmark of the Halfmoon Bay Post Office, Stewart Island, (New Zealand) in 1932 claimed to emanate from "the most southerly post office in the world", but though it lies at 47° south, the Falkland Islands and parts of Argentina and Chile are well south of it, and do have regular postal services.

Spelling can be erratic on slogan cancellations. A South African slogan of 1938 urged "Support S.A. Industres" instead of 'Industries'. A British commemorative handstamp of 1973 marked the 330th anniversary of the siege of Halton Castle (near Runcorn, Cheshire, by Oliver Cromwell) with the misspelling "seige", and the same mistake occurs on a 1971 Warwick and Leamington Spa handstamp commemorating the siege of Warwick in 1642. A 1926 slogan cancellation of Newfoundland reading "New Foundland for your Vacation" was much criticised for the unorthodox spelling of Newfoundland. In the 1930s Palestine had a trilingual slogan for Jaffa oranges and grapefruit in English, French and German. The French read "ACHETEZ LES ORANGES ET LES GRAPEFRUITS DE JAFFA", but the French for grapefruit is *pamplemousse(s)*.

A 1973 British cover and cancellation marked the bicentenary of Clive's death, placing the event in 1773, but he died in 1774. A Silver Jubilee slogan emanating from Cape Town, South Africa, in 1935, gave the date as "April, 1935" instead of May, 1935. The British 1961 slogan "50th ANNIVERSARY OF FIRST AERIAL POST" is rather too sweeping, ignoring early posts by pigeon, balloon and even arrow. The cachets for the inauguration of Australian administration of the Cocos (Keeling) Islands in 1955 showed the route followed by mail 'planes from Cocos Island to Australia, arriving at Perth, but due to legislative delays the Australian Post Office did not open until 23rd November, 1955, and in the meantime the air route had been changed from Brisbane to Darwin (thus connecting with flights to Japan), so the route map on the F.D.C.s was out-of-date. A 1925 British slogan for the Wembley Exhibition read "Torchlight Tattoo—to 26th Sept.". This event proved so popular that it was extended, so a new slogan appeared, amended to "...—to 10th Oct." When a further extension was made the authorities gave up being precise, and the third version bore no closing date at all. The 1962 Delius Centenary Festival, Bradford, was marked by a suitable cachet including a stave of music with two notes intended to be F and D (his initials), but in Die A the second note was a C, thus losing the whole point of the musical inclusion. This was corrected in Die B.

Pictorial slogans are usually cruder than stamps, and one should not, perhaps, be overly critical. However the spring flowers on a 1974 cancellation of Jersey (bearing the slogan "JERSEY FOR A SPRING HOLIDAY"), though obviously intended to be crocuses or closely similar flowers, have perianths of five parts instead of six. Similarly the wasp or bee on a Danish cancellation of 1977 with the slogan "HUSK POSTNUMMER" has only four legs instead of six. The 1938 Royal Train cancellation of Canada (see page 84), includes the British Royal Standard, but with a single instead of double tressure round the lion rampant of Scotland. An amusing gaffe which also concerns the Queen occurred with the use of the British slogan cachet for World Refugee Year 1959-1960 which included an outstretched hand, for when this was placed close to the Queen's portrait on the stamp she appeared to be cocking a snook in a most undignified manner, so the slogan was withdrawn on 8th January, 1960.

A couple of miscellaneous items include the use by the Austrians during the First World War of unchanged names of regiments honouring heads of state with whom they were at war. Thus regimental cachets of Ferdinand King of Rumania Regiment and George Fifth King of Great Britain and Ireland and Emperor of India Regiment can be found on Field Post Cards. One wonders what the feelings of the troops were if they came into combat with the subjects of their eponymous colonels. Birobidjan was founded as a Jewish Soviet Republic in 1928 and Russian and Yiddish were the official languages. Before the war bilingual postmarks were in use, but after the war they were meant to be discontinued and only Russian used. However at least one letter arrived in London in 1947 with a bilingual postmark, which the Russians tried to retrieve when they heard about it (figs. 107-8).

Finally we may consider the interesting case of advertising slogans in general. Where these concern Government services, special events, tourist attractions or products of a country in general these are usually considered acceptable, but where the products of a particular industrial concern are advertised, their rivals are understandably incensed to have incoming and outgoing mail become a vehicle for promotion of rival products. This came to a head in the Netherlands in 1924, when a rival margarine manufacturer complained to the postal authorities concerning the use of a postal slogan advertising Blue Band Margarine, and when he failed to get satisfaction sued the Post Office. The Hague Law Courts issued an injunction which prohibited further use of the Blue Band Margarine slogan, holding that 'mail remains legally the exclusive property either of the sender or of the addressee only; at no time has the carrier any property rights on mail. The sender, therefore, does not need to consent if the Post Office should want any advertising matter that in his opinion interferes with his interests'.

In conclusion, we must reiterate that this chapter only touched on the fringes of a vast field. Our main concern has been with design errors on postage stamps, and even there we are well aware that we have uncovered only a fraction of the errors which exist, have for many of these only got part of the story behind the error, and have ourselves doubtless perpetrated or perpetuated errors—we claim no immunity from the human propensity to err. However we hope our readers will have found something of edification and diversion in these pages, and have been encouraged to examine stamp design more critically for themselves.

ADDENDUM

Errors have continued to be perpetrated and to be brought to our attention during the final phases of printing this book, emphasising yet again the impossibility of producing a truly definitive catalogue on this subject. However, we do our best, and the following additional list includes all but the most trivial of these latecomers for which we feel reasonably certain that they do indeed qualify.

Commencing with misspelt place-names, a 70c. 1963 stamp of the Spanish Post Offices of Andorra features the meadows of Anyos, misspelt "Aynos" on the stamp. Rocamadour is wrongly hyphenated "ROC-AMADOUR" on a 15f. French stamp of 1946. Domodossola is spelt "DOMOSSOLA" on a 1937 15c. Peruvian stamp commemorating the aviator Jorge Chavez. Portuguesa is misspelt "PORTUGUEZA" on a 1c. charity tax Portuguese stamp of 1913, and a 1978 issue of the Bahamas marking the 6th Caribbean Scout Jamboree wrongly gives it as "CARRIBEAN". The Canadian Government has at last tried to acknowledge the Eskimos' own name for themselves—Inuit (the people)—on four 12c. stamps of 1977, but failing to grasp that this word is already plural (the singular is 'Inuk') they converted it into a double plural, "Inuits", in the French captions on the stamps.

Haiti honours the first permanent settler in Chicago, Jean Baptiste Point de (or du) Sable, on several values of a 1959 issue marking the Third Pan-American Games, Chicago, but wrongly spell his name as "DESSABLES". On two other values of this issue they spell PAN-AMERICAN without its hyphen, an all too common type of error. The hyphen is omitted from the name of the Brazilian pioneer aviator Alberto Santos-Dumont on Brazilian 200r. and 500r. stamps of 1929, a 30cr.80 stamp of 1951 and a 1p.40 Bolivian stamp of 1973, but his name is correctly hyphenated on a 1956 Brazilian issue. The revolutionary Nicolas Estevanez is misspelt "ESTEBANEZ" on a 25c. 1952 Cuban stamp. The Azerbaijan poet A. T. Sabir was commemorated on a 4k. Russian stamp of 1962, but apparently as first prepared the stamps showed an extra "ЫН" added to his name. There is some doubt as to whether this version was ever officially issued, for only ten copies are known: the corrected version gives his name in slightly larger type so as to fill the extra available space. Louis Braille has his name misspelt Braile in the Braille alphabet on a 60c. 1976 stamp of Uruguay.

'The Embroiderer' of Vermeer's painting is mistitled "The Embroider" on a 2b. 1969 stamp of the Yemen Arab Republic, while a 1s. 1936 Peruvian stamp featuring the Packet-boat *Sacramento* has PAILEBOT(E) misspelt "PAYLEBOT". A 2r. Iranian stamp of 1975, ironically marking an International Literacy Symposium, misspells it "SIMPOSIUM", and a Panamanian issue of 1953 marking the centenary of publication of 'La Estrella de Panama' has PUBLICA misspelt "PUULICA". Barbudan 1974-5 issues commemorating Sir Winston Churchill incorrectly put a full stop after "Sir.", and 1b. and 4b. 1970 stamps of the Yemen Arab Republic marking the Moon Mission of Apollo 12 have "LAUNCING" in place of LAUNCHING. A 5p. Spanish stamp of 1964 honouring Scientific Research has TECHNICA misspelt "THECNICA". A Venezuelan issue of 1966 marking the 150th anniversary of the death of José Lamas, composer of the National Anthem (rather belatedly, for he died in 1964) has oboes misspelt "oboeses", but as this is in a reproduction of his original manuscript it is possible that the misspelling was made by Lamas himself rather than by the stamp designer or engraver. A 1971 Nicaraguan issue poses the question 'Is there a formula for Peace?' in various languages. The French version has "YA-T-IL" in place of Y A-T-IL, and in the Spanish version "PARA PAZ" instead of the more proper PARA LA PAZ. Another set of 1971 illustrating the Ten Commandments has LEVANTAR misspelt "LEVENTAR" on the 75c. value. Many modern Nicaraguan issues, including this one, bear lengthy inscriptions on the back of the stamps, and minor errors, particularly of accents, are so numerous that we feel there is little point in attempting to catalogue them in detail. The 1971 issue featuring the Ten Commandments, the 1972 Interpol anniversary issue and the 1973 issue which exemplifies some of the causes of the American Revolution come into this category.

The scientific names of plants and animals continue to provide fertile sources of error. A 1976 issue of the Congo (Brazzaville) has the water-lily *Nymphaea micrantha* misspelt "NYMPHEAS" (5f.) and *Strelitzia reginae* wrongly given as "STRELIZIA" (15f.). The flower *Canna speciosa* is misspelt "*Cana*" on a 10c. 1974 stamp of Equatorial Guinea, and *Sesivium portulacastrum* on 15c.+5c. and 50c. stamps of Spanish Sahara is misspelt "SESIVIUN". On a 1962 issue of Spanish Sahara *Neurada procumbens* (25c., 1p. and 3p. values) is misspelt "*procumbres*". In the same issue the plant labelled "*Anabasis articulata*" (50c., 1p.50 and 10p. values) is certainly NOT that species, which is a prostrate halophyte of the family Chenopodiaceae with small simple leaves and inconspicuous little flowers, whereas the plant figured has large ornate flowers and large divided leaves. A 2d.10 1975 Yugoslavian stamp features the balsam *Impatiens noli-tangere* but wrongly gives the specific epithet as one unhyphenated word. We have previously noted that a 1s. 1955 stamp of Somalia shows *Erythrina melanacantha* misspelt "*Erihrina*", but omitted to point out that the specific epithet was misspelt "*melanocantha*". We may now clarify the *Plumeria/Plumieria* controversy, also alluded to on page 13. The genus was named by Linnaeus after Charles Plumier (1646-1704), but his name was deliberately latinized as Plumerius, so this is NOT an orthographic error (see Article 82, note 4 of the Code of Botanical Nomenclature) and hence must not be 'corrected' to *Plumieria.*

Mixed languages are found on a 1972 issue of the Yemen Arab Republic marking the 10th anniversary of Revolution, inscribed "10^{m} ANNIV. OF REVOLUTION", which should of course be '10th'. A Spanish 1p. stamp of 1963 marking the Freedom from Hunger Campaign quotes the Lord's Prayer in latin, "Panem nostrum quotidiánum da nobis hódie" (Give us this day our daily bread), but latin is an unaccented language.

Wrong inclusion of an apostrophe in dates such as "1880's" was mentioned earlier for a 2s. 1976 Kenyan stamp showing various types of telephone: this also applies, of course, to the corresponding issues of Tanzania and of Uganda. An unwanted hyphen occurs in the word AUTORETRATO (as "AUTO-RETRATO") on a 95c. 1966 stamp of

Venezuela featuring a self-portrait of the artist A. Michelena, and an unnecessary one on a 1976 issue of Norfolk Island which marks the Bicentenary (as "BI-CENTENARY") of the American Revolution. The subject of the 45c. stamp, the California Quail (*Lophortix californicus*) seems somewhat irrelevant, for California was not involved in the revolution any more than Norfolk Island was. A hyphen in the wrong place occurs on a 15c. 1973 Venezuelan stamp commemorating Copernicus has CŒLESTIUM hyphenated as "CO-ELESTIUM", in the middle of the diphthong 'Œ'. Iran has hyphenated NATIONS-UNIES (United Nations) on stamps of 1956, 1958, 1961, 1962, but omitted the hyphen from various other issues from 1953 to 1972. Kingsford Smith has once again had his name hyphenated on a Fijian issue, this time of June, 1978. New Caledonia and Dependencies (NOUVELLE CALEDONIE ET DEPENDANCES) has appeared in full or abbreviated with no hyphen, one hyphen or two hyphens from 1860 onwards with no apparent consistency to the present day. A 25l. 1954 Italian stamp marking the First Helicopter Mail, Milan-Turin, has TRASPORTO and ELICOTTERO broken at improper places and with no hyphens at all to indicate the breaks. Hyphens are also missing from PAN-ARAB (Egypt, 1966, 7th Pan-Arab Scout Jamboree), PAN-AMERICAN (St. Christopher, Nevis & Anguilla, 1977, 75th anniversary of the Pan-American Health Organization) and PRE-OLYMPIC (Yemen Kingdom, 1972, Pre-Olympic Games, Munich). An interesting case occurs with the early issues of Venezuela, for the correct abbreviation of Estados Unidos de Venezuela is EE.UU. DE VENEZUELA: all too often this appears either as "E.E.U.U." or "EEUU". The letter 'C' of 'SC' is reversed in the lower right corner of a 30ore Swedish Stamp of 1968 featuring a fox, and the Greek letter Phi (φ) is inverted in a formula given on a 60h. 1967 stamp of Czechoslovakia illustrating Space Research. A non-consistent use of semi-colons and hyphens occurs in a Greek issue of 1975 commemorating national benefactors, where the 1d. and 6d. values have the dates given as, for example "1787-1856" and the 4d. and 11d. values give the dates as, for example "1769;-1841".

We come next to errors of identification. Five of the unnamed birds shown on a 1967 Panamanian set have been copied from *Birds of the World* by Oliver Austin and Arthur Singer, and do belong to Panama, but the bird on the 5c. value not only is not copied from this source but is not readily identifiable as any known species.

Most collectors are familiar with the orange tree depicted on the stamps of the Orange Free State (1868-1900): however this was originally intended to represent the Tree of Life, and the prominent oranges were added to the original design by the printers, De La Rue & Co. The State was named after the Orange River, which was named by the Dutch Capt. R. J. Gordon in honour of the Prince of Orange, and has no connection with the fruit or tree. The flower labelled "*Heliconia salomonica*" on a 45c. 1972 stamp of the British Solomon Islands appears to be a mystery plant for no such species is recorded in the *Kew Index*—we should like more information, however, before attempting to classify this as an error.

The all too familiar error of representation of England by the flag of the United Kingdom instead of its own Cross of St. George flag is evidenced on 5p. and 35p. stamps respectively of two distinct 1973 issues of Equatorial Guinea, a 12b. 1969 stamp of Yemen (Royalist) and a 1cor. 1970 Nicaraguan stamp.

Next we come to denomination errors. Spanish ½c. stamps of 1872-76 wrongly had "cent$^{\underline{s}}$" (plural) instead of singular, while for many recent issues the plural 'Pesetas' has been wrongly abbreviated to "PTA". In 1945 Lebanon applied a "7P½" overprint on a 12½p. stamp, but does not appear to have repeated this error. The United States has in 1978 released a stamp to function as a 15c. value. It features an eagle and bears the letter 'A' but no printed value, thus contravening U.P.U. regulations. Technically it should therefore not be used except for internal postage, but it has been widely used—and accepted—internationally. Many issues of Hong Kong from 1862 to 1960 include values given in letters only, which is also contrary to U.P.U. rules, although obviously those issued prior to the formation of the U.P.U. cannot be classed errors. The paired 5c.+5c. local stamps of Geneva were in February, 1844, reduced in price to 4c.+4c. (sales had been disappointing) but no overprint was applied to correct the values printed on the stamps. A Swedish semipostal issue of 1928 marking the 70th birthday of King Gustav V carried a surtax in aid of the Cancer Research Fund, but this surtax is not printed on the stamp, which bears no indication of its semipostal nature. In 1855 Modena printed a 9c. deep violet newspaper tax stamp, but this was not issued because the letters 'B.G.' (Bollo Gazzette) were omitted.

A 50f. 1975 stamp of the Congo (Brazzaville) features a silver denarius of L. Flaminius Chilo of 42 B.C., wrongly dated "37 B.C." on the stamp, while 100l. and 200l. 1945 stamps of a Bulgarian issue marking the Liberty Loan show a 1 leu coin of 1923 but misleadingly bearing the date "1945". The Catholic leader Baron W. E. von Ketteler is featured on both 10pf. 1961 and 50pf. 1977 stamps of West Germany, in each case with 'von', an ingredient of a title of nobility, quite improperly abbreviated to "v". An issue prepared for the Co-Principality of Andorra's Spanish Post Offices in 1875 during the reign of the Carlists was improperly inscribed "Republic De Andorra", and because of this error was not issued. A rather extraordinary mistitling occurs on a 1973 miniature sheet of the Cook Islands showing Dürer's painting 'Lamentation for the dead Christ' but entitling it "Christ weeping for His people". Still another apparent confusion concerning a National Anthem occurs on 1952 (10c.), 1970 (3c., 20c.) and 1976 (13c.) stamps of Cuba, where there is a discrepancy in the seventh note which is D on the 1952 stamp and C on the others. A 60fi. 1950 Hungarian stamp for Children's Day as first prepared carried the ominous slogan "Youth is our Reserve for Future Battles". This was speedily replaced with a less bellicose statement "Happy Youth in a Free Fatherland", but essays with the earlier inscription do exist. A 300f. 1978 stamp of Mali marking the 150th death anniversary of Schubert gives the closing notes of 'The Trout', but in a very simplified form with the wrong rhythm and in C Major in place of the correct D flat Major.

A 1d. 1940 stamp of New Zealand shows Captain Cook and a chart which at first sight appears erroneous, for it shows lines of longitude of 185° and 190° west of Greenwich, but this is Captain Cook's own chart, and such numbering was quite correct in his time. A 1p.90 Mexican stamp of 1977, part of an issue marking resumption of diplomatic relations with Spain, shows a map of Mexico and Spain, but with no indication that they are drawn on different scales, and Mexico should rightly be about four times as big as shown.

Several examples of the Boy Scout emblem being represented by a fleur-de-lys without mullets have already been given: to these may be added a 30cr. Brazilian stamp of 1965. To the long list of incorrect reproductions of the linked rings symbol of the Olympic Games may be added the 1968 Olympic Games issue of Malaysia. The portrait of Sir Walter Raleigh on a British 7½p. stamp of 1973 is after a miniature by Nicholas Hilliard (in the National Portrait Gallery, London) but reversed. The obverse of a coin shown on a 4d. 1870 postal fiscal of the state of Victoria is also reversed. The zeppelin LZ1 is shown on a West German 40pf.+20pf. semipostal of 1978, but the stabilising rod, a single structure running the length of the airship, is shown on the stamp as two short widely separated structures.

A 1942 issue of the Yemen inscribed "Taxe à percevoir" (postage due) was nevertheless used only for ordinary postage, since indeed there was no postage due system in the Yemen! A 4c. 1974 stamp of the Pitcairn Islands shows three Mitre shells and a Horn-shell, but the label names them confusingly in reverse order.

The Italian series of 1937 commemorating famous Italians has already been referred to earlier. The 2l.55+2l. semipostal marks the bicentenary (not the centenary as claimed) of the birth of Stradivarius, while the 1l.25 and 2l.75+2l. values mark the 600th anniversary, not the centenary as labelled, of the birth of Giotto di Bordone. It has also been claimed that the portrait is not of Giotto but of Boccaccio. A Colombian 2c. stamp of 1950 gave the patriot Antonio Baraya the wrong birth year of 1768 instead of 1770. There are problems concerning calculation of anniversaries of events which occurred before the Christian era because the reckoning does not include a year zero: thus 25l. Italian stamps commemorating the birth of Ovid (43 B.C.-A.D. 17) and the death of Cicero (43 B.C.) should have been issued in 1958, not 1957. A Rumanian 1l.75 stamp of 1957 likewise marks the bi-millenary of Ovid's birth a year too soon.

A 500r. Brazilian stamp of 1929 honours the first flight of the Brazilian aviator Santos-Dumont in his biplane 14bis on 23rd October, 1906, but gives the date of his *second* flight (12th November, 1906). It also identifies his plane as "14BIS" instead of the correct '14bis'. The departure of Cardinal Sarto from Venice for a Conclave in Rome occurred on XXVI-VII-MCMIII, not XXVIII-VI-MCMIII as shown on a 15l. 1960 stamp of the Vatican City.

The inauguration of the Ryukyu-Japan Microwave link, scheduled for 1963, was delayed, so the already prepared commemorative issue of the Ryukyu Islands was released in 1964 with the date "1963" cancelled by bars and "1964" substituted. The 1973 50l. Italian stamp commemorating the centenary of the foundation of the Military Marine Institute of Hydrography, which was actually founded on 26th December, 1872, was a year late. So was the 1978 issue of Grenada marking the 150th anniversary of the death of Beethoven.

A 1976 miniature sheet of Dominica marking the Viking mission to

Mars shows the Titan III/Centaur rocket being launched, but the mission symbol is missing from the casing. Russian stamps of 1971 (16k.) and 1973 (20k.) show the manipulators of the Lunakhod Moonrovers I and II respectively, guiding the performance of their machines with the aid of TV pictures shot from the vehicles, but while the 1973 stamp shows on the screen the landing ramp from the carrier as seen from the Lunakhod, the corresponding 1971 stamp shows the entire Lunakhod filling the screen, a feat obviously beyond the powers of its own camera. Turning from reality to fiction we find Panama, on a 21c. 1966 stamp, showing the manned projectile of Jules Verne nearing the Moon but leaving a trail behind it as if it were self-propelled, which in his story it was not, though subsequent film versions have brought it up-to-date in this respect. A large cloud stretches from behind the projectile to the Moon—another curious addition to the story as first narrated.

In some cases stamp designs which do not have clearly obvious design errors are nevertheless considered sufficiently faulty to be replaced by better drawn designs. Examples of this include the Sudanese 1970 issue marking the first anniversary of the Revolution, which was withdrawn on the day of issue and replaced by an improved version later in the year, and a somewhat fuzzy view of Vancouver on a $1 Canadian stamp of 1972, replaced by a slightly cleaner looking version in 1973. The Cowfish design on a 15c. 1975 stamp in a fish set issued by St. Vincent was also criticised, and replaced by a design of the much more handsome Skipjack (*Euthinnus pelamis*). On the other hand the redrawn design of the Calven Battle Memorial on a 20c. Swiss stamp of 1940 appears to create an error, for the original design bears on a separate white tablet an inscription which on the redrawn design is transferred to the statue, though the statue itself has no such lettering.

A 40f. 1975 stamp of the Congo (Brazzaville) commemorates the Olympic Games but shows boxers without the vests obligatory for all amateur boxing events, as does a 1972 issue of Ajman illustrating the Olympic gold medallist boxers and a 1p.+50c. 1959 stamp of Argentina marking the Third Pan-American Games, Chicago. A 55c. Colombian stamp of 1963 shows tennis rackets without strings, although fine details of the bindings of the handles are included. The swimmer on a 15d. 1952 Yugoslavian stamp marking the Olympic Games, Helsinki, appears to be diving off the side of the block rather than the end, judging from the position of the water illustrated. 150r. and 500r. 1921 stamps of the Azerbaijan Republic show blacksmiths with their shirtsleeves rolled up outwardly, but, as already explained in relation to the blacksmiths on an Estonian issue, sleeves are always rolled inwardly to reduce the risk of trapping sparks in the blacksmith's clothing.

A 20p. 1970 stamp of Rwanda shows Gericault's painting 'The Derby at Epsom'. Here it is the painting at fault, for the galloping horses are shown with legs at fullest stretch, an impossible position which if attained would probably rupture the animals. Our cave-painting ancestors knew better, but it took high-speed photography to convince modern man that the action of a galloping horse was not as here depicted. A 1976 45c. stamp of St. Vincent shows the blue-headed hummingbird *Cyanophaia bicolor,* but on the stamp its head appears uniformly green. The original design of a 25p. 1974 stamp of Tristan da Cunha showed a Rockhopper

Penguin with two chicks, but as these birds normally have only a single chick the design was reworked to remove the unwanted extra chick and only the corrected version was issued. A 50f. 1975 stamp of the Comoro Islands shows a coelacanth alongside a skindiver, but coelacanths live at depths far below those which a skindiver could penetrate and live. A 40b. 1963 Rumanian stamp shows a silkworm on what appears to be a lime tree leaf, but silkworms feed on the leaf of mulberry, particularly the White Mulberry (*Morus alba*), the leaves of which can be not unlike the leaf figured but are typically darker, glossier and more irregular both in toothing and general shape. The red squirrel on a ½c. 1975 stamp of Grenada, part of an issue marking a Scout Jamboree in Norway, seems enormously out of proportion to the leafy branch on which it sits.

The 1c. stamp issued by the Pitcairn Islands in 1967 marking the 150th death anniversary of Admiral Bligh of Mutiny on the Bounty fame shows Bligh and the *Bounty's* launch, in which he was cast adrift by the mutineers with 18 companions. If it was intended to depict this episode then three figures in the launch are insufficient. The 15c. 1975 stamp of the Cook Islands showing "The Holy Family under the Oak" by Raphael omits Joseph, who stands on Mary's left in the original. The heroic defence of Belfort against the Prussians in 1870 was marked by a lion, sculptured by Bartholdi, who subsequently created the Statue of Liberty. It has been claimed that the French semipostals of 1917 and later for the War Orphans Fund are incorrect representations of the statue.

Taking anachronisms next, we find that the "ANCIENT MUSICAL INSTRUMENTS" on a 1977 Israeli issue are all modern reconstructions. Pope Marcellinus (296-304) is shown on a 1d. 1972 Christmas stamp of Ajman wearing the triple crown, which as explained earlier in relation to Pope Sylvester II was not developed until very much later. A 50f. 1961 stamp of Ruanda-Urundi shows a lion and lioness (*Panthera leo*) but under the outdated name "*Felix leo*". In 1961 the Netherlands Antilles commemorated the 185th anniversary of the First Salute to the American Flag with a 20c. denomination which is alleged to show the wrong American flag at the mast of the *Andrew Doria.*

The emblem of the National Overseas Bank, shown on a Portuguese issue of 1964, is a sailing ship with pennants and sails indicating differing wind directions, and the Cenotaph on a 35c. 1978 stamp of the British Solomon Islands has flags flying in opposite directions. However we are in no position to point the finger of scorn, for the flag that waves from the Tower of London on a British 1978 9p. stamp does so in a direction markedly different from the wind direction indicated by the four weathercocks. A mind-boggling design on the 1967/68 Italian stamps marking the introduction of Postal Codes shows covers bearing properly coded addresses but stamped with these stamps. A Swedish 1976 issue marking the telephone centenary shows a dial numbered 0 to 9 instead of 1 to 9 and then 0.

In the 'non-event' category we have two fresh examples, both of coins, which though prepared and featured on stamps were never actually issued. These are a 4p. Paraguayan coin of 1867, featured on a 1978 stamp of Paraguay, and a 50f. gold coin of Liechtenstein, dated 1961 but unissued, the obverse and reverse of which are shown on a 1976 miniature sheet of Liechtenstein honouring the 70th birthday of Prince Franz Josef II.

A 1924 Swedish issue marking the 8th U.P.U. Congress, Stockholm, flouts U.P.U. regulations by omitting the name of the issuing country. A self-adhesive 15c. 1977 stamp of Barbados shows the Queen knighting a kneeling Gary Sobers, but the solemnity of the occasion is somewhat jarred by the command printed at the side—"BEND AND PEEL". The Central South African Railways, an official organisation operated by the governments of the Orange River Colony and the Transvaal, blithely overprinted stamps of the Orange River Colony "CSAR" without permission, although postal authorities reserved exclusive rights to overprint stamps. This was pointed out to the C.S.A.R., but they were allowed to use up existing stocks and thereafter used perfins.

The British official PHQ card, number 18(a), repeats the error made on the stiffener for the Post Office F.D.C. by wrongly stating that the design shows the Knight instead of the Squire (fig. 109). An Indian postal stationery card of Queen Victoria is incorrectly inscribed "ONE AND A HALF ANNA", and finally a special postmark used to cancel F.D.Cs. of an East German issue of 1957 marking the first anniversary of the death of the dramatist Bertold Brecht unfortunately misspelt his name, so was rapidly withdrawn.

INDEX

Aden: 101.
Afghanistan: 2, 6, 7, 11, 12, 16, 22, 23, 24, 30, 41, 43, 47, 49, 53, 54, 62, 68, 73, 81, 91, 106, 148.
Aitutakai: 38, 129.
Ajman: 3, 16, 18, 64, 66, 74, 76, 98, 106, 124, 180, 181.
Albania: 5, 6, 9, 10, 11, 13, 34, 36, 40, 61, 91, 106, 114, 121, 122, 157
Algeria: 3, 10, 13, 38.
Andorra: 14, 37, 43, 87, 132, 175, 178.
Angola: 43.
Anguilla: 18, 20, 95, 122, 153.
Antigua: 8, 84, 96, 97, 111, 123.
Antioqua: 8.
Argentine Republic: 65, 75, 77, 82, 88, 97, 98, 99, 117, 128, 159, 180.
Armenia: 33.
Ascension: 61, 66.
Australia: 8, 16, 17, 24, 27, 29, 30, 43, 50, 66, 86, 94, 101, 108, 112, 116, 118, 120, 121, 125, 129, 131, 134, 138, 148, 150, 163, 165, 166, 167, 168, 169, 171, 172.
Austria: 1, 19, 20, 27, 28, 43, 53, 71, 81, 87, 90, 93, 100, 101, 105, 114, 115, 117, 155, 164, 165, 166, 173.
Austrian Occupation of Rumania: 50.
Azerbaijan: 180.

Bahamas: 34, 44, 58, 62, 72, 79, 91, 137, 175.
Bahawalpur: 41.
Bangladesh: 132.
Barbados: 8, 10, 18, 19, 31, 64, 66, 78, 79, 102, 136, 162, 182.
Barbuda: 55, 175.
Basutoland: 39.
Bavaria: 73, 118, 163.
Bechuanaland: 96.
Belgian Congo: 12, 99, 113, 116, 120, 137, 138.
Belgium: 14, 18, 22, 42, 43, 46, 52, 84, 87, 90, 109, 118, 138, 147, 150, 151, 154, 162.
Bergedorf: 46.
Bermuda: 18, 32, 80, 114, 123, 126.
Bhopal: 5, 23.
Bhutan: 6, 41, 131.
Bohemia and Moravia: 74, 150, 164.
Bolivar: 23.
Bolivia: 26, 89, 91, 100, 111, 113, 140, 143, 144, 145, 160, 175.
Bosnia and Herzegovina: 119.
Botswana: 78.
Brazil: 9, 18, 36, 43, 49, 58, 75, 90, 97, 98, 99, 112, 113, 117, 124, 127, 130, 133, 139, 147, 150, 151, 152, 161, 166, 167, 175, 179.
Bremen: 47.
British Antarctic Territory: 26, 104.
British Colonial 'Victory' issue: 107.
British Columbia and Vancouver Island: 17.
British Guiana: 8, 70, 102, 112, 137, 168.
British Honduras: 8, 9, 12, 39, 44, 101, 102.
British Military Administration of Tripolitania: 49.
Buenos Aires: 46.
Bulgaria: 9, 13, 14, 36, 37, 47, 70, 106, 112, 113, 114, 123, 135, 136, 139, 142, 147, 157, 160, 161, 178.
Burma: 16, 83.
Burundi: 9, 22, 121, 122.

Cambodia: 21, 47, 70.
Cameroun: 12, 21, 38, 110, 113, 119, 124, 139.
Canada: 5, 6, 7, 19, 21, 22, 23, 26, 28, 30, 32, 34, 35, 39, 43, 48, 55, 56, 57, 58, 64, 65, 66, 69, 78, 81, 84, 85, 96, 98, 102, 104, 105, 107, 109, 110, 115, 116, 117, 118, 119, 121, 122, 124, 125, 129, 131, 132, 134, 138, 151, 152, 154, 157, 163, 166, 168, 173, 175, 180.
Canal Zone: 163.
Cayman Islands: 81, 101, 121.

Central African Republic: 10, 21, 35, 81, 91, 94, 99, 112, 145.
Central South African Railways: 182.
Ceylon: 14, 15, 35, 43, 49, 51, 70, 73, 119, 122, 152.
Chad: see Tchad.
Chile: 26, 60, 75, 97, 100, 101, 104, 131, 154, 159.
China: 24, 34, 40, 66, 72, 83, 89, 93, 104, 107, 149, 157, 160.
China (Taiwan): 122.
Christmas Island: 14, 16, 32.
Cochin: 15.
Colombia: 7, 13, 20, 29, 41, 50, 53, 67, 78, 82, 88, 134, 143, 155, 179, 180.
Comoro Islands: 38, 124, 135, 181.
Congo (Brazzaville): 5, 11, 12, 13, 14, 65, 91, 106, 176, 178, 180.
Congo (Kinshasa): 12, 14.
Cook Islands: 9, 14, 20, 33, 38, 78, 82, 92, 110, 113, 178, 181.
Costa Rica: 4, 21, 22, 31, 44, 56, 73, 123, 138, 142, 144.
Crete: 161.
Cuba: 5, 8, 9, 10, 11, 13, 14, 17, 21, 35, 54, 60, 63, 67, 72, 104, 111, 122, 136, 145, 178.
Curacao: 7.
Cyprus: 43, 109, 116, 121, 161, 170.
Czechoslovakia: 9, 10, 12, 22, 26, 34, 52, 53, 60, 61, 63, 65, 71, 74, 91, 92, 98, 99, 105, 106, 111, 112, 113, 121, 132, 135, 140, 147, 149, 150, 157, 177.

Dahomey: 19, 53, 63, 74, 75, 98, 113, 135.
Danzig: 46, 109, 155.
Denmark: 97, 103, 173.
Djibouti: 111.
Dominica: 4, 73, 90, 96, 123, 179.
Dominican Republic: 4, 7, 43, 45, 48, 58, 75, 78, 92, 93, 142, 146, 160.
Dubai: 18, 19, 36, 38, 95, 149.

East Africa (Kenya, Uganda and Tanzania); 1, 18, 60, 72, 124.
East Germany: 3, 5, 6, 9, 13, 17, 20, 24, 25, 36, 54, 56, 58, 71, 74, 82, 88, 94, 95, 97, 99, 106, 107, 108, 112, 114, 115, 116, 117, 120, 125, 127, 138, 141, 143, 155, 157, 164, 182.
Ecuador: 3, 4, 5, 9, 10, 22, 36, 53, 59, 62, 73, 89, 93, 97, 139, 143, 166.
Egypt: 3, 4, 7, 9, 15, 16, 19, 45, 47, 50, 54, 75, 80, 83, 91, 95, 109, 116, 118, 133, 139, 151, 161, 177.
El Salvador: 11, 12, 41, 67, 69, 70, 119, 135, 150.
Equatorial Guinea: 73, 142, 176, 178.
Estonia: 102, 118, 156, 180.
Ethiopia: 5, 10, 37, 78, 124, 125, 139, 144.

Falkland Islands: 77, 105, 120, 129.
Falkland Islands dependencies: 101, 159.
Fernando Poo: 90.
Fiji: 9, 19, 21, 66, 77, 102, 123, 128, 131, 168, 177.
Finland: 41, 62, 74, 87, 102, 114, 142.
France: 20, 21, 22, 23, 27, 32, 42, 43, 53, 54, 57, 59, 63, 67, 68, 74, 78, 91, 92, 93, 95, 97, 100, 101, 104, 107, 108, 109, 110, 114, 115, 116, 117, 118, 126, 132, 133, 134, 138, 139, 157, 170, 175, 181.
Free French issues: 144.
French Colonies, General issues: 21.
French Equatorial Africa: 22, 33, 98.
French Guiana: 22.
French Morocco: 72, 139.
French Somali Coast: 135.
French Southern and Antarctic Territories: 61.
French Sudan: 145.
Fujeira: 4, 7, 29, 43, 92, 95, 99, 100, 106, 124, 133.

Gabon: 12, 73.
Gambia: 9, 11, 101, 119, 171.
Geneva: 178.
German Colonies (key type): 102.
German New Guinea: 19.
German Occupation of Belgium: 48.

German South-West Africa: 19.
Germany: 3, 7, 19, 24, 32, 42, 46, 52, 56, 73, 87, 89, 91, 98, 104, 108, 112, 113, 117, 118, 119, 133, 139, 148, 151, 152, 165, 166, 167, 171.
Ghana: 3, 16, 21, 42, 53, 78, 118, 128, 137, 142.
Gibraltar: 32, 41, 48, 50, 65, 79, 124, 127, 131, 137.
Gilbert Islands: 80.
Gilbert and Ellice Islands: 80, 94, 103, 107.
Great Britain: 9, 23, 38, 50, 51, 56, 59, 63, 71, 73, 79, 84, 91, 92, 95, 96, 97, 98, 100, 102, 107, 111, 113, 116, 120, 121, 124, 131, 132, 134, 137, 140, 141, 147, 150, 152, 156, 165, 167, 168, 169, 170, 171, 172, 173, 179, 181, 182.
Greece: 2, 5, 9, 13, 28, 43, 46, 65, 68, 79, 95, 96. 103, 108, 109, 116, 118, 136, 137, 152, 155, 162, 177.
Grenada: 8, 12, 19, 31, 52, 74, 90, 110, 179, 181.
Grenadines of St. Vincent: 5.
Guatemala: 6, 62, 63, 91, 150, 159.
Guernsey: 77.
Guinea: 9, 11, 61, 106.
Guyana: 9, 14, 64, 66, 70, 79, 123.
Haiti: 6, 48, 89, 91, 160, 175.
Hamburg: 167.
Hawaii: 26.
Holkar: 166.
Honduras: 4, 48, 51, 58, 63, 93, 97, 144, 151, 160.
Hong Kong: 3, 70, 71, 171, 178.
Hungary: 2, 4, 8, 9, 10, 11, 17, 27, 36, 37, 39, 41, 43, 52, 53, 54, 60, 61, 65, 74, 75, 90, 98, 101, 106, 107, 111, 113, 114, 115, 116, 118, 132, 135, 136, 142, 147, 157, 178.
Hyderabad: 116.
Icaria: 96.
Iceland: 6, 38, 82, 114, 116, 143.
Ifni: 10, 14, 90, 98.
India: 5, 43, 51, 53, 83, 91, 92, 95, 104, 117, 148, 182.
Indian Settlements: 121.
Indo-China: 147.
Indonesia: 10, 91, 142.
Iran: 3, 6, 11, 15, 19, 24, 43, 45, 54, 142, 175, 177.
Iraq: 3, 18, 21, 37, 80, 83.
Ireland: 22, 54, 118, 122, 148, 159, 160.
Isle of Man: 84, 88, 134.
Israel: 4, 11, 13, 14, 15, 16, 18, 21, 23, 37, 39, 40, 52, 54, 59, 62, 67, 72, 73, 83, 89, 90, 108, 110, 115, 121, 133, 149, 150, 153, 155, 162, 169, 171, 172.
Italy: 1, 2, 5, 14, 23, 26, 34, 46, 48, 53, 55, 57, 63, 67, 68, 83, 84, 91, 93, 95, 98, 100, 109, 110, 116, 124, 125, 130, 132, 133, 138, 139, 147, 150, 165, 177, 179, 181.
Ivory Coast: 2, 13, 14, 20, 22, 36.
Jaipur: 82, 119.
Jamaica: 31, 33, 43, 59, 68, 69, 85, 92, 94, 95, 98, 99, 123, 157.
Japan: 15, 24, 29, 30, 90, 98, 100, 124, 138, 152.
Jersey: 13, 80, 121, 123, 164, 173.
Johore: 7, 102.
Jordan: 3, 7, 17, 18, 20, 21, 24, 36, 37, 52, 60, 73, 80, 106, 111, 142, 161.
Kenya: 10, 18, 38, 125, 135, 176.
Kenya, Uganda and Tanganyika: 48, 72, 101.
Khmer Republic: 70.
Kishangarh: 23, 45, 47, 86.
Korea: 24, 64, 94.
Kuwait: 3, 20, 50, 68, 122, 137.
Laos: 12, 13, 14, 37, 50, 117, 142.
Latvia: 35, 50, 105, 144.
Lebanon: 3, 11, 17, 47, 80, 91, 113, 143, 178.
Lesotho: 7, 37, 124.
Liberia: 2, 14, 34, 39, 43, 61, 73, 74, 79, 110, 114, 133, 137, 138, 142, 143, 147, 152, 166.
Libya: 2, 3, 18, 54, 80, 81, 107.
Liechtenstein: 95, 97, 104, 117, 118, 143, 182.
Lithuania: 61, 62, 143, 161.

Lundy: 72.
Luxemburg: 19, 23, 66, 74, 88, 102, 109, 117.

Macao: 49, 69.
Madagascar: 51, 117.
Mahra: 90.
Malagasy Republic: 9, 36, 38, 64, 91, 122.
Malawi: 6, 12, 39, 70, 128.
Malaya: 80.
Malaysia: 179.
Maldive Islands: 13, 36, 39, 60, 64, 67, 80, 127, 135, 136, 142, 144.
Mali: 9, 19, 35, 52, 57, 58, 64, 91, 105, 111, 117, 178.
Malta: 18, 125, 136.
Manama: 18, 29, 42, 55.
Marshall Islands: 1, 145.
Martinique: 139.
Mauritania: 11, 12, 13, 38, 80, 91, 122.
Mauritius: 9, 19, 68, 69, 77, 86, 95, 122, 168, 171.
Mecklenburg-Vorpommern: 118.
Memel: 51.
Mexico: 7, 24, 26, 94, 98, 115, 125, 127, 140, 142, 145, 167, 178.
Modena: 178.
Monaco: 4, 6, 9, 10, 21, 27, 30, 40, 52, 77, 91, 104, 111, 114, 115, 124, 133, 137, 139, 142.
Mongolia: 6, 9, 11, 13, 14, 23, 36, 41, 54, 123.
Montenegro: 166.
Montserrat: 58, 79, 118.
Morocco: 10, 17, 37, 38, 91, 113, 124, 151.
Mount Lebanon: 96.
Mozambique: 10, 11, 50, 113.
Mozambique Company: 48, 101.
Muscat and Oman: 49.

Negri Sembilan: 86.
Nepal: 2, 15, 81.
Netherlands: 88, 91, 93, 103, 113, 141, 142, 150, 162, 165, 173.
Netherlands Antilles: 19, 80, 93, 156, 181.
Netherlands Indies: 7, 156, 166.
New Brunswick: 51, 99, 152.
New Caledonia: 14, 111, 122, 136, 139, 177.
Newfoundland: 6, 8, 17, 19, 22, 27, 29, 31, 50, 51, 55, 59, 62, 66, 68, 77, 79, 85, 96, 97, 119, 120, 121, 123, 126, 172.
New Hebrides: 11, 61, 78, 90, 156.
New South Wales: 23, 79, 85, 121, 165.
New Zealand: 1, 18, 40, 41, 44, 47, 48, 58, 71, 82, 86, 98, 103, 104, 109, 111, 120, 123, 126, 129, 130, 131, 137, 139, 140, 148, 150, 151, 157, 165, 172, 178.
Nicaragua: 4, 5, 9, 10, 14, 16, 19, 27, 28, 34, 43, 50, 53, 55, 64, 69, 73, 76, 90, 112, 113, 136, 143, 158, 160, 176, 178.
Niger: 11, 13, 40, 57, 61, 65, 75, 91, 97, 105, 110, 122, 125, 131.
Nigeria: 33, 38, 90, 108, 113, 118.
Niue: 50, 116, 129.
Norfolk Island: 18, 34, 38, 79, 121, 128, 129, 177.
North Borneo: 2, 39, 41, 69, 80, 149.
North Korea: 36, 143.
North Vietnam: 10, 11, 12, 14, 41, 106, 135, 136, 142.
Northern Rhodesia: 41, 119.
Norway: 2, 4, 9, 35, 54, 130, 139, 157.
Nova Scotia: 51.
Nyasaland: 29, 70, 96, 102, 138, 139.
Nyassa: 119.

Obock: 111.
Oldenburg: 87.
Oman: 80.
Orange Free State: 177.
Oubangui-Chari: see Ubangi-Shari.

Pakistan: 14, 15, 18, 29, 43, 51, 54, 63, 65, 123, 148, 160.
Palestine: 45, 50, 73, 149, 167, 172.
Panama: 4, 8, 10, 11, 19, 34, 61, 71, 79, 89, 175, 177, 180.
Papua New Guinea: 14, 59, 101, 105, 135, 172.
Paraguay: 9, 19, 42, 45, 49, 60, 61, 69, 82, 90, 99, 110, 127, 160, 181.
Persia (Iran): 15, 24.
Peru: 4, 11, 30, 31, 35, 39, 60, 91, 96, 109, 136, 137, 154, 175.
Philippine Islands: 9, 11, 33, 34, 97, 113, 116.
Pitcairn Islands: 34, 38, 40, 71, 79, 102, 123, 179, 181.
Poland: 1, 9, 11, 19, 23, 28, 36, 37, 39, 40, 53, 65, 67, 91, 98, 99, 100, 103, 107, 110, 112, 117, 132, 136, 137, 140, 144, 152, 155, 157.
Polish Post Offices in Danzig: 155.
Portugal: 12, 22, 32, 75, 90, 98, 108, 125, 165, 175, 181.
Portuguese Guinea: 42.
Portuguese India: 42.

Qatar: 36, 37, 60, 91, 120, 161.
Qu'aiti State in Hadhramaut: 61.
Queensland: 92.

Rarotonga: 116.
Ras al Khaima: 5, 9, 36, 37, 43, 60, 61, 91.
Réunion: 21, 77, 81, 139.
Rhineland-Palatinate: 103.
Rhodesia and Nyasaland: 35, 86.
Rio Muni: 90.
Ruanda-Urundi: 113, 181.
Rumania: 5, 10, 11, 12, 36, 37, 40, 46, 50, 52, 55, 62, 64, 65, 69, 71, 75, 88, 92, 93, 99, 105, 106, 107, 112, 113, 119, 121, 123, 150, 157, 179, 181.
Russia: 4, 13, 17, 20, 34, 36, 52, 57, 62, 64, 65, 67, 68, 91, 92, 94, 97, 107, 108, 114, 124, 144, 155, 157, 161, 173, 175, 180.
Rwanda: 14, 75, 110, 114, 180.
Ryukyu Islands: 64, 80, 123, 179.

Saar: 24, 42, 47, 50, 87, 107, 164.
St. Christopher, Nevis and Anguilla: see St. Kitts-Nevis.
St. Helena: 32, 38, 79, 110, 118, 129, 132, 136, 156.
St. Kitts-Nevis: 9, 39, 54, 80, 128, 177.
St. Lucia: 1, 31, 137, 138.
St. Pierre et Miquelon: 9, 138.
St. Thomas and Prince Islands: 122.
St. Vincent: 1, 17, 79, 86, 128, 180.
Samoa: 10, 13, 19, 28, 34, 81, 94, 128, 134.
San Marino: 10, 11, 13, 35, 39, 60, 104, 112, 128, 130, 146.
Sardinia: 111.
Sarawak: 12, 120.
Saudi Arabia: 3, 5, 15, 17, 18, 63, 90, 104.
Saxony: 138, 150.
Senegal: 10, 14.
Serbia: 163.
Seychelles: 19, 32, 35, 64, 77, 129, 137.
Shanghai: 45, 47.
Sharjah: 5, 18, 29, 49, 100, 106, 115, 129, 142.
Siam (Thailand): 16, 18, 45, 46, 143.
Sicily: 152.
Sierra Leone: 2, 18, 102, 119.
Signy Island: 171.
Singapore: 63, 103.
Sirmoor: 2, 110, 119.
Slovakia: 112, 152.
Solomon Islands: 18, 38, 39, 58, 59, 131, 177, 181.
Somalia: 12, 14, 37, 176.
South Africa: 6, 11, 14, 42, 76, 78, 86, 91, 100, 101, 103, 108, 129, 135, 140, 148, 150, 166, 167, 168, 172.
South Australia: 85.
South Georgia: 18, 41, 80.

South Korea: 4, 8, 16, 23, 43, 90, 94, 95, 133.
South West Africa: 4, 6, 93, 121, 126, 138, 150, 166.
Southern Rhodesia: 86.
Spain: 14, 22, 30, 35, 36, 41, 42, 46, 47, 48, 58, 70, 95, 96, 110, 113, 127, 142, 143, 156, 165, 176, 178.
Spanish Guinea: 14, 43, 117.
Spanish Morocco: 22.
Spanish Sahara: 13, 43, 90, 176.
Sri Lanka: 70, 138.
Sudan: 1, 15, 18, 45, 62, 114, 130, 148, 180.
Surinam: 12, 64, 93, 112.
Swaziland: 18.
Sweden: 5, 11, 35, 42, 49, 66, 75, 99, 119, 151, 153, 177, 178, 181, 182.
Switzerland: 8, 56, 87, 88, 98, 101, 107, 108, 113, 118, 120, 125, 127, 139, 165, 180.
Syria: 3, 4, 6, 7, 16, 17, 18, 20, 21, 23, 24, 43, 51, 70, 80, 142.

Tahiti: 23.
Taiwan: see China (Taiwan).
Tanganyika: 70, 71, 138.
Tanna Touva: see Tuva.
Tanzania: 10, 125, 176.
Tasmania: 17, 145, 163.
Tchad (Chad): 10, 41, 43, 105, 112, 113, 114.
Thailand: 9, 47, 113, 142.
Tibet: 7.
Togo: 4, 19, 43, 73, 74, 113, 142, 143, 168.
Tokelau Islands: 2, 78.
Tonga: 1, 80, 84, 101, 152.
Transvaal: 86.
Travancore: 2, 51, 122.
Trinidad and Tobago: 33, 79, 107, 120, 147.
Tripolitania: 40.
Tristan da Cunha: 4, 120, 138, 180.
Tunisia: 13, 43, 47, 142, 147.
Turkey: 3, 23, 29, 31, 45, 73, 139, 149, 160.
Turks and Caicos Islands: 32, 101, 107, 118, 121.
Tuscany: 88.
Tuva: 130.

Ubangi-Shari (Oubangui-Chari): 97.
Uganda: 13, 125, 176.
Umm al Qiwain: 8, 69, 93.
United Nations: 72, 81, 102, 156, 168.
United States of America: 2, 4, 6, 23, 26, 30, 31, 33, 35, 40, 41, 43, 48, 51, 54, 55, 56, 57, 59, 60, 65, 66, 68, 74, 80, 81, 82, 87, 91, 93, 95, 96, 97, 98, 99, 103, 104, 105, 106, 107, 108, 114, 116, 118, 119, 125, 126, 129, 132, 133, 134, 137, 138, 140, 144, 147, 148, 151, 153, 157, 162, 163, 167, 171, 178.
Upper Volta: 12, 110.
Uruguay: 10, 12, 19, 35, 75, 115, 119, 145, 175.

Vatican City: 9, 22, 23, 26, 27, 44, 95, 97, 179.
Venezuela: 7, 8, 9, 10, 12, 13, 21, 24, 44, 88, 93, 97, 117, 121, 133, 159, 176, 177.
Victoria: 51, 84, 161, 165, 179.
Virgin Islands: 1, 5, 18, 31, 66, 67, 81.

Wallis and Futuna Islands: 12, 135.
West Berlin: 20, 71, 91, 98, 99, 108, 125, 133, 140, 154, 164.
West Germany: 3, 4, 6, 19, 20, 21, 24, 25, 27, 29, 40, 50, 52, 59, 60, 63, 68, 79, 87, 93, 97, 98, 99, 106, 108, 115, 121, 125, 127, 130, 134, 137, 138, 140, 145, 148, 154, 156, 163, 164, 178, 179.
Western Australia: 40, 71.

Yemen: 3, 7, 9, 18, 25, 29, 43, 47, 48, 49, 62, 72, 73, 79, 80, 91, 142, 143, 175, 176, 177, 178, 179.
Yugoslavia: 9, 20, 29, 31, 66, 70, 91, 95, 97, 99, 112, 113, 115, 130, 136, 142, 176, 180.
Zaïre: 63.
Zambia: 11, 66, 123.